FINANCIAL TIMES OF CANADA ■ PERSONAL FINANCE LIBRARY

The Only Retirement Guide You'll Ever Need

BY ROBERT KERR

PENGUIN BOOKS

PENGUIN BOOKS

Published by the Penguin Group

Penguin Books Canada Ltd., 10 Alcorn Avenue, Suite 300, Toronto, Canada M4V 3B2

Penguin Books Limited, 27 Wrights Lane, London W8 5TZ, England

Viking Penguin Inc., 40 West 23rd Street, New York, New York 10010, USA

Penguin Books Australia Ltd., Ringwood, Victoria, Australia

Penguin Books (NZ) Ltd., 182-190 Wairau Road, Auckland 10, New Zealand

Penguin Books Ltd., Registered Offices: Harmondsworth, Middlesex, England

Published in Penguin Books, 1993

10 9 8 7 6 5 4 3 2 1

All enquiries should be addressed to the Financial Times
of Canada, 440 Front Street West, Toronto, Ontario M5V 3E6 (416) 585-5555

Canadian Cataloguing in Publication Data

Kerr, Robert John, 1945 —
    The only retirement guide you'll ever need
(Financial times personal finance library)
Includes bibliographical references and index.

ISBN 0-14-016707-2
1. Retirement — Canada.
2. Retirement income — Canada.
3. Retirees — Canada — Finance, Personal.
4. Retirees — Health and hygiene — Canada.
I. Title. II. Series

HQ1064.C38K47 1993   646.7'9'0971   C93-095423-8

Cover design: Gary Hall
Interior design: Creative Network
Cover illustration: Norman Eyolfson
Cover photo: Francois Berube
Technical support: Godfried Verhaeghe, Calvin Foston and Sarah Pennefather

Contents

Acknowledgements

This book began its long journey toward publication in 1983 when Doug Lovat of Air Canada asked us to write the financial planning sections for their very successful pre-retirement planning workshops. It has been polished and improved since that time with the help of devoted Kerr Financial staff members, knowledgeable outside professionals, and the insight of thousands of retirees and pre-retirees who have attended our seminars and met with us for individual counselling.

As we became more and more involved in retirement planning, I realized that, while financial planning is of vital importance, it is the health and lifestyle choices that really bear on the enjoyment of life after our working years. You can live well with or without a lot of money, but you need health, energy, friends, activities and a positive attitude to enjoy life fully. After months of research and writing, we called in the experts to read, improve and extensively rewrite the lifestyle planning chapters in our attempt to prepare the most comprehensive book on retirement planning in Canada.

One person who made a significant contribution to this book is Mary Holder. Mary is a registered nurse and a certified psychologist. Her career has covered a wide range of professional activities including business, educational, nursing and community involvement. As a psychologist, she carries on a private practice specializing in mid- to late-life issues and concerns. Since 1978, Mary has been a retirement and life planning consultant to business, government and other agencies. Mary has also taught gerontology and retirement planning at the University of Calgary and the Mount Royal and Grant McEwan Colleges.

Our strength at Kerr Financial is the financial planning aspects of retirement. Mary's strength is lifestyle planning. Together we have tried to bring to you the best advice on all facets of retirement planning. Mary took the research I had collected and brought to the work her own knowledge, experience and insight. It was Mary who shaped the lifestyle planning, aging and health chapters of this book into a readable, reliable and useful guide. I thank her immensely for her substantial contribution to this book.

Others who provided critical comment and improvements are: Lois Faris, Sharon Cohen, Usha Rughani, Donna Hennyey, Edith Skutezky, Dr. R.K. Dougan, Catherine Dougan and Dr. Gertrude Robinson. The professionals, past and present, at Kerr Financial Corporation who gave generously of their time and expertise are: in Montreal — Katherine Aziz, CFP, RFP; Kris Kotecha; Kathy Hallgren; Suzanne Malo; Patricia Gasc; Ann Carson; Jim Matheson, CA; Brenda Zanin; and, Chris Gobeil, CA, RFP; in Toronto — Barbara Tarr, CFP, RFP; Peter Volpe, CFP, RFP; and Reagan Stillar; in Calgary — Russell Popham, CFP, RFP; and Paul Boeda, CLU, RFP; and in Vancouver — Lynne Triffon, CFP, RFP; and Bob Paterson, CA, RFP.

I would like to single out another Kerr Financial staffer, Krista Kerr, CA, my eldest daughter, and a financial consultant in our Toronto office, for the biggest thanks. Krista put in an extraordinary effort and carried us through to an excellent completion. She is a very talented person.

I would like to thank Elaine Wyatt, publisher and author, for her patience, wisdom and persistence — and for the professionals she brought to work on this book: Michael Posner, Helen Keeler, Jared Mitchell, Susan Grimbly, Arlene Arnason, Myrna Forsythe and Patricia Coull.

I thank the financiers of Kerr Financial Communications Inc. without whose help, as they say, this book would not have been possible: William H. Kerr, Dr. L. Paul Ramsay, Ron Couchman, John Lafave, Dr. Roopnarine Singh, James Morton, Elizabeth and James Taylor, Bruce Hyland, John O'Reilly, Wendy McKeown and Ian Poole.

To Gitta Kerr, our family and friends, I thank all of you for your patience and understanding.

Finally, a special thanks to the real experts, the retirees whom I have met over the years, whose lives are an inspiration to us all. They are proof of what can be accomplished with planning, persistence and energy. I thank all of you and hope that, through our collective efforts, this book will benefit Canadians facing the challenges of retirement for many years to come.

Robert J. Kerr
October, 1993

Chapter 1

Sharing your sardine sandwiches

The thought of retirement conjures up two different emotions in most people — warm thoughts about the freedom to do whatever you choose and fear. Perhaps it's just a small, nagging concern that sits at the back of your mind. Sometimes there are fears that just won't leave you alone.

I'd like to confront these concerns right now — get them out on the table, or at least written down. Let me share some of my concerns; I've got a lot of them, so sharing is easy. They're like the sardine sandwiches my mother gave me for school. I couldn't share them enough.

Take death.

I'm concerned about death. As Woody Allen said, "It's not that I'm afraid to die. I just don't want to be there when it happens." My concern is pretty wide-ranging. It starts with my own death and fans out from there to the eventual loss of my parents, and to the unthinkable possibility of my wife and children dying before me. (On the other hand, I also imagine with more than a touch of satisfaction the death of my neighbour's surly dog as it yaps and barks at me every day.)

I'm also concerned about money. Don't get me wrong, we live in relative comfort. And, with the mortgage paid and two of three children finished university, we have already achieved enviable success. But I've looked at the retirement needs of many clients, and I've become aware of the huge sum of money needed to be financially independent. I can't help but wonder if I'll have enough to live as well as I live today. Will there be any money for the children?

Other people worry about another kind of worth, feelings of self-worth. Will you still be important after you retire from your job? If your sense of self-worth derives from your job and career, how will you maintain it after retirement? This is one concern I do not share. I have always been made to feel totally inconsequential by my staff and colleagues.

Now it's your turn. Jot down some of the things that worry you as you look ahead. Write them down in any order in the space on the next page. Use your own words; there are no writing awards being handed out here. Some of you may have trouble getting started. Take your time, it's not easy to confront your worries. If you like, just jot down three or four short statements, you might even rank them in order of importance. Get your partner — your wife, husband or a friend with whom you share your life — to rank his or her concerns about retirement as well. How do you and your partner compare?

You're not alone in worrying about the future. It's natural. In fact, most of us worry about the same things. We worry about money and whether or not we'll have enough when we retire. We worry about getting old and sick. We wonder if our retirement will have an impact on our relationship with our husband, wife or friends. We worry about being bored or lonely. We even worry about not feeling useful when we're not working. We wonder if we should move when we retire. And, if we do move will we be happy in a different home? And most of us worry about death.

My concerns about retirement

_____

_____

_____

_____

_____

_____

_____

_____

_____

_____

_____

We'll deal with many of these concerns throughout the book. You'll find plenty of information, prodding and worksheets that will not only help you design your retirement lifestyle but ensure that you have the emotional and physical health to enjoy it.

Many of our fears arise from the myths about the impact of aging. Our society is obsessed with youth and our vision of our "golden" years is bleak. James Lynch and Gail Riddell look at these myths in *Retirement Education: A Multi-Group Discussion Approach*. Let's look at some of them:

Myth: People tend to become more religious as they become older.

False. People do not become more religious because of age. It is true that today's older Canadians tend to be more religious, but this is probably a result of stronger religious traditions when they were younger. As people age they often return to those traditions that were highly valued when they were young.

Myth: Older workers have more accidents at work than younger workers.

False. Older, more experienced workers usually have better safety records than younger workers.

Myth: People over age sixty-five do not do as well on intelligence tests as people under age sixty-five.

False. An older person will do as well on an intelligence test as he or she would have when younger but it might take longer to finish.

Myth: People tend to avoid taking risks as they get older.

False. Older people are usually more realistic in their decisions, taking only necessary risks, not foolish ones.

Myth: Our sense of touch, smell, hearing, taste and sight decline in old age.

True. All five senses do decline with age. This is particularly true of vision, hearing and touch. The senses of taste and smell decline less rapidly.

_____

_____

_____

_____

_____

_____

_____

_____

_____

_____

_____

_____

_____

Myth: Sexual activity is rare among people of retirement age.

False. Interest and participation in sexual intimacy continues to be a normal, satisfying part of life for most people. Many people remain sexually active even in old age. Just as in our youth, sexual activity is influenced by personal preference, habit, health and the availability of a partner.

Myth: Drivers over age sixty-five have fewer accidents than younger drivers.

True and false: Drivers over age sixty-five have about as many accidents as middle-aged drivers but fewer accidents than drivers under age thirty. Possibly, older drivers compensate for any decline in perception and speed with which they react by driving more carefully.

Myth: Most people sell their homes and move when they retire.

False. Most retired people remain in their homes as long as they can.

Myth: Younger workers are better at their jobs than older workers.

False. The majority of older workers can work as effectively as younger workers. They are at least as accurate and steady in their work, are absent less and have fewer accidents.

Grey power

It cannot be ignored that our society is aging. But if you thought that getting older and retiring was a limiting, unhappy experience, think again. Retirees today are the richest, healthiest and most active we have ever known — independent, powerful and involved. This is not the stereotype of old.

There are almost three million Canadians over age sixty-five, 11 percent of the Canadian population. By the year 2030, close to 25 percent of our population will be over age sixty-five. Not only is the population gradually aging, we're living longer than ever before. The

Your retirement concerns

Rank your concerns about retirement from one to ten.
One represents the concern that worries you most, ten the least.

	Your ranking	Your partner's ranking	Canadian average ranking
Finances Will we have enough to live on? Will we live as well as today?			1
Health Will I have the energy and health to enjoy retirement? Will I get sick and become dependent on others?			2
Marital or intimate relationships Will they change? Will I be able to replace lost relationships?			3
Loneliness Without my friends and acquaintances at work, will I be lonely?			4
Housing Should I move in retirement? If I do, where would I go?			5
Loss of work Will I miss work? What will I do to replace the challenge, satisfaction and contact with others?			6
Boredom What will I do with my time? Will I have enough interests and activities to keep me from getting bored?			7
Feelings of self-worth Without a job, am I still of value to the world?			8
Death and bereavement How long will I live? Will I lose my husband or wife or friends as they age?			9
Wills and estate planning Have I done everything I should to protect my family and business partners?			10

SOURCE: AIR CANADA PRE-RETIREMENT SEMINARS

life expectancy for a baby girl is 79.73 years; 73.04 years for a baby boy. A more startling statistic, however, is the life expectancy of adults at various different ages. A forty-year-old woman can expect to live to 81.20 years of age; the life expectancy of a seventy-five-year-old woman 86.92 years. Life spans will be lengthened a few more years when we conquer cancer, and by ten to twelve years when we beat heart disease.

It is not just our life span that is becoming longer; so is our health span. More than 50 percent of those age seventy-five to eighty-four and 35 percent of those over age eighty-five lead active, healthy lives.

Canadians in retirement today are wealthier than retired Canadians have ever been before. All Canadian residents over age sixty-five have access to a minimum income provided by the federal Old Age Security pension and Guaranteed Income Supplement. Everyone who has worked is covered by the Canada or Quebec Pension Plan and some 45 percent of Canadians are covered by company pension plans. Thousands of Canadians have registered retirement savings plans and other forms of savings and investments.

Of those nearly three million seniors, more than one million own and live in their own homes. Most of these (92 percent) are debt-free. One estimate puts the value of this home ownership of seniors at more than $60 billion. This enormous sum will provide the money to fund a long and healthy retirement, tapped by selling the home or borrowing against the equity through a reverse mortgage. I am not ignoring the unconscionably high number of Canadians who live without dignity in poverty, especially senior women who are inadequately supported by our financial systems. Still, it remains true that seniors as a group have never been wealthier than they are today.

The marketplace has noticed, providing new services and products at a burgeoning rate aimed at active, healthy seniors. Persons over fifty now represent the largest buying force in the country. Even baby boomers lack the cash resources of the seniors.

Finally, seniors have political power at every level of government — town and city, provincial and federal. Not only do they have the numbers, they also have the time and interest to organize, to attend meetings and to vote. Their organizations and associations are gaining momentum. While the Canadian Association of Retired Persons (CARP) is only six years old and relatively small, its counterpart in the United States, the American Association of Retired Persons (AARP), has more than 32 million members. When the AARP talks, Congress listens.

Financial planning really matters

But, you ask, what about the drastic reduction in income? Pensions will produce 60 percent or less of your former employment income. How can you live on less when you earn barely enough today? And what about the long-term effects of inflation and taxes? The best way to deal with this worry is to make estimates and projections, so you become comfortable with the way things will be. Knowing that you need supplementary income might persuade you to continue some form of income-producing activity, the rewards of which may be both financial and emotional.

This book provides the framework for a step-by-step approach, with worksheets, tips and enough guidance to enable you to complete your own financial evaluations and forecast. Once you've completed these worksheets, you can use them to pinpoint planning and investment improvements.

Even if you decide you want to hire a financial adviser, go through the worksheets that follow. Your adviser will need all this background detail to construct a financial plan for you. Compiling it yourself will give you a better understanding of the advice you will receive, and may reduce the fees of those financial advisers who charge by the hour. Whether you do it alone or with an adviser, it's time-consuming to build a financial plan; but once done it will be easy to update. Just make sure you keep it simple so it will be easier to achieve.

It might seem like a great deal of work, but surveys on personal finance show that the overriding concerns of retiring North Americans can be expressed in a few disconcerting questions: Will I outlive my money? Will I retire in dignity? Will I have to work long after age sixty-five?

In 1992, there were two surveys of financial attitudes in Canada that brought to light some interesting contradictions. A Gallup Canada and Investors Group survey found that half of Canadians expect to need as much as 75 percent of their current income when they retire. A Decima Research and Royal Trust survey discovered that 70 percent of Canadians do not feel confident that the federal government will be able to provide adequate pension for their retirement. They do not believe the government's assurances that the Canada Pension Plan is adequately funded and capable of taking care of the growing number of retired Canadians.

Both surveys found that while everyone dreams of a romantic and comfortable retirement, few people are doing enough to ensure it happens. In fact, despite a lack of confidence in government, only 44 percent of those surveyed planned to contribute to an RRSP that year — although an RRSP is a very powerful tool that enables you to build your wealth without taking any unnecessary risk.

At the same time, employers are seeking every possible way to reduce costs and they are shifting responsibility for retirement onto the shoulders of employees. A Statistics Canada study in early 1993 showed the proportion of working Canadians covered by employer pension plans fell from about 48 percent in 1980 to less than 45 percent in 1990. Employers are blaming regulatory changes which have created a situation that one administrator called "an administrative, wildly expensive night-mare." And with governments plagued by massive budget deficits, there's a good chance universal support mechanisms like Old Age Security will disappear and only the needy will receive government assistance.

Yet the Canadian population will be older and there will be more retired seniors. Today, there are six Canadians working for every Canadian retired. By the year 2030, there will be fewer than two workers for each retired person — a small percentage of the population shouldering the responsibility for funding the hospitals, schools, roads and other government activities as well as the pensions for retired Canadians, you and me.

Canada is not the only country in this uncomfortable predicament. Over the next few years, the United States is gradually raising the age requirement for maximum social security from sixty-five to sixty-seven. Italy has announced that it plans to reduce the state pensions paid to its retired citizens. Many other European countries are considering raising the retirement age and increasing the years one must work to qualify for a pension.

In Canada, the first step toward the disappearance of universality is the claw-back of OAS and child tax benefits. It's feared this will spread to the Canada and Quebec pensions. The government can't restrict payment of these pensions but it can remove the annual increase in the pension to match increases in inflation, the indexing. There is no doubt that Canadians will have to rely more and more on the retirement funds they manage to save themselves through instruments like RRSPs. With two-income families, the opportunity to build these funds is greater. Some people might look forward to receiving inheritances, but with parents living longer and possibly remarrying, it is not a sure thing.

If you have wealth, your day-to-day income and expenses in retirement might be largely unaffected. Your major concern might be preserving wealth so that it can be left for children and grandchildren. This is not an unimportant responsibility. If this is your situation, you will want to concentrate on tax reduction, investment management and estate planning.

For most of us, however, financial resources are limited. Our concern that our retirement income won't be sufficient to meet our expenses for the rest of our lives stems from two changes in our financial status. The first change, when you receive a pension cheque rather than a paycheque, can come as a shock. Your primary source of income is no longer a regular salary but a monthly pension over which you have little, if any, control. This includes company pensions, the OAS pension and the CPP or QPP.

The change from salary to pension income is not in itself alarming. The shock comes from the sudden drop in income. Your pension, if you are among the 55 percent of Canadians age forty-five to sixty-five who have a pension plan, will be 30 to 70 percent less than your salary in your last few years of work. Only rarely does a pension approach the income that you were receiving before retirement. How do you like the prospect of living on less than you have now?

Second, your pension might not keep pace with the cost of living. Few people have fully indexed pensions and, while the government and a few company plans might provide some growth to cover inflation, it might not be enough. Even if you have a fully indexed pension, don't be complacent. The combination of the rising cost of living and income taxes will erode the protection you think you have.

Fortunately, many factors help soften these financial problems. First, your expenses in retirement are usually lower than your expenses while working. Your mortgage will probably be paid, your children grown and moved out of the house and life insurance either paid up or no longer necessary. The costs of working will also be gone: You'll no longer have to travel to and from work, buy coffee or lunch at the office, or buy special clothes for work. And you'll have more time than ever to spend on your financial affairs, finding new ways to cut costs and to improve the returns from your investments. Retirement might also mean having more time for household and auto repairs, gardening, sewing and other odd jobs. This can keep your out-of-pocket expenses as low as possible. There will be more time to pursue a profitable hobby or a second career for both enjoyment and income.

Special financial benefits for people over age sixty are becoming commonplace: premiums on savings accounts, property tax rebates, ticket discounts, and free prescriptions. Such advantages may increase as the market and political power of seniors grow. There are also income tax credits and tax deferrals that become available once you hit age sixty-five and begin receiving pension income.

Of course, a pension is not your only possible source of income. There are your personal savings — bank deposits, savings bonds, RRSPs, your investments and other less obvious savings, such as the equity in your house or cottage and the cash value of insurance policies. Canadians are great savers, traditionally tucking away much more than our southern neighbours. Your aim is to make sure that these savings will be enough to meet your retirement needs.

A few thoughts about work

You said you were going to retire. This doesn't mean you're going to roll over and die. You've got things to do, and some of them may even involve working. Everybody has to work to provide food, shelter and good health for themselves and their loved ones. Sometimes retirees work just because they like to.

Work, in fact, is the dominant force in our lives. It structures our day. It governs our allocation of time. Most of what we do in any twenty-four-hour span is devoted to or related to work. When we aren't actually working, we are travelling to and from work, taking a break from work, fitting in a lunch hour, working overtime, taking work home at nights, getting a good night's sleep so we can be ready for work tomorrow, buying clothes for work, and so on. We look forward to holidays and vacations away from work. We even look forward, one day, to retiring from work.

But is work really so bad? Doesn't it provide many of the things we love? Money, for one: to spend not just on necessities, but on possessions and good times. Work offers self-esteem and adds meaning to our lives. We gain satisfaction from gaining new skills, new promotions and salary increases.

When we complain about work, aren't we

actually complaining about the tedium of our jobs, the long hours doing substantially the things we mastered years ago? In a better world, we would devote fewer hours to work each day, fewer days each week, fewer weeks each year. We'd have greater control over when we work and what we do.

We'd want new challenges at work and the training to perform them well, to accomplish new tasks, to enjoy the feeling of self-development. And we'd want less pressure, the stress that arises from having too few choices, running up against decisions made by others, or not being able to control our lives.

Well, hallelujah. Because that's what retirement is all about. At long last, we have a measure of financial independence. We receive money from several sources without having to work for it. We can structure our lives however we choose, with or without the influence of work. We can sleep in, play golf, travel, take up a new hobby, do what we enjoy, whenever we want. This is a whole new ball game. And we want to play it. But what are the rules?

That's what this book is all about. It's a comprehensive guide to help you plan for a whole new life, one that isn't governed by the work you must do, one that will be shaped entirely by you. We'll look at the changes retirement brings, and consider the actions you can take to turn them into opportunities. As the importance of work diminishes, you'll have to organize your days effectively, putting a new structure into the twenty-four-hour clock. Wait a minute. Isn't that the same rigid scheduling you've been trying to escape? Well, once you try a few days of no schedule at all, you'll quickly recognize that human beings need structure.

A great deal of study has been devoted to the retirement years. Conclusion: You'll perceive life in retirement either as a disaster or as challenging and satisfying. The outcome depends on your planning and personal attitude to retirement, aging and change. This book can guide you toward a positive and enthusiastic acceptance of the new opportunities ahead. My approach is lifestyle oriented; it's about choices, assessment and actions. And I hope it provides motivation for you to begin your retirement planning. Good luck!

Notes

The shape of retirement

What will you do when you retire? At our seminars, about-to-retire men and women are given pieces of paper with circles on them, which they divide into sections according to how they intend to spend their time.

Several years ago, I watched a gentleman stare blankly at the circles, or time-pies, as we call them. He hadn't a clue to how he was going to spend his retirement time. Suddenly he smiled, and split his circle in half. On one side he wrote "sleep" and on the other he wrote "play." He was satisfied, and we all chuckled.

Twelve hours of play sounds like fun, doesn't it? When the gentleman was asked what he was going to play at, his response was, "I don't know. I figure I'll try this and that. Something will come up." When asked what he does in the evenings and weekends now, he could only come up with watching television, reading the newspaper and doing whatever needed to be done around the home. He admitted to being a bit of a workaholic; and, he dreaded the thought of retirement. Perhaps that's why twelve hours of sleep sounded so appealing. But normal healthy adults only need six to eight hours of sleep a day. Sounds as if he might have a problem.

Maybe you already know what you want to do with your retirement. You're lucky if you do. For many people, retirement can loom ahead like a great, disturbing void. Even if you have a good idea of what you'd like to do, it's really worthwhile to think carefully about your goals to make sure they're right for you. So let's focus on developing retirement goals. What are your dreams and desires? And what do you need to do to achieve them?

Different strokes

We all cope with retirement in different ways. Let's look at some examples.

John really wasn't looking forward to retirement. "I liked my work and I was sure I would miss it and my friends at the office. I lived in a small town close to the company where I worked. I didn't know what I was going to do to keep busy, there wasn't much for me to do in town. We finally decided to move closer to the city. I've been retired for a year and I don't think about work at all. I'm busy helping out at the shop at the technical school down the street. Helen does some volunteer work at the museum and she's been asked to give a couple of lectures at the gardening club. We're busy but there's still time for a walk in the park. And I'm finally getting all the odd jobs around the house done. I wonder why I worried so much."

Martin's approach was quite different. He decided to keep working. "My cousin and I have talked about running our own business since we were kids. Well, I spent five years planning a landscaping business. By the time we were both old enough for early retirement, we were ready. I was scared but really excited. I'm working long hours but I'm doing something I've always wanted to do. I'm happier than I've been in years."

Laura wanted a new life. "For years my retirement plan was to travel as much as possible. I don't mind travelling alone, but it's expensive and I wasn't sure I was going to be able to afford it. I knew I'd have to watch my finances carefully, so I decided to look around for alternatives. And I found them! Everyone knows about bed-and-breakfasts, but I also found that I like travelling by freighter and through the Elder Hostel program. I even went to Peru as an assistant tour guide in exchange for my air fare, hotel and meals."

John, Martin and Laura made decisions about how best to use their time, where to live, and with whom they'd like to spend time. Retirement represents an opportunity to do things differently. It offers the chance to focus more on the things you'd like to do and perhaps do less of what you don't like.

Sound intriguing? Let's think about that and write down some thoughts. Get your pen and paper ready. Look at worksheet four, "What I like and don't like about my life," and spend some time considering your likes and dislikes. Then look at worksheet five, "Changing your lifestyle." What did you learn? Are you surprised? Does it confirm what you've been feeling? Does it motivate you to change?

Satisfaction is our barometer of the appropriateness of our lifestyles. Once you've retired you must find ways to satisfy those needs that were previously filled by work. Consider the need to be involved in a meaningful way. Once you're retired you might consider doing volunteer work at a hospital, art gallery or school. Or the need to be challenged with new problems or new ideas. Once retired you might go back to school, join the book club at your local library or attend lectures at a museum.

Now, what are your needs? There's space for you to list them in worksheet six, "Satisfying your needs in retirement." At the same time, try to identify ways in which you might fulfill each one. Don't worry if you're not satisfied with this first stab at it. It isn't always easy to recognize your personal needs; it's even more difficult to understand how they're satisfied. We'll look at ways in which you can

spend your time in retirement throughout the rest of this chapter. Keep the exercise in mind and turn back to this page, filling in a line here and there, until you've identified your needs and feel confident you'll be able to satisfy them in retirement.

Time on your hands

Regardless of the choice, everybody fills time with different kinds of activities, interests, hobbies and pursuits. Some individuals have sufficient time to accomplish all they like to do; others never seem to have enough time. There are those who have too much time on their hands – and it sits there like a dead weight. Taking a quick glance at a typical day before and after retirement will make the vast difference in free time available to you in retirement strikingly apparent.

Now's your chance to work on a time-pie of your own. You can do it on worksheet seven. First, look at how you spend the minutes and hours of each day now, before you're retired – time spent sleeping, eating, working, on personal hygiene, household tasks, reading, watching television, relaxing, pursuing hobbies, chatting with friends or playing sports. In the second time-pie, try to imagine how you would spend time during the day once you're retired. There'll be a good chunk of every day available for leisure activities.

If you're worried about how you will spend your time in retirement, you should address it now. Your days in retirement are not time that has to be filled, your choices must be satisfying. You should also be flexible. If you're unable to pursue an activity, whether because it's not possible or you discover that it's boring, you should be able to move on to something different. Can you produce a list of interests, activities, hobbies, and pursuits that is fairly long and varied? If you can, you will probably not have any trouble settling into retirement. If not, you should be giving this some serious

What I like and don't like about my life   **WORKSHEET 4**

	Like	Dislike
Your living arrangements		
Leisure time		
Relationships		
Health		
Lifestyle		
Stress		
Self-image		
Finances		

thought or you could run into problems with boredom and loneliness later.

This isn't an easy task. After years of demands on our time from work and family, it can be hard to imagine what we'd do with free time. Putting thoughts down on paper often helps. But where do you start? Well, you can start at the beginning. What did you like doing when you were younger – before work and family. Can you list things that

you have often said you'd like to do but haven't had time? Take a look at "Your leisure lifeline" and "Your activity wish list."

Could you again do some of those things you once enjoyed? Could you plan to start doing them now? Are there family members, friends, acquaintances or fellow workers that you'd like to get to know better? People with whom you'd like to spend more time? Can you talk with them and

Changing your lifestyle   **WORKSHEET 5**

Likes   **How to do more**

_____

_____

_____

_____

Dislikes   **How to do less**

_____

_____

_____

_____

suggest possible activities to do together? Is there something you'd like to learn, courses you want to take or something specific you'd like to accomplish? What is preventing you from doing it?

There are many, many possibilities from which you can choose. The crux is to narrow down the possibilities to those that are really meaningful to you and then schedule them into your retirement. It's best to choose activities that not only appeal to you, but are affordable. Your retirement will be shaped not only by your interests but also by your finances – in fact, your retirement might mean a new career.

A few thoughts about work

Why even think such thoughts? Isn't ceasing to work the essence of retirement, its raison d'être? Surely that's what retirement is, retiring from long hours, tedious repetition, lack of freedom and control over our own time. Yet many people begin new careers within twelve months of retiring. In a recent survey, close to 70 percent of Canadian Association of Retired

Persons members said they wanted to work part-time. Why? The need for extra income is a good reason for continuing to work, particularly if you've retired early or your pension is inadequate. However, this can also be your opportunity to work at something that has always intrigued you. Finally, there are those who enjoyed working but not in the job or circumstances from which they retired. Usually it's a combination of factors that lead people back to work. But you should look on your retirement as a second chance, an opportunity to move in new directions and leave old mistakes behind.

The first step is to look at the working world around you. How has it changed in the last ten or fifteen years? How do you think it might change over the next decade? The workplace is changing rapidly. Low-cost, sophisticated computer systems are eliminating many jobs at the same time they're creating new opportunities. However, taking advantage of these new opportunities usually requires you to invest time and money in training. Unfortunately, few companies are willing to invest in training

Satisfying your needs in retirement

Your physical need for activity
_____

_____

_____

Your intellectual need to learn and to be challenged
_____

_____

_____

Your social and emotional need for companions
_____

_____

_____

Your spiritual need to feel fulfilled and of value to the world
_____

_____

_____

older workers. If you decide to reenter the work force after retirement, you'll have to come fully prepared, with your old talents enhanced by new skills that you've gained through study or training.

The next step is to know your skills: Take a close look at those things you can do well and pinpoint the skill involved in that activity. You might find you're skilled at analyzing information, arranging social functions, influencing others, or coping with complex problems. Remember you learned how to be persuasive when you sold your first lemonade drink on the front lawn that summer day years ago, or when you sold a charity on a way to raise money, or just yesterday when you sold your three-year-old grandchild on a nap.

Make an inventory of your skills. Can you drive a car, treat sick people or animals, keep books, counsel people, write or edit, teach math or history, draw up financial plans, navigate a boat? Can you play a musical instrument, prepare a legal action, speak a foreign language, act or design clothes? Pause for a mo-

ment and consider those things you do well and write down all your skills on the worksheet "Your skills, interests and natural abilities" even if they don't seem to be something you could "sell."

It's also important to consider how you can apply your skills. Perhaps you have a natural flair for carpentry, drawing and designing, gardening, working with animals, teaching or writing. Surely such hobbies and interests can pay off in some way. Carpentry skills might lead to a part-time job building cabinets and furniture or creating novelty items. A gift for designing might lead to the creation of ads or flyers for local stores. A green thumb could lead to helping others landscape their yards or growing and drying herbs. A flair for working with animals might lead to boarding and training pets.

If your skills are managerial or technical, you might continue working part-time, perhaps under the auspices of the Federal Business Development Bank or through an organization known as Counselling Assistance to Small Enterprises, which encourages retired business

Your leisure time – before and after retirement

On the clocks, draw the time usually spent during a typical day before and after retirement on various activities. On your before-retirement clock include activities such as getting ready for work and getting to and from work as part of your working time. Don't forget to include the time you spend doing personal and household tasks and just kicking around. The difference will be even more apparent if you colour each type of activity a different colour.

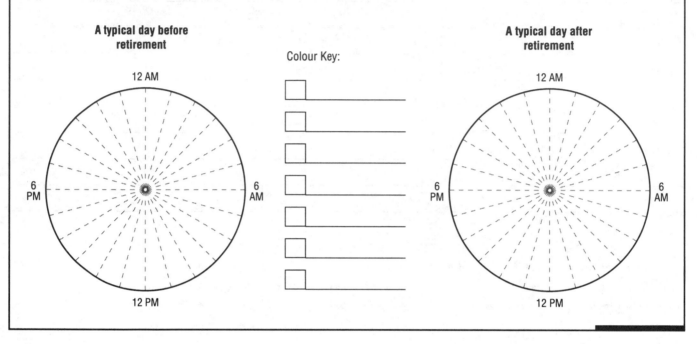

A typical day before retirement

A typical day after retirement

Colour Key:

people to help small businesses with problems. There are also many nonprofit agencies, groups funded by such organizations as Health and Welfare Canada's New Horizons program for seniors. There is the YMCA Over-55 program, the Golden Opportunity Employment Bureau, the Senior Citizens' Job Bureau, 55-Plus Personnel Placement, and Experience Unlimited located in cities and towns across Canada. Spend some time with your phone directory or local seniors' help organizations to find out what's available in your area.

Finding a job

You don't have to find your way through this new marketplace alone. If your employer does not provide any retirement counselling, you can use the services provided by federal, provincial and municipal governments.

Community colleges and universities offer free counselling for those exploring the possibility of returning to school; a few also provide career planning courses and job search counselling for students and alumni. Check the Yellow Pages and local newspapers for community programs. There are private placement companies that offer their services for around $75 an hour or $200 for a resume. (Don't depend too much on your resume. You should have a good one but that alone will not guarantee you a job.)

You can also turn to one of the many books on job-hunting. One of the best is *What Color Is Your Parachute?* by Richard Bolles. It's been a bestseller since 1978 and is updated every two years. There are many different approaches to finding a retirement job but Lois Faris, who launched Life Transitions Associates in Calgary

Write down the activities, interests and skills that you remember enjoying and not enjoying at each stage of life. The same activity might appear several times. Take your time and jog down memory lane.

Age 20
_____

_____

_____

Age 30
_____

_____

_____

Age 40
_____

_____

_____

after taking an early retirement, recommends this ten-tip process:

- Write down your answers to the following: What do I want to do and where do I want to do it? Your success will depend on the clarity of your goal. Once you've declared what you would love to do, find someone who will pay you to do it.

- List every organization or group that might provide an opportunity for you. Then invite two or three creative and connected people to meet with you to brainstorm. See how many ideas and opportunities you can come up with – it could be pages.

- Explore these ideas a few at a time. Choose the ones that have the strongest appeal. Contact people you know or would like to know who have information about the options you've chosen to explore. Ask for fifteen-minute interviews. Take along a note book. Most people will give you more time and ideas than you expect. If you are still working full-time, even three hours a week, strategically planned, can produce results.

- Spend some time with phone books, news-papers, magazines and at libraries. Read just enough to get ideas and names, then contact people to discuss the opportunities as you see them.

- Let everyone know you're job-hunting. Don't depend on the telephone – go to interviews, meet people for lunch, spread the word. But be effective. That means showing genuine interest in the person you're with. The focus has to be on the needs of the person to whom you're talking, not you.

- Nurture your network. If you value and appreciate all your contacts they will remember you and open many doors for you.

- Update your knowledge and skills. Attending conferences, taking courses or volunteering will make you more employable.

- You need an advisory group, a team to cheer you on. Choose the most creative and challenging people you know or can get to know to be on your team. What's in it for them? You can offer to reciprocate and coach and cheer them toward their goals. There is nothing patronizing when helping

Your activity wish list

_____

_____

_____

_____

_____

_____

_____

_____

_____

_____

_____

in a reciprocal arrangement. Three to six people make a good working group. It takes as little as thirty minutes once in a while to be effective. Continue meeting only if it works for everyone.

■ Target potential employers and be selective when sending out resumes. It's more effective to mail out twenty to appropriate targets than to mail out two hundred at random.

■ Tune up your attitude toward change and transition. Instead of resisting it, welcome insecurity and uncertainty.

Your job search

Prepare yourself for the interview. Remember, you'll want to find a job that is satisfying and you'll want to ask as many questions as you're asked. Develop your own set of questions before the interview, questions that will elicit information you need. You can also try to anticipate the questions. Run through an interview scenario several times, using a job-hunt-ing notebook to write down answers to the pertinent questions. You can always take the notebook to the interview.

Starting your own business

Starting a business appeals to many people. It's a logical outlet for a hobby or interest and it offers the opportunity to run your own show. But it can be risky, especially if all the details aren't worked out in advance. Sufficient capital is essential; profits will take time. If you'd like to pursue the possibility of running your own business, but aren't sure which direction to take, read on.

I started my company thirteen years ago and have had the pleasure of counselling hundreds of business owners. I've gained great respect for people who succeed. They've worked hard to overcome the pitfalls and problems. We actually discourage people from starting their own businesses because of the many pitfalls involved. Yet, there's probably never been a

Your combination of skills and interests

Your natural abilities

What do you do well naturally? In other words, what do you do almost without thinking?

_____

_____

_____

_____

Your skills

Identify your skills and list them below. Remember, it is your combination of skills and natural abilities that you have that makes you unique. The way you combine them will identify business and employment opportunities for you.

_____

_____

_____

_____

Your interests

Although we should be interested in the work we do at any time in our lives, during retirement we have the freedom to indulge our personal interests.

_____

_____

_____

_____

_____

better time to start one. Businesses and governments have cut back their work forces to cope with the recent recession and are in no mood to hire new employees. Instead, they'll be looking for small businesses and independent consultants to fill any gaps in the expertise and services. And they will have needs. Business will boom in the 1990s as the economy recovers. I'm not the only one who believes the opportunities for small businesses will abound. In 1991 alone, 328,000 businesses were started in Canada – and half of them were started by women.

However, about 80 percent of these new businesses will fold within three years. Most of the rest will bring their owners a comfortable livelihood; only a handful will bring their owners wealth.

It's a great Canadian dream to be your own boss. There's a feeling of creativity, self-determination and control. There's also the pride in telling others that you're the boss – that you own the company. But don't delude yourself; it isn't easy. You can't afford to hire employees with the diverse talents needed by a young company. Depending on the business, you may need knowledge in some or all of the following areas: marketing and sales, production, administration and business management, accounting, personnel, law and finance. If you were paid a reasonable salary for each of these activities, you'd be earning about $500,000 a year!

Instead, you'll operate with little pay until your business becomes profitable. Risks of failure are great, which is why banks won't make loans to start-up businesses without airtight security. Most leasing companies won't make equipment leases available until you've been around at least three years.

Where do you get started? Obviously, you need a business concept, one that has a realistic chance of being successful. Many people flounder right here. Some have too many ideas and go off in too many directions. Others can't develop confidence in any of their plans. Ideas come from recognizing trends in society – goods and services that people will need or want. A muffin was considered to be healthier than a doughnut – now muffin shops abound. You might find an already successful business that's neglecting the market or not fully serving your area. Or, you might develop a product or service based on your own expertise.

Build a business around your own skills, experience and insight. It may be hard to find your niche. But it's this that will make success possible. Many people look to their own business history as a guide, but the opportunity could spring from a hobby, or even from your work as a volunteer. Choose something you love because you'll spend a lot of time trying to make it work.

Try to stay away from fads; they fade as quickly as they appear. By the time you discover this year's pet rock, someone else will have developed it into an organized business. Instead, create what your market really needs. Study demographic trends and changes in what people are doing. And once you've discovered a good idea, test it. Companies like Procter &

Gamble Inc. spend millions before they launch new products. Your dollar commitment, relatively, is just as large. Spend the time, even if it's several months, to find out if your idea works, if the market wants your product or service, and what price it will pay. At the same time, you'll be promoting yourself to potential customers and learning the best way to sell.

In addition to good luck and a sense of humour, every business owner needs:

- Sufficient capital for two years, since sales can be unbelievably slow.
- Entrepreneurial qualities: drive, ambition, determination, creativity, commitment and enough optimism to keep the dream.
- A positive attitude and enthusiasm to convince customers, suppliers, employees and partners to buy into the dream.
- A capacity for hard work and the ability to focus attention for long periods of time.
- Confidence in yourself and what you are doing.
- Presentation skills to sell ideas and products to everyone you meet.
- Willingness to take calculated risks once you've studied the situation.
- Leadership and team-building skills.
- Honesty and integrity.
- Supportive people to share the dream and give you the time and resources to pursue it.
- A consuming love of the business and what it can provide for you. Without this commitment, you'll falter.

The capital required to start your business is two to three times what you think you need. Many businesses fail because owners underestimate the money required to sustain the business until a profit is achieved. As a general rule, businesses lose money in the first year, break even in the second, and become profitable in the third. You need enough capital to get that far. To know how much you need you should prepare a comprehensive and realistic business plan.

Once all the elements are analyzed, you'll be able to prepare estimates of resources needed: employees, equipment, premises, vehicles, inventories and working capital. You'll forecast revenues and expenses – cash receipts and disbursements – month by month for a period of one to three years.

An accountant can help you draft a business plan, but a good place to start is your bank, library, community college and the Federal Business Development Bureau, the FBDB. The banks produce booklets for people interested in starting a business. The province of Ontario has a small-business hot line: 1-800-567-2345. British Columbia has one too: (604) 356-5777. The FBDB has a lot of free books and programs. Call them at 1-800-361-2126 or write 800 Victoria Square, Tour de la Place Victoria, P.O. Box 335, Montreal, Quebec H4Z 1L4.

In most cases, your capital will come from you and your partners. Banks don't provide start-up capital, although they will lend against your assets – your house, personal investments and bank deposits. Banks also provide term loans for equipment and working capital loans, secured by accounts receivable and inventories. If you're short of start-up money, you'll need to find partners (silent or otherwise), or a rich uncle. Often, family members become investment partners. Or you may have to scale back your plans to something you can afford.

Buy the business you want

An obvious way to ensure success is to buy an already profitable business. The risk here is that you may be fooled into paying too much or acquiring hidden problems. You should hire a professional with expertise in buying and selling businesses – a broker or chartered accountant specializing in the area. He or she can give you a fighting chance of making a sound purchase, and the right purchase will repay the consulting fees many times over.

Buying a successful business from an elderly owner may provide the best opportunity. The firm will often enjoy the goodwill of customer relationships that have existed for years. Employees will know their jobs and may run the company with little need for supervision.

Your energy and ideas might be just what's needed to push the business to its next level of profitability. But make sure you don't destroy the formula that makes the business a success today. Nurture and support the existing secret of success, and complement it with adjustments and improvements that meet customer needs.

Your entrepreneurial success depends on knowing your business thoroughly and understanding the competition. Study your competition closely: You can learn from their weaknesses and strengths.

Many people buy franchises. You'll pay more money to get started than you would on your own but you can get good value for your money. Any franchise you buy should be well established; it should have proven technology, an already established brand name, solid sales and promotion strategies. All aspects of its operation, from hiring and training staff to the colour of stationery and menus, should be in place and effective. You and your employees should be offered comprehensive training and on-the-job support until the business is operating successfully.

You'll need to do your homework. Meet with existing franchisees to find out how they're doing and whether the franchiser's promises have been met. If you can, meet with a few former franchise owners and find out why they left the business.

Again, a business consultant will be invaluable in finding the right franchise for you. Buying a franchise is not a guarantee of success. The TCBY Inc. yogurt shops disappeared almost as quickly as they landed on the fast-food scene. Even if a franchise appears to be very successful in one place it could fail in a different location – if that location is just wrong. Or your advertising and promotion may not work. Costs might be too high for your volume. Your managers might not inspire good service. And, don't forget that people's tastes change – something that was successful yesterday might not be successful tomorrow.

Indeed, whether you buy or build your own business, surround yourself with the best available professional help: accountants, lawyers, business consultants, suppliers. Get them enthusiastic. Not only will they advise you well in their area of specialty, they will promote your business to others, becoming an important part of your sales team, your marketing network.

You might ask how someone age fifty-five, sixty or sixty-five could persuade others that he or she has a future in business. It's simple. No one cares how old you are. They just want to know if you can do the job – if you can deliver what you promise in quality, price, timeliness and reliability. The doubts are only within ourselves. If you know your business and you're enthusiastic, concerns about your age will quickly disappear. People will give you a try. Then your abilities will take over and demonstrate why you will be successful.

Now, let's examine a few ideas that offer a good shot at delivering both fun and profit:

- Provide office help to associations. Associations are staffed by volunteers and need business services such as word processing, bookkeeping and public relations expertise to make things run smoothly, especially when volunteers aren't up to a job that might need a professional touch.

- Open a bed-and-breakfast. You can turn your country home into friendly overnight accommodation and your natural sense of hospitality will be rewarded. This will appeal to anyone with a country home or a big home in the city.

- Match buyers of businesses to sellers. You can develop your own supply of businesses for sale by contacting accountants and lawyers or contact franchisers.

- Turn your own experience into advice for others having problems with alcohol, drugs, money, marriage, death or terminal illness.

- Become an export consultant, especially if you gained experience in foreign trade before retiring. You can help small- and medium-sized Canadian businesses sell their products in foreign countries. They need leads, and often lack time and know-how to develop them. They often need help developing overseas contacts with foreign businesses and Canadian trade commissioners, and in understanding foreign markets, customs and languages.

- Organize care for older seniors in their homes. Elderly seniors want to stay in their homes but can't always cope with home, health and personal care.

- Help home buyers and mortgage lenders by inspecting houses for defects in structure and heating, plumbing or mechanical systems. This is a natural for someone with a background in engineering or construction.

- Offer landscape and outdoor house care. People often don't have time to keep their houses looking their best. If you've got the know-how, you can probably find lots of neighbourhood talent to do the work.

- Plan parties. Many companies need help in planning, organizing and running events for staff, customers, suppliers and friends. All you need is imagination and the patience to arrange the many details.

- Open a specialty sports shop or clinic. If you really want to indulge an interest you might consider opening a bookstore specializing in books on particular topics such as sailing or racquet sports, or crafts.

Become a travel tour guide. Many people prefer to travel with escorts. Acting as a tour guide can be another way to indulge your own passion for travel. But the tours have to be unique. If you've travelled extensively, even as part of your job, you can turn your expertise at deciphering airline schedules and finding hotels into a tidy profit. You might have an area of expertise that could make you a tour guide of unique insight. A professor of Italian history might offer tours of Italy, an archaeologist, tours of Greece.

Other possibilities will emerge from your skills and interests. If you're creative you might consider ceramic crafts, costume jewellery, weaving rugs or scarves or hand-tooling leather. If you have teaching skills, consider adult-education classes, private tutorials or teaching a language, music or singing. Writers could earn income from research, writing or editing – copy editors and proofreaders are especially apt choices for people schooled at a time when attention was paid to the details of English grammar. Others might set up businesses that offer housekeeping, child care, babysitting or nursing. If you know how to make and repair sports equipment, you could repair skis, maintain fishing poles, or prepare fishing lures.

If you are interested in starting a business that you can run from your home take a look at Valerie Bohigian's *Real Money from Home: How to Start, Manage and Profit from a Home-based Service Business,* published by New American Library. There's even a home-business magazine, *Home Business Report,* available from 2949 Ash Street, Abbotsford, British Columbia V2S 4G5.

Working as a volunteer

Today's volunteers make a big impact. In 1987, close to five million Canadians contributed nearly a billion hours to volunteering. Forty-six percent of those volunteers were over age fifty-five, participating in a variety of services such as Meals On Wheels, the Red Cross, and Big Brother or Big Sister programs. They visit shut-ins, work in museums, staff phone-alert services for people living alone or serve as telephone clearing houses for seniors' projects.

People who donate time and effort to volunteering usually find that it brings tremendous satisfaction. Helping others provides purpose in life, brings recognition, contributes to a sense of belonging and can improve your skills and abilities. It's stimulating and challenging for the mind and the body and also brings pleasure and happiness.

Doing community service can be especially desirable for people who have just retired. It helps reduce the shock of leaving a structured work environment and of having to fill free time. Prospective volunteers need not worry about training. Most agencies provide special courses. And you can choose a task that appeals to you and decide your own hours and days of work.

You can find volunteer work by looking through the Yellow Pages. Perhaps you'd like to raise funds for a theatre group, counsel troubled teens, become a "grandparent" to a young family, read to the ill or very old, act as a guide at your local art gallery, repair children's toys at a drop-in centre, prepare care packages. The list is endless.

In larger communities, there is often a central volunteer agency that coordinates the needs of the community through its numerous support services and the individual needs of the volunteer. If you see a need that is not being met that you would like to fill you should explore New Horizons. This is a federally funded program geared to groups of at least ten people age sixty years and older. It was established to finance the start-up of approved senior citizens' projects. The organization usually funds projects in sports and recreation, crafts and hobbies, culture and education, or social services. For more information, consult the blue government pages of your phone directory under New Horizons or Health and Welfare Canada.

The Canadian Executive Services Overseas enables retired business people to volunteer as advisers, travelling to many parts of the Third World to provide advice on a range of issues. CESO is at 415 Yonge Street, Suite 2000, Toronto, Ontario M5B 2S7. You can also call (416) 596-2376.

If one volunteer experience isn't working out, don't hesitate to move on. Ask yourself what skills you can offer, what time you have available, and who would benefit from you. You should get satisfaction from volunteering. Effective placement should include an interview with the volunteer coordinator of the service or agency you are considering. Find out all about the organization, the expectations for volunteers, the types of activity available and the scheduling and flexibility of hours of work.

Continuing education

It used to be thought that we stopped learning after high school or university. Now, we recognize that learning is a life-long process. Most educational institutions have noticed the trend and are reaching out to every age group – in fact, they even offer seniors discounts on fees. There are night courses, weekend seminars and correspondence courses. Libraries often offer short courses and evening presentations. The mental exercise that learning demands will keep the mind fit, much the way physical exercise keeps the body in shape. Even memory improves, the more we work at it.

Unfortunately, some individuals don't take advantage of the opportunity to continue their education in retirement because they believe they're too old. This just isn't true. You have the capacity to learn throughout your life. If you need inspiration, we have a client who is

studying the Greek classics – in the original Greek. Another is learning to sing opera. A retired nurse is studying therapeutic massage and holistic medicine. Some of them enjoy the stimulation of fellow students. Others simply find it exciting to learn, to approach and explore new areas of thought.

Of course, some resistance to going back to school arises from a fear of failure, anxiety over exams and an unwillingness to find yourself being compared to others, especially to the young. Don't worry. Educators recognize most of these concerns and most continuing studies programs are structured to create an atmosphere in which you will feel comfortable. The next time you get a calendar from an education institution in your mailbox, take time to read it. Or you can call your local university or community college for a curriculum and list of courses offered through their continuing education departments.

Exploring the world

Many people travel throughout their lives, taking advantage of vacations to rush here and there. In retirement we often have the freedom and time to really explore the world. The possibilities are limited only by your imagination. Information is widely available in newspapers, magazines, books, brochures, advertisements, on radio and television, through travel shows, exhibitions, from libraries, travel agencies, automobile clubs, transportation services, universities and colleges, governments, community clubs, associations and simply by word-of-mouth as our friends and neighbours share their travel experiences.

The Globe and Mail even publishes a regular column called Mature Travellers. A few agencies across Canada concentrate on trips for older tourists. It's not always as costly as you might think. You can travel by bus rather than plane; by freighter rather than cruise ship. A

Travelling in retirement

Where do I want to go?

_____

_____

With whom?

_____

_____

When? What time of year?

_____

_____

How long do I need to fully enjoy it?

_____

_____

How much will it cost?

_____

_____

Can I afford it? If not, what do I have to do to make it possible?

_____

_____

Do I need to purchase special clothes or equipment? If so, what?

_____

_____

Personal thoughts on travelling

_____

_____

_____

camping trip is less expensive than staying in motels or hotels. Bed-and-breakfasts not only provide cheaper accommodation, they also give you an opportunity to meet local people. You can share the cost of travel with companions or travel in the off-season.

Elder Hostel is one organization that combines inexpensive travel with education for mature students. For a reasonable price, seniors age sixty or over and the husbands and wives of qualifying seniors can travel around Canada or around the world to dozens of countries, rooming in university residences and studying liberal arts and the sciences. Elder Hostel can be reached at 308 Wellington Street, Kingston, Ontario K7K 7A7.

You might also consider joining the Home Holiday World Exchange. This program lists homes that are available for exchange throughout the world. If a particular home interests you, you can write to the owner suggesting an exchange with your home. There are various kinds of exchanges available – a straight exchange of homes, exchange of home and car, and exchange of home with payment of a small stipend. Although there are strict guidelines on insurance, safety and cleaning, it is your correspondence with the other home owner that establishes the ground rules, conditions and agreement. Get more information by writing to 1707 Platt Crescent, North Vancouver, British Columbia V7J 1X9.

If you have considerable flexibility, you can also consider joining a last-minute travel club. These clubs offer the airplane seats, cruises and vacation packages that haven't been sold. You could find yourself on a charter cruise of the Caribbean leaving within days of your call – at less than half the regular fare. Check the newspaper travel pages for advertisements. Museums, art galleries and universities often sponsor educational group travel. There are also associations and clubs that cater to the retired by offering group packages. Group travel can be especially appealing to single persons who prefer not to travel alone. Finally, consider a working tour. If you are an expert in some field, you can agree to deliver lectures on a cruise ship in exchange for free transportation. More demanding is the job of tour director, leading a group to a particular destination, again in exchange for travel expenses.

There are plenty of things to do with all that free time you'll have in retirement. The key to making the most of it lies in knowing your aspirations, what you need to do and then putting your game plan into action. Retirement can be the time of your life, but only you know exactly what shape it will take for you.

Notes

_____

_____

_____

_____

_____

_____

_____

_____

_____

_____

_____

_____

_____

A house is not a home

There's more to a home than the bricks and mortar. My home is the place where I can put my feet up on the coffee table for a Sunday afternoon of golf on television. This is where I can nap on the couch under a big, old bear rug or just spread my work over the dining room table in the evenings.

My wife is not always too pleased with my sense of home but she has her own pleasures. And we'd miss them if we lived anywhere else on earth. Maybe you feel the same way about your place, too.

Still, there's good reason to take a hard look at your current home. Is it where you want to retire, to live for the next ten years? Or the next forty? The place you have lived in for twenty years might have been great for raising children and work. But is it where you want to live the rest of your days? Perhaps you've decided to get a bigger home, to move to another locale or to build the dream home you've always wanted.

Whatever you've been thinking, it's important to realize that the place you call home makes a significant contribution to your sense of well-being. Unfortunately, some people make a decision to move because they think most people do move in retirement.

So they sell everything, pull up their roots and retire to a place they've always dreamed about, perhaps a condo in Florida. But some of them end up lying awake at night, wondering why they don't feel happy. The dream has become a nightmare! They miss the family, old friends, the familiarity. They feel lonely and out of place. What they're beginning to realize is that something is missing.

What's missing are the factors that contribute to a sense of home. Home is an encompassing concept that includes not only the type of structure but also significant people in your life: family, friends, neighbours and friends from work. It includes conveniences you expect to have within reach and it also means the intangible factors — memories, comfort, security, familiarity and roots — that are important to you. So it's important to identify your needs and then discuss them with your husband, wife, friend or anybody else with whom you plan to share your place.

Should you move at all? Thinking that you have to move when you retire because that's what everybody does is downright unhelpful. Your decision to move should be based on what you want to do. When you identify your retirement lifestyle you can determine if moving is part of your retirement planning. So read on, we'll look more closely at defining "home" and assess the alternatives you have.

Looking at your home

Let's consider the financial pros and cons of keeping a house. We live in an era of economic uncertainty, so is it prudent to hold onto your house? Resale prices of average-priced houses have been level over the past few years. In major centres such as Toronto, prices for more expensive houses have suffered declines of 25 percent or more during the recession. In other cities, such as Montreal and Winnipeg, prices have been more stable but they have never achieved the sky-high prices of Toronto in the 1980s.

Economists are less certain about the direction of future house prices than they have been in the past. Some point to continuing decline, or at least increases below the annual rate of inflation. The market analysis centre of the Canadian Mortgage and Housing Corporation (CMHC) agrees. Even in hot markets like Vancouver, prices are stable or falling slightly.

The state of the housing market is not your only financial concern. Is your mortgage paid off? Are there any major debts against the house, or major repairs that need to be made? What about property taxes and maintenance charges? Will you be able to afford them on your retirement income? If you rent, will government rent controls keep costs within reach? The basic question is: Can you continue to live in your current home, maintain your lifestyle and remain financially secure?

We'll talk about the financial decision to move in chapter ten. For now, let's concentrate on the lifestyle decision. Would it be more convenient to live in a smaller place? What about the neighbourhood: Is it a friendly, well-maintained community with facilities and services you need now and in the future? Is there convenient, dependable public transportation? Are there stores nearby, or delivery services? Is there a local community centre? Is the neighbourhood relatively free of crime? Are sidewalks kept clear of snow during the winter?

Look critically at your own dwelling. Are there too many stairs, slippery floors, inadequate lighting? Are these or other problems fixable? Is the superintendent in your rental building sufficiently cooperative? Are you now, and will you in the future, be able to do all the chores your place requires?

The late Billy Baldwin, a celebrated American interior decorator, said: "Comfort is perhaps the ultimate luxury." That's partly why many people do choose to stay in the family house. Where else can they be so comfortable? You might feel the same. It's your home. You've lived in it for years, improved it and put up with that rotten neighbour. You've added features that can't be found elsewhere. Your location is unique; no one could duplicate it for double the price. And, most important, it's the good times that have you here. Homes are more than just houses: They hold memories. These emotional ties to the neighbourhood as well as to your home are important considerations when you think about moving.

Now think about what you would need if you were to move. If you are parents, will your children live with you in retirement? Even children who move out sometimes move back, for financial or marital reasons. Where else do they have a car at their disposal, a fridge full of food, laundry service, telephone, and all the comforts of home — for free?

Our friends, David and Margaret, had that problem. After raising five children, they looked forward to being empty-nesters. But the family home was so comfortable and so much fun that the kids weren't interested in moving out. To give them an incentive, the Taylors sold their six-bedroom house and moved to a three-bedroom bungalow. The kids still stayed. One moved into the unfinished basement. Three others crammed into the two small bedrooms. Life went on. A year later, the Taylors moved again — to another six-bedroom home. Everyone had breathing room again.

Children aside, ask yourself some other questions. How much travelling are you planning to do? Do you pursue most of your interests at home, or at the club, cottage or church? Do family members stay or visit regularly? Do you entertain at home or meet friends outside?

Now that you're no longer tied to a job, would a move to a new area be right for you?

It might take you out of traffic congestion, noise or a crime-ridden neighbourhood. But perhaps you'd be far from friends and relatives.

Take a look at the worksheet "Will your home meet your needs in retirement?" This will help you to assess your home for retirement and identify the factors important to you if you plan to make a change. Is it clear that you should stay in your existing home? Most Canadians do stay put after retirement, although an increasing number are moving. There has also been a trend toward owning two homes in retirement; one home close to family and friends, a second down south or in the country. If you want to remain or aren't sure, consider what you could do to make your home a better place for retirement.

Most of you, regardless of your age, health or personal circumstance, want to be in your own homes, living active, independent lives. Unfortunately, some retirees, often the very elderly, reach a point when circumstances make this difficult. Sometimes they can't keep up with the maintenance and repairs; or, they have problems making meals or taking care of hygienic matters. A few have medical, safety and financial problems. With government assistance, family and community support, many people overcome these problems. Governments, both national and provincial, have departments whose mandates are to deal with the issues and concerns of the senior population.

CMHC prepared a study in 1991 that looks at housing choices for older Canadians, and also provides other excellent publications that can help you decide how you want to live. Contact your local CMHC office to obtain these publications: *Housing Choices for Older Canadians* and *Housing Choices for Older Canadians: New Financial and Tenure Options.*

Governments aren't the only ones who can help you. Developers, architects and builders are increasingly interested in catering to the older population. Financial help, such as home-equity conversion plans, can enable you to turn the value of your house into cash without selling and moving out. I'll look at financial options in later chapters of this book.

What I'm trying to get at in all this is to show you the importance of your choice in homes. You need to plan ahead, to consider the possible consequences of changes to your health, finances and other personal circumstances which might force you to consider other options. Giving some thought to potential changes, talking about it with your family and looking at possible options can help you avoid a future crisis. Otherwise, you could end up moving into a home where you will be miserable because you have not given yourself time to find a more suitable home. Unfortunately, our aging population has created waiting lists at more desirable retirement homes. So start thinking and talking to others about your home needs now.

Now let's talk about other housing options you might want to consider.

Home sharing

If you're short of money or you need physical assistance, think about home sharing. Among families, the idea is hardly new. In fact, it was the social norm until the middle of this century. Mom, Dad, the kids and a grandparent were a common sight around dining tables across Canada. Then families began dispersing across the continent, either because they wanted to move or because they were chasing jobs. Suddenly, living together became much harder to arrange.

But for someone with a large home, sharing your place with others sometimes makes sense. It not only provides a little extra income or help with the rent, it can also provide help with the cooking, housekeeping, repairs or gardening. Home sharing also provides you

Will your home meet your needs in retirement?

	Yes or no	What would be better

The enjoyment of your home

Are there too many rooms or stairs?

Is your home safe?
Does it need better lighting or carpets instead of scatter rugs?

Do you like the size of your home and yard?

Do you enjoy working on the grounds, gardens, repairs?

Your neighbourhood

Are you close enough to friends, relatives and family?

Are you close enough to stores or places of entertainment?

Are the neighbours friendly, helpful?

Is the neighbourhood safe?

Is the street too noisy, or too quiet?

If you live in the city, would you rather live in the country?

If you live in the country, would you rather live in the city?

Would you like to escape the Canadian winters for a southern climate?

Are you close to clubs, associations or recreational centres?

Will it be easy to find new activities, work or hobbies?

Will you be able to exercise nearby?

Are you emotionally tied to this neighbourhood or could you live elsewhere?

Would you like to experience new places?

Transportation

Are there nearby buses, subways, trains or streetcars?

Will you need to buy a second car?

Could you get around by walking or bicycling?

The cost of your home

Will your home be affordable on your retirement income?

Are your costs increasing?

Do you have any major expenses pending, perhaps for repairs?

Are there any subsidies available to help cover those costs?

Is it costly to maintain the grounds or clear snow?

Would you prefer to spend less on your home, perhaps to travel more?

Would you consider finding a boarder to rent a few rooms?

with companionship and security. Your tenants might be a fellow retiree, students or even a single parent. Agencies can fix you up with someone and provide advice and legal agreements. Be sure and check the zoning regulations to confirm that you can do this.

Consider the case of Edna, a divorced Calgary woman in her fifties. Although she loved to travel, Edna had little pension or savings and was sure her travelling days were over. Her only asset was a big old family house. She loved that house, and did not want to sell it. But its upkeep threatened to consume all her retirement income. Home sharing offered a real solution. She was able to find a couple of people to live in her home: a young student at the local community college and an elderly neighbour.

Some independent homeowners are also creating "accessory" apartments. These are self-contained apartments within an existing home. This can be done by converting a floor or by building an extension. Basements and garages can be turned into apartments without changing your own living space. You can rent the apartment and live in the rest of the home or move into the apartment yourself, renting out the rest of the house. An apartment provides privacy and independence without loss of security and companionship. Again, be sure and check out your local zoning rules.

One of our clients, Jane Adam, moved in with her eldest daughter after retirement. Her handy son-in-law converted the two-car garage and basement into a compact home within a home   separate entrance, bedroom, kitchen, dining room, living room with a fireplace and even a screened-in veranda! Just perfect for someone living alone but attached and cared for while Jane is off on her many travels.

Another way to keep the old house is to install a garden suite or granny flat in the backyard. The garden suite is a self-contained one-storey house entirely separate from the main one. These small homes are factory-built and movable; they're easy to install and can be easily moved or sold. Naturally, a certain amount of land must be available and the plan might be hard to implement in congested suburbs. In some cities they are not allowed.

Moving to greener pastures

If your existing dwelling is not going to be suitable for your retirement lifestyle or needs, it's time to find out where you should go and what type of place you'd like to have. Let's consider a few of the options.

Condominiums

The condo has been around for many years, although many Canadians might know it better in the United States than at home. Unfortunately, there have been a number of disaster stories about condominium developments. Typically, problems spring from committing to a property before it's built. It's always risky to buy something you can't see, especially housing. The condo might not be built as you imagined it. Of course, there are many cases in which condo buyers see their dreams come true. Some developers deliver more than you expect.

In any event, buying a condo that is still under construction is tricky. You should always work with a developer who has a long and untarnished reputation. Examine his or her previous developments and talk to other owners to see if they're happy with their investment. It would be a good idea to have a lawyer take a look at the fine print of the bylaws. Often they contain clauses or regulations which might be too restrictive for your chosen lifestyle; some condos do not allow pets or overnight visitors. Others have strict decorating codes that you might find too restrictive. Remember, too, that condominium owners must pay maintenance fees; those fees will not be fixed over time, they'll probably rise. This has implications for your financial planning and management.

Going south

If you're planning to retire outside Canada, carefully consider such factors as the cost of American health care, the impact of a lower Canadian dollar on the purchasing power of your pension, the income tax and estate tax implications, the rules governing Old Age Security pensions and allowances, and the cost of medical care. The cost of health care is particularly important if you plan to move to the United States. I'll talk about these matters in detail in chapter fourteen.

If, after careful consideration, you still want to move away from Canada, perhaps to the United States, Mexico or any other location, go through the following steps to make sure you will be comfortable in your new home:

- Carefully consider the area in terms of your health, social, financial and recreational needs. If you decide to move to a place where your mother tongue is not spoken, consider the demands that will be made on you as you do your daily shopping, try to meet new friends or putter around. Will you be able to find books, magazines, newspapers, entertainment in your own language? Is there a place of worship of your choice in the area? What's the local crime rate? What about transportation; will you be able to get around with ease?

- Write to the state, province or country to which you believe you would like to move and ask for information on housing, taxes, climate and any programs or tax exemptions for seniors.

- Write to the local chamber of commerce and ask them for information on their community. Make sure to tell them of your personal interests; if you want to play chess, ask if there is a local chess club. If you're

interested in the performing arts, ask for information about the theatre, opera, ballet. You might even ask for a local newspaper. A glance through its pages will give you a feel for the place.

- Visit the place on your next vacation. Look at everything.

- Before buying, rent a home there so that if, for any reason, the move fails to work out, you can return without losing any money.

- Glance back at the worksheet "Appraising your home": Does your new home overcome all of the problems with your old home and meet all of your needs.

Often, retirees are drawn to warmer regions such as Florida, Arizona, Mexico, the Caribbean, or southern British Columbia. But could your need for warm weather in the winter be met by visiting these locations for a few months each year? Instead of moving, perhaps you could travel for a time and either close up your home or rent it out. (If you can't find a tenant, ask a friend to live in your house. It's safer to have an occupant in the house; in fact, your insurance policy will probably require that the home be visited daily if you're away for more than forty-eight hours. There are companies that make home checks for a fee.)

I'd like to stress the importance of renting before buying. A retiring pilot and his wife sold their house in Canada and bought another in Phoenix, Arizona. Because their appliances were old, they sold them with the house and bought new ones in the States, saving on moving costs. They even held a garage sale to clear out odds and ends. Unfortunately, their new life in Arizona wasn't what they had thought it would be. Friends from home who talked about following them to Arizona never did. And their new American neighbours seemed older and had different interests than they did. After playing golf for three months, they realized that golfing every day wasn't what they wanted. Nor did they enjoy the sun blazing down every day. They decided to return to Canada, owners of tropical furniture and new appliances too expensive to move. They returned a few thousand dollars lighter, but happy to be back.

By renting, you can test the area and the housing, then decide whether you want to return. You'll have little trouble finding a place to rent. Most major Canadian newspapers carry ads for homes to rent in Florida, Arizona and other sunny places. Local newspapers, rental and real estate agents, and visits to communities under development will add possibilities to your list of choices.

Of course, owning a home does have its conveniences. It allows you to decorate your southern home and to leave clothing and belongings, making travel easier. And you might not want to pass up the low prices available in the overbuilt sunbelt states. But if you're determined to buy, the least you should do is test it first.

Our recommendation: find tenants for your home here and rent one in the south for at least a few months. (Remember, provincial health coverage usually allows for absences of up to six months only.) If you're planning on living in your new home year-round, be sure to visit in the least favourable circumstances. Go in the off-season. See Florida or other sunbelt locations at its hottest and most uncomfortable.

There are books available in bookstores and public libraries which provide checklists of important features to consider. But it's a good idea to prepare your own checklist of factors important to you. Glance back at some of the worksheets you've completed while reading this book. Make sure your new home will allow you to do those things you've decided are important and avoid those things you dislike. Where you live is critical to deciding your future lifestyle. You need a firm picture of the life you intend to lead to decide where your new home will be.

Living in dignity

A home is not just a house. We expect our homes to make it possible for us to enjoy the companionship of others. We want to be secure, comfortable, able to indulge in those activities that bring us pleasure. We want to be able to eat nutritious meals and be close to any care we might need. Sometimes the home that will provide all of this is a retirement home or senior citizens complex.

There are many types of such homes; with some searching you should be able to find the one which provides the environment which you need. There are retirement homes or villages which provide self-contained houses or apartments complete with their own kitchens and bathrooms. Often, there's a dining room where meals can be had and a recreation room for games, television and activities. There might even be a shopping complex. Health care is not provided, but a doctor, dentist and other personal-care providers appear regularly, perhaps once or twice a week.

Then there are homes that provide a little more personal and medical care. The residents are helped with the preparation of food, cleaning, laundry and nurses or paramedics help with medications or medical procedures. Residents might have their own bedroom or bed-sitting room with private bathroom but not a kitchen. They might even share bath facilities. Finally, in an extended-care nursing facility, full medical attention is provided.

Unfortunately, Canada is a bit behind the United States in providing homes for its retired citizens. One of the more interesting developments in the United States is the life-care communities. Hundreds of separate houses and apartments are gathered together with facilities for health care, recreation, social functions and activities, shopping, hobbies and crafts. A geriatric clinic or hospital is on the grounds and residents can move into the full-care centres as needed. As in any home, the more elaborate the facilities, the more expensive it will be.

Fortunately, the vast majority of older people remain in their own homes with family and community help when required. Only about 5 to 10 percent of our elderly, usually the very elderly, are cared for in nursing homes. But retirement housing is a different matter. Such homes ensure that those who are unable or unwilling to prepare their own food are still able to eat nourishing meals. Often, older people move to a senior citizens' apartment for security, particularly if they are single or don't have family members who live nearby. What would happen if they had an accident or a sudden illness? Informal social networks develop in seniors' apartment housing. Neighbours and caretakers are aware of the usual activities of the residents and will investigate if something seems unusual or out of the ordinary. This can be very reassuring, not only for the resident but also for concerned family members.

There is considerable diversity in retirement and nursing homes and it's wise to get accurate information from local senior citizens' housing registries, home-care services and placement agencies. There are homes that are privately run and others that are run by the government or nonprofit organizations. The former can be very expensive while the latter usually peg the rent to the resident's income.

Selling your home

If you have decided to move, you will face the task of selling your home. Real estate agents tell me that retirees often make four mistakes when trying to sell their homes.

■ They don't know and refuse to learn the value of similar houses in their neighbourhood. As a result they are often willing to accept far less than they might be able to demand for their home. Spend time looking at other homes for sale in your neighbourhood. Compare them with your house. Talk to real estate agents and your bank manager.

■ They don't consider whether it's the right time to sell. Determine whether demand is strong for your property. Don't try to sell your house in a hurry, it is a luxury you can probably afford. Put your property up for sale when there's an active market for your type of house. Give yourself at least two or three years.

■ They forget the needs of prospective buyers. Don't spend too much on unusual decorations or structural changes; they might not suit the buyer. A fresh coat of paint outside and inside is sufficient. Remember, a clean house with one or two bad features sells more easily than a dirty one with everything in its favour. Attractive landscaping can also make your home easier to sell.

■ They fail to show their houses at their best. Set aside certain days for showing the house so that you can prepare for the event. It's best to sell a house while you're in it.

Well, I hope I've convinced you that your home is more than just a building? Your satisfaction in retirement is going to depend upon a comfortable home that allows you to live as you choose. Take the time to consider your needs very carefully.

Chapter 4

People to people

It's an old truism that the end of one thing is the beginning of another. It's a particularly apt observation for the changes that occur at retirement. Think back to when you first left home and got a job. Or to when you got married.

During each of those times you went through some fundamental changes in the way you related to your family and friends. I know that I did. Well, the same thing is going to happen when you retire, and some of the changes are the biggest you'll ever experience.

Do relationships change after retirement? The answer is yes and no. Your retirement can have a ripple effect on the people close to you. For example, Chuck, age fifty-three, arrives at work and learns that he'll be offered an unexpected early retirement. The financial incentive is good and he fears the offer won't be repeated, meaning termination instead. Chuck had been planning his retirement for age sixty, not fifty-three! He doesn't feel financially or emotionally ready for this change. When he goes home and shares this disconcerting surprise with the family, he gets quite a reaction. This change to his life has affected theirs! His wife wonders how they'll manage on reduced income, his kids are upset about expensive holiday plans that will have to be cancelled and Chuck knows the golf club membership will have to go — and the club members will be affected when he steps down as president of the club.

This is the ripple effect in action. If Chuck and his family had already discussed the possibility of a forced early retirement, they would have been less shaken and emotional once the situation arose. There would probably have been little, if any, change to the quality,

strength and endurance of their relationships. On the other hand, if Chuck's family endures frequent strain and doesn't communicate well, the results could be far different. Emotional difficulties, relationship breakdown and financial insecurity could result.

Believe me, it can happen to any of us. Don't think that retirement is going to give you all the time in the world to work out your personal problems. It can have the opposite effect. I've seen it time and again: Throughout working life, jobs and raising children can mask difficulties and a lack of communication. Once you're retired, those masks are gone and with all your newfound time you're faced with the underlying problems.

What about single people? Take John's case. His company is moving to Calgary and he's been given an early retirement package — and offered part-time, seasonal work if he moves west. His sister lives in Calgary and he'd like to go. But he shares his home with a friend, and that person is upset with his decision. It could ruin their friendship. As you can see, even for a single person change can have an effect on personal relationships.

No two people think, feel or respond in precisely the same way to a change of events. We often forget this when we're involved with people. Then we wonder why the quality of our relationship isn't quite what we'd like it to be. We forget that members of our family and our friends are still distinct individuals.

Sometimes, one person tends to dominate and control decisions and plans. The others may go along with the status quo but aren't exactly thrilled with the arrangement. Relationships can move along like this for some time until a change, event or transition produces a crisis and then, all too often, things fall apart.

Experts tell me that the key to avoiding such heartbreaking impasses is deceptively simple: communication. Obviously, that means talking about your feelings, thoughts and concerns with your loved one. This can occur only in relationships which uphold mutual respect, trust and understanding. Relationships based on these principles maintain quality because your needs and those of your loved ones are accounted for through compromise.

Don't get me wrong: I'm not trying to be glib. Talking about effective communications is probably easier than doing it! Because we humans are emotional beings and because our relationships are important we tend to respond emotionally. Yet, it's difficult to resolve problems when your emotions get in the way. Communicating well requires objectivity and the ability to solve problems without resorting to tears or shouting. This is not to say emotions are wrong; they're not. They are healthy expressions and need to be acknowledged and accepted. But, once you've let off steam, you have to set your emotions aside and work rationally together toward a solution.

How do you do this? First, both of you have to care, to be willing to discuss your differences, concerns and needs. You should be honest and open. Try to talk things over in times when you feel good and at ease with your loved one. If there is shouting, crying or an angry silence, wait until things are calm.

If this is difficult to do, call for help from someone who doesn't have a vested interest in what is taking place but is willing to help — a family member, friend or neighbour who is caring and fair. Other people who can help are clergy, health-care professionals or informal support group members.

Consider this scenario — a husband and wife are squabbling over household finances, getting nowhere. He isn't listening to her and she isn't listening to him because the emotions are running on overload. Along comes a third person, say a friend, and what happens? Boy, do they behave! They wouldn't want someone to see them arguing and hollering.

For more information on effective communication check out local public libraries and bookstores as well as the bibliography at the back of this book.

Now I've got a fancy concept to run by you that can really help in planning for your retirement: "anticipatory planning." Anticipatory planning deals with the "what ifs" in life — what would I do if this happened to me? You do this unconsciously all the time. Do you recall watching life unfold for others, seeing people wrestle with their problems and then commenting to yourself on their responses?

Remember saying, "Gee, he handled that well, that was a smart way to deal with the situation," or "Boy, was she dumb, I wouldn't have done it that way." That's what anticipatory planning is all about — watching someone else in a particular situation, imagining yourself in the same circumstance and filing away useful strategies for possible future use.

How can you take advantage of these lessons? Consciously observe people around you for situations which may have relevance for you. Here's how to go about it:

- Identify situations that could occur in mid-life to later years such as retirement, grandparenting, illness, or caring for frail parents.
- Identify the effects of these issues on the people involved, such as the financial worry, the responsibility, the demands on your time, the emotional impact.

■ Point out to yourself feelings you'd probably experience in these situations, such as anxiety, frustration, satisfaction, or happiness.

■ Identify ways to deal with the situation.

Doing this helps you take greater control of your life, helps you see ways to deal with problems and reduces the number of crises and the subsequent stress they involve. Now let's look at the potential relationship changes that could arise with retirement and do some anticipatory planning.

Retirement and the couple

To assume that a marriage will continue along the same lines, either good or bad, after your retirement or the retirement of your husband or wife, is a grave mistake. There are a number of potential difficulties. The first revolves around the separate lives of husbands and wives.

For retired couples, there's a dramatic increase in the hours they will spend together after retiring and that can expose their marriages to new stresses. Almost certainly it makes the degree of marital happiness somewhat unpredictable.

If you're married, it's a good idea to sit down with your partner and talk about spending more time together. How will you handle it? What activities, if any, will you share? A husband might find that his wife leads a very active life — one that does not, and perhaps will not, include him. His inclination to see retirement as a family affair might be contradicted by his wife's belief that the event does not greatly concern her. He could be in for a surprise.

In fact, his wife may find it difficult to adjust to the disruptions caused by his being around all the time. For most wives, the pleasure of spending time with their husband and the satisfaction of feeling needed overrides the loss of personal freedom. On the other hand,

marriage counsellors often find that it is the wives, rather than husbands, who are more likely to complain about having to spend too much time with their men and to suggest that the demands on them have increased.

The second cause for debate — sharing the housework — is a difficult issue. I know couples make a lot of jokes about this but plenty of others fight over it bitterly. There aren't any hard and fast rules; all couples must learn to cope with this in their own ways or resentment could cloud your relationship.

A third potential difficulty, although less common, contains the seeds of personal and domestic tragedy. I've seen dynamic and interesting men and women become bored and apathetic after retirement; their confidence and feelings of self-worth suffer along with their relationships with their wives and husbands. Ultimately, it damages their health. What is to be done?

You have to work these critical issues out together. You'll have to find ways to structure your time. Planning together is key. Well in advance of retirement, try to talk about what both of you want and expect. Be sure that you both present genuine needs and desires, maintain your individuality rather than trying to be what you think your partner expects.

When it comes to privacy, many couples choose to pursue at least a few separate activities. The husband goes to a movie while his wife has the bridge club over. He walks the dog; she does chores at home. You might even decide to get a second telephone line. This doesn't mean you don't love one another — everybody needs a little time apart.

Obviously, it's important to be aware of each other's activities when drawing up your schedules. The key, as always, is to strike a balance. You can avoid problems if both of you remain alert to changes in the way you live after retirement. That way you're in a better position to deal with problems when they arise.

Now that approximately 50 percent of Canadian women are in the work force, you could well be faced with another concern: How do two working people decide on the timing of their retirements? Do you retire together or should you both leave work at different times? Can you even afford for both of you to retire? If not, are you willing to alter your lifestyle before retirement to make it possible or would you rather change your retirement plans? If you choose to retire at different times, who should retire first?

To decide, you have to consider your feelings about work. Perhaps one of you really likes your job and would miss the work and friends if you retired. Spend time talking about your expectations for retirement. Then try to agree on a mutually satisfying lifestyle. You can do this if you're both willing to compromise.

Retirement and your family

Shifting social and economic realities have altered the retirement of many people. Rather than enjoying a life of carefree freedom it is possible you will have family responsibilities long after you retire. The current buzzword to describe this phenomenon is the "sandwich generation." Did you ever think you'd be dealing with both adult children and aging parents just when you want to kick back and enjoy some time to yourself? Well, chances are pretty good that you will.

The economic situation is pretty grim for many of our adult children. If they can find a job at all, it is often poorly paid and not in their field of study. Plenty of well-educated kids are working as bicycle couriers, driving cabs and working as clerks and receptionists — often part-time. Others have given up on a professional career and are going back to school to learn a trade. Many who are already skilled trades men and women are finding their trades overtaken by technology and must learn new skills.

Our kids are having trouble supporting themselves and often return to the family home seeking help, usually financial. Remember when people used to think the empty nest was a bittersweet time when the kids left? Well, your kids might leave but chances are they'll be back whenever things get tough. Imagine the discussions on rules, rights and responsibilities that are going to take place with parents and kids at home all day.

Imagine taking on more responsibility and concern by dealing with aged parents. People are living longer. This trend, coupled with the trend to early retirement, means many of us will be in retirement at the same time as our parents. That was not usually true for your parents as they entered their retirements.

The implications for the sandwich generation — those of us who are in between — demands planning. How should you respond to such family needs? I don't have any simple answers. The answer always lies in establishing responsibility; whose is it and how much is necessary? As a parent, for how many years are you responsible for a child? As the child of your parents, are you responsible for their well-being? You can only resolve these issues by sitting down together and discussing everyone's concerns. If you cannot resolve your family's concerns, outside professional assistance can be useful, particularly in resolving the concerns and needs of aging parents. Family counsellors, social service agencies or clergy can help.

Grandparenting and retirement

I've painted a bleak picture, but retirement will also bring an opportunity for you to spend more time with your family, especially the grandchildren. But, well, there's always a but. The time you spend with your children and grandchildren will depend on what both you and your children want. It is possible each of you will have a different opinion about the amount of time you spend together.

Again, it's important to discuss the matter and agree on some guidelines. Sometimes, your kids might want you to baby-sit and you won't know how to tell your children you don't want to be a baby-sitter. Or, your kids might think you're around too much; that you're interfering with their parenting or spoiling the grandchildren. You have to be able to talk out your feelings openly and without undue emotion.

Singles and retirement

Unlike couples, single individuals — the never-married, separated, divorced and widowed — enjoy greater freedom and flexibility in choosing a retirement lifestyle. Unless you're strongly committed to a particular relationship, you are free to decide what you'd like to do. You should not, however, plan in isolation. You have friendships and responsibilities which are important and must be considered in retirement plans. Your needs are similar to the needs of others, only the circumstances are different. You need companionship, love, meaningful interests and activities, a sense of purpose and recognition from others. You must rely on yourself to make things happen. Loneliness, boredom and dissatisfaction are not particular to single people but they are often more pronounced.

Certainly, not all singles make poor choices for retirement, but some do because their lives tend to have too narrow a focus. Everyone needs to have pursuits that we can participate in by ourselves, but we also need friends and interests which we share with others. Variety and friendships make retirement much more pleasant.

Unfortunately, the most impoverished group in society today is the older single woman. Finances represent a major concern: The number of employment years is generally fewer than for men because women must take care of their families. Also, women's pay was and continues to be lower than that of men. Usually women do not have as many years of pension contribution because they have fewer years of employment or because pension plans were not available to them. Women enter retirement with fewer resources and are often forced to make compromises to survive economically. They end up with fewer choices in housing, interests and activities.

For those who have been accustomed to a sharing partner, the transition to being single — through widowhood, divorce or separation — is often difficult. It takes a willingness to try, a determination to succeed, as well as a strong self-image to adapt. Perhaps if everyone kept his or her individuality even when they have significant relationships there'd be less trouble becoming a single late in life.

Social relationships

It's important to take stock of your friendships before you retire. Does your social life revolve around work? If so, you should consider how many of your colleagues you'll see when you're in retirement. Once you leave work you're usually forgotten unless you make the effort to keep in touch. Also, the fact that you have more time available to participate in activities can isolate you from former work associates who have very little free time and who choose to use their limited time in other ways. Rather than feeling lonely and discouraged later, do something about it now.

One of the best ways to meet new friends is to join organizations with goals and activities that appeal to you. Try drawing up a list of likely places and contact one new group each month to find out more. You might consider a church group, chess club, horticultural society or gourmet club. There are curling clubs, bowling leagues and many other sports groups.

Some people are attracted to religious or personal development subjects; others to political parties, and still others to social service organizations like the United Way or the Special Olympics. Keep looking until you find the right one. Try to join at least one before retiring. Having a whole new set of interests to look forward to will ease the transition.

Golden Age clubs, which usually accept people fifty and over, are a particularly good place to meet people. It's surprising they haven't considered a name change, since retirees today are a younger group of people. The activities offered have changed as well. You'll still find card games and crafts but there will also be fitness classes, basketball games and lectures. Such groups provide more than an opportunity to make new friends. They're also a gold mine of practical information on discounts, government benefits or the best entertainment spots around. For older seniors, such clubs provide a buddy system, or even referrals for help with home maintenance.

Relationships are important to your sense of well-being and satisfaction. To take care of them requires effort, sensitivity, commitment and caring. Understanding how change can affect you and those close to you is necessary to resolve any difficulties that can result. Retirement will bring change and you should be as prepared emotionally as you are financially.

Notes

A retirement financial plan

Not very long ago there was a newspaper advertisement for a bank that caught my eye. It was a drawing of a pair of bare feet. Beneath the feet were the words: "When you retire we want to make sure you can stand on these." Your own two feet. It played on one of the most common financial fears in North America.

It's natural to be concerned about your finances. You suspect that you won't be able to afford to enjoy the freedom that retirement will bring. You might be confused by the variety of investments and financial products available today — mutual funds, registered retirement savings plans, registered retirement income funds, annuities, even bank accounts. You may be discouraged by low interest rates and the resulting lower return on investments. You're probably wondering if you're getting all the tax breaks that are your due. And you worry that your husband or wife and family might not be financially secure were you to die.

These and other worries are normal and can be relieved by carrying out some realistic financial planning. Yet I know that you probably see financial planning as another worry, not a solution. You might think you've waited too long and it's far too late to do a financial plan. You probably think it's too difficult: you don't know how to do a financial plan and you don't like math and you never did understand insurance. Stop worrying. It's not too late and it's not hard to do. I'm going to show you how financial planning is a matter of making improvements. It will allow you to achieve your goals through effective management of your resources.

We've worked with thousands of people individually and in seminars to help them plan for a secure retirement. After a seminar, people always tell us they wish someone had discussed these things with them years earlier. But it's possible that, years earlier, they might not have been open to listening and acting on our advice. Since you have bought this book, I'll assume you are ready to act. Can you achieve all of your dreams? I don't know. I do know that you will be better off if you act now than if you don't act at all.

I know you're still nervous. You know you'll need a fair bit of money to retire, but you don't know how much and you sense you aren't saving enough. Perhaps your taxes and living expenses are so high there's little left for saving. Or you're uncertain about how to invest the little you do save. You feel your financial affairs aren't under control but you procrastinate, promising yourself you'll start next year.

There's another reason for being nervous. You may never have done this before. If financial planning is a new and unfamiliar task, think of it as an adventure. The completion of your financial plan will provide the blueprint for achieving the rest of your life's goals. You have to overcome your natural anxiety and choose to move forward. Financial planning is not complicated, although many advisers would have you believe it is. There are only five steps to carrying out a financial plan, yet they will touch on every facet of your finances. By discovering your financial weaknesses now, you'll have time to make changes and you'll be better able to profit from your strengths.

Five steps to retirement planning

If you skipped the chapters on lifestyle planning in a rush to get to the financial planning, go back to them now.

1. Lifestyle planning is an integral part of financial planning.

It's the first step that gives your plan both direction and energy. Establish your goals in precise detail; what do you want, when do you want it, how much will it cost. Set financial checkpoints for the years between now and retirement. This will help you stay on track and stay motivated. Don't skip this step. If you cannot see the benefits of financial planning, it will be hard to stay motivated to finish all of the work that goes into a serious plan.

2. Take a good look at your financial situation now.

Try to establish exactly how much it costs to maintain your lifestyle and how much wealth you've already built. Then you'll be able to determine whether the income you expect to receive after retirement can cover those living expenses. At the same time, you'll be able to identify urgent problems and search for opportunities to improve your financial position — and act on them.

3. Identify every opportunity to reduce your tax burden.

This will maximize your after-tax income and further improve your ability to save.

4. Develop a savings and investment strategy

Your investment plan should suit your objectives for income, growth and security and take the best possible advantage of RRSPs.

5. Organize your estate for the best protection of your family.

You'll want to make sure that clear financial records and an up-to-date will are on hand. Keep copies in your desk and your safety deposit box. Let your executor know where everything is. Only then can an executor settle your affairs efficiently and provide the best possible treatment for your heirs.

These five steps are the cornerstones for improving your financial well-being in retirement. Once you've taken them, you'll understand the possibilities for improvement, you'll discover opportunities to reduce expenses, and you'll find investments that might better accomplish your objectives. In addition, your husband or wife and your advisers will be more aware of your financial plans and able to help you achieve them. I'll explain the potential role for outside financial advisers later on. Your plan will allow you to look forward to retirement, confident that your finances are under control and that you're taking advantage of all opportunities.

One last word before we dig into the details. Effective financial planning requires that you, and your partner, become personally involved in the planning process. You must both make a commitment to analyze your finances in an unemotional manner and to understand the ground rules affecting your financial well-being. The process is easier for a single person because there's no need to compromise, unless other family members are involved.

If you're prepared to do your homework, you will eliminate the uncertainties. As a dividend, you'll probably be able to save hundreds of dollars or more every year than you can now, which will help to make your retirement years more comfortable and financially secure.

Getting down to work

Financial planning is not complicated. It is simply making the most of your financial resources. The pages that follow will take you through the steps involved in establishing a retirement financial plan. They will help you not only to understand the process, but also to understand the financial information with which we are bombarded. As taxes and financial products become more complicated, the competition to provide financial services is intensifying.

Once you understand the process of financial planning, you will be able to scan the newspapers, magazines and literature given to you by your banker, insurance agent or investment adviser and quickly pick out the bits of information relevant to you.

Keep in mind that they are advertising to sell products, and not necessarily providing useful, relevant information. It takes work to keep up with changes in the financial marketplace and tax system, but the work lightens once your financial plan is complete.

Your financial goals

In the first few chapters of this book we looked at your home and your lifestyle dreams. Now you should take a look at the cost of the life you've planned for yourself. Keep in mind that even in retirement you will lead several different lifestyles. At first, your life will be full and active. You might work on a second career or launch yourself in a serious hobby or volunteering. Then you'll become less active but still fully independent and healthy.

Finally, as you age, you might need support, especially if your health becomes frail. Of course, your situation could change. One client who planned on playing golf for the rest of his life injured his back a year after retirement. He's not able to play golf so he and his wife travel around North America in a van.

Be realistic. It's fine to wish for financial security — enough savings, pensions and investments to ensure that you'll never run out of money — but your goals should be well-defined. There are a number of goals that many people seem to share:

- to leave the cold Canadian winter behind,
- to spend more time with friends and family in other parts of the world,
- to work part-time and still be able to golf on sunny days,
- to leave as much of your wealth for children and grandchildren as possible,
- to travel for a few months a year after they retire,
- to retire early.

If you'd like to travel, think about the places you'd like to go and how you'd like to get there. If you want to take a slow boat to China or camp at the bottom of the Grand Canyon find out how much it will cost. Don't ignore any possible expenses. Remember, we're dreaming with an eye on our pocketbooks.

Many people would like to be able to shave a few years off their work life. Even if they don't intend to actually retire early, they'd like to be able to go to work by choice for those last few years. It would relieve some of the pressure and make the job more fun. It would allow them to devote more time to a hobby or some other type of work.

Don't take the advertising slogan "Freedom 55" too literally. Most people, unless they have started early to plan for retirement or have come into a major inheritance, won't be able to retire as early as age fifty-five without a drop in lifestyle. If early retirement is your goal, set a target financial independence day. To determine how much this will cost, see your financial planner or buy a financial planning computer program.

It is your lifestyle aspirations which motivate you to establish more functional goals; paying all your debts by a particular date, making a prepayment on your mortgage this year, cutting your living costs by 5 percent so that you can save 5 percent more, selling the boat and investing the funds, saving $5,000 by the end of the year, $10,000 by the end of the decade. These goals can stand as milestones — measurable accomplishments that take you that much closer to your ultimate retirement goal.

Unfortunately, you can't rush into planning your fantasy retirement. You must first make sure that you will be able to fulfill all of those obligations that might arise before or after you retire. Think about the future, the family members who might need your support. Do you have children or grandchildren that you want to help through university or college? Should you be saving for a wedding or a child's bar or bat mitzvah? Do you want to help a child with his or her first home? Will you have to care for an aged parent? You should list these obligations on the worksheet provided along with an estimate of how much they might cost and the impact on your financial situation. If you can, jot down when the money will be needed.

Then you can turn to the goals and objectives worksheet. Your expectations should realistically match your income. There isn't any sense in setting out to achieve the unachievable. Of course, there's nothing wrong with stretching to gain something you really want, but deal with priorities first. If you have a mountain of debt, it makes little sense to buy a condo in Florida or a thirty-foot yacht. Get to work paying off the bills so that they don't mount and ruin your retirement. If you still believe you'd like to spend the winter months in Florida, rent a home there for a month or two before you buy.

As for the yacht, persuade your neighbour to buy it and become an indispensable crew member. Or buy it with three other families; there'll be more people to share the work as well as the cost. Most boats are used for less than sixty days a year. Ask any sailor, especially in Canada. Consider chartering the boat of your dreams for a couple of weeks every year. In this way, you can achieve your goal, not just dream about it, and have money left over for other goals.

This doesn't mean your life can't provide the same joy. We know a retired missionary who lives in Vancouver. One of her favourite things

---

Computer programs ease the task

Computer programs can ease the task of retirement planning by automatically making many of the calculations required. They can quickly calculate the wealth you will have to have by the time you retire and the savings you should be putting away every year.

One program is KozyPlan, which you can order from Leaside Systems Inc., 11 Randolph Road, Toronto, Ontario M4G 3R6; another is Retiring Wealthy, available with a book by the same name by Gordon Pape and published by Prentice-Hall Canada and sold in most bookstores. A third is the Financial Toolkit, published by Footprints Software Inc. in Toronto. This complex program has three sections — retirement planning, mortgages and loans, and savings and budgeting — along with fifteen tools for making what-if calculations.

These programs are nifty but they simply do the calculations. You still have to do the groundwork; filling in the income you'll need, the years you expect to spend in retirement, an inflation rate, tax rate and the rate of return you expect to earn on your investments.

Your financial obligations

Don't rush into planning your fantasy retirement. Use this worksheet to list those obligations that you will have to fulfill before or after you retire. There could be family members who will need your support, children or grandchildren that you want to help through university or college, perhaps a wedding. List your obligations here along with an estimate of how much they might cost and when the money will be needed.

is to go to Stanley Park on a sunny day, feed the ducks and talk to the other people there. She finds as much pleasure in this as others do in walking the high-priced beaches of Hawaii.

Financial goals and objectives are expressions of hope and of expectations related to your income and expenses over time. They should be clear, simple statements, expressed in their order of priority and importance to you along with a cost and target achievement date. Record your goals separately from your partner, then reconcile them. Being realistic will focus your financial planning on the matters of most importance and help you to achieve financial stability. They also encourage you to use your income to the best immediate advantage while accepting the reality of your situation. They can motivate you to achieve the lifestyle you want. And, if you

are truly motivated and focused on your retirement goals, you and your partner will achieve financial independence and security in retirement.

Discovering your worth

Everyone knows that you cannot find your way to a destination unless you know where you want to go. It's just as true that it makes it a lot easier to get there if you know where you are right now. The same is true of financial planning. You can't plan your financial future without knowing exactly where you stand today.

So the next step in the process is to take stock of your present position — what you own and what you owe to others. You might have to do some accounting, but you don't need to be a trained accountant. Nor does the

Unlike obligations, which are financial responsibilities, goals are more flexible. Probably the most challenging is being able to retire at the age and in the lifestyle that you want. But, let's be more specific. Here are a few to get you started: At what age would you like to retire? Will you want the same life style in retirement? Will you be able to spend less? Or, will you probably spend more? Will you earn any money in retirement, either by selling handicrafts, part-time work or a new career? Do you want to buy a cottage for your retirement? Do you want to build an inheritance for your family? Do you have special concerns or interests, such as raising money for a hospital, teaching land conservation in Africa, developing the business you've always talked about, helping your preferred political party. They all need help!

_____
_____
_____
_____
_____

Now establish those financial goals that will help you to achieve a financially secure retirement; such as getting rid of your debts, paying off your mortgage, or saving an extra $1,000 this year.

_____
_____
_____
_____

Your life is not dedicated to retirement. There are many things to buy and do over the next few years. Perhaps, you want to buy a new cottage or sailboat or car. We cannot only live for tomorrow but as you list these pre-retirement goals consider whether or not they will undermine your ability to achieve your retirement goals.

_____
_____
_____
_____

accounting have to be detailed. You simply want basic information to plan your financial affairs, to find opportunities for improvement and to measure improvements as they're realized. Once you've done your financial plan, you can review it every six months to a year. Try to be businesslike. Public companies publish an annual report. You should do the same for your family finances, reviewing the year just completed and planning for the future. First, prepare a statement of assets and liabilities for you and your partner, if you have one. Your assets are the things you own: your house, bank accounts, savings bonds. Your liabilities are your debts: your bank loans, mortgage, credit card balances. You should own more than you owe, and this excess is called your net worth. You need not worry about the accounting terminology, but you do have to draft a statement of assets and liabilities. It is this statement that will tell you where you are now.

Completing the statement of assets and liabilities can be a learning experience that is quite enjoyable, especially if you use a good computer program such as Quicken. With or without a computer, the statement can be done fairly quickly by estimating the value of the things you own and looking at statements from banks, mortgage companies and credit card companies. The worksheets on the following pages have enough space to allow you to record details of bank accounts, stock market investments, insurance policies, real estate holdings, bank loans. Complete the detailed worksheet first, preparing a full list. Once the detailed statement is complete, you can distill it down to the one-page snapshot of your financial situation.

Although these worksheets are to be used as working papers, if updated annually, they will be extremely useful to the executor of your estate to avoid a time-consuming search for information.

Completing the statement of assets and liabilities is relatively simple but there are a few guidelines you should follow:

■ The statement should capture your entire financial position at one date in time, preferably the most recent monthend. You can simply record the information contained in statements or passbooks from your bank, trust companies and stock brokers, which will show both your deposits or holdings and balances due on loans and bills outstanding. Some people find income tax time a good time for doing this.

■ Record the financial position of each partner separately. In marriage or common-law

relationships, there are tax and legal reasons for knowing precisely the assets and liabilities of each person. Then, because a financial plan is usually developed for a family, you combine the assets and liabilities for a complete picture.

■ The value of your assets and liabilities need not be precise. A conservative estimate is good enough. For example, for savings bonds or term deposits, you might use the amount originally deposited plus an estimate of the interest earned to date but not yet received. For stocks and bonds, you can use the price quoted in the newspaper. You might estimate the value of your home from prices of comparable houses recently sold in your area. Deduct about 10 percent to cover the cost of selling your home but only 2 or 3 percent for the cost of selling investment securities.

■ Assets that can be easily sold are called "liquid" and should be listed separately from those investments that are locked in for a term of more than one year. Liabilities to be paid within twelve months are called "current" and should be listed separately from those to be repaid over a longer period, such as a mortgage or car loan.

■ In the case of "marketable" securities, such as stocks, bonds and mutual funds, record your original purchase cost, including brokerage charges, which increase your overall costs. It's also important to keep track of reinvested dividends and tax already paid on the securities, or you might pay tax twice.

If you held publicly traded common or preferred shares, rights, warrants or convertible bonds on December 22, 1971, include the value of the security on that day, which is known as valuation day. You can get these values out of a booklet published by Revenue Canada, available from your broker or financial adviser. The valuation day for capital property other than publicly-traded shares was December 31, 1971. Although these values aren't needed for completing the statement of assets and liabilities, they'll be helpful when considering the impact of possible future tax liabilities and in administering your financial affairs.

■ It can be difficult to calculate the cash value of life insurance. You might have several policies and will probably be unfamiliar with the rules and regulations. It's worth the trouble, however, to document information about these policies so that you can decide whether to cash them in, borrow against the policy, convert, or continue the policies as they stand. Whole life policies that you've held for years could be worth a great deal. Refer to the tables in your policy, try to make a rough estimate of their value, then write to the customer service department of the insurance company to obtain accurate information.

■ You might own several RRSPs, pension plans, deferred profit-sharing plans, and employee savings plans with both present and previous employers. Take the time to find the value of plans still held by old employers. The estimated value of your pension with your current employer can be found on your annual benefits statement or calculated using information in the pension chapter of this book. If you belong to a defined contribution or money purchase plan, or you've been a member of a pension plan for less than ten years, you can use the value of your accumulated contributions.

■ Make a note of the liabilities on which you pay interest by listing the interest rate on the worksheet. This will draw attention to the cost of carrying debt, particularly personal debts where interest is not tax-deductible.

■ Record the income taxes that would have to be paid if you cashed in your pension or RRSPs, or if you sold investments that have risen in value. This should go under long-term liabilities. Assume you will have to pay tax at a 40 to 50 percent rate.

■ Finally, total liabilities should be subtracted from total assets to arrive at your net worth. This net value, when compared to those of previous years, is a useful way to monitor changes in your financial status.

Once you've completed the one-page snapshot, take a look at what it tells you about your financial situation. Among the pieces of information you're looking for are the six following points:

1. The percentage of your assets devoted to those things you enjoy compared to the percentage devoted to investments, including retirement savings. If, for example, you are spending money on your cottage in mortgage or taxes, and if you find you aren't using it much anymore, you might consider selling it or renting it and putting the money toward your retirement.

2. Analyze your debt load, which you can determine by taking your total debt as a percentage of your total assets. Are your loans for investments or for pleasure and personal consumption? Usually it is best to pay cash for things like vacations and consumer goods. If borrowing is unavoidable, perhaps to buy a car to do your job, then get a loan at the best rate and pay it as quickly as possible. If you are borrowing to invest, does your after-tax return exceed your borrowing costs? If not you are eroding your wealth, not building it.

3. Do you have the cash to meet financial emergencies, make new investments, or meet major commitments? If you go on strike or lose your job, you need enough ready money to pay your expenses for three

to six months. Likewise, if an excellent investment opportunity presents itself, you want to have funds to act quickly.

4. The percentage of your income which you save. A financial planning rule of thumb is to save 10 percent of your annual income. This is one of those rules that are often cited and people frequently ask us if they should save 10 percent of their income after taxes and benefits have been deducted, their net income, or 10 percent of their gross income, their income before any deductions. You might start with 10 percent of net income and gradually increase to 10 percent of gross. If you don't belong to a pension plan, this 10 percent should be over and above your RRSP contributions.

5. How are your savings invested? Are they invested for growth or are they in fixed income securities such as guaranteed investment certificates and Canada Savings Bonds. Are they invested in "marketable" securities — can they be sold or must you hold them until maturity? What is your return? Is it sufficient to keep you ahead of taxes and inflation, that is, to maintain the buying power of your dollar, as well as increase your capital? What are the alternative investments available, and what

are the risks involved. Do you run the risk of losing your capital if the venture fails? Are your savings growing sufficiently to meet your goals?

6. How much is invested in tax-deferred retirement savings programs? Remember that money grows in your RRSP without being taxed until it is withdrawn. This allows it to grow much faster than if you paid tax on it. How are these assets invested? What tax liability would result if they were cashed in?

Remember that your goal is to build wealth for retirement. Each of the six areas is key in meeting that goal. Money going to pay the interest on a debt, for example, is money that you could be putting into an RRSP or other investment. You might want to consolidate debt and get a new loan at a lower rate of interest.

Reading some of these points might raise questions you don't have the answers for yet. But an increased awareness of where you are financially right now will help you develop an action plan further along in this book. If you do have any ideas for making changes or improvements, jot them down in the space at the end of this chapter for use at the end of the book in your action plan.

A detailed list of your assets

Chequeing accounts

Institution	Details	Value today		
		You	Spouse	Total
_____	_____	_____	_____	_____
_____	_____	_____	_____	_____
_____	_____	_____	_____	_____
_____	_____	_____	_____	_____
_____	_____	_____	_____	_____
		$ _____	+$ _____	=$ _____

Savings accounts

Institution	Details	Value today You	Spouse	Total
_____	_____	_____	_____	_____
_____	_____	_____	_____	_____
_____	_____	_____	_____	_____
_____	_____	_____	_____	_____
		$ _____	+$ _____	=$ _____

Short-term deposits

Institution	Maturity date	Maturity value	Interest rate	You	Spouse	Total
_____	_____	_____	_____	_____	_____	_____
_____	_____	_____	_____	_____	_____	_____
_____	_____	_____	_____	_____	_____	_____
				$ _____	+$ _____	=$ _____

One-to-five-year GICs

Institution	Maturity date	Maturity value	Interest rate	You	Spouse	Total
_____	_____	_____	_____	_____	_____	_____
_____	_____	_____	_____	_____	_____	_____
_____	_____	_____	_____	_____	_____	_____
_____	_____	_____	_____	_____	_____	_____
_____	_____	_____	_____	_____	_____	_____
_____	_____	_____	_____	_____	_____	_____
				$ _____	+$ _____	=$ _____

Pensions

Sponsor	Details	You	Spouse	Total
_____	_____	_____	_____	_____
_____	_____	_____	_____	_____
		$ _____	+$ _____	=$ _____

Registered funds: RRSPs, RHOSPs, DPSPs

Institution	Type of plan	Annual growth	You	Spouse	Total
_____	_____	_____	_____	_____	_____
_____	_____	_____	_____	_____	_____
_____	_____	_____	_____	_____	_____
_____	_____	_____	_____	_____	_____
_____	_____	_____	_____	_____	_____
			$ _____	+$ _____	=$ _____

Annuities and deferred compensation   **Value today**
  Institution   Maturity date   Maturity value   Annual income   You   Spouse   Total

_____   _____   _____   _____   _____   _____   _____

_____   _____   _____   _____   _____   _____   _____

$ _____ +$ _____ =$ _____

Whole life insurance
  Issuer   Details

_____   _____   _____   _____   _____

_____   _____   _____   _____   _____

_____   _____   _____   _____   _____

$ _____ +$ _____ =$ _____

Tax-sheltered investments
  Details

_____   _____   _____   _____

_____   _____   _____   _____

$ _____ +$ _____ =$ _____

Mutual funds
  Fund   Purchase date   Cost   Dividend

_____   _____   _____   _____   _____   _____   _____

_____   _____   _____   _____   _____   _____   _____

_____   _____   _____   _____   _____   _____   _____

_____   _____   _____   _____   _____   _____   _____

_____   _____   _____   _____   _____   _____   _____

_____   _____   _____   _____   _____   _____   _____

_____   _____   _____   _____   _____   _____   _____

_____   _____   _____   _____   _____   _____   _____

$ _____ +$ _____ =$ _____

Bonds and debentures
  Issuer   Face value   Interest rate   Maturity date

_____   _____   _____   _____   _____   _____   _____

_____   _____   _____   _____   _____   _____   _____

_____   _____   _____   _____   _____   _____   _____

_____   _____   _____   _____   _____   _____   _____

$ _____ +$ _____ =$ _____

Common shares

Company	Purchase date	Cost	Dividends	Value today You	Spouse	Total
				$ _____	+$ _____	=$ _____

Preferred shares

Company	Purchase date	Cost	Dividends			
				$ _____	+$ _____	=$ _____

Investment real estate

Location	Details					
				$ _____	+$ _____	=$ _____

Gold and other precious metals

Details	Purchase date	Cost			
		$ _____	+$ _____	=$ _____

Loans and mortgage investments

Debtor	Maturity date	Outstanding amount	Interest rate			
				$ _____	+$ _____	=$ _____

Business interests

Firm	Details	Value today		
		You	Spouse	Total
_____	_____	_____	_____	_____
_____	_____	_____	_____	_____
_____	_____	_____	_____	_____
		$ _____	+$ _____	=$ _____

Other investment assets
Details

	You	Spouse	Total
_____	_____	_____	_____
_____	_____	_____	_____
_____	_____	_____	_____
_____	_____	_____	_____
	$ _____	+$ _____	=$ _____

Personal real estate

Details	Purchase date	Cost	Annual income or expense	You	Spouse	Total
_____	_____	_____	_____	_____	_____	_____
_____	_____	_____	_____	_____	_____	_____
_____	_____	_____	_____	_____	_____	_____
				$ _____	+$ _____	=$ _____

Personal belongings
Details

	You	Spouse	Total
Furniture _____	_____	_____	_____
Collections _____	_____	_____	_____
Automobiles _____	_____	_____	_____
Boats _____	_____	_____	_____
Furs _____	_____	_____	_____
Jewellery _____	_____	_____	_____
Art _____	_____	_____	_____
Antiques _____	_____	_____	_____
Other _____	_____	_____	_____
_____	_____	_____	_____
_____	_____	_____	_____
_____	_____	_____	_____
	$ _____	+$ _____	=$ _____

A detailed list of your liabilities   WORKSHEET 16

Bank and other short term loans

Value today

Creditor	Interest rate	Payments	Due date	You	Spouse	Total
_____	_____	_____	_____	_____	_____	_____
_____	_____	_____	_____	_____	_____	_____
_____	_____	_____	_____	_____	_____	_____
_____	_____	_____	_____	_____	_____	_____
				$ _____	+$ _____	=$ _____

Credit card and charge account balances

Creditor	Interest rate	Payments	Due date			
_____	_____	_____	_____	_____	_____	_____
_____	_____	_____	_____	_____	_____	_____
_____	_____	_____	_____	_____	_____	_____
_____	_____	_____	_____	_____	_____	_____
				$ _____	+$ _____	=$ _____

Tax and other liabilities

Creditor	Interest rate	Payments	Due date			
_____	_____	_____	_____	_____	_____	_____
_____	_____	_____	_____	_____	_____	_____
_____	_____	_____	_____	_____	_____	_____
_____	_____	_____	_____	_____	_____	_____
				$ _____	+$ _____	=$ _____

Mortgages

Creditor	Interest rate	Payments	Due date			
_____	_____	_____	_____	_____	_____	_____
_____	_____	_____	_____	_____	_____	_____
_____	_____	_____	_____	_____	_____	_____
				$ _____	+$ _____	=$ _____

Your one-page financial snapshot   WORKSHEET 17

You can complete this snapshot by transferring the relevant totals from the previous pages to this page.

	You	Spouse	Total
ASSETS			
Liquid assets			
Cash and chequing accounts			
Savings accounts			
Short-term deposits			
Total liquid assets			
Non-marketable investments			
One-to-five-year GIC			
Pensions			
Registered funds			
Annuities and deferred compensation			
Whole-life insurance			
Tax-sheltered investments			
Total non-marketable investments			
Marketable investments			
Mutual funds			
Bonds and debentures			
Common shares			
Preferred shares			
Investment real estate			
Gold and other precious metals			
Loans and mortgage investments			
Business interests			
Total marketable investments			
Other investment assets			
Personal real estate			
Personal belongings			
Total assets			
LIABILITIES			
Current			
Long-term			
Tax and other liabilities			
Total liabilities			
NET WORTH			
Total assets			
Total liabilities			
Net worth (subtract liabilities from assets)			

Keeping in touch

It's important to realize that even if you decided to take the first step and do your financial plan, you'll have to stay on top of things. Financial fitness is like physical fitness. You don't have to know everything about the human body to make it work well, but you do need to know what's good and bad for it, how to treat it well, how to keep it in top condition and what to do when things break down. The same goes for your finances. You need a working knowledge of personal finance, the financial system and the economy. You need to identify bad habits you've fallen into and opportunities to manage your money more effectively.

You'll need discipline to control your spending, avoid debt and invest your money so that you earn a decent return after taxes and inflation. You have to follow a sound savings and investment plan just as you would eat well, get lots of sleep and exercise regularly.

You should have an annual financial checkup to maintain your health. You should never be too shy to seek financial advice for problems and special needs just as you would visit a doctor or medical specialist for a health problem or illness. This is common enough stuff when we think of physical fitness. Keeping financially fit should be common knowledge, too.

You can stay up to date on financial planning by reading books, newspapers and magazines, watching business and financial television programs such as *Wall Street Week* and the CBC's *Business World* and by listening to radio shows. Financial planning is a popular feature on noon-hour and evening radio and television shows. These are generally well presented, giving clear examples of basic and topical opportunities. You'll find plenty of information on retirement, the various stages of financial planning and on income tax in the personal finance sections of many magazines.

In Canada, there is *The Financial Post* and *The Financial Post Magazine,* the *Financial Times of Canada, The Canadian Money Saver* and *The Globe and Mail Report on Business Magazine.* From the United States, you can receive *Money, Sylvia Porter's Personal Finance Magazine, Forbes, Fortune, Kiplinger's Magazine* and *Business Week.*

Excellent reading material is also available from sellers of financial products and services. You don't have to buy their products to enjoy their literature but be prepared to fend off aggressive sales efforts once you're on their mailing lists. Some good home-study courses are also available from educational television networks and organizations such as the Canadian Institute of Financial Planning, the Canadian Securities Institute and the Canadian Shareholders' Association. Universities, school boards, community centres and associations run low-cost courses, ranging from half-day lectures to full-term programs.

Advisory newsletters, such as *The MoneyLetter* from Hume Publishing Company and *The Money Reporter* from MPL Communications Inc., dealing with various financial planning and investment subjects can be purchased at prices ranging from $75 to $250 or more for a one-year subscription. Brokerage firms, mutual funds firms, banks and trust companies have their own newsletters, such as *CIBC Horizons,* available for free at branches. Even Revenue Canada is trying to be helpful. Your District Taxation Office of Revenue Canada has excellent booklets on taxation such as *Thinking of Retiring?, Income Tax and the Senior Citizen, Registered Retirement Savings Plans, Income Tax and the Non-Resident* and *Canadian Residents Going Down South.*

Retirement is different from working in more ways than simply not having a job. The most enjoyable aspect is probably receiving monthly cheques from your former employer

---

What to look for in a financial adviser

Reputation
Word of mouth can be a good way of finding a financial planner, especially the referral from someone you know and trust. You'll want a person with a good track record and enough years of experience to steer you safely and effectively on your financial path.

Credentials
You will want your financial planner to have education and expertise in any of a number of specialized areas. Designations to look for include: CA (chartered accountant); RFP (registered financial planner); C.Adm.FP (chartered administrator of financial planning, a Quebec designation); CFP (chartered financial planner); CIM (certified investment manager, a more advanced designation for brokers); CLU (chartered life underwriter); Ch.FC (chartered financial consultant); CFA, (chartered financial analyst); and degrees in business or law.

Association membership
Financial planners have organizations to govern themselves with respect to ethics, codes of conduct and standards of practice. It is to your advantage if your planner is a member of such an organization; that can be an indicator of professionalism. Two such associations are the Canadian Association of Financial Planners and the Order of Chartered Administrators of Quebec, financial planning division. Associations also require that members carry liability insurance. You should also ask the government agencies that regulate financial planners if there are any complaints against your prospective adviser.

Range of services
Some people prefer to have as many financial services as possible performed under one roof. This is not only convenient, it can also be beneficial. Your financial planner has the whole picture of your affairs. Others prefer to find experts in the various areas of retirement savings, insurance and investments. Ask your prospective financial planner what services are offered, including retirement planning, income tax advice, investment management and estate planning.

Full disclosure
You need to ask, and have every right to know, how the financial planner is paid. Do the planners receive a commission on the sale of products such as life insurance and securities, or do they charge an hourly fee for service? If they are selling a product, be aware of a potential conflict of interest.

Personal fit
You need to feel comfortable with this person, to whom you will have to show intimate details of your financial life, your goals and dreams. For that reason, you may want to meet face to face with a number of planners before deciding on one. You will want to know if you will be dealing exclusively with this one planner, or with others in the firm. Once you have found someone you like, follow up the initial meeting with a brief letter outlining your understanding of the agreement, including fees, time involvement, number of meetings, and so on. Having this letter on record can help should there be any future misunderstandings.

and the government without having to go work anymore. You worked many years to get this privilege. But one type of work continues — the management of your financial affairs. If you have plenty of money, you'll feel the weight of responsibility it carries. On the other hand, if you're short of funds, you might worry about how to cope with rising costs. Your retirement years should be enjoyed to the fullest. By spending time examining your finances and planning to make the most of them now, you'll quickly overcome any concerns you might have. You will find ways to clear any financial hurdles blocking the rewards of this new stage in your life. After a career of working for money, with proper planning, your money will work for you.

Finding good help

I steadfastly believe that you'll improve your financial well-being if you find a good adviser and work together year after year to manage your finances. The adviser will charge for the advice: either fees or commissions, or profits gained from selling financial products and services. Make no mistake, you'll pay one way or another. But you'll gain more than it costs if your adviser is honest and competent; he or she will help develop strategies tailored to your needs and help you put them into action.

One of the biggest concerns about hiring a financial planner is cost You can hire a fee-only planner for $75 to $250 an hour. He or she can answer specific questions or prepare a comprehensive individual plan. Because this profession is new and growing rapidly, you must take care to find an adviser who is truly qualified, with references you can check.

Many advisers, anxious to offer free advice, are really selling financial products and services for a commission. Some are truly able to assist you, and some might have long-standing knowledge of your family and your finances. You must listen carefully, recognizing that they might have a conflict of interest, and ask them how they are paid. Even the most scrupulous salesperson might be overly enthusiastic about the product he or she sells; the advice should be checked carefully. On the other hand, a fee-only adviser can take a scandalous number of hours to complete a simple plan.

A complete financial plan includes:

■ The financial planner having a detailed picture of your current finances, including income, assets, liabilities, insurance, wills, pensions, securities, and so on

■ Determination of your goals and objectives

■ Identification of weaknesses or trouble spots in your financial affairs, such as whether or not you have enough insurance

■ Recommendations from the planner in writing, together with an explanation of these recommendations

■ Help with implementation of the recommendations

■ Periodic review of the plan

The process can take from four to six weeks and requires that you supply the necessary information and attend meetings. For more information, contact the Canadian Association of Financial Planners, 60 St. Clair Avenue East, Suite 510, Toronto, Ontario M4T 1N5 or call (416) 966-9928, to receive their booklet "A Consumer's Guide to Financial Planning."

It doesn't hurt to develop ideas through discussion with different financial advisers. Go to free seminars offered by banks, life insurance companies, trust companies, and brokers. Most seminars will have a question-and-answer session that can be invaluable. It's important, however, to take care in applying the ideas of others to your personal affairs. Let your own common sense be your guide.

By now I hope you know where you stand. The next step in the financial planning process is to look at your need to save. We'll look at government benefits, pension plans and RRSPs before putting it all together for a complete picture of the income you'll receive each year in retirement. We'll combine this with a detailed look at your future living expenses to identify a possible retirement income gap. Try to complete all of the accounting work as quickly as possible so that you don't let it delay you from creating the personal financial plan that suits your retirement needs in every detail.

The government giveth, and it taketh away

As Canadians, we enjoy a wide variety of municipal, provincial and federal programs which provide a foundation for our retirement income. Together with our universal medical care system, these benefits constitute one of the most generous social security systems in the world. Of course, this sort of "retirement insurance" isn't free. Indeed, the price gets steeper every year, requiring higher income and sales taxes and payroll deductions to finance the system.

There's growing concern that the government benefits system as we know it will be unable to continue. The problem is that we've generated a mountain of debt by providing benefits for others in our country without having the income to afford them. In effect, we're stealing from our future — from our own retirement security — and from our children's future incomes. It's time to tighten our belts, accept the goods and services tax, shop in Canada and demand that politicians reduce the national debt and secure our futures.

Unlike many, I'm confident that we are becoming financially responsible and that the wealth of this nation will see us through. In our stumbling Canadian fashion, we'll find a way to continue benefits to Canadians who need them in retirement. These programs provide the foundation of your financial security during employment and in retirement.

This chapter touches on some of the programs for retiring Canadians: Old Age Security (OAS), the Canada Pension Plan (CPP) and Quebec Pension Plan (QPP), hospital and medical care programs, and unemployment insurance. These programs form a significant cornerstone in your retirement financial plan. I realize this chapter will not be easy to read; there's a lot of pretty dry information in it. But if you don't know what you're entitled to

receive you could end up not receiving it.

The first thing to know is that you must apply to receive most of these benefits. We suggest that you apply about six months before you're eligible to receive the benefit. The OAS pension can be paid retroactively for up to five years if your application is late but you will not be paid interest on the money owing to you. If you apply after age sixty-five for CPP or QPP, your monthly pension will be larger but you will not be sent the back payments.

Application forms are available from the Income Security Programs offices of Health and Welfare Canada. These offices are listed under "H" in the blue Government of Canada pages at the back of your telephone directory. You'll be required to prove your age by providing your birth or baptismal certificate. Furthermore, some benefits can be paid to you even if you choose to live outside Canada in retirement, although this option should be checked carefully — and then checked again. The rules change often.

Old Age Security

The OAS pension is one of Canada's oldest social security programs and remains our only "universal" retirement plan. It was introduced in 1952 as a $40-a-month pension for people over age seventy, but today the OAS payments are much heftier. In late 1993, the full OAS

Are you entitled to OAS benefits?

Are you age 65 or older?	➤ NO ➤	Do not qualify

▼ **YES** ▼

Have you resided in Canada for 40 years after age 18?	➤ YES ➤	Qualify for full OAS

▼ **NO** ▼

Were you twenty-five years of age or older on July 1, 1977, and resident in Canada for any time before that date?	➤ NO ➤	Do not qualify for full OAS - see partial OAS chart

▼ **YES** ▼

Have you: a) lived in Canada for the 10 years before your application for OAS?	➤ NO ➤	Do not qualify for full OAS - see partial OAS chart

▼ **OR** ▼

b) lived in Canada for less than ten years but at least one full year prior to your application and you have lived in this country since age eighteen for three times as many years as you have lived elsewhere in the world. Example: If you are age sixty-five, lived in Canada for the full year prior to your application for OAS but lived in the U.S. for the five years between age fifty-nine and sixty-four, then you must have lived in Canada for at least fifteen years (three times five years) between age eighteen and fifty-five.	➤ NO ➤ ➤ YES ➤	Do not qualify for full OAS - see partial OAS chart Qualify for full OAS

pension was $384.66 a month but payments are adjusted four times a year — January, April, July and October — to reflect changes in the Consumer Price Index and are usually increasing as a result.

Let's take a look at the basic rules:

■ You can receive an OAS pension if you are at least sixty-five years old and have lived in Canada for at least ten years. It makes no difference whether or not you've worked. In fact, you can receive the OAS even if you keep working beyond age sixty-five.

■ You must be a Canadian citizen or legal resident on the day before your application is approved. If you no longer live in Canada, you must have been a Canadian citizen or legal resident on the day before your departure from Canada.

■ Your benefits will be paid in Canadian dollars no matter where you reside.

■ If you neglect to apply for OAS when you turn sixty-five, you can receive up to five years of back payments, although you won't be paid interest on the money owed to you.

Take a look at "Are you entitled to OAS benefits?" to determine whether you qualify for the pension.

The OAS pension claw-back

Just when you thought you'd have a bit of extra income in your pocket, the federal government enacted a tax to ensure that high-income earners repay all of the OAS pension they receive. In late-1993, people whose income is $53,215 or less are not affected.

If you are not entitled to full OAS benefits, do you qualify to receive partial OAS?

Are you age 65 or older?	➤ NO ➤	Do not qualify

YES

Do you reside in Canada now and have you resided here for more than ten years but less than forty years after age eighteen?	➤ YES ➤	You are entitled to a partial OAS benefit equal to: $$\frac{\text{\# of years of residence}}{40 \text{ years}} \times \text{full OAS}$$

NO

If you do not live in Canada now, did you live here for at least twenty years after age eighteen?	➤ YES ➤	You are entitled to a partial OAS benefit equal to: $$\frac{\text{\# of years of residence}}{40 \text{ years}} \times \text{full OAS}$$

NO

Do not qualify for partial OAS

However, anyone with an income over $53,215 must repay 15 percent of that excess up to the full OAS received.

For example, if you receive $4,600 in OAS benefits and have a taxable income of $70,000, you'll pay an additional 15 percent tax on the $16,785 of taxable income earned above the $53,215 limit, $2,518. This is on top of the income tax you must pay on the benefit. The full $4,600 OAS pension is clawed back if your net income is $83,988 or more. The $53,215 threshold will be increased to match any increase in the CPI in excess of 3 percent. The chart "Old Age Security threshold" will help you to determine if you might be affected.

The Guaranteed Income Supplement

Just over three million people receive OAS benefits and almost half of these pensioners have sufficiently low incomes to qualify for the federal guaranteed income supplement, the GIS. Another 136,000 people receive either the Spouse's Allowance or the Widowed Spouse's Allowance. The purpose of both the GIS and allowances is to ensure our retired Canadians do not live in poverty.

Once you are approved for the OAS you will be sent a form which will be used to determine whether your income is low enough to make you eligible for the GIS. Whether you are eligible and how much you will receive depends on your income for the preceding calendar year. If you are a couple, whether married or common-law, your joint income is used to determine whether you are entitled to the GIS. The income levels exclude OAS and GIS benefits and are adjusted from time to time to reflect changes in the cost of living.

Will you lose your full OAS? **TABLE 1**

Your age today	Threshold when you retire	Income at which the OAS will be lost
40	$110,970	$175,852
45	95,724	151,692
50	82,572	130,851
55	71,228	112,873
60	61,442	97,365
65	53,215	83,988

The future thresholds in this table assume the OAS will increase by 3 percent a year.

If you are a single pensioner, the maximum GIS monthly benefit you could expect in late 1993 was $457.13. You are entitled to receive this maximum benefit if your income in the previous year was less than $24. Your monthly GIS benefit will be reduced by $1 for every $24 of income that you earn above $24. For example, if your total income, not including the OAS and GIS, was $5,000 then you will be entitled to a monthly benefit of $243. This is calculated by taking the income over $24, or $4,976, and dividing by 24. The result is $207. This is subtracted from $450.34 to get $243.34. The maximum income you can earn and still be entitled to some GIS benefit is $10,992.

If you are married, or in a common-law relationship, the GIS benefit depends on your age and your husband's or wife's age. If you are both pensioners, the maximum monthly benefit that you can each receive is $297.76. You will receive this maximum if your income as a couple is less than $24 a year. Again, the monthly benefit will be reduced by $1 for every $24 of income that you earn over this. If you earn more than $14,304, you will not receive any GIS benefit.

You must apply for GIS every year. Once you have qualified for the benefit, you will be sent an application form every January. You must complete this form and return it before March 31. If you don't, your GIS payments will stop until your application is received.

Both the GIS and the OAS pensions will be sent to you on one cheque. But, while the OAS pension is taxed, the GIS is not. However, if you file an income tax return you must include the federal supplements as income on line 146 of your return. You then deduct the same amount on line 250 return.

The supplementary benefits are paid to Canadian residents only. If you leave the country, they will be suspended after six months. They will resume if you return and still qualify but you cannot recover missed benefits.

The Spouse's Allowances

When one spouse has turned sixty-five and qualifies for OAS and GIS, the other spouse is potentially eligible to receive the Spouse's Allowance. To receive the Spouse's Allowance you must be between the ages of sixty and sixty-five and meet the same income and residency requirements as for OAS and GIS. Although it is called the Spouse's Allowance, it is really just the payment of the OAS and GIS early. Like the GIS, it is not taxable and is paid only while both husband and wife are alive.

If, as a couple, you earn less than $24 a year, the spouse under age sixty-five will receive $682.42 a month and the spouse who is over age sixty-five will receive a maximum GIS benefit of $297.76, and the maximum OAS benefit, $384.66 — $682.42 a month altogether. If you earn more than $20,208 a year, the younger partner will not receive any Spouse's Allowance but the maximum GIS which the person receiving the OAS will receive is $457.13, the single-pensioner maximum.

To protect the widows and widowers of OAS pensioners, OAS also pays a Widowed Spouse's Allowance. (This is called the Extended Spouse's Allowance if the Spouse's Allowance was being received before the OAS pensioner's death.) The rules are the same as those for the Spouse's Allowance. The widow or widower must have been legally married to an OAS pensioner or have lived for at least one year with a common-law spouse. The maximum benefit was $753.38 in late 1993. The most you can earn and still be entitled to some Widowed Spouse's Allowance is $15,048.

Just as you must qualify for GIS every year, you must also apply every year for the Spouse's and Widowed Spouse's Allowance. If you apply late, both allowances can be paid retroactively for up to five years. The Spouse's and Widow(er)'s Allowance will stop when the beneficiary reaches age sixty-five and be replaced by OAS and GIS benefits.

These rules can be confusing. If you want to know precisely what your benefit will be, you can contact the Health and Welfare Canada's Income Security Program offices. They have up-to-date tables that will show the benefits for your income.

Topping up your benefits

In 1984, the government introduced special benefits for pensioners who have very low incomes but are not eligible to receive the full OAS and GIS benefits. These topping-up benefits bring the full OAS and GIS benefit up to the full pension. If you are receiving a partial OAS pension and have little or no other income, you should contact the Income Security Program office in your province to obtain details of this provision and arrange to obtain it.

The provinces and income supplements

Pension benefits to bolster the federal OAS and GIS are paid by six provinces and the two territories. The provinces which did not have provincial retirement income programs in 1993 were Newfoundland, New Brunswick, Prince Edward Island and Quebec.

The provincial plans provide monthly or quarterly cheques to seniors to supplement the federal benefits programs. For example, the Guaranteed Available Income for Need (GAIN) Act in British Columbia provides a maximum monthly cheque for $49.30 for a single person and $60.25 for a married couple where both receive the OAS and GIS. The B.C. Ministry of Social Services automatically determines who is eligible and how much they are entitled to receive based on information they receive from the federal government. In Ontario, the Guaranteed Annual Income System (GAINS) provides a maximum monthly cheque of $83

whether you're married or single. The benefit is based on a monthly income test including all forms of pension and other income.

If you are receiving the OAS and GIS or the Spouse's Allowance and you live in one of the provinces or territories that offer assistance for seniors, you might well be entitled to these extra provincial benefits. Contact the social services or guaranteed income department of your provincial government.

Canada and Quebec pension plans

The CPP and QPP are our second national pension scheme. The plans are administered separately but are similar in most respects. They both provide pensions at retirement and pay benefits to the families of deceased contributors and to disabled contributors and their children. Unlike OAS, the CPP and QPP are funded by mandatory contributions deducted from your paycheque or through direct payments to Revenue Canada. The benefits received, whether triggered by retirement, death or disability, are always determined by the contributions to the plan.

Canadians retiring in 1993 at age sixty-five are eligible for as much as $667.36 a month. The maximum disability pension for contributors was $812.85; the children of a disabled contributor receive as much as $157.48 a month from CPP or $29 from QPP. The widows or widowers of contributors receive up to $649.85 a month; orphans receive the same benefits as the children of disabled contributors. Although the OAS pension is adjusted four times a year to keep pace with inflation, CPP and QPP are adjusted once a year in January. Keep in mind that these benefits are the maximums. There are many people who will receive less, either because they have only been in the plan for a few years or their income was not high enough to allow them to contribute at the maximum rate.

Five ways to avoid the OAS claw-back

Since 1952, the Old Age Security pension has been the foundation of financial security for thousands of Canadians. No more. In 1991, the government began to claw-back the pension from Canadians whom it believed to be sufficiently well off not to need the government's help in retirement.

Here are a few strategies to avoid the OAS claw-back:

1. If you're married, try to create two streams of equal income to you and your husband or wife.

   Your most important strategy is a spousal RRSP but it's one that you should put in place today. The longer you delay the less impact it will have but every dollar you can move into the hands of a spouse who has less income than you will reduce the impact of the claw-back. If you are already retired, you can take advantage of the RRSP pension rollover in 1993 and 1994 by moving up to $6,000 of pension income into a spousal RRSP.

   There are a couple of other ways to equalize family income:

   ■ Split your CPP pension with your spouse.

   ■ Have the higher-income earner pay all of the household expenses and allow the lower-income earner to invest any family savings.

   ■ If you already own your own business, or start one in retirement, consider paying your family members a salary — one that is reasonable for the work that they do for the company.

2. Make sure you are using every possible tax deduction and credit.

   Many people miss an opportunity to reduce their taxes by not claiming every deduction and credit to which they are entitled. For someone subject to the claw-back, the impact of this carelessness is especially expensive. Make sure you make your maximum RRSP contribution in your first year of retirement.

3. Leave your savings in your RRSP for as long as possible.

   Don't touch your RRSP until the year in which you turn seventy-one and then move the funds into a RRIF. If you need to draw an income from your investments, spend your non-RRSP savings before you touch the savings that are growing tax-sheltered in an RRSP or RRIF.

4. Alternate your high and low income years.

   If you need $60,000 a year to live on, can you draw $50,000 in one year and $70,000 the next, thereby avoiding the claw-back in one of the years? If you have an investment portfolio, you can do this by realizing capital gains in one year and not in the next.

5. Consider tax shelters with care.

   Limited partnerships and other tax shelters usually provide investors with losses in the first few years of the project with the promise of capital gains in the future. However, you must consider the increased risk involved. Investing in tax shelters might decrease the security of your retirement capital and should be approached with caution.

The calculation used to determine your benefit considers the number of years you have contributed to the plan and your average earnings during that period. There are a few exceptions. If you've contributed for more than ten years, it's possible that those years in which you earned a very low income, or no income at all, will be dropped from the average.

You can also drop a year for each year that you work beyond age sixty-five and the years which you spent caring for children under age eight. You can drop up to 15 percent of your working years from the pension benefits calculation if your income during those years

---

CPP and QPP rules and provisions

Although there are some differences between the plans, there are a number of rules and provisions that apply whether you're dealing with the CPP or the QPP:

■ You can begin receiving your CPP and QPP pensions at age sixty-five whether or not you continue to work and receive wages. However, you can opt to receive benefits before or after this age.

■ It's essential that you apply about six months before you're eligible to receive a pension since retroactive payment of the CPP or QPP is not possible. Without timely application, you will not receive benefits you might need. However, the longer you wait, the more generous your pension will be.

■ Dual contributors to the CPP and QPP are those who have made at least one contribution to both plans. They will receive their benefits under the regulations in an agreement signed in 1975. If you have paid into both plans, you will collect from CPP if you live outside Quebec when you apply for your pension. Otherwise, you'll receive QPP. If you live outside Canada when you apply, the plan from which you collect will depend on where you last lived in Canada. In any case, all of your contributions will be considered when your pension is calculated.

■ You can request that your CPP pension be split between you and your husband or wife provided you are both at least age sixty. This presents a good opportunity for income-splitting, a tax strategy that moves income into the hands of the spouse paying a lower rate of tax. Quebec does not permit splitting except in the event of marriage breakdown.

■ You can receive pension benefits anywhere in the world, payable in Canadian dollars.

■ CPP and QPP benefits increase with the cost of living, except for the QPP orphan and dependent children benefits.

■ Should you and your husband or wife obtain a divorce or legal annulment, the CPP or QPP rights which were earned during marriage can be split between you. This applies to marriages which ended after December 31, 1987. If you are a member of CPP, application must be made within three years of the date of the divorce. QPP benefits are automatically divided upon divorce without application.

---

was low because you worked part-time or for only part of the year.

These dropped years can include those years early in your working life when your income might not have been sufficient to make maximum contributions. Or if you are terminated or stop working at age fifty-eight, the two years between ages fifty-eight and sixty when you won't contribute to CPP will not prevent you from getting the full CPP pension benefits at age sixty.

Don't worry, you don't have to keep track of this. As a member of the CPP, you'll receive a statement of your contributions and earnings every three years. If you would like a statement more often, you can ask for it — but only once every twelve months. To get this information,

contact the Income Security Program's office nearest you. To receive a statement of participation in the QPP, contact the Regie des Rentes du Quebec.

You should compare these records with your T4 slips and tax returns. This will ensure that both sets of records are correct and will prevent confusion or delay when you apply for benefits. You can also ask for an estimate of your retirement pension at age sixty-five.

CPP/QPP — collect it early or wait?

Other than "Where's the bathroom?" the most often asked question at our seminars is "Should I claim CPP (or QPP) when I turn sixty or wait until I'm sixty-five or even older?" My trouble with this question is that I don't know for sure when you and your husband or wife are going to die. And I don't like talking about death. But to answer this question, you do have to think about it, along with several other factors.

First let's briefly look at the rules:

■ If you take your CPP or QPP pension early, your pension will be reduced by 0.5 percent for every month prior to your sixty-fifth birthday to a maximum reduction of 30 percent at age sixty.

■ This reduction in your pension continues for the rest of your life.

■ Early collection of your pension also reduces the survivor benefits your husband or wife will receive if you should die.

■ You cannot claim your pension early if you are earning more than the pension itself will pay, around $8,000 a year.

These rules provoke some questions. Let's eliminate an easy one first. Will you really be retired at age sixty? If you are earning more than $8,000 a year, you won't be able to claim the pension. You can retire, claim the early

pension and return to work. But you should keep in mind that if you do this, your pension will probably be taxed at a higher rate than would be the case if you were not working — after all, your income is higher. True, you might say, but even if you don't need the pension for living expenses, at least you'll get the money and can invest it.

Here's the dilemma: if you take the early pension, you'll receive the pension for more years but you'll get less each month. If you take the pension later, you'll receive more each month but for fewer years. The question comes down to this — which option puts more money in your pocket? Well, that depends on how long you live. Let's look at the chart, "Should I take my CPP/QPP pension early?"

We'll ignore inflation, since both streams of income are indexed, and compounding investment income just for the moment. The top row of coins represents the stream of payments you would receive if you take your pension at age sixty; the second row of coins represents the payments you would receive if you take your pension at age sixty-five. Between age seventy-six and seventy-seven, the number of coins in each row is equal. Past that age the total income received from the regular pension begins to exceed the total payments for the reduced, early pension.

This is the case if you spend the pension as you receive it. The answer is different if you save and invest the pension for many years. If you do, it will take longer for the pot of funds saved from receiving the regular pension to grow to equal the pot of savings that accumulate if you receive and invest the early, reduced pension. This makes sense: the huge head start makes the early pension the better choice for many years. In fact, if you are investing the early pension it isn't until age eighty-six that both accounts hold $38,500.

Another important issue in deciding when to claim your CPP or QPP is the survivors'

The difference between CPP and QPP

When QPP and CPP were launched in 1966 the plans were almost identical. The key difference was in the management of the funds contributed to the plans. CPP contributions form a pool of funds from which the nine provinces can borrow. QPP contributions flow into Quebec's pension investment fund operated by the Caisse de dépôt et placement du Québec.

Differences arose, and disappeared, over the years. The QPP allowed plan members to retire anytime between age sixty and seventy, a change which CPP did not adopt until 1987. Another difference is in the pensions paid to surviving spouses of contributors. At some ages the QPP benefits are higher. The benefits paid to orphans or children of contributors who are disabled are higher under CPP. A final difference is in the eligibility rules for receiving disability benefits.

The QPP also acts as the provincial regulator of employer pensions, a role played by pension commissions in the other nine provinces.

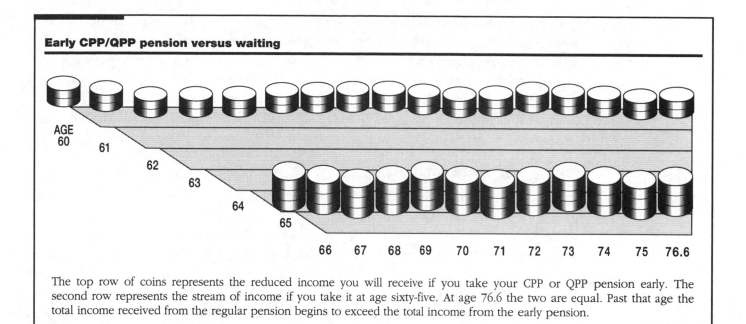

Early CPP/QPP pension versus waiting

AGE 60 · 61 · 62 · 63 · 64 · 65 · 66 67 68 69 70 71 72 73 74 75 76.6

The top row of coins represents the reduced income you will receive if you take your CPP or QPP pension early. The second row represents the stream of income if you take it at age sixty-five. At age 76.6 the two are equal. Past that age the total income received from the regular pension begins to exceed the total income from the early pension.

benefits. If you die before your husband or wife, the survivor pension will be 60 percent of the pension you were receiving before you died — whether you were receiving an already reduced pension or a full pension. If the survivor benefits to your husband or wife are important, keep this in mind, especially if you are in poor health and he or she is not.

Have I confused you or enlightened you? Let's set down some guidelines. Take the CPP or QPP pension early if:

- You're single, plan to spend the money and are unlikely to live past age seventy-seven.

- You're single, plan to save the money, and are unlikely to live past age eighty-six. Remember, one-third of Canadians age sixty will live past this age.

- You're married, plan to spend the money and won't live past age seventy-six or plan to invest the money and won't live past age eighty-six and your husband or wife will not receive a survivor's pension. This would be the case if he or she is also a contributor to CPP or QPP and will receive the maximum retirement pension or if he or she is in poor

health and likely to die before you.

- You need the money at age sixty and are not in a financial position to worry about the situation later.

Take your pension at age sixty-five if:

- You intend to spend the pension and you're likely to live past age seventy-six, or you plan to invest it and you expect to live past age eighty-six.

- You and your spouse will live a long time, and are worried about inflation and taxes.

- Your spouse will live past age seventy-six and will rely on survivor benefits from your CPP or QPP.

Of course, you can also delay claiming your pension. If you do this, your pension is increased by 1/2 percent for each month you wait to a maximum of 30 percent at age seventy. However, it's often not profitable to do so, unless you're sure to live a very long time. If you continue to work and to contribute to the CPP or QPP after age sixty-five instead of claiming your pension, you will continue to build pension credits, which will even further increase your pension.

One last word on CPP and QPP. Your contributions, historically set at 3.6 percent of your salary, have increased by 0.2 percent a year until they reached 4.6 percent in 1991. In mid-1993, that maximum was $33,400. If you're an employee, your employer pays 50 percent of the contribution. If you are self-employed, you must make the full contribution yourself. Contributions are increasing at 0.15 percent a year until they reach 7.6 percent in 2011. Although this means increased deductions from your pay, it may mean CPP and QPP will not suffer from cutbacks in benefits in the future.

CPP and QPP disability benefits

Although we are most familiar with CPP and QPP as plans which provide a pension in retirement, both plans also provide their members with disability pensions if you are unable to work. Unfortunately, to qualify for a disability pension under either plan you must be unable to work at any job. The disability must be serious enough that it will probably last for the rest of your life. The rules are relaxed for those over age sixty when a pension will be awarded if you cannot fulfill the requirements of your last job.

To claim a disability benefit, you must have contributed for two of the last three years, or for five of the last ten years. QPP has a couple of other rules. In Quebec, you must have contributed for at least half of the years since your eighteenth birthday. Under both plans the disability benefits stop at age sixty-five when CPP or QPP kick in. The 1993 maximum monthly disability pension is $812.85.

CPP and QPP survivor benefits

Benefits are available to families of a deceased contributor to the CPP and QPP as a lump-sum payment upon death and a monthly pension to the survivors. For your family to be eligible to receive any benefit, you must have contributed for at least three years; to receive the maximum

benefits, you must have made contributions for ten years or one-third of the years that you were eligible to participate, whichever is less.

These benefits are paid to a surviving legal or common-law spouse. The definition of "common-law" is under constant revision and differs from province to province. But generally, a surviving spouse is the person of the opposite sex who has lived with the contributor for at least one year before the contributor's death. This one-year period must not have been interrupted by separation. And if the contributor dies of illness, the common-law spouse must be able to prove that he or she did not know that the contributor was terminally ill when they began to live together.

The death benefit is either 10 percent of the yearly maximum pensionable earnings or six times the contributor's monthly retirement pension, whichever is less. In 1993, the maximum death benefit was $3,340.

The monthly pension varies according to the surviving spouse's age and circumstances. A lower sum is paid to someone of working age who does not have a disability or children to support. For someone under age sixty-five, the pension is 37.5 percent of the contributor's retirement pension. For spouses age sixty-five and over, the pension is 60 percent of the deceased contributor's retirement pension.

If you are receiving CPP or QPP survivor benefits and are eligible for a retirement pension in your own right, your survivor benefits will be integrated with your own pension once you reach age sixty-five. However, the combined benefits cannot exceed the maximum monthly pension, $667.36 in 1993. Similarly, if you're entitled to disability benefits as well as the surviving spouse monthly benefit, the maximum amount you can receive is $812.85.

Survivor benefits continue even if the surviving spouse remarries. All surviving spouses' pensions that were discontinued because of a remarriage that occurred before January 1, 1984, for the QPP and before January 1, 1987, for the CPP are payable again but you must apply. Retroactive payments will not be made. The pension will be calculated as if it had not been discontinued.

The natural or adopted child of a contributor who has died may be eligible for an orphan's benefit under the CPP and QPP if the child is under age eighteen or between the ages of eighteen and twenty-five and attending school full-time. The maximum orphan's benefit in 1993 is $157.48. If a child has lost both parents, then he or she may be eligible for two CPP or QPP benefits .

Unemployment insurance

Unemployment insurance (UI) protects Canadians by providing them with an income when they are out of work. The program is funded by mandatory contributions from most working Canadians and contributions from their employers.

You will receive a weekly benefit from UI if you lose your job or resign with just cause but you must be looking for work. Your benefits depend on the contributions you've made to the plan and the unemployment rate when you apply. The unemployment insurance office will take between three to five weeks to process your claim and send your first weekly payment. You'll receive benefits for between seventeen and fifty weeks.

Your benefits will be delayed if you receive any vacation pay, retiring allowance or pension income. If you have received such payments, the weekly income you were earning while you were working will be divided into the amount you received in order to determine the waiting period before you will begin receiving UI benefits. For example, if you were earning $1,000 a week while working and receive a $20,000 severance package, you will have to wait for twenty weeks ($20,000 divided by $1,000) before receiving your unemployment benefits. If you are given a severance package, check with your local UI office to find out when your first UI cheque will arrive.

There is an important exception to this rule. If you retire early, begin to receive a pension, return to work and then become unemployed you will not suffer any reduction in your UI benefits because of the retirement pension from your previous job.

Not everyone who works is covered by unemployment insurance. People who do not make contributions, and are therefore not insured, include those who:

- work less than fifteen hours a week, are paid an hourly wage and receive their wages at the end of every week.

- earn less than 20 percent of the maximum weekly insurable earning ($33,400).

- are employed by a company in which they own more than 40 percent of the voting stock. In the past, an employee whose husband or wife owned more than 40 percent of the voting stock of the company was also not insured by UI but this is no longer true.

Hospital and medical care programs

The hospital and medical care programs which

CPP/QPP maximum monthly survivor benefits		TABLE 2
	CPP	**QPP**
Spousal benefit		
■ for spouse under age 55	$372	$563
■ for spouse aged 55 to 65	$372	$650
■ for spouse age 65 and over	$400	$400
Surviving children benefit		
■ for children under age 18 or under 25 and attending school	$157	$29
■ an orphan whose parents were both contributors	$314	

protect all Canadians are administered according to the rules established by each province. Although the plans provide similar services, there are differences in the fees and benefits. Generally, hospital benefits include room and board in a ward, nursing care, prescription drugs, operating room and anesthetic facilities, laboratory and diagnostic services, and outpatient emergency services.

They also cover the care you receive from a medical practitioner in your home, at the hospital or at the doctor's office. Only limited coverage is available in some provinces for paramedic or optometric service and for prosthetic or orthopedic devices. Drug expenses for the elderly are fully reimbursed or subsidized in most provinces but several of the provinces are considering changes to the drugs which are covered. The extent of reimbursement or subsidy is also being reviewed by many provinces and changes are possible. Some dental and oral surgery that is performed in hospitals is covered by all the provinces; Alberta is the only province to provide routine dental care to those sixty-five years or older and their dependents.

You're covered by a province's medical plan after you've lived in the province for three months. (In the meantime, your previous province will cover you for three months as you establish residency in another province.) If you move from one province to another after retirement, make sure you register with the authorities as soon as possible. Be sure to ask for information; some provinces provide more benefits, others fewer.

Your provincial coverage will cease if you're absent from a province beyond a certain period of time, usually six months. If you're going to be away longer, check to see if you can extend your coverage. It's important to remember that you cannot buy medical insurance that will protect you as well as you are protected by your provincial plan. For this reason, you should take special care to comply with the residency requirements if you spend long periods of time outside Canada.

Your provincial medical coverage also protects you while you're travelling outside Canada. However, it will pay only the cost of similar care here, even though your medical bill could be higher. To make things worse, many provinces have reduced or are planning to reduce coverage when you travel outside Canada. Health care is especially expensive in the United States and many American hospitals and doctors demand payment or proof of insurance before they'll even look at you — no matter how urgent your problem. If you travel, private health insurance has become essential. Call your provincial health department to find out what is covered and how to get supplemental benefits.

Of course, many Canadians are protected by the supplementary health insurance provided by their employer or their professional associations. Although some of these will protect you into retirement, many do not. If you are not protected by such a plan, you will find there are only a few plans that provide private coverage for extended hospital care, private rooms, private nursing, drugs and ambulance service. Unfortunately, these plans offer low lifetime claims limits and low reimbursement percentages.

If you decide to live outside of Canada and are not protected by your former employer's insurance plan, make sure you purchase the best available hospital and medical insurance possible. These are available through insurance companies and travel organizations. Although this is not difficult to arrange for short periods of time, perhaps six months, coverage for longer periods of time is harder to obtain and more expensive. In fact, you might need to buy several policies to provide the protection you need. Few expenses can sap your financial resources more quickly than major medical treatment. We will talk more about arranging for health coverage in the United States in chapter fourteen on retiring outside Canada.

Although it is crucial that you have medical insurance, be warned that most private policies will not cover you for complications arising from problems which you already have. If you are diabetic and go into a diabetic coma while in the United States, you will be liable for the expenses. If you have a heart attack but have had no previous heart problems, the expenses will be covered. This is the case whether you have purchased travel insurance or a supplementary plan for a few months.

Special programs for seniors

Each province and territory also has social and health programs to assist retired Canadians. They offer community health and social services, home-care support, and organized senior citizen centres and groups.

Ontario publishes a booklet called "The Guide for Senior Citizens" which outlines the many ways in which that government helps its retired citizens through drug benefits, housing, long-term care, educational programs, health care and other information services. It's home-care programs include Meals On Wheels, transportation to medical appointments or shopping, and community centres which provide counselling on problems associated with aging and retirement as well as recreational and cultural activities.

British Columbia publishes a guide called "When I'm Sixty-Four." This booklet contains extensive information for seniors and outlines the health care, transportation, counselling services and housing assistance provided by the province, including a discussion of the Shelter Aid for Elderly Renters (SAFER) program which offers cash assistance to certain senior renters over the age of sixty.

The list of provincial services and programs available throughout the country is long and varied. Find out what is available in your province and community so that you can get all the benefits to which you are entitled.

Veterans' benefits

Financial, social and health-care support is available to veterans and their dependents through the Department of Veterans' Affairs and other organizations.

Pensions are awarded through the Canadian Pension Commission to those who served in the military and to civilians who supported the Canadian armed forces during wartime. There are pensions for veterans who were held prisoners of war or suffered disability and for the families of those who died while serving this country. Some of these pensions continue to a husband, wife or children after the death of the pensioner — the full pension for a year but usually a reduced pension after that time.

If you think you might be entitled to a pension benefit, you should apply to the Canadian Pension Commission. If you need help with your application, you can ask the Bureau of Pensions Advocates or a veterans' association such as the Royal Canadian Legion. Their help is free.

If you are a Canadian veteran and have a low income, you might be entitled to receive an allowance if you meet war service, age and residency requirements. If you are an Allied veteran, you might be entitled to this financial support if you lived in Canada when you joined the forces or if you have lived here for at least ten years since the war.

The allowance you receive depends on whether you're married or single; they're paid to veterans, their widows or widowers and orphaned children. For more information on allowances, call the Department of Veterans' Affairs office. You'll find their telephone number in the blue government pages of your telephone book.

Other programs, also available through the

The only retirement guide you'll ever need

Department of Veterans' Affairs, include the Veterans' Independence Program. The aim of this program is to allow you to stay in your own home by providing financial help to cover the cost of a housekeeper, help with maintaining the grounds around your home, Meals On Wheels, a nurse or personal care giver, transportation to social activities or a retirement home.

Health-care support is available for medical, surgical and dental care, prosthetic devices, home adaptations, and travel to a hospital or clinic for medical examination or treatment. Veterans' Affairs will even provide support for the family members providing care to a veteran. You might also be entitled to assistance with funeral and burial expenses and education assistance for the children of pensioners who have died.

Agreements with other countries

Canada has reciprocal social security agreements with many other countries. These agreements make your benefits portable and avoid duplication of benefits to people who have lived and worked in several countries over their lives. These can help you in a number of situations, including:

■ Old Age Security. If you have not lived in Canada long enough to receive the OAS, participation in the social security program of another country might count in reaching the residency requirement to receive the benefit, even if you live outside Canada when you apply for the benefit. These adjustments only establish eligibility. Your benefit will still be based on the number of years you've lived in Canada.

■ Canada Pension Plan. Participation in a similar program in a country with which we have an agreement will help establish your eligibility to receive a retirement pension, disability benefits and your family's eligibility for survivor and death benefits.

■ Canadians might be able to use their participation in Canadian plans to meet eligibility requirements for programs in other countries where they are eligible because of their citizenship or residency.

United States social security

The reciprocal social security agreement between the United States and Canada allows for the coordination of social security benefits earned in both countries. Under this agreement it is possible for Canadians who have worked in the United States for as little as eighteen months to be eligible to receive an American social security pension income.

The American plan, called Old Age Survivors and Disability Insurance, pays as much as $1,000 ($U.S.) a month, somewhat more than the combined OAS and CPP or QPP payments in Canada. In addition, the American pension is received entirely tax-free if your total income is less than $25,000 as an individual or less than $32,000 for a married couple. It seems generous but you should know that the deduction from American paycheques throughout their working lives is almost twice the deduction from Canadian cheques.

To claim a full American pension, and to qualify for free United States Medicare, you

Your government benefits		WORKSHEET 18
	Monthly	Annual
Old age security		
■ Pension	_____	_____
■ Guaranteed Income Supplement	_____	_____
■ Spouse, Widow or Widower Allowance	_____	_____
Canada or Quebec Pension Plan		
■ Pension	_____	_____
■ Survivor benefits	_____	_____
■ Veterans' benefits	_____	_____
■ Provincial government assistance	_____	_____
Total	_____	_____

must have worked in the United States and contributed to the social services plan for at least ten years. However, if you have worked for at least a year and a half, credits from the United States and Canada will be combined to qualify you for a partial pension. If you do qualify for benefits, your husband or wife automatically qualifies to receive benefits that are equal to about half what you receive, even if he or she did not contribute to the plan.

People who live outside the United States must have worked in the United States for at least ten years to be eligible to claim the social security pension. If you file a Canadian tax return and receive American social security, only half of it must be reported as taxable income, just as only half is taxed in the United States. The American government is looking at changing this tax rule. For higher-income Americans, there is a claw-back of the Social Security just as the Canadian government claws back the OAS. Usually, there isn't a withholding tax deducted in the United States nor would you be required to file a United States tax return unless you're a United States citizen or resident.

Your government retirement income

To sum up the government benefits you expect to receive in retirement you should complete "Your government benefits." Although the dollars and cents provided in this section are based on the 1993 maximums and will not apply when you retire, they will enable you to estimate the benefits you will receive when you do retire. You'll be referring back to this table when you look at your retirement income in chapter nine.

NOTES

Understanding your pension plan

An employer pension plan can be the cornerstone of your financial security in retirement. A good pension to which you've belonged for many years will provide you with an income that will allow you to live in comfort for the rest of your years. Unfortunately, pension plans are neither as widespread nor as generous as Canadians tend to believe.

It helps to have an historical perspective to understand both the importance of your pension plan to your retirement security and the impact of recent legislative changes on your ability to save for retirement.

At the turn of this century, only governments, banks and railways provided pensions. These were primitive affairs, offering little in the way of benefits, often funded solely by employee contributions. With 1914 came World War I, government debt and the introduction of income tax. In 1919, tax legislation in Canada allowed employers to deduct contributions to pension plans from an employee's paycheque. Finally, in 1927, those contributions became tax-deductible. It wasn't until the 1960s that it became commonplace for employers to contribute to their employees' pension plans.

Still, pension plans were offered only by major corporations. There were many Canadians retiring with inadequate resources, and the geographic scattering of families meant that getting support from family members was difficult. Canada introduced the OAS pension in 1952, the RRSP program in 1957, the CPP and QPP in 1966, and the GIS in 1967. These programs were needed to fill the gap for many Canadians who were retiring without company pensions or whose pensions were inadequate. Many of these Canadians worked for smaller companies, were self-employed or worked only part-time. Many were the women who had joined the labour force during World War II.

The latest developments in the web of programs designed to support Canadians in retirement are the many changes that were made to pension standards and the income tax system that were made in the past decade. The thrust has been to include part-time employees in pension plans, to ensure that benefits "vest" or belong to employees sooner, and to encourage people to keep their pension funds for retirement instead of collapsing retirement plans when leaving an employer. The tax changes are designed to equalize the tax advantages available to all Canadians as they save for retirement, whether they are using RRSPs, are members of employer-sponsored pension plans or both.

There are various kinds of pension plans. The actual rules and calculations are complex, but the basic concept behind all pension plans is simple: To save for retirement, we must save a little bit every payday and invest our savings in safe and progressive ways. Once we retire, we can then convert these savings into a monthly income. This is what your pension plan does. A small portion of your pay is collected from every paycheque, either from you as your pension contribution or from your employer as part of its payroll benefits costs or

Retirement income of Quebecers TABLE 3

A 1987 study of Quebecers sixty-five years of age and over looked at the sources of retirement incomes.

Income source	Single	Married
Government pensions	55%	40%
Company pensions	16%	37%
Investment and personal sources	29%	23%
Average retirement income	$12,364	$19,751

SOURCE: STATISTICS CANADA

from both. Everyone can afford small contributions each month, particularly if they are deducted from your pay before you receive it. It's even more affordable if your employer pays all of the premiums.

The power of pension plans as a savings tool is enhanced by the income tax benefits. Contributions to the plan are tax-deductible: for every $100 you contribute to your pension plan, you will gain a $40 to $50 reduction in your taxes, depending on your marginal tax rate. And you don't have to wait until July to get this tax recovery. It's built into your pay through a reduction in the tax withheld each month. Your employer also gets a similar tax benefit. A contribution by your employer brings a tax saving in the employer's monthly corporate tax payment.

The investment growth within the pension plan is tax-advantaged as well. Unlike personal investment income, which attracts income tax each year, pension funds earn interest, dividends, capital gains and rental income free of tax. If $20 billion in assets earns $1.6 billion a year in a pension plan, the government does not collect the $600 million in income taxes it would collect if this had been earned outside the pension plan. All of the income and growth a pension plan realizes remains in the plan and you share in this windfall at retirement. This tax advantage allows the funds to grow in value so that the largest possible amount is available at retirement.

Finally, many years down the road, the process reverses and you begin to receive pension income to replace your employment earnings. The pension income you receive is taxable, but this is fair because it's really a long-delayed payment of earnings that you didn't receive at the time you earned them nor paid tax at the time. In fact, they gained you a tax saving and the growth and income earned by your contributions over the years was never taxed either.

The company provides or pays for the administrative and management system to collect the funds, invests them with professional care, and pays them out month by month wherever you reside. After a thirty- to forty-year career, your pension will provide up to 70 percent of what you were earning just before you retired. If you're not around to collect it, it will pay your surviving wife, husband, children or your estate.

A pension plan is a legal arrangement that must be honoured. Trustees hold the funds and ensure that the pension plan rules are followed. The plan document itself can run fifty pages or more. Investment managers manage the funds according to the pension plan's investment policy and adhere to legislative and professional investment standards. Auditors ensure that nothing gets lost, and consultants and actuaries advise on the pension funds needed and policies.

Most of this is of little concern to you but it is comforting to know that the rules surrounding your pension are rigid and closely monitored to ensure the pension plan will provide you with your retirement income. What you need to know in detail are your rights and responsibilities. To understand these you have to know what kind of pension plan you have. Although we tend to call them all pension plans, there are really three kinds of retirement plans which your employer might have: a registered pension plan, or RPP; a deferred profit sharing plan, or DPSP; and a group RRSP. Let's look at the registered pension plans first.

Defined benefit plans

A pension plan can be either a defined benefit plan or a money purchase plan. The most common is the defined benefit plan. These plans specify the pension benefit you will receive during retirement. That benefit is based on a formula generally using your average income for a particular period of time, the number of years that you've been a member of the plan and a defined pension benefit factor, usually between 1 and 2 percent. It's up to your employer to ensure that enough contributions are paid into the plan and that these contributions are being wisely invested so that the plan will be able to pay the "defined" pension income. Regardless of how well or poorly the investments in the plan perform, you will receive the agreed-upon pension income from your employer.

Let's assume that your plan's defined benefit is a pension income that will be 70 percent of your income before retirement. If you've worked for thirty-five years, this will mean that for each year you've worked you will be paid 2 percent of the income you were earning before retirement. This would be generous. Most plans will pay only 1 or 1.5 percent rather than 2 percent of your earnings; the more generous pension is very expensive. (For the same reason, not all plans will increase your pension income to keep pace with inflation. Although this is often done, it is at the discretion of the pension manager.)

Often the defined benefit calculation is made in two steps, using two different percentages. There's a lower percentage for your earnings that are covered by the CPP or QPP, and a higher percentage for earnings above the government's yearly maximum pensionable earnings. The YMPE is the annually adjusted maximum earnings on which CPP and QPP premiums must be paid and on which CPP and QPP pensions are paid. The higher pension benefit makes up for the fact that CPP and QPP are not available on the higher earnings.(If you retire early, before you receive your OAS and CPP or QPP, some plans will boost your payments until these government benefits kick-in. This is called a bridging clause.)

Unfortunately, this complication comes into the calculation of most defined benefit pensions. It might also mean that you will receive a lower pension income than you might have expected to receive.

Just as the formula in each pension plan differs, so does the way in which your earnings are calculated. Some plans base your pension on your basic salary only, while others consider your total compensation — your salary, bonus and overtime pay. Some plans use your average earnings for your whole career, adding each year's compensation and dividing by the total of years and months of service. This is called your career average earnings. Other plans take an average of your last three or five years. A few look at only your best three or five years. Some plans don't consider your earnings at all. These "level-benefit" plans calculate your pension on a flat amount for each year of service. This amount is usually different for the various types of jobs within a company.

Because the contributions made to a defined benefit pension plan are usually based on your income, there isn't any difference between the level of contributions made by men and women. Similarly, because the pension benefit is determined by your earnings and years of work, your gender will not affect your pension income either.

Money purchase pension plans

Money purchase plans, also called defined contribution plans, do not have any pension income guarantees. Instead it is the contributions that you and your employer must make to the plan that are "defined." Those contributions depend on the terms of your pension plan and are subject to a maximum contribution limit. You and your employer can contribute up to 18 percent of your salary during the year to a maximum of $13,500 in 1993. This dollar limit is scheduled to rise by $1,000 a year to $15,500 in 1995.

The size of pension you will receive on retirement will depend on the amount that has been contributed over the years, the growth in your savings through the plan's investment strategy and annuity rates at the time that you retire. For this reason, the investment performance of your pension funds is very important for it is your retirement income that is at risk if the funds are not well-managed. To control this risk, your pension manager will have engaged a professional investment manager who will manage the pension fund in keeping with the investment policy set out in your pension plan document. This professional investment manager must also abide with pension legislation and other professional investment standards.

In order to become more familiar with the investment performance of your pension funds, you should read the investment policy statement set out in the pension document. You should also review your annual plan statement, which should comment on the growth in market value of pension fund assets. If you want to get a more detailed understanding of the investments supporting your pension, you are entitled to ask for a copy of the audited financial statements of your pension plan.

When retirement day comes, the funds that have been building in the plan over the years are used to purchase an annuity. The monthly pension income that you will be able to buy will depend on the amount of money you have and the annuity rates in place at the time. Annuity rates fluctuate with interest rates; the higher the interest rate at the time you buy your annuity, the higher your income.

Annuity rates also depend on life expectancy. Since women have a longer average life expectancy than men, the monthly pension income which a women will receive from an annuity is usually slightly lower than for a man the same age.

Group RRSPs

Group RRSPs are very similar to money purchase pension plans. Your employer arranges payroll deductions for RRSP contributions to a plan that is registered with the tax authorities. You have a convenient way to contribute to an RRSP and your monthly income tax deduction will be reduced to reflect the RRSP contribution deducted from your salary. Usually you have to wait until July or later for a tax refund.

As a member of a group RRSP, you are responsible for establishing your own investment strategy, often from the mutual funds of an investment management firm as well as guaranteed investment certificates. Your employer might choose to contribute to the RRSP on your behalf, or leave it entirely up to each employee to use the group RRSP as he or she wishes. The employee requests that a portion of each paycheque be contributed to the RRSP and can change that level of contribution and the investment option at will.

Contributions to a group plan have to be within the RRSP contribution limits. Your contributions in a year cannot exceed 18 percent of your earned income in the previous year up to $12,500 for 1993. This limit is scheduled to increase by $1,000 a year until it reaches $15,500 in 1996, when it is scheduled to rise with inflation. Earned income represents your employment income less employment expenses plus any business or rental income earned net of losses, alimony payments received, supplementary unemployment benefits, CPP/QPP disability benefits and certain other forms of income. (We'll discuss RRSPs in detail in chapter eight.)

Perhaps one of the most significant differences between group RRSPs and money purchase plans is the ability to make your own investment choices. Some people see this control over their investments as an advantage of group RRSPs. Others prefer to have the benefit of the professional investment managers engaged by pension plans.

Deferred profit-sharing plans

Companies are required to make contributions to a pension plan every year, regardless of whether they have profits or losses. In tough economic times, many companies look for ways to cut costs and gain greater flexibility. They might be tempted to change from a defined benefit plan, in which they pay specific amounts of pension benefits and high administration costs, to a cheaper, risk-free money purchase plan. Even better, from the corporate viewpoint, would be a plan in which contributions are tied to profits — low when profits are low, higher when profits are high. This describes some of the attributes of a DPSP.

Although a DPSP is not a pension plan, it is often used by employers to build retirement funds for their employees. Funds are contributed to a DPSP by the employer, depending on corporate profits and the employee's salary and responsibilities. Employees are not allowed to make contributions to a DPSP. The company receives a tax deduction for contributing to the DPSP up to the maximum level defined in regulations. Employer contributions are limited to the lesser of 18 percent of the employee's

---

You can still contribute $1,000

You can still contribute at least $1,000 to your RRSP even if you are a member of a generous pension plan. It's an opportunity you shouldn't miss. Your money grows far more quickly inside an RRSP than it does when it's invested within the grasp of Revenue Canada. If you invest a modest $1,000 a year from age fifty-five to sixty-five and earn just 8 percent, your nest egg will grow to $17,000 by the time you are sixty-five, $26,500 by the time you're seventy-one.

---

salary income or the annual contribution limit ($6,750 for 1993, increasing by $500 per year to $7,750 in 1995, and indexed thereafter).

You are not taxed on the funds set aside in your name in the DPSP nor is there tax on the investment income or growth. These funds become "vested" in your name; that is, they are owned by you either after a certain period of years or gradually over a number of years, perhaps 20 percent a year over five years. Employees tend to leave DPSP funds in the DPSP until they retire or leave the company. In this way, DPSPs resemble retirement plans. The funds can be paid out in a lump sum, in which case they are taxed in full immediately, or they can be transferred tax-free to an RRSP or your new employer's pension plan.

Retirement compensation arrangements

A retirement compensation arrangement, or RCA, is a plan other than an RRSP, DPSP or registered pension plan under which an employer makes payments to an account that will provide money to an employee on retirement or after the employee has left the company. It's basically an unregistered pension plan. Your employer's contributions to this plan do not have any immediate tax consequence to you. However, your employer pays a special refundable tax on the contributions and on earnings in the plan. Therefore, these arrangements do not gain the benefit of tax deferred earnings growth seen in registered

---

Individual pension plans

Individual Pension Plans (IPPs) are defined benefit pension plans that can be set up for people who own their own companies or the senior executives of very large firms. These plans can provide tax benefits but because the full cost of administering the plan is borne by a single plan member rather than spread over many members, such plans are very costly. In fact, the compliance and reporting requirements have made IPPs less desirable — most owner-managers and many executives still use defined contribution plans or RRSPs to build their retirement nest eggs.

---

pension plans. If you make a contribution to an RCA that is required under the terms of your employment, you will be entitled to deduct this contribution as long as it does not exceed that made by your employer. Because employer contributions to RCAs are subject to the special refundable tax, these arrangements are not widespread.

Past service contributions

There might be instances under which contributions are made to your plan for "past service." Past service is work that you performed in previous years that qualifies as pensionable service under your defined benefit pension plan but did not earn pension credits at the time. This might occur, for instance, if you become a member of a plan after a couple of years with your company, and you then choose to make past service contributions for the years you were with the company but didn't belong to the pension plan. You might also make past service contributions if the defined benefit plan is adjusted to increase the pension benefit and you want to increase the contributions you made for earlier years to match this higher level of benefits.

The amount of a past-service contribution that you can deduct on your tax return depends on the years for which you are making the contribution. The pivotal year is 1990. You can deduct all the past-service

contributions you pay to your defined benefit plan for service in 1990 or later. You must deduct these contributions in the year they are paid. If you make the contributions for 1989 or earlier, your deduction will depend on whether or not you were a contributor to the plan during these years.

If you were a contributor, you can only deduct up to $3,500 less the sum of all current service or other past service contributions you are already deducting for the year. You can carry forward contributions that aren't deductible this year to deduct in the future. If you were not a contributor, you can deduct up to an additional $3,500 on top of your current service contribution.

You can also earn past service pension benefits, perhaps when your employer upgrades its pension contributions for previous years. Receiving such benefits for 1990 or any year after that might result in a past-service pension adjustment or PSPA. This PSPA will reduce the amount which you will be able to deduct for RRSP contributions in the year in which the PSPA occurs. If you have made the maximum RRSP contribution that you were entitled to before receiving the PSPA, it is likely that you will have overcontributed. Don't worry. You're allowed to overcontribute by up to $8,000, a provision which we'll discuss in chapter eight.

Changing employers

Often employers use their pension plans to discourage employees from leaving to work elsewhere. There might be a penalty, usually a loss of contributions that have not yet been vested in the employee. Even if your pension has been vested, the impact of changing jobs late in your career can be significant. Let's look at an example. John Smith has been working with ABC Inc. for twenty years and is now earning $60,000 a year. He has ten more years to go before retirement. A competitor, XYZ

Corp., has offered John a job, but if he takes it he will lose the benefit of his last ten years of membership in ABC's pension plan. Is this important?

If XYZ has a similar pension plan, the pension benefits he'll receive for his last ten years of work will be about the same from ABC or XYZ. But if Smith leaves ABC, he is surrendering the chance to apply the first twenty years of his working career to his eventual final salary, which will be around $101,400 by 2003 when he retires.

If both plans pay a pension equal to 1.5 percent of the final three year average salary for each year of service, Smith will be giving up thousands of dollars of pension income each and every year of retirement. This is calculated as follows:

If Smith did not leave ABC, his pension would be 1.5 percent x $101,400 (his final average salary) x thirty years of service. This would be an annual pension of $45,600.

If Smith does leave ABC, then his pension from ABC would be 1.5 percent x $56,000 (the 1993 final three-year-average salary) x twenty years of service, or $17,000. His pension from XYZ would be 1.5 percent x $101,400 x ten years of service, or $15,200. The combined total annual pension he would receive would be $32,200, $13,400 less than he would receive if he stayed with ABC. On top of this, if Smith chooses the standard pension option and his wife receives 60 percent of his pension on his death, she will end up with a much reduced survivor's benefit.

You can move accrued benefits in a defined benefit plan to the defined benefit plan of a new employer, but only if the employer agrees. Usually, they don't. On the other hand, if you're a member of a money purchase pension plan, DPSP or group RRSP, a change of employers late in your career will have less impact on your retirement income — leaving you freer to move to a better job. Usually, you

---

Voluntary contributions

Additional voluntary contributions (AVCs) are contributions you make to a pension plan over and above the amounts you are required to contribute as a condition of the plan. AVCs are used to build pension benefits under a money purchase provision of a pension plan.

They can relate to current or past service, but since 1986, past-service AVCs are not tax-deductible. You can deduct AVCs as long as the contributions are allowed under your pension plan as registered. The amount of AVC you make will be included in your pension adjustment and will therefore reduce your RRSP limit for the following year. Because the AVCs are not required to fund your pension, you have the flexibility to transfer the AVCs and any earnings from those contributions to an RRSP.

---

can instruct your old employer to make a direct transfer of your benefits in any one of these plans to a new money purchase plan, DPSP or group RRSP at your new employer's. But you should still consider the pension benefits provided by each employer when considering a change. You should think twice before walking away from good pension benefits to an employer with a less generous pension plan.

Your pension options

One of the most important steps in your financial planning for retirement comes just before you retire when you must choose the pension option that best fits your needs. Most plans offer two "normal" pensions. The normal option for a single person is a pension that will continue for as long as you live, ceasing the day you die. The normal pension option for a married person provides for a pension for life for the pensioner and will continue to provide at least 60 percent of that pension for the lifetime of your husband or wife.

This "joint-life" pension will not be as generous as a pension guaranteed for only one life. Even if your husband or wife is older than you, it cannot be ignored that there are two persons receiving the income, one of whom will probably outlive the other. A couple has a greater chance of collecting for longer than one person alone. These odds are even more pronounced if your spouse is younger and healthier. The people running pension plans and the life insurance companies providing life annuities will want to pay a little less every month to ensure that the pot of money funding the pension will last a little longer.

You can reject the standard joint-life pension, and choose to have your spouse receive 100 percent of your pension after your death. If you do, your monthly pension income will be lower. You could also choose to refuse the pension for your spouse's lifetime. If you do, you will receive more pension income each month, but your spouse will not receive a dime after you die.

Despite the temptation of receiving a more generous pension, a married person cannot reject the 60 percent pension to his or her spouse unless the spouse agrees in writing, usually by signing a waiver. He or she will also have to sign a form if you choose to continue 100 percent of the pension for your spouse's lifetime, even though this will mean less pension income during your lifetime.

Let's consider an example. There is $200,000 in the pot to buy a pension for sixty-five-year-old Tom. This sum will provide $25,000 a year for Tom's life alone. But Tom is married to Sandy, who is only sixty-three and they want to make sure that Sandy is financially secure if he dies first. The pension would probably have to last about six years longer — Sandy is two years younger than Tom and statistics tell us that women live four years longer than men. If they choose a joint-life pension, they will receive $21,500 a year for life, or $3,500 less every year.

If you're tempted to choose the higher pension and refuse the pension for your partner, think carefully. You might even seek professional advice. Some employers will provide this advice to make sure that you have

considered all factors before making a decision that cannot be changed. In the old days, too many people opted for the higher pension — the life-only pension — and when the husband died he left his wife, who had no pension of her own, in distress.

In making your decision, you should have a sound knowledge of your finances, particularly your spending needs and the income that your husband or wife will receive if you are no longer around. You should also look at the value of your investments, insurance and properties. (Don't forget to consider the taxes your spouse will have to pay when doing your calculations.) It is possible that your husband or wife will have all the income needed, especially if he or she has a pension as well. Only if your spouse has enough income and you are sure the pension will not be needed should you sign the waiver and reject the joint-life pension.

Your pension guarantees

There is another choice to be made when settling your pension affairs. On top of the guarantee that the pension will last at least for your lifetime, you can also choose, or refuse, a guarantee that the pension will be paid for a certain period of time even if you die within that time.

Although, the normal option for a single person is a life annuity, most people choose to add a five-year guarantee. Even if you were to die the day after you retired, the five years of pension income would be paid to your estate. If you died a year after you began to receive your pension, four years of pension will be paid to your estate or heirs. If you decide not to take this option, your pension income will be slightly higher. Or you can choose a longer guarantee of ten, fifteen or even twenty years. The longer the guarantee period, the less income you'll receive each month.

Pension plans can be complex and confusing. The only way to understand your pension benefits is to ask questions. We've compiled the questions and concerns that many people seem to have about their pensions. Some are general questions, followed by those that are more specific. Make sure that you know the answers to each one before you make any predictions about your retirement income.

How much will I receive as a pension benefit?

Am I a member of a defined benefit plan or do I belong to a money purchase plan? If I am a member of a defined benefit plan, what will my pension income be? If I am a member of a money purchase plan, how well are the investments performing? How much might I receive when I retire? Will my pension be indexed for inflation?

_____

_____

How much is being contributed to my pension plan every year?

How much do I have to contribute? How much do you contribute to the plan?

_____

_____

Will my pension income be affected by my government benefits?

If I retire before the age of sixty-five, will I get extra pension until I begin to receive the OAS and CPP or QPP benefits? Will my pension be reduced by the OAS, CPP or QPP that I receive?

_____

_____

What happens if I retire early?

At what age can I retire early and receive a full pension? If I retire earlier than that, what will the penalty be? Is there a formula based on my age and the years I've been a member of the pension that will allow me to calculate when I can retire early without penalty?

_____

_____

What happens to my pension when I die?

How much will my husband or wife receive? Will my children receive any pension benefits if both my spouse and I die?

_____

_____

Do you provide any other retirement benefits?

Will my life insurance continue into retirement? If it does continue, will it drop to a lower amount after I've been retired for a few years? If it does drop, can I buy more life insurance if I need it? Am I covered for any out-of-province or out-of-country medical care in retirement?

_____

_____

These pension options are like the options on a car. They're nice to have but they're not free. You have an established pot of funds with which to purchase your pension and you pay for the options by receiving less pension income each month. Let's look at some examples and the factors influencing your choice.

Jack is retiring and is considering three options:

- A pension that would pay Jack and his wife Mary $3,000 a month while Jack is alive but only $1,800 a month to Mary after he dies. This is the normal option.

- A pension that will pay them $2,750 a month while Jack is alive and continue to pay Mary the same $2,750 after Jack dies. The couple will receive $250 a month less a month but as a widow Mary will receive $950 more each month than she would receive under the normal option.

- A pension that will pay them $3,500 a month while Jack is alive and then cease. This pension does not have any provisions for Mary and would only be chosen if Mary has her own income.

As you can see, Jack and Mary can receive $3,500 a month if they do not need any guaranteed income for Mary or $2,750 a month if they do not want any decline in her income after he dies. Usually, we recommend that couples choose to continue the pension for the surviving spouse but reduced to 60 percent.

This seems to make sense for most people. Your living expenses will be lower with one person gone but they will not be cut in half. The cost of shelter, utilities and car maintenance will probably continue undiminished. It doesn't cost any less to heat a home for one person than it does for two. There might be a few extra expenses without two people to carry on the tasks of looking after a home — it might be necessary to hire

someone to look after the yard or keep the home clean. Entertainment expenses might climb a bit as well. In fact, a surviving spouse might need 60 to 70 percent of the couple's former spending requirements.

Even single persons have to consider their options carefully. Consider the case of Sally. She is looking at three options:

- She can take the normal lifetime pension with a five-year guarantee and receive $1,840 a month.

- She can refuse the guarantee and receive $2,000 a month for her life only.

- She can take a life pension with a fifteen-year guarantee and receive only $1,500 a month.

Sally will receive the highest income if she chooses the pension without guarantees. But she has a younger brother with mild disability whom she has been putting through technical college. She can choose the five-year guarantee, and receive slightly less, but this will just see him through school. Or, she can receive significantly less herself and provide more significant protection for her brother.

Life-insuring your pension

Another option that would allow you to protect your spouse is "life-insuring" your pension by purchasing life insurance. This strategy calls for choosing your pension for your life only, and receiving a higher monthly pension than if you choose the joint-life pension. Then you turn around and buy an insurance policy that would provide a sufficient amount of money on your death to purchase a life annuity for your spouse that would provide the same stream of income that he or she would have received if you had opted for joint-life pension. You could end up with more money in your pocket if the increase in your pension income more than covers the premiums on the insurance you have to buy. (Don't forget that you will be

Learning the lingo

The next step in unravelling the mysteries of your pension plan is to understand the many words, rules and concepts that will be used in the pension literature and conversations with your colleagues, at retirement seminars or in discussions with your human resources advisers.

The rules governing the minimum standards for many of the pension plans in Canada are set out in the Pension Benefits Standards Act passed by the federal government in 1985. This act covers all employers under federal jurisdiction, including the federal government, Crown agencies, and all federally regulated companies such as those in the banking, transportation and broadcasting industries. This act also covers pensions in the Yukon and Northwest Territories.

The provinces have established their own pension standards for those employers that are not regulated by the federal authorities. The provincial standards are adaptations or improvements to the federal rules and are similar to each other in many ways. Both the federal and provincial standards govern eligibility, vesting requirements, survivor benefits, pension benefits and the administration of plans.

Eligibility

Under federal standards, full-time employees working for two continuous years and part-time employees who have either worked for twenty-four consecutive months and earned at least 35 percent of the yearly maximum pensionable earnings (around $11,000) or who have worked for 700 hours are eligible to belong to the pension plan. Although membership is not compulsory under the legislation, it often is under the terms of the plan.

Vesting

Vesting is the point at which the contributions made to the pension plan by your employer belong to you. Under federal and Ontario regulations, your pension benefits must vest within two years of joining the plan. Once vested, the funds are also "locked-in" and must be kept for retirement. This means that even a short-term employee will begin to build retirement income rights. If the pension is not vested when you leave a job, you get back only the contributions that you have made to the plan, not the contributions made by your employer on your behalf.These rules apply only to contributions and earnings on contributions made after 1987. For contributions made prior to 1987, the old rules apply. Under these rules, pension benefits did not vest until you were at least forty-five years of age and had ten years of service with your employer.

Financing

Under federal and Ontario legislation, the employer is required to finance at least 50 percent of your pension through contributions and earnings.

Portability

This is the ability to move your pension funds when you leave your job. In most jurisdictions, you can:

- transfer the money to the pension plan of your new employer, although your new employer might not accept the transfer.

- move your money into a locked-in RRSP. Once your funds are in a locked-in RRSP, you cannot withdraw them. The RRSP is then used to buy a life annuity when you retire.

- buy a life annuity. You can buy a deferred annuity that will pay you an income for life.

- or, leave the money in the plan to provide a benefit when you retire. Be wary of leaving pension credits with an employer. The pension might seem generous today but can be pretty meagre twenty or twenty-five years down the road. Unfortunately, sometimes you cannot move your pension funds to another plan if you are within ten years of normal retirement, the eligible time for early retirement. Normal retirement age is sixty-five except for a few professionals, such as police officers and pilots, for whom normal retirement is at age sixty. The decade before normal retirement age is referred to as the retirement-eligible age.

You will be lucky if your options include the ability to transfer to your new employer's plan. Choosing the best portability option demands a close look at your particular situation. The decision will depend on several factors, including the benefits you will be entitled to under your previous employer's plan, the details of your new employer's plan, and the annuity rates available at the time you change jobs.

You will have to determine what benefit each of these options will provide at retirement, then choose the option that will provide the highest retirement benefit. You might also want to weigh the certainty of the benefit you would receive from a life annuity purchased now or a defined benefit pension plan against the uncertainty of a potentially higher benefit under your RRSP where you can control the funds.

Survivor benefits

To protect the surviving husbands and wives of pension plan members, the normal pension of a married employee is a joint-and-last-survivor pension guaranteeing the survivor an income that is at least 60 percent of the pension before the death of the plan member. You can reject this provision or choose a lower survivor pension only if your husband or wife signs a waiver. The surviving benefit will continue to be paid even if your husband or wife remarries.

If you die before you retire, the value of your pension benefits will be paid to your husband or wife, your dependent children or your estate. The pension funds can be paid in one payment, used to purchase a life annuity, or transferred to a locked-in RRSP.

Indexing

Neither federal nor provincial standards require pension benefits be adjusted to keep up with inflation. Ontario has adopted inflation protection in principal and sets out some guidelines, but indexing is very costly, and to date, few organizations have incorporated this feature into their pension plans. Government benefits are fully indexed to provide you with inflation protection. However, a large percentage of your income in retirement will come from your employees' pension.

Early retirement

You have the right to retire up to ten years before the normal retirement age and receive a pension based on your vested contributions — even if your employer does not want you to leave. If you do retire early, your pension will be reduced to reflect the fact that you will make fewer contributions to the plan yet receive pension benefits for more years. If you choose to postpone your retirement, the pension benefit will increase to reflect the fact that you will contribute more to the plan yet receive a pension for fewer years.

Splitting credits

If your marriage should break down, the value of the pension or the benefits will be split in accordance with the family law in the province where you live. There is a provision for the division of pension benefits on marriage breakdown in all pension jurisdictions except Newfoundland. Generally, the amount of pension that will be given to the spouse after a marriage breakdown is limited to 50 percent of the amount of pension benefits that have accrued during the time of the marriage. Alberta, British Columbia and federally regulated plans do not have such a limit.

Administration

Employees are slowly gaining the right to be represented on pension committees. Where this has taken place, members receive annual statements on the operations of the pension fund. Plan documents, actuarial valuations and financial statements are being made available for inspection by the members. They might even be allowed to attend an annual meeting of plan members.

paying those insurance premiums with after-tax dollars.)

This is not usually the case, particularly with the low interest rates we have today. In most cases, you'll have to buy a great deal of insurance to provide adequate security to your spouse. And it's expensive to buy insurance when you're more than fifty or fifty-five years old — if you can get it at all. Yet you might have to keep this policy in place until you're seventy or seventy-five. The insurance premiums will probably be too high to make this work. If you decide the strategy does work for you, make sure that you have the insurance in place before signing the pension option form. Once you're retired it's too late to change your mind and ask for joint-life payments.

Company retirement benefits are valuable but often poorly understood because they're complex. Contributions are usually deducted from our paycheque, or made by our employer on our behalf, and the wealth builds in our name without our even being aware of it. As a result, we do not fully appreciate the value of these benefits. It's worthwhile, however, to gain a solid understanding of these plans so that you can make the most of these benefits and fit them into your retirement plans.

Other employer retirement benefits

There are several other corporate benefits that can be very helpful in retirement. These include life insurance that continues into retirement, supplementary medical and hospital insurance, out-of-province and out-of-country health care insurance, and dental care insurance. (Dental insurance is not often continued into retirement so be sure to take care of all your dental needs in the years before retirement.)

Most companies offer life insurance coverage that protects you by one, two or three times your salary level. You can often add to this with additional voluntary coverage at a reasonable cost. When it comes time to retire, however, your insurance coverage will dwindle to little or none at all. Of course, your need for insurance will have greatly diminished by this time, replaced by the pensions, savings and investments you've amassed over your lifetime. Still, you shouldn't ignore the benefit of life insurance. In fact, there might be a continuing need. (We'll cover insurance needs in more detail in chapter fifteen.)

If your employer doesn't provide at least some insurance in retirement, you might consider continuing some of your group insurance into retirement if this conversion privilege is available to you. This insurance remains in place for your life or might continue only for a particular period of time, depending on the arrangement made by your company. Usually you must act within thirty days of leaving the company to take advantage of this opportunity.

Many employers provide their employees with supplementary health care insurance. Typically, it pays for prescription drugs, private duty nursing, medical supplies and appliances, hospital care while they're outside Canada, chiropractors and other professional services not fully covered by provincial medical plans. Sometimes the company continues this benefit into retirement, usually with a lifetime limit of expenses that will be paid. The limit might be $50,000 or $200,000. In an effort to reduce their costs many companies are considering reducing these benefits.

Another benefit that might be of use is the right to purchase the company's products at a discount. My father-in-law worked for Alcan Aluminium Inc. and we still have rolls of aluminum foil around the house.

One much-enjoyed benefit, but all too seldom offered, is the retired employees club. These clubs provide people with the opportunity to attend social events and meetings with former colleagues who are also retired. You can catch up on the news about the company and old friends. A vibrant example is Air Canada's Pioneer Club which holds an annual meeting in Florida. Senior officials come down to the meetings to keep

---

The pension benefits guarantee fund

In Ontario, an employer-funded guarantee fund, the Pension Benefits Guarantee Fund, has been established to provide a safety net for companies who fail without sufficient funds to cover pension benefits. The fund covers benefits up to $1,000 a month. Benefits that were created in the three years before a plan is wound up are not covered.

the retired employees up to date on company developments and to discuss their concerns about benefit programs. Such a club offers not only camaraderie, but a sense of belonging and opportunities to help others less fortunate than yourself. Air Canada's Pioneer Club was instrumental in convincing the company to add dental benefits for retired Air Canada employees.

Notes

Your money your way: RRSPs

The most powerful wealth-building tool that Canadians can use is a registered retirement savings plan. It's difficult for most people to retire with an adequate income if they do not have an RRSP. Not only does an RRSP contribution reduce your tax bill — giving you more money to invest — but everything your RRSP investment earns is untouched by the hand of the tax man for years. Despite this, only one in four Canadian taxpayers makes annual contributions to an RRSP.

Let's look at the first source of power. When you make an RRSP contribution you can deduct that contribution from your income and reduce your income tax burden that year. This makes it possible for you to invest more money than you could without the tax advantage. Not convinced? If you're in a 40-percent tax bracket, you have to earn $830 to have $500 left after paying your taxes — money you've decided to invest. But if you invest in an RRSP, you won't have to pay tax on that $830 so you can invest it all. You have $830 growing and building instead of $500, over one and a half times as much.

Everyone likes to cut their tax bill, but the real power behind the RRSP is not the tax deduction, it's the tax-sheltered growth in your RRSP over the years. You do not pay any income tax on your RRSP investments as they grow. They're "sheltered" from tax and every dollar you earn you keep, at least until you retire and begin to withdraw it. If your investment rate of return is 10 percent a year, $1,000 will earn $100 a year. But if you're in a 40-percent tax bracket, you will only have $600 to invest if you don't put your money into your RRSP. Your $600 will only earn $60 a year — and it will be taxed so you'll end up with only $36 in your pocket. In your RRSP, you can keep the entire $100.

By contributing to an RRSP every year, your wealth will grow far more quickly than by trying to invest without this tax advantage. You might find this of less immediate interest, but it will have a powerful impact on your financial security in retirement. The combination of tax deduction and tax-sheltered growth will make your investment grow three times as fast as a similar investment outside an RRSP.

Consider taxpayer Morgan and taxpayer Watson. Morgan has earned an annual bonus of $2,000 and can invest the entire sum in an RRSP. If the $2,000 earns 10 percent a year, it grows by $200 the first year. This money is also sheltered from tax and, by the end of the second year, he has $2,200. This $2,200 also earns 10 percent and by the end of the third year his original investment has grown by another $220 — to $2,420 altogether. Every year, Morgan invests his $2,000 bonus in his RRSP and after twenty years he has $114,000.

Now, take Watson. He decides not to use an RRSP. He has to pay tax on his $2,000 bonus, so he has only $1,200 left to invest after the tax man has taken his share. He also invests his bonus at 10 percent but earns $120 a year. Again, the tax man takes his 40-percent tax, leaving Watson with only $72. After one year, Watson has only $1,272. This $1,272 also earns 10 percent and by the end of the second

RRSP rules and provisions

Contribution limits

You can contribute up to 18 percent of your previous year's earned income to a maximum of $12,500 for 1993. This maximum will increase to $13,500 in 1994, $14,500 in 1995 and $15,500 in 1996. After 1996, it is scheduled to keep pace with the average industrial wage. You can make contributions to your own RRSP to the end of the year in which you turn seventy-one or to a spousal RRSP to the end of the year in which your spouse turns seventy-one.

Deadlines

You can make your contribution any time during the year and up to sixty days after the year-end. If you decide not to make your contribution during the year, or make a smaller contribution than you are allowed, you can forward this "contribution room" for up to seven years.

Overcontributions

If you contribute more than the amount you are allowed to deduct, the excess is called an overcontribution. These overcontributions cannot exceed $8,000. The over contribution is a buffer the government has created to protect you against exceeding your limit by mistake — after all, they've made the rules so much more complex that mistakes are bound to occur. If you exceed the $8,000 buffer you will have to pay a penalty of 1 percent for every month the excess overcontribution has been in your RRSP. A person under age eighteen cannot overcontribute at all and will be subject to an overcontribution penalty of 1 percent a month for any excess RRSP contribution.

Pension plan members and RRSPs

You can still make a contribution to an RRSP if you are a member of a registered pension plan but your limit will depend on your pension adjustment, or PA, and any past-service pension adjustment, or PSPA. Your employer can provide you with this information; it is also provided on your T4 slip. You will be entitled to contribute at least $1,000 to an RRSP each year unless you have a large PSPA.

Eligible investments

You are restricted in the kinds of investment you can hold in your RRSP. Eligible investments are:
- savings deposits, guaranteed investment certificates and term deposits with life insurance companies, banks, trust companies, credit unions and stock brokers.
- common and preferred shares traded on public Canadian stock markets and on certain stock exchanges in fifteen countries, including the United States, France and Britain.
- the bonds of governments, corporations and municipalities, including Canada Savings Bonds.
- mortgages for your own personal residence.
- the shares of privately held corporations, provided you do not control the corporation.

There are many investments that you cannot hold in your RRSP: Precious metals, real estate, art, antiques, collectibles, commodity futures — pretty well anything that you can touch. However, you can invest in mutual funds, which invest in these things. If you hold an ineligible investment in your RRSP it will be subject to penalty taxes and the investment might be included in your income for the year. You might also have to pay income tax on any growth or earnings from that investment while it was in your RRSP.

Foreign assets

In 1993, you can invest up to 18 percent of your RRSP in foreign securities. This will increase to 20 percent in 1994. You can't get around this rule by investing in a mutual fund that is heavily invested outside Canada. Mutual funds can hold up to 18 percent of their assets in foreign securities and still be 100 percent RRSP eligible. If a fund holds more than this in foreign securities the mutual fund itself will be considered foreign content. The value of the foreign assets is based on the original cost of the asset, not on its current value.

year his original investment has grown by another $76 after tax to $1,348. Watson also invests his bonus but after twenty years he has only $44,000 — a $70,000 difference.

Of course, the comparison doesn't end there. Morgan is eventually going to have to pay tax on the income he receives from his RRSP. Chances are, however, he'll be in a slightly lower tax bracket in retirement, maybe only 30 percent. Even if he withdraws it all in one year, he would receive $79,800, still almost twice as much as Watson's nest egg. Of course, he probably won't withdraw all the money at once. Most of it will remain in the RRSP for many years, growing steadily, sheltered from tax.

RRSP contribution limits

If an RRSP is such a powerful wealth-building tool, why not invest as much as you possibly can in such plans? Alas, as with most good things, you're not allowed to. The tax rules ensure that only a certain percentage of your income can be put into RRSPs — not really unfair, since if we're gaining, the tax man must be losing. And he is, not only by not taxing your income this year but also by not taxing your investment growth year after year. The tax officials will only give up so much.

Individuals can contribute up to 18 percent of their previous year's earned income to an RRSP up to a maximum of $12,500 for 1993. This maximum is scheduled to increase to $13,500 in 1994, $14,500 in 1995 and $15,500 in 1996. After that, the limit is scheduled to increase in pace with the average industrial wage. (This contribution limit will be reduced if you participate in a pension plan; we'll discuss this later in this chapter.) If you earn $50,000 a year, you would be allowed to contribute 18 percent of that $50,000, or $9,000, to an RRSP and deduct this amount from your income. If you made $100,000, you would not be able to contribute $18,000 because of the maximum contributions.

The first step in determining your RRSP contribution limit is calculating your earned income. The income that you're looking at is the income you earned in the previous tax year, not the current year. In the 1993 tax year, you're making contributions based on your earned income in 1992. And earned income is clearly defined by Revenue Canada; it doesn't include everything you might bring home.

Earned income is income from employment, from a business carried on by you or by you and partners, rental income from real estate, research grants, income from unemployment insurance, and alimony or maintenance payments that you have received. From this income you must deduct professional dues, refunds of salaries or grants, losses from your business or real estate, expenses if you have a research grant, and alimony or maintenance payments that you paid. Commissioned employees must decrease their income by their employment expenses.

Earned income does not include pension income, retiring allowances, death benefits from life insurance, amounts received from RRSPs, registered retirement income funds, annuities, or your investment income.

RRSPs and pension plan members

If you belong to a pension plan or deferred profit-sharing plan, you are still able to make RRSP contributions. To determine how much you can contribute, start by determining your contribution limit just as anyone who does not belong to a pension plan would — 18 percent of your previous year's earned income up to $12,500. From this, deduct the pension adjustment, or PA, for 1992, as well as the past-service pension adjustment, the PSPA, if there is one. Your employer will have provided both the PA and the PSPA on your T4 slip. The federal government will have confirmed it when they sent you an assessment notice for your 1992 tax year.

Commonly asked RRSP questions

What if I don't have enough money? Should I borrow to make my RRSP contribution?
The answer is a qualified yes. Making your RRSP contribution on time will give you a tax refund a few months later that will probably allow you to pay back close to half of your loan. If you pay off the loan within a year, the cost of your borrowing will be less than what you will have made by making the contribution. You'll be ahead; if you take more than a year to pay the loan, it's not worth it.

Should I make an RRSP contribution even if I don't have any income?
Usually, no. Remember, the advantages of an RRSP arise from the tax savings; first, the deduction when the contribution is made, then the tax-free growth of your investment. If you do not have any taxable income, an RRSP does not offer you these advantages. In fact, even though you have never deducted the contribution to the RRSP, you will still have to pay tax on the money when it is withdrawn.

What happens to my RRSP if I die?
If your RRSP has not been left to your spouse or dependent children, Revenue Canada will consider it to have been cashed in on the day you die. It will be fully taxable in your final tax return. Outside Quebec, you can specify the beneficiaries in your RRSP agreement or your will. In Quebec, the beneficiary must be named in your will. Your husband or wife can start a new RRSP or merge the funds with an existing RRSP. RRSPs can be left to a child or grandchild under the age of eighteen provided that you are not married and the inheritor is financially dependent on you. If you die, the funds must be placed in an annuity that will provide benefits only to age eighteen. You can also leave your RRSP to an adult child who is dependent on you as a result of mental or physical infirmity. In this case, the funds can be transferred into a life annuity or RRSP for the child.

How much do I need to put into an RRSP?
As much as you can, right up to your maximum annual contribution limit! You just can't afford to put in any less. The amount of money you will need to retire in style is enormous, so you must make the most of the wealth-building power of RRSPs.

Which should I do first, pay off my mortgage or contribute to my RRSP?
You won't like the answer — do both! If you can't, which comes first? It depends on your age. If you are under age forty-five, put the maximum into your RRSP and then make whatever extra payments on your mortgage that you can. If you are over age forty-five, pay down your mortgage as quickly as you can and then contribute what you can to your RRSP. Try to make up the shortfall in your RRSP contributions within the seven-year delay period.

Is a spousal RRSP contribution really that important? What happens if we split up?
A spousal RRSP allows you to move income from the hands of the person who is in a high tax bracket into the hands of the one who is in a lower tax bracket. This should reduce your tax burden and give you more after-tax income for the family in the retirement years. Whether you use a spousal RRSP or not, if you separate or divorce you will probably have to divide your RRSPs and pensions. The risk is not any greater in splitting them as you go.

This is complicated. We looked at PAs and PSPAs in chapter seven but let's look at how they affect your RRSP contribution. The pension adjustment is a measure of the benefits building in your pension plan or deferred profit-sharing plan, or both. The adjustment is calculated by multiplying the annual value of retirement benefits earned in the pension plan by nine, to the maximum annual contribution limit, then subtracting $1,000. This ensures that you can contribute at least $1,000 to an RRSP every year. If your company-sponsored plan is miserly, your PA will be low, leaving you with more room to contribute to RRSPs.

The second adjustment to your RRSP limit is the PSPA. This applies to defined benefit pension plans that enjoyed an increase in benefits during the year. If those improvements affect previous years, your RRSP room will reflect the retroactive pension improvements gained. You'll be informed each year of the adjustments that affect you.

Your company will need to have your PSPA certified by Revenue Canada. They do this on something called a T1004 form. Once Revenue Canada has certified the amount, they will return the certified T1004 to your company and the company should provide you with a copy.

If the PSPA is certified before your notice of assessment is sent by Revenue Canada, then the RRSP limit on the notice will reflect the reduction for the PSPA. However, if the government certifies a PSPA after the notice of assessment is sent, then it will not reflect the effect of the PSPA. Revenue Canada will send you a notice of adjustment regarding your RRSP limit as soon as its records are updated. Because this situation is a bit tricky, you might be wise to call or visit your local taxation office to confirm that you are using the right RRSP contribution limit if you receive a PSPA.

RRSP deductions will also be reduced by contributions made to a money-purchase pension plan or by contributions made on your behalf by your employer to a deferred profit-sharing plan. Even with these adjustments, you should still have some room to make contributions to an RRSP.

The impact of contributing early

To qualify for an RRSP income tax deduction in a tax year, your contribution must be made no later than sixty days after the end of that year. Given our tendency to procrastinate, many people make contributions in February, or even as late as March 1. Often we justify our tardiness by insisting that we didn't have the money until then and that making it under the wire is better than not making a contribution at all. This is true. But if you do have the cash, you're far better off contributing at the beginning of the tax year rather than at the end. This way, your money will earn tax-deferred investment income inside the RRSP for an extra fourteen months.

The rewards for making your contribution early are significant. If you make a contribution of $5,000 on January 1 every year for twenty years, your RRSP will grow to $247,000, if you earn 8 percent on your investment. If you make this same contribution for twenty years but make it at the end of the year, your RRSP will only grow to $229,000.

Spousal RRSPs

You can contribute to your own RRSP or invest the funds in the name of your husband or wife. Your tax deduction for the year will be the same, but the RRSP investment will belong to your spouse.

Why would you give away your money, even if it is to someone you love and cherish? First, you would only do it if your spouse will have a lower income in retirement than you. By moving income from someone with a higher tax bracket to someone with a lower tax bracket, you will lower your retirement income tax burden and save thousands of dollars. Your goal is to create two equal streams of income.

This is a form of income-splitting, a very effective tax-planning strategy. Consider George and Martha. George plans to retire in ten years and expects to have an income of around $60,000 a year. Martha has just returned to work part-time and expects her retirement income to be just less than $25,000 a year. In retirement, George will pay 50-percent tax on any extra income he earns while Martha will pay only 26-percent tax on her retirement income. George intends to contribute around $10,000 a year to an RRSP for the next ten years, building their retirement nest egg by another $100,000.

Should he put the money in his own RRSP or in Martha's? If he puts the money in his own RRSP and the $100,000 provides George with an extra $10,000 of retirement income he will have to pay $5,000 to Revenue Canada. If instead he contributes the money to Martha's RRSP and Martha receives the $10,000 income, she will pay only $2,600 in income tax — a savings of 24 percent or $2,400 a year.

Furthermore, if Martha doesn't have any pension income, the RRSP could be used to purchase an annuity. The income from the annuity would qualify as pension income and Martha could claim the pension credit. This is worth another $250 in tax savings. In addition, in chapter six we noted that any OAS recipient with taxable income over $53,215 in 1993 will have to repay 15 percent of that excess up to the amount of the full OAS received. By reducing George's taxable income, he will reduce the amount of OAS repayment he has to make to the government.

Making a spousal RRSP contribution does not interfere with your spouse's ability to make an RRSP contribution to his or her own plan. In fact, if he or she doesn't have the money for a

contribution, but is qualified to contribute, it's wise to provide the funds to make the contribution. In this way, both the spousal RRSP and the spouse's own RRSP will build future income financed by dollars that would otherwise be taxed at a higher rate. Neither does making a spousal RRSP mean that you cannot make a contribution to your own plan. However, a spousal RRSP does not give you an extra RRSP deduction. Your contribution limit is based on your earned income. You can make that contribution to your own plan, to a spousal plan or contribute a bit to both.

Keep in mind that putting money in a spousal RRSP is the same as giving it away. The investment and future withdrawal of those funds is solely within the control of your husband or wife. Despite this, if money is withdrawn from a spousal RRSP, the tax will have to be paid by the contributing spouse if contributions have been made in any of the past three years. The only exception is when the RRSP is converted into an annuity or RRIF. Even then, only if the minimum is withdrawn will the income be taxed at the spouse's rate and not the contributor's. Of course, you can make a tax-deductible contribution to a spousal RRSP, leave it for three years, then withdraw it and pay tax at the spouse's tax rate. However, this means giving up the chance to make spousal RRSP contributions for three years.

At times, this strategy can be profitable, especially if your spouse's income fluctuates widely or he or she stops work to return to school, raise a family, start a business or take a sabbatical. But the spousal RRSP should be regarded primarily as a way to build wealth in the hands of the spouse with the lower income and to reduce your family taxes in retirement.

Carry-forward of RRSP deductions

If you decide not to make an RRSP deduction, or to only make a portion of the contribution allowed, you can make up the deduction any

The value of RRSP overcontributions TABLE 4

Let's assume that you overcontribute $8,000 to your RRSP and earn 8 percent a year.

	10 years	15 years	20 years
You will have: If you cash in the RRSP and pay 50 percent to the government in income tax you will have:	$8,650	$12,700	$18,650
If you invest the $8,000 outside an RRSP and earn 8 percent you will have:	$11,800	$14,400	$17,500
Did the overcontribution strategy work?	No	No	Yes

time within the next seven years. This is called a carry-forward. The carry-forward amount is the difference between the amount you're allowed to contribute to your RRSP that year and the amount you actually contribute. This is very different from the rules in the past when if you didn't make your RRSP contribution for the tax year, you lost it!

Suppose you're allowed to make a $6,000 contribution in 1993 but you can only afford to contribute $4,000. This leaves you with a $2,000 carry-forward which will be added to your contribution limit in 1994. In 1994, you could make your contribution for that year plus the $2,000 contribution you were unable to make in 1993. If you can't afford to make the contribution in 1994, it will carry forward to 1995, then 1996 for up to seven years.

The carry-forward will be deductible in the year you actually make the contribution — which can give you a very generous deduction in one year. But it is better to make your RRSP contribution every year. If you don't, you end up paying higher taxes in those years when you do not have the tax deduction and you will not gain from the benefit of earning investment income that is sheltered from tax over the years. It can make sense to defer your contribution if you are in a period of low taxable income and know that you will be earning a higher level of income — and will therefore be subject to a higher tax rate — in the future. But you should avoid falling into the psychological trap of continually using the carry-forward rules as an excuse for not contributing this year. We all know that it's easier to set aside a little each month or each year than to face a whopping demand for cash several years down the road.

The value of overcontributions

Should you contribute more to your RRSP than you're allowed to deduct? It's allowed and there are situations where it's profitable but

---

Overcontributions

We're often asked if you can make an $8,000 overcontribution every year. The answer is no. Before the RRSP rules changed, you could contribute up to $5,500 every year to your RRSP even if your maximum deductible contribution was less than that.

Under new rules, the overcontribution cushion is a cumulative maximum, not an annual limit. If you exceed that $8,000, you will be subject to penalties.

---

you should do so with care. By contributing more than you can deduct in years when you have the cash, you can build a pool of deductions that can be drawn upon in years when you're short of cash and cannot make your maximum contribution.

The overcontribution allowance can also be used by people who have just taken a job after a year or so of not working. (Remember your RRSP limit is based on your previous year's income.) You can still get money into your RRSP by using the $8,000 overcontribution and deducting it in a future year — even a year as far away as the first year of retirement. In fact, in your first year of retirement you will be allowed to make a contribution based on your income in your last year of work. You can draw on the overcontribution room instead of taking the cash from your pocket.

If you make an overcontribution by mistake and do not want to leave the money in your RRSP it can be withdrawn tax-free only in the year in which the contribution was made and only if it was reasonable to assume that the amounts contributed would be deductible during that year. At all other times, funds withdrawn from your RRSP will be taxable. This would mean paying tax on that income twice — you didn't receive a deduction going in and you're taxed again when you pull the money out. You could also be subject to a

Locked-in RRSPs and life income funds

When you leave an employer and have vested pension funds, you might be able to transfer the funds to the pension fund of your new employer. If not, you will have to leave the funds with your old employer, move the funds into a deferred annuity or put them into a locked-in RRSP.

Locked-in RRSPs differ from ordinary RRSPs only in your maturity options. In fact, the only maturity option with these plans is a life annuity; you cannot take money from the RRSP nor convert it to a RRIF or term-certain annuity. This rigidity ensures that the funds are used for their original purpose — to provide retirement income.

Many taxpayers in Quebec thought this was too rigid. So a new concept has been introduced — the LIRA, a locked-in retirement account. LIRA funds can be used to purchase a life annuity or a LIF, a life income fund. The LIF is very similar to a RRIF, and offers all the investment and tax advantages, but it must be used to purchase a life annuity no later than at age eighty.

Unlike a RRIF, the LIF has a maximum withdrawal each year, ensuring that the fund cannot be exhausted prematurely. This new concept is good news for the many Canadians who wanted more flexibility and opportunity for tax deferral. LIFs are now available in Alberta, Manitoba and Ontario. Other provinces are working on legislation to allow LIFs.

1 percent per month penalty if you exceed the $8,000 overcontribution buffer.

If you want to take advantage of this strategy, you might consider making the overcontribution to a spousal RRSP. You could even consider giving funds to your husband, wife or any children over eighteen so that they can make overcontributions. (We believe that you do not need to worry about the income tax attribution rules if you lend money for an overcontribution to your spouse or kids because there will not be any taxable income generated by the gift. Remember, though, that children have control over their RRSP and can withdraw the $8,000 without informing you.)

A properly planned overcontribution can be profitable because it allows you to earn tax-sheltered investment income for years before you eventually deduct the contribution. If you

don't intend to claim the deduction, you have to hold the money in your RRSP for about twenty years for it to be profitable.

More ways to build your RRSP

Most of us build our RRSPs gradually and steadily over the years but that's not the only way to build your RRSP. You can have a retiring allowance deposited into your RRSP and you can transfer funds from your pension plan or DPSP into a locked-in RRSP. You can also transfer pension income to a spousal RRSP. If your marriage should break down, RRSPs can be split by court order. Finally, if your husband or wife dies, you can move his or her pension and RRSP assets into your RRSP.

Let's look at them one at a time.

Retiring allowances: Retiring allowances are payments made to an employee to compensate for the loss of a job or as a reward for long service. You can transfer up to $2,000 of a retiring allowance into your RRSP for each year of service with your employer. You're also allowed to transfer an additional $1,500 for each year of service prior to 1989 if you did not have vested pension plan or deferred profit-sharing plan benefits.

For example, if you joined a company in November 1980 and left in January 1991 you would have twelve years of service. If you were not a member of a DPSP or pension plan (or were a member but had no vested rights or payments from the plan), you could transfer to an RRSP as much as $37,500 (twelve years x $2,000 + nine years x $1,500). If your retiring allowance is $25,000, the entire amount can be transferred to your RRSP. If the allowance is $40,000, $37,500 could be transferred and the remaining $2,500 would be taxed as income.

If you receive a retiring allowance, the transfer should be made directly from the company to the trustee for your RRSP. It should not pass through your hands. If you receive the retiring allowance directly, the employer will deduct tax which you would then have to recover when you file your tax return, presuming you made the eligible payments to the RRSP .

Transfers from a pension plan or DPSP: You can transfer benefits from a pension plan or DPSP directly to your RRSP but only if the pension plan or DPSP allow it. This also applies to a transfer from a foreign pension and from certain plans established while you are a resident of the United States. The funds will be moved into a special kind of RRSP called a locked-in RRSP.

Transfers of pension income to a spousal RRSP: Since 1989, taxpayers who are already retired have been able to transfer up to $6,000 from an employee pension or DPSP to a spousal RRSP. This puts more money into the hands of a lower-income spouse — allowing you to reduce taxes and ensure that your spouse can take advantage of the pension credit. This so-called pension rollover will only be available for the 1993 and 1994 tax years. It doesn't apply to Old Age Security benefits or the QPP and CPP, nor is there any relief of this type for unmarried pensioners.

Transfer on marriage breakdown: Transfers of RRSP or pension funds can be made to the RRSP or pension of a former spouse provided this transfer has been recorded in a court order or separation agreement. Recent changes to the RRSP rules have included a common-law spouse in this provision. By definition, you must have been living with this person for at least a year or he or she must be the parent of your child.

Transfer of survivor benefits: You can transfer the funds from the RRSP or the pension plan of a husband or wife who has died. (This has to be permitted by the pension plan.) To do this, the surviving spouse must be named the beneficiary on the RRSP application or in the will. In Quebec, the surviving spouse must be designated as the RRSP beneficiary in the will or the RRSP will not be transferred tax-free.

Investing your RRSP

Of course, getting money into the RRSP is only half the strategy. The second step is investing your RRSP wisely. The only difference between an investment in an RRSP and any other investment is that the income earned is not taxed until it's withdrawn.

To be effective, your RRSP investment strategy cannot be created in isolation. It must be part of the strategy you create for all of your investments, a strategy that considers your pension plan (or lack of pension), your home,

---

Make the most of your foreign affairs

The rule allowing some of your RRSP investments to be in foreign securities can be of particular advantage to an investor who does not have significant non-RRSP investments. It allows you to diversify your portfolio, protecting yourself against drops in the Canadian stock markets. More important, there are only a handful of world class companies listed on our stock exchanges and your portfolio could benefit from holding the shares of large, multi-national companies. A third benefit arises from having some of your investments in currencies other than the Canadian dollar, particularly if you expect to spend some of your retirement days outside Canada.

If your RRSP is too small to hold the stocks and bonds of foreign companies or governments, you can achieve this diversification by investing in Canadian mutual funds that specialize in global investments or in the stocks of a specific country. The more sophisticated investor might even invest in foreign mutual funds. If you're looking for currency diversification you can find bonds of Canadian issuers that are denominated in U.S. dollars, deutsche marks, yen and other currencies.

The kinds of RRSPs

The deluge of RRSP advertising that you face each winter can easily be confusing. It needn't be. There are only three main types of RRSPs.

RRSP deposit accounts

You can place your RRSP funds in a savings account, GIC or term deposit. These deposit plans are administered mainly by banks and trust companies as well as insurance companies and credit unions. Deposit rates vary: In January and February the competition is fierce. Historically, smaller trust companies have offered better rates than banks. Lately, insurance companies have provided competitive yields.

Mutual fund RRSPs

You can purchase the shares or units of a mutual fund. Canadian equity mutual funds (mutual funds which invest in the shares of companies listed on Canadian stock exchanges) are one of the most common in the market. But there is a wide variety of different kinds of mutual funds available: international equity funds, money market funds, bond and mortgage funds, and dividend funds. Many of these funds are 100 percent RRSP-eligible while those that invest in foreign securities can only be held as foreign content. Mutual fund RRSPs are available through banks, trust companies, insurance companies, brokers, and the fund companies themselves.

Self-administered RRSPs

A self-administered RRSP allows you to hold individual securities such as stocks and bonds, including Canada Savings Bonds, although you can also hold mutual funds and deposits in your self-administered plan. All of the investment decisions are under your control. Or, you can hire an investment adviser to manage the account and make investment decisions for you. These accounts are very efficient ways of diversifying your RRSP funds. You can hold a wide array of investments and your financial institution will provide you with a summary of your holdings every month. Self-administered RRSPs are available from most financial institutions. Make sure you pay the administration fee yourself, do not allow it to be taken from your RRSP or it will not be tax-deductible.

---

your non-RRSP savings and your ability to save. Usually, your RRSP strategy is one of achieving solid returns without risking the safety of your investments. This is every investor's goal: To see our wealth grow without risk of loss. But we take security more seriously with RRSPs than with other investments. After all, this is the money we intend to live on when we retire. We can't afford to have an empty RRSP when retirement day comes.

There's another reason why you should make every effort not to lose on RRSP investments. There's no tax relief if you do suffer a loss on investments in an RRSP. Nor are you rewarded for taking risks. As we'll discuss in detail in chapter twelve, the tax system treats the returns from different types of investments differently. You pay less tax on dividends from Canadian corporations because of the dividend tax credit. The $100,000 lifetime capital gains exemption can mean you won't pay any tax at all while pursuing growth in the stock market. Even if your capital gains exemption is exhausted, only 75 percent of your capital gains are taxed. You can't claim the dividend tax credit nor the capital gains exemption in your RRSP, yet the funds are fully taxable when removed. On the other hand, interest income that would be fully taxed outside an RRSP will not be taxed at all as it quietly grows in your RRSP. Without the tax advantages, there's less reason for taking the risks that come with growth when choosing RRSP investments. For the same reason, I would avoid investing your RRSP dollars in a small private business. There are significant tax advantages in holding small business corporation shares outside your RRSP.

These factors guide you toward an RRSP strategy of investing in bonds, term deposits and GICs. You will want to load up your RRSP with the highest income-yielding investments while keeping those tax-advantaged investments in Canadian and foreign equities outside your RRSP. If your investments are 50 percent deposits and 50 percent stocks, you should try to place all of the deposits in the RRSP and hold the stocks outside the RRSP. If, like many people, you have precious few personal investment dollars, then your fifty-fifty strategy might mean that both stocks and deposits are held in your RRSP, which is fine.

As you build your non-RRSP savings and investments, you should start to reduce your equity investments in your RRSP and build them up outside the RRSP. One of our clients had few personal investments but his RRSP holds $50,000 in GICs and $50,000 in equity mutual funds. His company had a very good year and he was given a $20,000 bonus. He decided to swap the $20,000 cash for $20,000 of the equity mutual funds. Then he used the cash in the RRSP to purchase bonds.

We'll cover investment strategies in detail in chapter eleven but there are some specific RRSP strategies I'd like to discuss here.

Strategy one

For people who have only a little money in their RRSP or are not settled securely, either financially or professionally, I recommend guaranteed investment certificates or term deposits. This is a simple, worry-free and cost-effective way of building RRSPs for people just beginning to build their wealth.

I recommend trust-company deposits rather than the deposits offered by banks, credit unions and insurance companies, because the

trust companies have historically had to pay higher deposit rates to get your business. Since your deposits will be covered by the federal and Quebec government deposit guarantees, you needn't worry about the safety of your money. You should pursue the highest rates only with qualifying financial institutions. (We'll explain insurance deposit in chapter twelve.)

As you build your portfolio of GICs, you should spread your money among certificates with maturities ranging from one to five years. Start by buying a GIC for the term with which you feel comfortable. Then each year add a GIC with a maturity date that is different from the certificates which you already hold. Eventually you will have accumulated five GICs maturing over five years. As the certificates mature, you can continuosly balance the term-to-maturity of your portfolio by reinvesting each one into a GIC with a five-year maturity. You are never forced to invest more than 20 percent of your savings at one time and you don't have to try to predict interest rates.

Strategy two

Once your financial position is more stable, you can begin to add one or two Canadian growth equity mutual funds to your expanding

Never ignore your investments			TABLE 5

Although it may seem insignificant, a couple of percentage points difference in the rate of return on your RRSP can make a major difference in the long run. You can see the difference on a single $1,000 investment over thirty years.

Year	6%	8%	10%
5	1,338	1,469	1,611
10	1,791	2,159	2,594
20	3,207	4,661	6,728
30	5,743	10,063	17,449

Although it is possible to increase your RRSP considerably by increasing your return by a few points, don't be a rate chaser and change every year to get 1/8 percent or 1/4 percent more. The time lost in transferring funds (and at which time the funds are not generating a return) usually doesn't make it worthwhile.

RRSP investment tips and advice

1. Make your RRSP contribution at the beginning of the year, not at the end.

2. Make sure that you inform your payroll department that you have made your RRSP contribution for the year and that it is reflected in the tax withheld from your paycheque each month.

3. Borrow, if you have to, to take advantage of your full annual contribution limit.

4. Make contributions to a spousal RRSP if your spouse would otherwise have lower income in retirement than you.

5. If your spouse is eligible to make an RRSP contribution but does not have the cash, consider giving him or her the funds to make the contribution.

6. Make an overcontribution up to the cumulative $8,000 amount. Remember, though, that if you are not going to be able to deduct the contribution the funds will have to be in your RRSP for at least twenty years before you withdraw them.

7. If you have decided to make contributions to a spousal RRSP, consider making the overcontribution to the spousal RRSP so that the extra income generated in retirement will be taxed in the lower income spouse's hands.

8. Consider giving funds to your adult children to make their overcontribution — you will be multiplying the family's opportunity to earn tax-free income. Be aware that the funds will then be controlled by your children.

9. Ensure that your spouse is specified as the beneficiary of your RRSP. If you don't, the money will not be transferred tax-free into his or her RRSP.

10. Don't use the seven-year carry-forward rules as an excuse not to make your annual contribution.

11. Consider carrying forward contribution room to the future if you are in a lower tax bracket this year and you know that you will be in a higher tax bracket in the future.

12. Be aware of and take advantage of all of the ways that you can build your RRSP, including the $6,000 pension rollover and transfer of eligible retiring allowance.

13. As a general rule, keep investments that yield interest income in your RRSP and investments that will provide dividends or capital gains outside your RRSP.

14. Develop an investment strategy that will build your RRSP quickly and safely.

15. Maximize the foreign content in your RRSP. The added diversifications will provide even greater safety and higher returns.

16. Make arrangements to convert your RRSPs to retirement income well before December 31 of the year you turn seventy-one. If you miss the deadline, the funds will be deemed to have been paid to you and will be fully taxable.

17. Consider the benefits of a RRIF — flexibility and continuing tax deferral — and compare them to the simplicity and steady income of an RRSP annuity.

---

pool of term deposits. Despite the oft-repeated advice that you should keep your RRSP invested in high-yield deposits, don't wait until you can afford to build your non-RRSP investments to get the benefits of growth that equity investments will bring to your portfolio.

(Again, we'll discuss mutual funds in detail in chapter twelve.)

Strategy three

As your wealth grows, you will probably begin to save more than just your RRSP contribution each year. When you reach this point, you should make sure that all of your equity investments are held outside your RRSP and all of your future RRSP investments are in bonds, mortgages and the money market. Those who can accept the risk and the responsibility might open a self-administered RRSP so that you can manage your own investments. This will allow you to swap non-RRSP investments for RRSP investments — perhaps cash for an equity mutual fund. You'll be able to get your equities into your hands where any growth will be lightly taxed, if taxed at all, and fill up your RRSP with fixed-income investments.

Strategy four

Once you have about $200,000 in your RRSP, you've developed a sound knowledge of investments, and you're financially stable you should definitely be holding your investments in a self-directed RRSP. If you don't want to manage a diversified portfolio, you might hire a professional investment manager. If there are two significant income earners in a family, each contributing to an RRSP, you can quickly achieve level four. But I still advise taking the step-by-step approach. This gives you time to make small errors, errors that will not be too damaging but will provide lessons from which you can learn.

These strategies apply to persons young and old. Even if you are close to retirement, you could have many years to go until you begin to draw on your RRSP savings. Even then, the pool of investments will continue for many years into your retirement. Some people suggest that as you approach retirement you should become more and more cautious in your investments, perhaps even moving all of your investments into cash. They say you can't afford to take investment risks. But they are assuming you have a very short time horizon, that you are going to need all of your money on your sixty-fifth birthday. Well, you won't.

Many of your investments must remain intact into your eighties or nineties. You cannot afford to let your money languish, earning a pittance when you need growth to get you through to ripe old age.

All good things must come to an end

Usually, RRSP investments are held for many years, often throughout your career and for as long as a decade into retirement. Although normal retirement age is sixty-five, you do not have to collapse your RRSP until December 31 in the year you turn seventy-one. Then you must take action. If you don't, Revenue Canada will consider all of your RRSPs to have been cashed and received as income. You'll be taxed on the full amount. There are better ways to handle maturing RRSPs.

You have three options for maturing your RRSP — and one is simply cashing it in, either completely or a little at a time. This can be done at any age, but the withdrawn amounts are fully taxable. Suppose you retire at age sixty-two. Three years later, you would like to buy a new car but realize that you do not have the cash and you don't want to borrow. One solution is to take $25,000 from your RRSPs. After paying the tax, you'll have $13,000 to $15,000 to spend. Another year, you may want $4,000 for a trip and take $8,000 from the RRSP. At age sixty-nine you might find that your income doesn't cover your living expenses so you start withdrawing $300 a month.

You can withdraw as little or as much from your RRSP as you like but tax will be withheld on your withdrawals at the following rates:

- 10 percent on the first $5,000,
- 20 percent on the next $10,000,
- 30 percent on anything over $15,000,
- In Quebec, the withholding rates are 21 percent on the first $5,000, 30 percent on the next $10,000 and 35 percent on any amount over $15,000.

You can keep your withholding taxes low by never withdrawing more than $5,000 at a time, but this tax saving is only temporary. When you file your tax return, the total amount withdrawn is taxable and your tax bill will exceed what you've already paid. This is a strategy that can be followed only until the December in which you reach age seventy-one. In a way, you're treating your RRSP like an annuity or RRIF.

Annuities

Your second option is to purchase an annuity from a financial institution. An RRSP annuity is very similar to an employee pension. You turn over your RRSP and the financial institution guarantees a steady monthly income. Unlike a pension, these payments do not have to continue for your lifetime. You can choose from among various different kinds of plans:

- a term-certain annuity that will provide an income for a guaranteed period, usually five, ten or fifteen years,
- a term-certain-to-age-ninety annuity that will provide an income until you reach age ninety,
- a single-life annuity that will provide an income for your lifetime,
- a joint-life annuity that will provide an income for the lifetime of both you and your husband or wife.

Banks and trust companies offer term-certain annuities while life insurance companies offer both term-certain and life annuities.

As with a pension, you can fine-tune your annuity with guarantee periods and inflation protection. Usually you can choose a five-, ten- or fifteen-year guarantee on a life annuity. If you choose a ten-year guarantee and die within five years of buying the annuity, your heirs will either receive monthly payments for five years or be given a sum of money equal to the value of those payments.

You can also protect your own future by choosing a variable annuity, one that will provide an income that will increase with inflation. The maximum rate of increase is 6 percent a year and must be chosen when the annuity is purchased. Indexing for inflation is not popular now because of the very low rates of inflation we are experiencing. I have no doubt that higher rates of inflation will return to haunt us by the end of the decade and the popularity of the indexed annuity will return, particularly if we see rates rising to the levels they reached in the 1970s and early 1980s.

Revenue Canada allows you to cash in or commute an annuity, but to do so this flexibility must be part of the original purchase agreement. The tax rule was changed recently and many financial institutions are reluctant to allow annuitants to cash out prematurely or convert to a RRIF.

Registered retirement income funds

Your third option is a registered retirement income fund, a RRIF. While annuities provide a steady stream of income in retirement guaranteed by the company to which you have given your money, RRIFs allow you to control both your investments and your income. You can withdraw different amounts of money each year to meet varying needs or take as little as possible and leave as much of your savings to grow untaxed as possible.

"As little as possible" is a significant phrase: Although you can withdraw as much as you like in any one year, taking it all if you choose, there is a minimum percentage of your savings that must be withdrawn each year. This minimum is quite small in the early years but grows year after year. If you chose to open a RRIF at age seventy-one, you will have to remove at least 7.38 percent of the assets in the RRIF during that year, 7.48 the next year, 7.59 the year after and so on. In the year you turn ninety-four and every year after that you must withdraw 20 percent.

If you are an astute investor and you withdraw the minimum, the amount of your withdrawal will be less than the growth and your RRIF savings could continue to build well into your eighties. In this way, you will be sure that your income will keep pace with inflation. (The purchasing power of your income from your pension or an annuity could decline with each passing year.)

RRIFs are the best choice for anyone with RRSPs of $50,000 or more. You have the potential for a maximum tax savings but can choose to withdraw a tailor-made income for your lifetime or for the lifetime of your husband or wife. By basing your RRIF payout on the life of a younger spouse, your tax savings will be that much larger. You still have complete freedom to withdraw more than this minimum in any given year — a freedom that gives you great flexibility — but this extra income will attract extra tax.

RRIFs can be purchased at most financial institutions: insurance companies, banks, trust companies, mutual fund management companies, brokerage houses. You can continue to manage your investments or hand over the task to the institution or an investment manager. As long as your funds are not locked into a long-term investment, such as a five-year GIC, you can take your RRIF funds and buy an annuity at any time.

Many people with RRSPs should choose a RRIF, or at least use it in combination with an annuity. Some people use a RRIF until age eighty then switch their funds into an annuity. This gives them the minimum payments and maximum tax deferral for ten years, then carefree monthly income for the rest of their lives.

Your RRIF investment stratgegy

You will only be seventy-one, at the most, when you convert your RRSP to a RRIF and you will want it to be invested so that it will provide income for the rest of your life. For many of us this will be for at least another twenty years! Given this time frame, it's important to continue to invest your RRIF using the same investment principles you use to invest your RRSP. Like your RRSP, your RRIF can be invested in deposits, mutual funds or in a self-directed portfolio of investments. You should not ignore equity investments in your RRIF; these are the securities that will provide you with the most growth potential.

However, your RRIF investment strategy requires special attention to liquidity and flexibility. You must have enough cash to make the required minimum withdrawals. You should also build in some flexibility so that if you need to withraw a sum of money, perhaps for a trip, you will be able to do so.

Choosing the right RRSP maturity option

It is not easy to choose the right option, but you should consider the following when making your decision:

Are interest rates, and therefore annuity payment rates, high or low? If you need your RRSP to provide as much income as possible,

The minimum annual RRIF payments			TABLE 6
Age	Payment (%)*	Age	Payment (%)*
71	7.38	84	9.93
72	7.48	85	10.33
73	7.59	86	10.79
74	7.71	87	11.33
75	7.85	88	11.96
76	7.99	89	12.71
77	8.15	90	13.62
78	8.33	91	14.73
79	8.53	92	16.12
80	8.75	93	17.92
81	8.99	94	20.00
82	9.27	95	20.00
83	9.58		

*This represents the least amount that can be withdrawn as a percentage of the assets in your RRIF.

then it is usually simpler to put the funds into an annuity and receive monthly cheques. If rates are relatively high then you might want to secure some of your money so that you can enjoy this relatively higher level of income throughout your retirement years. However, if rates are very low and you cannot wait any longer to convert, consider moving your RRSP into a RRIF temporarily. When rates rise, you can switch.

Are you going to be financially comfortable in retirement without spending your RRSP funds? Are you seeking to reduce your taxes? If so, then a RRIF will allow you to delay tax and build your investment funds for later years when they might be needed to cover inflation. If you want to pass as much as possible on to your heirs, you should choose a RRIF. The RRIF allows you to build your retirement savings well into retirement.

Once you have chosen the right maturity option, you should go shopping to find the specific investment or financial institution to manage your annuity or RRIF funds. You will have a great many choices so be prepared to take some time in making this decision.

Your key to reaching financial independence

RRSPs are an essential element of your strategy to build enough savings for a secure retirement. It bears repeating: Your RRSP savings will grow three times as quickly as your non-RRSP savings. It is true that the funds will be taxed when you withdraw them in retirement, but the wealth that you will have in your hands will still be twice as much as it would be otherwise.

You must find every way possible to build your RRSP. Make your maximum annual contributions, consider making the overcontribution of $8,000 and take advantage of the $6,000 pension rollover and the right to transfer retiring allowances to your RRSP. Use spousal RRSPs as a way to build up wealth in the hands of your husband or wife so that you will have similar incomes in retirement.

Invest your RRSP for growth and safety. Make a smart decision about how best to withdraw the funds from your RRSP, shopping carefully for the best RRIF or RRSP annuity. Finally, once you've worked hard to build your RRSP funds remember to enjoy spending them! Too often we forget that the purpose of making RRSP contributions is to build the wealth that will provide income for us to spend in retirement.

Notes

_____

_____

_____

_____

_____

_____

_____

_____

_____

_____

_____

_____

_____

_____

_____

_____

_____

_____

How much is enough?

"I've been poor and I've been rich," Sophie Tucker once said. "Rich is better." How much is enough to be even just well off? This is the question we're asked more often than any other. How do I know if or when I will have enough in my RRSPs, pensions and savings to retire comfortably for the rest of my days?

Achieving a financial goal requires only two things: a time frame and a cost. In retirement planning your time frame is the years between today and the age at which you wish to retire. What is your goal? To retire by age fifty-five, sixty or maybe sixty-five, or even seventy?

Identifying the cost is more difficult. Financial planners use sophisticated computer programs to determine exactly what their clients need and the amount they will have to save by the time they retire to be financially secure and comfortable.

This is your financial independence target and by the end of this chapter you will be able to calculate it yourself. It takes some work, but it's very important. And, becoming acquainted with the many factors essential to your financial plan will allow you to achieve your independence.

This mathematical fortune-telling is an imprecise science. It involves making estimates and projections of many unknowns. How much will you spend each year in retirement? How quickly will this need increase with inflation? How many years will you and your partner live? How much will you get from your government pensions? Employee pension? What rates of return can you expect on your RRSP and non-RRSP savings? How much income will they provide in retirement?

To pull all of this together you need some knowledge of financial mathematics. This math deals with the future value of incomes and expenditures at different rates of growth. This is a familiar world for the actuary and professional financial adviser, and is worth your attention because it will enable you to understand what compounding interest can do to benefit your savings or frustrate your spending plans.

Here's what we're going to do:

- forecast your spending needs in your first year of retirement,

- forecast your after-tax income from every possible source,

- deduct your expenses from your income to arrive at your retirement income gap, the shortfall that must be made up by income from your investments,

- calculate how much investment capital you will have to accumulate by your target retirement date and how much you will need to save each year to make sure you will have enough.

As you go through the calculations in the worksheets, you'll find an example — fifty-five year old Sally. We hope this helps to clarify the steps and calculations. So let's get going.

Your expenses in retirement

Let's start with the known requirements — your annual expenses. Many people simply assume that they will need only 60 to 75

Your living expenses before and after retirement

	Before retirement	After retirement
Housing expenses		
Mortgage payments		Ø
Maintenance and repairs		100
Property taxes		
Property insurance		
Heating		
Electricity		
Telephone		
Other		
Total housing expenses		
Transportation		
Gasoline and oil		
Repairs and maintenance		
Insurance		
Payments on car loans or leases		
Other		
Total transportation expenses		
Personal expenses		
Food		
Lunches at work		
A child's school expenses		
Life insurance premiums		
Health insurance premiums		
Deductions for Unemployment Insurance		
Dentist and dental care		
Optometrist and glasses		
Pharmaceutical needs		
Clothing		
Other		
Total personal expenses		

Entertainment

Dining out   _____   _____

Movies   _____   _____

Performing arts   _____   _____

Vacations   _____   _____

Travel   _____   _____

Gifts   _____   _____

Holiday entertaining   _____   _____

Total entertainment expenses   _____   _____

Savings

Contributions to RRSPs   _____   _____

Contributions to pension plans   _____   _____

Contributions to CPP or QPP   _____   _____

Other savings   _____   _____

Total savings   _____   _____

Other expenses

Alimony or child expenses   _____   _____

Loan payments   _____   _____

Professional fees   _____   _____

Club dues   _____   _____

Union dues   _____   _____

Total other expenses   _____   _____

Total expenses   _____   _____

percent of their current earnings. But this could be very wrong. You should go through the exercise of determining what you will need in retirement. It's tedious, but poverty in your old age is an unfairly harsh punishment for avoiding a couple of hours of math homework.

The best starting point is last year's expenses. By examining the details of your expenditures and adjusting those numbers you can determine what you'll spend in retirement.

This does not mean simply adjusting your expenses for inflation. We'll look at inflation later. What you need to look at are those changes that will alter your financial needs.

Let's look at some examples. Even if you stay in the home you live in today your expenses could change when you retire. You might be able to undertake repairs which you hire tradesmen to do today, thus reducing your costs. Or costs might rise because you have time to do the repairs or renovations you've put aside for years. If your housing arrangements change, you will have to raise or lower your cost of shelter to reflect that change. If you own two cars, will you keep both or sell one? Will you be travelling more or less? You will no longer have to commute to work but you might travel more to visit friends and family. We have a client who lives close to public transit. During his working years he commuted to work and his wife had use of the family car during the week. Once he retired, he wanted to play golf in the summer and curl in the winter. His wife was not interested in these activities. Nor was she interested in giving up her car. Guess what? They now have two cars. Good retirement planning allowed them to buy the second car.

There are many expenses that will be reduced. A couple that you can count on are the payroll deductions to cover pension plan contributions, unemployment insurance premiums, employer life insurance plans, union dues — all those deductions which reduce your pay. These end with retirement, reducing your expenses by as much as 10 percent. Most people feel they no longer need to save 10 to 20 percent of their paycheque, although in reality most people do need to continue saving for several years into retirement. Another area of potential saving is clothing. You're not likely to need the kind of clothing you wear to work. On the other hand, you might need more leisure clothes.

How about social, fitness or golf fees paid by your employer; will you drop the club or pay the fees yourself? The cost of membership and simply going to the club may be too rich for your budget and you drop it. On the other hand, you might enjoy a senior's discount.

It's tough to draw a reasonably accurate picture of your living expenses. Very few people are actually aware of their spending habits. They might have records in cheque books and credit card vouchers, but they seldom sit down and take a good look at where the money goes. It can even be emotionally difficult if you'd rather not know how or how much you spend. On the other hand, there are people who actually keep a book in which they track the flow of money through their hands. A growing number of people use computers to maintain records. Keeping such records makes it much easier to predict the flow of money in the coming months or years. This insight is particularly valuable because it helps you to plan for the future and make the most of your money.

So how do you go about it? To figure out what you spent last year, you have to return to your bank records and cash books, and consider whether costs will increase or decrease in retirement. Of course, many of the items will recur in much the same way they have occurred in past months. Even if you are a copious record keeper, your goal is not to carry out a detailed accounting and arrive at precise information. You're simply trying to establish reasonable estimates of your expenses. This can be done using the worksheet on pages 104 and 105.

Make sure you cover an entire twelve-month period; this way you can be sure that you won't miss any expenses that arise year after year. If retirement is imminent, the details you compile on your situation before retirement will allow you to make a very accurate estimate of your financial situation in your first year of retirement. If retirement is some years away, the retirement prediction will not be as accurate but will allow you to develop a financial plan aimed at ensuring you will live comfortably in retirement by forcing you to consider the adequacy of your retirement savings.

Let's look at the life span of retirement. If you retire at age sixty and live to age ninety, you're going to live about thirty years in retirement, aren't you? Almost as long as you spent working! Will your lifestyle or the way you spend your time change? Will you do less and less — and therefore spend less and less — or will expenditures rise because of health costs in later years?

Of course, these are uncertainties. In planning, most people consider a certain amount for their whole retirement. Others assume they will spend less after they reach age eighty or so but I know many retired people age eighty and older who still travel the world and are busy at their usual activities, spending money as usual. A neighbour who will be eighty-eight in September took a trip to South America. When asked why she was going she replied, "because I have never been there." We prefer to be conservative and plan on a continuing need for a fixed amount.

Inflation

You cannot be complacent about inflation just because it's low today. You will be retired for many years and inflation will rear its ugly head during that time. What do you think it will be in the future? I'm not only talking about inflation between now and the day you retire but also from the day you retire to the day you die. Many people think that today's low inflation rate will go on forever. Others fear the rampaging inflation will inevitably return because of politicians' penchant for giving our money away and the huge public debt.

It's useful to take a look at the history of inflation in Canada in chapter twelve. Inflation in this country has averaged 3.4 percent over the last sixty-five years. But during the past twenty-five years inflation rose to almost 11 percent and then dropped back down to 1.5 percent. During that time, the average rate of inflation was 6.3 percent; over the past ten years it's been 4.4 percent. I prefer to use these longer-term average rates of inflation of 5 to 6 percent in the retirement plans we develop.

We're certain that inflation will rise again at some time during your retirement years and do not want our clients to be caught short.

To establish your expenses at retirement you need to know the amount you would like to spend each year, the number of years between today and retirement, and the expected average inflation rate over this period. Put this information into a computer or a good financial calculator, and you can calculate the amount of money you will need on your retirement day to provide for all of your living needs. Financial calculators, made by companies such as Texas Instruments, allow you to enter the period of years, the compound interest rate, and either the present value of a sum of money or the annual payments that will be made over the period. The calculator can then quickly calculate the future value. You can also enter any of these items as a given and have the calculator figure out the missing number. If you do not have these resources, you can use future value tables.

Future value tables allow you to "project" the future value of your pensions, savings and expenses. In this workbook we're going to use future-value tables to do this. If you expect to spend $40,000 this year after tax and you have decided that this is the income you want to have in retirement, then you can refer to the table to find the future value of $40,000 at a particular rate of inflation between now and your retirement age.

If you pick 5 percent as your average expected inflation, and there are twenty years to retirement, you will need an after-tax income of $106,120 to meet your expenses in twenty years. This is a very healthy target. That is why you must start your retirement planning immediately and be very serious in your savings and investing.

Future value tables will also tell you how your money will grow over time at different rates of return. You can use these tables to

The future value of $1

TABLE 7

Years	1%	2%	3%	4%	5%	6%	7%	8%	9%	10%	11%	12%	13%	14%	15%
1	1.010	1.020	1.030	1.040	1.050	1.060	1.070	1.080	1.090	1.100	1.110	1.120	1.130	1.140	1.150
2	1.020	1.040	1.061	1.082	1.103	1.124	1.145	1.166	1.188	1.210	1.232	1.254	1.277	1.300	1.323
3	1.030	1.061	1.093	1.125	1.158	1.191	1.225	1.260	1.295	1.331	1.368	1.405	1.443	1.482	1.521
4	1.041	1.082	1.126	1.170	1.216	1.262	1.311	1.360	1.412	1.464	1.518	1.574	1.630	1.689	1.749
5	1.051	1.104	1.159	1.217	1.276	1.338	1.403	1.469	1.539	1.611	1.685	1.762	1.842	1.925	2.011
6	1.062	1.126	1.194	1.265	1.340	1.419	1.501	1.587	1.677	1.772	1.870	1.974	2.082	2.195	2.313
7	1.072	1.149	1.230	1.316	1.407	1.504	1.606	1.714	1.828	1.949	2.076	2.211	2.353	2.502	2.660
8	1.083	1.172	1.267	1.369	1.477	1.594	1.718	1.851	1.993	2.144	2.305	2.476	2.658	2.853	3.059
9	1.094	1.195	1.305	1.423	1.551	1.689	1.838	1.999	2.172	2.358	2.558	2.773	3.004	3.252	3.518
10	1.105	1.219	1.344	1.480	1.629	1.791	1.967	2.159	2.367	2.594	2.839	3.106	3.395	3.707	4.046
11	1.116	1.243	1.384	1.539	1.710	1.898	2.105	2.332	2.580	2.853	3.152	3.479	3.836	4.226	4.652
12	1.127	1.268	1.426	1.601	1.796	2.012	2.252	2.518	2.813	3.138	3.498	3.896	4.335	4.818	5.350
13	1.138	1.294	1.469	1.665	1.886	2.133	2.410	2.720	3.066	3.452	3.883	4.363	4.898	5.492	6.153
14	1.149	1.319	1.513	1.732	1.980	2.261	2.579	2.937	3.342	3.797	4.310	4.887	5.535	6.261	7.076
15	1.161	1.346	1.558	1.801	2.079	2.397	2.759	3.172	3.642	4.177	4.785	5.474	6.254	7.138	8.137
16	1.173	1.373	1.605	1.873	2.183	2.540	2.952	3.426	3.970	4.595	5.311	6.130	7.067	8.137	9.358
17	1.184	1.400	1.653	1.948	2.292	2.693	3.159	3.700	4.328	5.054	5.895	6.866	7.986	9.276	10.761
18	1.196	1.428	1.702	2.026	2.407	2.854	3.380	3.996	4.717	5.560	6.544	7.690	9.024	10.575	12.375
19	1.208	1.457	1.754	2.107	2.527	3.026	3.617	4.316	5.142	6.116	7.263	8.613	10.197	12.056	14.232
20	1.220	1.486	1.806	2.191	2.653	3.207	3.870	4.661	5.604	6.727	8.062	9.646	11.523	13.743	16.367
21	1.232	1.516	1.860	2.279	2.786	3.400	4.141	5.034	6.109	7.400	8.949	10.804	13.021	15.668	18.822
22	1.245	1.546	1.916	2.370	2.925	3.604	4.430	5.437	6.659	8.140	9.934	12.100	14.714	17.861	21.645
23	1.257	1.577	1.974	2.465	3.072	3.820	4.741	5.871	7.258	8.954	11.026	13.552	16.627	20.362	24.891
24	1.270	1.608	2.033	2.563	3.225	4.049	5.072	6.341	7.911	9.850	12.239	15.179	18.788	23.212	28.625
25	1.282	1.641	2.094	2.666	3.386	4.292	5.427	6.848	8.623	10.835	13.585	17.000	21.231	26.462	32.919
26	1.295	1.673	2.157	2.772	3.556	4.549	5.807	7.396	9.399	11.918	15.080	19.040	23.991	30.167	37.857
27	1.308	1.707	2.221	2.883	3.733	4.822	6.214	7.988	10.245	13.110	16.739	21.325	27.109	34.390	43.535
28	1.321	1.741	2.288	2.999	3.920	5.112	6.649	8.627	11.167	14.421	18.580	23.884	30.633	39.204	50.066
29	1.335	1.776	2.357	3.119	4.116	5.418	7.114	9.317	12.172	15.863	20.624	26.750	34.616	44.693	57.575
30	1.348	1.811	2.427	3.243	4.322	5.743	7.612	10.063	13.268	17.449	22.892	29.960	39.116	50.950	66.212
31	1.361	1.848	2.500	3.373	4.538	6.088	8.145	10.868	14.462	19.194	25.410	33.555	44.201	58.083	76.144
32	1.375	1.885	2.575	3.508	4.765	6.453	8.715	11.737	15.763	21.114	28.206	37.582	49.947	66.215	87.565
33	1.389	1.922	2.652	3.648	5.003	6.841	9.325	12.676	17.182	23.225	31.308	42.092	56.440	75.485	100.700
34	1.403	1.961	2.732	3.794	5.253	7.251	9.978	13.690	18.728	25.548	34.752	47.143	63.777	86.053	115.805
35	1.417	2.000	2.814	3.946	5.516	7.686	10.677	14.785	20.414	28.102	38.575	52.800	72.069	98.100	133.176
36	1.431	2.040	2.898	4.104	5.792	8.147	11.424	15.968	22.251	30.913	42.818	59.136	81.437	111.834	153.152
37	1.445	2.081	2.985	4.268	6.081	8.636	12.224	17.246	24.254	34.004	47.528	66.232	92.024	127.491	176.125
38	1.460	2.122	3.075	4.439	6.385	9.154	13.079	18.625	26.437	37.404	52.756	74.180	103.987	145.340	202.543
39	1.474	2.165	3.167	4.616	6.705	9.704	13.995	20.115	28.816	41.145	58.559	83.081	117.506	165.687	232.925
40	1.489	2.208	3.262	4.801	7.040	10.286	14.974	21.725	31.409	45.259	65.001	93.051	132.782	188.884	267.864

The future value of $1 saved every year

TABLE 8

Years	1%	2%	3%	4%	5%	6%	7%	8%	9%	10%	11%	12%	13%	14%	15%
1	1.010	1.020	1.030	1.040	1.050	1.060	1.070	1.080	1.090	1.100	1.110	1.120	1.130	1.140	1.150
2	2.030	2.060	2.091	2.122	2.153	2.184	2.215	2.246	2.278	2.310	2.342	2.374	2.407	2.440	2.473
3	3.060	3.122	3.184	3.246	3.310	3.375	3.440	3.506	3.573	3.641	3.710	3.779	3.850	3.921	3.993
4	4.101	4.204	4.309	4.416	4.526	4.637	4.751	4.867	4.985	5.105	5.228	5.353	5.480	5.610	5.742
5	5.152	5.308	5.468	5.633	5.802	5.975	6.153	6.336	6.523	6.716	6.913	7.115	7.323	7.536	7.754
6	6.214	6.434	6.662	6.898	7.142	7.394	7.654	7.923	8.200	8.487	8.783	9.089	9.405	9.730	10.067
7	7.286	7.583	7.892	8.214	8.549	8.897	9.260	9.637	10.028	10.436	10.859	11.300	11.757	12.233	12.727
8	8.369	8.755	9.159	9.583	10.027	10.491	10.978	11.488	12.021	12.579	13.164	13.776	14.416	15.085	15.786
9	9.462	9.950	10.464	11.006	11.578	12.181	12.816	13.487	14.193	14.937	15.722	16.549	17.420	18.337	19.304
10	10.567	11.169	11.808	12.486	13.207	13.972	14.784	15.645	16.560	17.531	18.561	19.655	20.814	22.045	23.349
11	11.683	12.412	13.192	14.026	14.917	15.870	16.888	17.977	19.141	20.384	21.713	23.133	24.650	26.271	28.002
12	12.809	13.680	14.618	15.627	16.713	17.882	19.141	20.495	21.953	23.523	25.212	27.029	28.985	31.089	33.352
13	13.947	14.974	16.086	17.292	18.599	20.015	21.550	23.215	25.019	26.975	29.095	31.393	33.883	36.581	39.505
14	15.097	16.293	17.599	19.024	20.579	22.276	24.129	26.152	28.361	30.772	33.405	36.280	39.417	42.842	46.580
15	16.258	17.639	19.157	20.825	22.657	24.673	26.888	29.324	32.003	34.950	38.190	41.753	45.672	49.980	54.717
16	17.430	19.012	20.762	22.698	24.840	27.213	29.840	32.750	35.974	39.545	43.501	47.884	52.739	58.118	64.075
17	18.615	20.412	22.414	24.645	27.132	29.906	32.999	36.450	40.301	44.599	49.396	54.750	60.725	67.394	74.836
18	19.811	21.841	24.117	26.671	29.539	32.760	36.379	40.446	45.018	50.159	55.939	62.440	69.749	77.969	87.212
19	21.019	23.297	25.870	28.778	32.066	35.786	39.995	44.762	50.160	56.275	63.203	71.052	79.947	90.025	101.444
20	22.239	24.783	27.676	30.969	34.719	38.993	43.865	49.423	55.765	63.002	71.265	80.699	91.470	103.768	117.810
21	23.472	26.299	29.537	33.248	37.505	42.392	48.006	54.457	61.873	70.403	80.214	91.503	104.491	119.436	136.632
22	24.716	27.845	31.453	35.618	40.430	45.996	52.436	59.893	68.532	78.543	90.148	103.603	119.205	137.297	158.276
23	25.973	29.422	33.426	38.083	43.502	49.816	57.177	65.765	75.790	87.497	101.174	117.155	135.831	157.659	183.168
24	27.243	31.030	35.459	40.646	46.727	53.865	62.249	72.106	83.701	97.347	113.413	132.334	154.620	180.871	211.793
25	28.526	32.671	37.553	43.312	50.113	58.156	67.676	78.954	92.324	108.182	126.999	149.334	175.850	207.333	244.712
26	29.821	34.344	39.710	46.084	53.669	62.706	73.484	86.351	101.723	120.100	142.079	168.374	199.841	237.499	282.569
27	31.129	36.051	41.931	48.968	57.403	67.528	79.698	94.339	111.968	133.210	158.817	189.699	226.950	271.889	326.104
28	32.450	37.792	44.219	51.966	61.323	72.640	86.347	102.966	123.135	147.631	177.397	213.583	257.583	311.094	376.170
29	33.785	39.568	46.575	55.085	65.439	78.058	93.461	112.283	135.308	163.494	198.021	240.333	292.199	355.787	433.745
30	35.133	41.379	49.003	58.328	69.761	83.802	101.073	122.346	148.575	180.943	220.913	270.293	331.315	406.737	499.957
31	36.494	43.227	51.503	61.701	74.299	89.890	109.218	133.214	163.037	200.138	246.324	303.848	375.516	464.820	576.100
32	37.869	45.112	54.078	65.210	79.064	96.343	117.933	144.951	178.800	221.252	274.529	341.429	425.463	531.035	663.666
33	39.258	47.034	56.730	68.858	84.067	103.184	127.259	157.627	195.982	244.477	305.837	383.521	481.903	606.520	764.365
34	40.660	48.994	59.462	72.652	89.320	110.435	137.237	171.317	214.711	270.024	340.590	430.663	545.681	692.573	880.170
35	42.077	50.994	62.276	76.598	94.836	118.121	147.913	186.102	235.125	298.127	379.164	483.463	617.749	790.673	1,013.346
36	43.508	53.034	65.174	80.702	100.628	126.268	159.337	202.070	257.376	329.039	421.982	542.599	699.187	902.507	1,166.498
37	44.953	55.115	68.159	84.970	106.710	134.904	171.561	219.316	281.630	363.043	469.511	608.831	791.211	1,029.998	1,342.622
38	46.412	57.237	71.234	89.409	113.095	144.058	184.640	237.941	308.066	400.448	522.267	683.010	895.198	1,175.338	1,545.165
39	47.886	59.402	74.401	94.026	119.800	153.762	198.635	258.057	336.882	441.593	580.826	766.091	1,012.704	1,341.025	1,778.090
40	49.375	61.610	77.663	98.827	126.840	164.048	213.610	279.781	368.292	486.852	645.827	859.142	1,145.486	1,529.909	2,045.954

Projecting your expenses at retirement   WORKSHEET 21

	Sally	You and your partner
Expenses today	$30,000	
Number of years to retirement	10	
Inflation rate between today and retirement	5%	
Future value factor	1.629	
Annual expenses in first year of retirement	$48,870	

Your government benefits   WORKSHEET 22

Old Age Security benefits

	Sally	You	Your partner
Maximum OAS in 1993	$4,600		
Years until age 65	10		
Rate of inflation	5%		
Future value factor	1.629		
Expected OAS	$7,493		

Your CPP or QPP pension

	Sally	You	Your partner
Maximum CPP/QPP in 1993	$8,000		
Years until age 65	10		
Rate of inflation	5%		
Future value factor	1.629		
CPP/QPP at age 65	$13,032		

determine what a future sum of money is worth in today's dollars. Let's say you have $10,000 in your RRSP on which you expect to earn 8 percent every year for the next ten years. You can see in the future value table that $1 will grow to $2.159 in ten years' time if compounded each year at 8 percent. Therefore, your $10,000 will be worth $21,590. Perhaps you intend to invest $1,000 a year for ten years at 8 percent. The future value of $1 a year table shows that if you save $1 a year you will have $15.645, so multiply $15.645 by $1,000 and you can see that at the end of the decade you will have $15,645.

Your retirement income

Don't be frightened by the huge income it appears you will need in retirement. You've already built considerable wealth to finance your retirement. This will reduce the need for more saving to a more reachable target. Let's look at your existing retirement resources. First, there are the government pensions — OAS and CPP or QPP. These can be a powerful resource because they increase annually to keep up with inflation. These are discussed in detail in chapter six.

Keep in mind that the federal Old Age Security pension may be partially or fully reclaimed by the tax department if you earn more than $53,215. Otherwise, both you and your spouse will receive this pension starting at age sixty-five. The Canada or Quebec pension plans can be received at age sixty at a 30-percent discount from the full pension payable at sixty-five, provided you have paid into the plan during your working years.

You might also have the right to receive a pension from a foreign country if you have worked abroad. Perhaps you will receive American social security. This can be especially attractive because only one-half of the amount received is subject to income taxes.

The government pension plans are indexed to the cost of living and to figure out the income you would expect to receive when you retire you will again use the future-value tables. Today (in late 1993) the maximum payable by the Canada and Quebec pension plan for someone age sixty-five is about $8,000. Now take a look at the future value of $1 table. Say you're only forty-five, you can see that $1 invested at 5 percent will be worth $2.653 in twenty years. If you multiply this factor of 2.653 by $8,000 you find that the maximum Canada or Quebec pension will be $21,224 in twenty years. At 4-percent inflation, a more cautious number, the maximum would be $17,528.

In the same way, you can calculate the future value of the Old Age Security pension. The 1993 OAS monthly payments total about $4,600; at 4-percent indexing the OAS payment in twenty years will be $10,300 ($4,600 times 2.19). (You should ignore the Old Age Security pension if there is any chance you will lose it because of the claw-back.)

Your pension income

Next, look at the pension from your current employer and from any former employers with whom you might have earned pensions and left them intact to buy a deferred pension at retirement. You can find your expected pension income in your annual benefits booklet where it is calculated with one intentional omission. The pension calculation in annual statements usually takes into account your years of service, past and future, to normal retirement age but does not allow for salary increases that you might receive.

Even though you may have five, ten, fifteen or more years still to go before retirement, your future salary increases have not been considered. Therefore, the estimate in the pension statement will have to be increased to reflect salary increases over your remaining years. You can do this by simply taking the income on the statement and using the factor from the future value table that reflects your expected rate of salary increases to retirement day. Or you can ask your benefits staff to calculate the pension using the salary you expect to receive in your last years of employment. Also, try to find out whether your

Income from a defined benefit pension plan　　WORKSHEET 23

	Sally	You	Your partner
Expected pension income*		_____	_____
Years to retirement		_____	_____
Rate at which your salary will rise each year		_____	_____
Future value factor		_____	_____
Your expected pension		_____	_____
Is this pension indexed?		_____	_____

*You can get this from your pension statement or call your payroll or human resources department. If you plan to retire early make sure this is reflected in your calculation. Sally doesn't have a defined benefit pension plan.

Income from a money purchase pension plan*　　WORKSHEET 24

	Sally	You	Your partner
Value of the funds in the plan today	$200,000	_____	_____
Years to retirement	10	_____	_____
Average investment return	8%	_____	_____
Future value of these funds (A)	$431,800	_____	_____
Annual contributions (you and your employer)	$4,000	_____	_____
Average investment return	8%	_____	_____
Future value of contributions (B)	$62,580	_____	_____
Total future value (Add A and B)	$494,380	_____	_____
Annuity factor	0.062	_____	_____
Income from your pension	$30,652	_____	_____

*If you choose an annuity factor that reflects early retirement make sure you make the same assumption when calculating the income from your government pensions. This table can also be used to project the income from a group RRSP or a DPSP.

pension will be adjusted to reflect inflation over your retirement years. You might be able to enjoy some pension increases to keep up with inflation, whether guaranteed or voluntary, and you should know what they are now. Pension increases are at the employer's

Annuity factors   TABLE 9

You can use these factors to determine how much capital you need to bridge your retirement income gap.

Income starting at age:	60	65	71
If you are:			
Married (joint life)	0.050	0.056	0.067
Male (life only with 10 year guarantee)	0.060	0.069	0.081
Male (life only, no guarantee)	0.062	0.072	0.089
Female (life only with 10 year guarantee)	0.055	0.062	0.073
Female (life only, no guarantee)	0.055	0.064	0.077

SOURCE: DERIVED FROM 4 PERCENT INDEXED ANNUITY QUOTATIONS PROVIDED BY CANNEX.

Your income from your RRSP   WORKSHEET 25

	Sally	You	Your partner
Value of the funds today	$30,000		
Years to retirement	10		
Average investment return	8%		
Future value of these funds (A)	$64,800		
Your annual contributions	$2,000		
Average investment return	8%		
Future value of contributions (B)	$31,290		
Total future value (Add A and B)	$96,090		
Annuity factor	0.062		
Income from your RRSP	$5,958		

discretion and usually depend on the company's profitability that year. If your pension is not indexed, you should convert it to an indexed stream of income. For example, a pension that would provide a steady stream income of $409 a month would provide only $291 a month in the first year of retirement if it is indexed to rise by 4 percent a year. You are safer to use the indexed stream of income in your planning, even though your income will be lower in the earlier years.

If you belong to a money purchase pension plan, you will have to calculate the future value of the amount invested in your plan today and add to this amount the future value of future contributions to the plan by you and your employer. You can calculate the future value of the funds now in the plan by looking at the table "The future value of $1" and the future value of your future contributions by looking at the table "The future value of $1 saved every year." Now, let's assume that there is $50,000 in the plan, which will amount to $233,000 after twenty years at 8 percent. If you invest $3,000 every year for twenty years at an 8-percent annual return, the future value of these investments will be $148,300. You're almost there. Add the $148,300 for annual contributions of $3,000 a year to the $233,000 for a total retirement fund of $381,300. We still want to know the income this will provide.

Now we refer to the table, "Annuity factors". The annuity table allows you to calculate the income that will be provided by a sum of money. This table looks at the income from an annuity starting at various ages with different assumptions about the survivorship rights in an annuity contract. (Remember, when purchasing an annuity you can choose to have the annuity provide an income for your life only, for the lifetime of both you and your husband or wife or for a term of five, ten, fifteen or twenty years or until you or your spouse reaches age ninety.) The tables look at the stream of income from an annuity indexed at a 4 percent level of inflation. (These numbers reflect annuity rates available in late 1993. Remember, annuity rates fluctuate with interest rates.)

It looks daunting but it's not really. Let's see how the tables are used to help you make your calculations. If you select a joint-and-last survivor pension starting at age sixty-five (and you and your husband and wife are the same age) you would receive $21,700 a year (indexed at 4 percent) for the rest of your lives.

Income from your RRSPs

After looking at your pension, estimate the annual income you might expect from your registered retirement savings plans. This includes locked-in RRSPs arising from pensions from previous employers, the RRSPs you've accumulated to date, and RRSP funds you expect to contribute over the remaining years to retirement. As you can see in the worksheet, you have to project the growth of both your existing RRSPs as well as your future contributions. Hopefully, you will end up with a great pool of RRSP funds by retirement and can convert it to an income for your lifetime and that of your partner. You might be planning to use a RRIF as your RRSP maturity option but for calculating financial independence, I use annuity rates. It's easier and gives a valid estimate.

The method is exactly the same as that used to project the value of a money purchase pension plan. You take the amount which you hold in your RRSP today and multiply it by the factor in Table 7 that matches the investment return and the number of years to retirement. Add to this the future value of annual contributions by multiplying your annual contribution by the factor on Table 8. Then add the two amounts together and refer to the annual annuity Table 9 to find annual income you will receive.

In projecting the value of RRSPs or defined contribution pension plans, you might want to assume that the annual contribution will increase each year. If this is the case, you can use Table 7 to calculate the future value of each annual payment and then add them together, a long and tedious task, or you can find the mid-point in your stream of contributions, calculate its future value and then multiply this by the total number of years between today and retirement. This will give you a rough estimate of the future value of the increasing annual contributions.

Your income in retirement	Sally	You	Your partner
			WORKSHEET 26
OAS benefits	$7,493		
CPP or QPP pension	$13,032		
Employer pension income	$30,652		
Income from your RRSP	$5,958		
Other income	–		
Total income	$57,135		
Income taxes 18% on $20,000 a year 22% on $30,000 a year 27% on $40,000 a year 30% on $50,000 a year 32% on $60,000 a year 36% on $70,000 a year	$17,141		
Your after-tax income	$39,994		
Your annual expenses in retirement	- $48,870		
Your retirement income gap	= $8,876		

For example, if you plan to contribute to an RRSP for the next ten years starting with a contribution of $12,500 and increasing this contribution by $1,000 a year, the future value of your contributions would be $256,137 if invested at 8 percent. This is the precise calculation. If you chose the short-cut, picking mid-point between year five and six, when your contribution will be $17,000, the future value of that one contribution after five years and six months will be $25,978. Multiply this by ten (for ten annual contributions) and you will find that your savings will have grown to $259,780 after ten years, approximately the same value as that found by using a sophisticated computer program.

Let's take a second example. If you were to contribute $10,000 this year, $12,000 next year, then $14,000, $16,000 and $18,000 in the three remaining years, your contributions grow to

$86,757 five years down the road. By finding the future value of $14,000 (the mid-point) in 2.5 years and multiplying by five we arrive at $84,914, an estimate that is close enough for our planning. Remember, all of these approximations and projections will be inaccurate in the long run in any case so you only need to be reasonably accurate.

Finally, before calculating your retirement income gap look to any sources of retirement income, such as an insurance annuity, trust fund, rental property, family company, or loans being paid back to you over your lifetime.

Income taxes

An essential element of your future cash flow forecast is an estimate of income taxes. You can estimate the tax that will have to be paid by using the average rate in the worksheet. But, be aware that this will be a very rough estimate. For a more accurate income tax projection, you'll have to look at the tax table in the appendix. Remember, tax is not withheld from government pensions unless requested, nor is tax withheld on the payment of Canadian investment income. If these and other amounts are significant, you will be required to pay quarterly installments of income taxes, or pay an interest penalty. This requirement should not, however, come into effect in your first year of retirement, although, if you've had significant income from investments in the past, you are probably paying quarterly tax installments already. Make sure you record these payments in your expense statements.

Have you got enough?

With all of this information, you're ready to summarize your expenses and income and discover whether there will be a retirement income gap. You can use the worksheet on the following pages or a computer. A computer will do all the work and allow you to change

pieces of information with ease, creating many different "what-if" scenarios to test your financial independence prospects at different ages, different rates of investment return, various inflation rates and different spending levels. Whether you use a computer or our worksheets, your estimate will be rough and ready. By completing the worksheets, you'll have an estimate, based upon many assumptions, of the wealth you will want to have when you retire. Then you will compare your annual spending needs with the after-tax income your existing savings will produce.

It is possible that you will discover a retirement income gap. This shortfall must be made up by investment income, a retirement job, the sale of your house or an inheritance. Or you could do what many Canadians have done before you; simply adjust your living expenses to a more affordable lifestyle. I'd rather see you achieve your goal, however, and so we will concentrate on filling the gap by beefing up your savings and investments. We can easily calculate the investment capital that will be needed at retirement to produce sufficient investment income to make up the retirement income gap. Then we'll figure out how much more you will have to save each year to reach your target.

Keep in mind that one of the most important assumptions we've made is that your income will rise in retirement at the same rate as your spending. This is not always true. Only part of your pensions might be indexed, or none at all. And life annuities, trust funds and the like are not. If you are concerned that you will not have enough to support you in retirement you should see a retirement specialist who can do a very accurate projection and help you make sure you won't come up short.

Having calculated your own financial independence target using the worksheets, you have probably found that you need a great

Filling your retirement income gap

	Sally	You	Your partner
Annual retirement income gap	$8,876		
Annuity factor for your estimated retirement age	0.062		
Capital required at retirement Divide your income gap by the annuity factor (A)	$143,161		
Personal savings today (Include the value of your house if you intend to sell it)	$62,000		
Your after tax return on investments	6%		
Years to retirement	10		
Future value factor	1.791		
Future value of your savings (B)	$111,042		
The shortfall. Subtract the future value of your savings from the capital required (A-B)	$32,119		
Additional savings needed each year to make up the shortfall. Divide the capital shortfall by the factor in the Future value of $1 saved every year table. (Make sure you use the factor for the after-tax return you expect to earn.)	$2,299		

If you are able to save through increased RRSP contributions or by increasing amounts each year then you will move even faster toward financial independence.

deal of money. You might even be convinced that the money which you've discovered you need is unrealistic. Or, you might be discouraged. Don't fall into these traps! We want you to view retirement realistically; it does take a huge amount of money to achieve financial independence. And we want to motivate you to begin today so that you can achieve it. You will make it!

The pack-it-away years

From the time of our first job most of us spend pretty well everything we make. Sometimes a little more, sometimes a little less. The money that doesn't go to Revenue Canada goes to paying for a car, a house and children. It takes more than $200,000 to raise a child from birth to age eighteen. And then you have to face the cost of university or college.

Even if there aren't any children, we go along saving very little if anything beyond our contributions to the Quebec or Canada Pension Plan and maybe an employer's pension plan or RRSP. A few people buy whole life insurance, which begins to build a cash value, although it never seems to make sense to cash in a life insurance policy to get at that money. When we finally get around to looking at retirement planning, usually at about age forty or fifty, we've worked many years but don't have much set aside to show for it. There is some hope. Our right to government pensions is substantial; we could receive as much as 30 to 40 percent of the average industrial wage ($33,400 in mid-1993). A good company pension plan will provide another 50 percent

The pack-it-away years

When you reach age fifty your income will still be climbing but your expenses will drop. These are your pack-it-away years. Make the most of them.

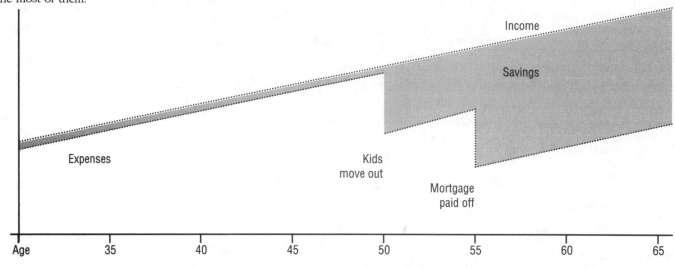

or so, if you are earning an average wage you will come out fairly well. Those who earn more than the average industrial wage have to do some serious saving.

Don't panic. There will be some relief down the road. Your mortgage will eventually be paid and the children up and off your payroll. At about age fifty or fifty-five your income is reaching a peak because of your seniority in the job or because of your wealth of experience in your chosen career. At the same time that you're earning more than ever, your expenses are lower. These are your pack-it-away years and it is critical that you make the most of them. You have ten to fifteen years to put away enough money to last you for thirty years of retirement. And I'm convinced that it is possible.

I once had a great guy in my office who asked me to prove it. He wanted to know how he was going to save $3 million when he had only $50,000 in his RRSPs and was saving only $10,000 a year, only half of it going into his RRSP. "It's not possible," he said. So we took a look at his finances and his expectations. He expected inflation to hover around 4 percent a

year but he was convinced he could earn 10 percent a year on his investments. I thought that was too aggressive; it's hard to earn a return that much higher than inflation. So we agreed to work with an 8-percent investment return. The $50,000 RRSP turned into $500,000 after thirty years and the $5,000 annual RRSP contribution will probably be closer to $20,000 by his last year of work. Therefore, his average contribution was around $12,500 a year — which would amount to about $1.4 million by the time he reached age sixty-five. This put $1.9 million in his RRSPs. Then we had to look at his personal savings to see what they would produce. If he saved $5,000 a year for thirty years and invested it for an 8-percent return, 4 percent after taxes, it would grow to only $280,000. At this rate of savings he would fall seriously short of his $3-million target.

But wait. His personal savings were not likely to remain at $5,000 a year. His savings rate would probably grow over the next thirty years as his income grew and his expenses declined. If it doesn't, then his $5,000 a year will actually represent a declining rate of saving. Let's have a look at that. At 4-percent

The cost of early retirement

If you want to retire early you will actually have to save less than you must save if you want to retire later. Surprised? After all, you will be in retirement for more years and you probably expected to need a bigger retirement pot. The opposite is true for a very simple reason: In your early years of retirement the income produced by your investments is more than you need to meet expenses. This extra income is reinvested and your retirement fund will continue to grow until you reach age sixty or sixty-five.

Does this mean that it's easy to retire at fifty-five? No, it's tougher because you have fewer years in which to build a sufficient pool of money. By age fifty-five you have not had as many years to contribute to your pension plan, your RRSP or the Canada or Quebec pension plans. Nor has your employer had the opportunity to set aside as much money for you.

Not only are your years of service and your years of accumulating pension benefits fewer, your average income is usually lower as well. For example, you can usually expect your salary and other compensations to increase year after year until you retire at the normal retirement age of sixty-five. In fact, you are usually at the peak of your career in that last decade or so and can expect to earn a good income for many years. By retiring early, you give up those salary increases which could have a significant effect on your pensions.

I'd like to quantify the magnitude of your difference. If we assume that you would receive increases of about 5 percent a year between age fifty-five and sixty-five, your income at age sixty-five would be about 60 percent higher than a decade earlier. And, by the time you retire you'd have ten more years of service, say thirty-five years instead of twenty-five, 40 percent more. Your pension would be increased by two factors: Your income would be 60 percent higher and you would have 40 percent more years of service. This would give you 2.25 times as much pension as you would receive at age fifty-five, just for working for ten more years. If you were expecting to receive $40,000 a year at age fifty-five you might find that working for ten more years would boost your pension to $80,000 to $90,000 a year.

inflation, $5,000 will be "worth" only $4,100 in five years in spending power. In ten years it will only be worth $3,380, in twenty years $2,280. I hope and expect that the value of savings will not decline in real terms over time. Rather, we agreed that he would keep increasing his savings, keeping ahead of inflation. So we assumed that over the next five years his savings rate would average $6,000 a year, which would amount to $33,000 after five years and $110,000 by age sixty-five. For the next five years he would save an average $7,500 a year, which would amount to $41,000 in five years, $140,000 by age sixty-five.

In the next five years he would save an average $10,000 a year, which would build to $146,000 by the time he reached sixty-five. For his final fifteen years of work he would probably save $15,000 a year, a savings that would produce $324,000 by the time he retired. The sum of his personal and RRSP savings would come to $2.6 million, not far from his target of $3 million.

He also had a house worth $125,000, which could increase in value by around 3 percent a year to more than $700,000. It is possible that half of this value might become available for investment, either by selling and buying a smaller home or by borrowing against it with a reverse mortgage. It is possible to reach that $3-million target but it takes commitment. In this case, it meant saving 13 percent of annual income. However, about 3 percent of this would be refunded in tax savings so only a 10-percent savings level was needed. To reach the target by age sixty would take an increase in that effort, perhaps saving another 5 percent of his annual income.

It's important to realize how quickly money can grow when it is invested properly. Second, remember that inflation will cause both your income and savings to grow significantly as well. The target is not really as large as it might seem at first glance. In fact, if you bring it back to the same value in today's dollars, $3 million in thirty years is only $925,000 (at 4-percent inflation). Isn't that much easier to swallow? Only $925,000. Sure, it's going to take some serious work, and maybe I will have to write several more books to make it myself.

Financial speed

You will make it to your financial independence target if you are travelling at the right financial speed. Financial speed is a concept that integrates the two powerful functions of saving and investment. It is obvious that if you increase your savings rate, in other words you save more each year, you are going to accumulate more money. It is also obvious that if your savings earn a higher than expected investment return they will grow into an even larger amount. Therefore, if you are worried about falling short of your financial independence target you must either increase your savings rate or increase your investment rate of return. Most people have to do both. In this way you will not have to save so much that you will have an unacceptable lifestyle today nor will you have to put your money into investments of such high risk that you could lose it. Rather, financial planning deals with a series of strategies to use your money more intelligently; you will be able to improve your savings rate by managing your money more effectively, reduce your income taxes in a variety of acceptable and safe ways, and take on a little more risk in your investments, and improve your returns, without jeopardizing what you have worked so hard to get.

Knowing "how much is enough" is only the first step toward achieving your objective. The second step is to apply all of your wits and energy to achieve this most coveted goal — financial independence. The worksheets we have gone through provide you with a glance into the future and should not be thought of as static or unchangeable. The pattern of saving and investing is guideline, one which you can change as your goals and circumstances change. However, it does provide you with what you need to make some of your retirement decisions. Will you be able to retire early? Will you need to consider some part-time paid work? Should you be saving more? Are you achieving a good rate of return on your investments or less than you should be?

It is possible you will have to challenge some of the ways you have been accumulating your retirement resources and make some changes. Even more important, most Canadians need to be shocked out of their complacent attitude toward saving for retirement. If you really want to continue your current lifestyle for the rest of your life you're going to have to make a greater commitment to financial planning strategies we'll cover in the coming chapters to increase your financial speed and allow you to bridge your retirement income gap. That is the magic of financial planning.

Chapter 10

Planning priorities and opportunities

The coveted goal of retirement planning is to build enough wealth to guarantee security and comfort in retirement. For most Canadians, this goal will require changes in the way you handle your money. You'll have to set priorities — and controlling the flow of dollars through your hands will probably be at the top of the list.

Cash is neither easy to come by nor easy to keep. If you were given $10,000 today what would you do with it? Buy a nicer car, a new couch, take a vacation, put it aside for your children, your retirement? What are your financial priorities?

To identify your financial priorities more clearly, let's use the financial planning pyramid. The pyramid corresponds to how you should view your financial priorities — start from the bottom and work up. Ensure that your foundation is firmly established before moving to the next level.

From there, you can make forays into riskier areas with their promise of greater returns, secure in the knowledge that while damage might occur, the foundation will not be shaken. In fact, it's the solid foundation that permits the

risk-taking that eventually builds your wealth. You have to establish the foundation through persistent effort, building layer by layer. Only then will you find that you can risk the pyramid's higher levels.

Spending and saving

The foundation of your pyramid should be control over spending and debt. It's the availability of cash that will allow you to do other things on the pyramid. This isn't easy. It starts with knowing exactly what income you will receive and when you'll receive it. It entails reducing your expenses, keeping your income tax burden as light as possible, and making your savings work hard for you at all times. It might even mean increasing your income if you can.

Protecting yourself and your family

At the next level of the pyramid, we find insurance. You need disability insurance to protect you if you are hurt or become ill and are unable to work and save for your future. You need life insurance to protect those who depend on you for financial support. (We'll cover life insurance in more detail in chapter fifteen when we discuss estate planning.) It takes a huge chunk of cash to protect your family from the hardship that your premature death would cause. The least expensive way to make sure that chunk of cash will be there is

Priority pyramid

Art

Gems

Commodities

Real estate

Tax shelters • Private business

Canadian growth stocks • International stocks

Blue chip Canadian stocks

Bonds • Preferred shares

Your home • RRSPs • Pension • Term deposits • Canada Savings Bonds • Treasury bills

Insurance • Wills • Debt repayment • Emergency and opportunity fund

Control over cash flow

Average duration of disability lasting three months or longer TABLE 10

Age	Duration
25	4.3 years
30	4.7 years
35	5.1 years
40	5.5 years
45	5.8 years
50	6.2 years

through insurance. Your insurance needs are probably most inexpensively met by group insurance from your employer. (You should make sure you pay the premiums on disability insurance yourself. If they are paid by your employer, your disability benefits will be taxed.) You can also buy reasonably priced insurance from professional organizations and unions. If you're in doubt about your needs and the kind of policy to buy, call a life insurance agent or financial adviser.

I've covered life insurance first, because your death would be such a financial and emotional hardship for your family. However, the risk of being disabled for up to two years is much greater than your risk of dying before you reach age sixty-five. A disability not only disrupts your family's income, it could create the burden of medical expenses or special care that can be expensive. Being disabled also makes it impossible to continue saving for retirement. Unless you are already financially independent, you place yourself in great financial jeopardy if you do not have adequate disability insurance.

A disability can arise because of an accident or illness; you should keep this in mind while choosing a policy. To be properly protected, your insurance should provide a benefit whatever the cause of your disability. You should be protected if you cannot work at your own job; some policies will only pay a disability benefit if you cannot do any work at all. Avoid these. You should also keep in mind

that only 15 to 20 percent of disabilities last for six months or less. A disability can easily last for several years.

Unlike your ability to buy as much life insurance as you want, the disability insurance companies will limit your coverage to no more than 70 percent of your income. To calculate your monthly disability insurance needs, look at your monthly expenses and add a reasonable amount to cover those expenses that occur only once or twice a year.

It is possible to buy a disability insurance rider that will cover your retirement savings but I wouldn't bother with it. It's expensive. And, once you are back on your feet you should be able to make up for lost time.

Wills and estate planning

It's important to your family's well-being and peace of mind that you leave a will that clearly expresses your intentions. It should identify who will manage the affairs of your estate until it is handed over to your beneficiaries and your heirs. Estate planning is so important that we devote an entire chapter to it. I'd like to emphasize that it is your personal responsibility to your loved ones to leave your estate in good order.

If you don't have a will, take an hour and a few hundred dollars and have a will prepared immediately for you and your husband or wife. Generally, your minor children do not need wills because they do not have anyone dependent upon them who would need financial support. If, however, your children are beneficiaries of a trust or have a right to income now, you should consider what will happen to their assets if they were to die.

Getting rid of your debts

The next tier on the planning pyramid is the elimination of debt. There isn't any other action that will strengthen your financial position as much as becoming debt-free. Canadians have taken on enormous debt loads in the past two decades. Before we can even start to build the solid foundation and retirement nest egg that we will need, we must get rid of our debts.

Although it's hardly as glamorous as investing, there can be no better return on your money than ridding yourself of a loan. The interest costs on a loan can range from 8 or 9 percent for mortgages to 20 percent for credit cards to as much as 32 percent for retail store cards and finance company loans. Paying off a debt saves you 12 or 19 or 32 percent on your money without taking any risk at all. This is pretty good compared to a decent, reasonably risk-free return of perhaps 10 percent from investing. Of course, you would have to pay tax on that 10 percent return, reducing your yield to 5 to 6 percent. Clearly, paying off your debt offers a much higher return than investing.

Consider Sally, who has accumulated a $3,000 credit card debt on which she is being charged interest at 20 percent a year. If Sally saves $3,000 and invests it at 10 percent, she'll earn $300. After tax, she'll have around $180. Yet the cost of carrying the $3,000 loan for a year is $600. Sally would be further ahead by $420 if she uses the $3,000 to pay off her credit cards rather than invest.

If you're in debt, you should follow these 5 steps to get out of debt as efficiently and quickly as possible:

1. **Pay off your most costly debts first**.

If you have a car loan at 10 percent and a 28 percent credit card debt, concentrate on getting rid of the credit card debt. There is an exception, however. The interest on your investment and business loans will be tax deductible and the after-tax cost could be less than the cost of a non-deductible loan carrying a higher interest rate. If that car loan is for a car that is not used for business, the after-tax cost is the full 10 percent. The

payments on a 12 percent investment loan can be deducted from your taxable income. If your tax rate is 50 percent, then the after-tax rate is 6 percent and the investment loan is less costly than the car loan. It will usually turn out that tax-deductible loans cost less. As a rule, you should pay off your non-deductible debts first.

2. **Convert your non-deductible loans into tax-deductible loans.**

If you have $20,000 and want to purchase both a $20,000 car and invest in an international mutual fund, then you must make a choice or borrow. If you decide to borrow, good planning would mean paying cash for the car and borrowing for the mutual fund. That way the interest on your loan will be tax-deductible.

Now suppose that you already have done it the wrong way. Are you stuck? At first blush, you might say no. Sell the mutual fund, you say, pay off the car loan then turn around and buy the same fund again with an investment loan. Unfortunately, things aren't as easy as that. The tax department would consider this to be an artificial arrangement devised to evade taxes — which is illegal. However, if your opinion of investment conditions has changed, you might sell the international fund, pay off the car loan and borrow to make an investment of another type, perhaps a U.S. bond fund. This only makes sense if your investment perspective has changed significantly. As usual, remember that investment returns are more important than tax deductions.

3. **Consolidate your loans to reduce interest charges.**

If you take all of your credit card debts and consolidate them in one bank loan, your interest charges could plummet. This is especially true if you have a solid credit position with the bank because of a responsible record, strong earnings foundation or significant net worth. You can even secure the bank loan by pledging investments or by taking a second mortgage on your home. With a dramatic improvement in your interest rate, your monthly debt payment will go much further in reducing the principal instead of excessive interest expenses.

For example, let's say that Sally, with her credit card debt of $3,000, didn't take our advice and use her money to pay down her debt. Instead she went on vacation and spent money. Then she went on a shopping spree. Now, she has a $4,000 debt on two bank credit cards, each charging 20 percent, as well as cards from a couple of department stores, both charging 30 percent. This is a good time for Sally to consider a consolidation loan from her bank. Although Sally's credit history has been hurt by her lapse into debt accumulation, she should still be able to get a personal loan bearing an interest rate of 2 to 5 percent above prime. By combining her debts, Sally will save herself $600 in interest expense. More important, if Sally continues to make the same debt payments that she was making before, this $600 will go directly to reducing the principal of the loans.

There is a serious warning due here! Don't let your good intentions get you into worse shape. If you slip back into your bad habits, you could end up carrying the consolidation loan and running up new balances on credit cards as well. You have to be certain that you have the discipline to resist charging up new debt. One of the best ways is to destroy your credit cards or reduce their credit limits to safe levels.

4. **Increase your loan payments.**

Look hard at your monthly income and expenses to find more money that can be devoted to debt repayment. It will focus your attention on the gravity of the situation and you might find you can easily increase your debt payments. If you can't increase the amount you pay, perhaps you can increase the frequency of your debt payments. This will allow you to reduce the principal and interest more quickly. For example, if you owe $10,000 at 16 percent and plan to repay it with monthly payments of $400, then you will pay out $2,400 of interest over the thirty-one months to settle the debt. If, instead, you pay $100 a week, it will only take you twenty-eight months to pay off the debt — and you will save $400 in interest.

5. **Sell investments that are not performing.** You can sell investments that haven't been performing well, or personal assets, to raise cash. This will give you a fast start to clearing your debt. (You often see major corporations selling prized assets for the same reason.) Unfortunately, it's not easy to do. It never feels like the right time to sell investments, they are either doing too well to be sold or doing so poorly we don't want to take a loss — we'll just wait until they come back a bit. You have to realize that:

■ you'll feel great;

■ your best return does not come from the laggard investment but from reducing your debt;

■ once you get your affairs in order, you'll have the cash to buy yourself something or buy a more promising investment. Be careful, though, that you don't reward yourself for getting rid of your debt by buying something that is beyond your means and puts you right back into it.

Building cash reserves

Hand in hand with the elimination of debt is the need to build a pool of money that you can use for emergencies and for opportunities. You should have enough cash squirrelled away to cover your expenses for three months. Fortunately, unlike many Americans, you won't face a financial crisis because of a medical problem — thanks to government medical care — but you would need money if you lost your job, if you took a leave of absence to care for a loved one or if you wanted to help a family member experiencing financial hardship.

A second reason to build a cash reserve is to have funds available for opportunities that might arise. There are often opportunities that we can take advantage of only if we act quickly. I have always been impressed with the guy on television who bought his grass seed in December and snow blower in July — he got the best prices. A cash reserve allows you to anticipate your needs and buy when the price is right, rather than being forced to buy on credit or pay more because you have an immediate need. There could be many opportunities, including wealth-building investment opportunities, that you will want to take advantage of as they arise.

Your investment foundation

The next tier brings us to the most popular Canadian investment, Canada Savings Bonds. CSBs are one of the best vehicles for holding your cash reserve fund. In addition, they can be the building blocks for this third level, your investment foundation. CSBs offer very little risk and the ability to put your hands on your money quickly, all at the best possible return.

They are safe because they carry the Canadian government's guarantee and Canadians invest millions of dollars in CSBs, partly because of the ease with which they can be bought, and partly because they're a safe investment paying a reasonable yield. Be aware, however, that this yield is low and you should not use CSBs as a long-term investment. It's better to use them as short-term deposits,

something that can be cashed at any time (preferably at the beginning of the month, to earn the full previous month's interest).

With $5,000 or more, Canadians can also invest in Canadian treasury bills which provide some of the same features as the CSBs. Treasury bills are also offered by the government of Canada and therefore carry the same guarantee and safety as CSBs. Treasury bills do not technically pay interest like CSBs. Rather, they are sold at a discount to their face value and then their market value increases steadily until they reach their face value on the date of maturity. (This rise in value is taxed as interest, however, not as a capital gain.)

More and more Canadian investors are putting their cash into money market funds long a favourite investment of our American neighbours. Money market mutual funds invest in treasury bills and short-term loans (often called "paper") issued by federal and provincial governments and companies with strong credit ratings in Canada.

These funds have huge sums of money to invest and can buy these securities in large denominations of $100,000. This allows them to command higher interest rates than would be available on smaller denominations. Money market mutual funds can also secure higher rates of interest by investing for longer periods of time than we might, knowing that they can sell these investments in the open market if a rush of investors demand the return of their cash. Because of this ability to secure higher rates, money market funds often provide investors with higher returns than short-term deposits and T-bills. Mutual funds do have to pay their managers, though, and these fees are passed on to the investor in the form of management fees, which reduce the investor's overall income yield.

On the same pyramid tier are safe, secure deposits of up to five years, such as guaranteed investment certificates issued by trust companies, term deposits with banks and term annuities issued by insurance companies. The goal is security and good returns on money that can be tied up for a few years, but not for the long term.

Also on this tier are your RRSPs and pension funds. We've already seen how the tax advantages of RRSPs and pension plans allow your wealth to grow at two or three times the speed as similar investments that are not tax-sheltered. It's an opportunity that you can't afford to miss.

Finally, on this tier is your investment in your home. Canadians have realized some spectacular financial gains in real estate. The reasons are threefold. First, historically the value of the investment seems to grow and keep pace with inflation over time. At times, house values run ahead of inflation, bringing extremely rich gains. At other times, growth is relatively slow or even negative.

I can't predict whether house prices will repeat the growth they had in the 1970s and 1980s, but I would expect that values would grow at a slightly slower rate than inflation in the next decade. Condominium housing and country properties may run ahead at a faster rate of growth owing to the demand for these properties by baby boomers ready to buy recreational properties and older boomers considering a move to condominium housing after their children have moved away. In any event, homes should generally remain safe and secure investments.

The second reason investing in your home is important is that any gain in your home's value is tax-free. And, there are very few ways of earning income or capital gains that are not subject to tax. A principal residence is the home generally inhabited by you and your family. Each family can only designate one principal residence at one time. There's a third reason your home is a good investment. A home is usually acquired by taking on a mortgage and the debt is repaid slowly and steadily by regular monthly payments. It's a forced savings plan that demands that you gradually increase your equity in your home over time. This is a healthy method of saving and an important way to build wealth.

Investment priorities

At the next tier on the pyramid, we start to have more investment capital available and to make longer-term investments, especially on the stock and bond markets. Investing in mutual funds may be the wisest way of investing in these markets because of the diversification and professional management that would not otherwise be available for individual investments.

Historically, stocks and bonds yield higher returns over time than do less risky investments lower down on the pyramid. But that risk can be exaggerated by investing in only a few individual securities. Putting all your eggs in one basket does not permit efficient diversification and leaves you exposed to the misfortunes of a few investment positions.

You should also be careful with preferred shares. These are considerably riskier than bonds and guaranteed deposits and do not offer the same rewards as common stocks. There are short periods of time when holding preferred shares can be profitable because of their high yield and preferential tax treatment. However, it is difficult to time these opportunities and the risks of being in preferred shares at the wrong time can be great.

Here, too, you can make greater use of income-splitting, whereby family members with lower tax rates become investors. Family members with higher income pay the household expenses, including the tax bills of the lower-income members. Lower-income spouses and family members can then use their own cash to invest and earn investment income that will be taxed at a lower tax rate.

For some individuals, more aggressive and longer-term income-splitting strategies may be more appropriate. If one family member has accumulated a large investment foundation and the lower-income spouse has none, it's valuable to move some of the assets into the lower-income spouse's hands. This can be done by giving the assets to the lower-income spouse or by giving the spouse an interest-free loan with which to buy the assets.

In both of these cases, Revenue Canada will require that the income from the assets be attributed back to the original owner. However, any new income earned will be taxed in the hands of the lower-income spouse. Because it is only the second generation of income that gets transferred to the spouse, this is a long-term strategy that will result in income-splitting after a number of years.

Moving to the next level, I recommend the use of more aggressive investments in the stock markets, both in Canada and worldwide. By this I mean buying and holding strong, established, fast-growing companies with well-known products operating in major markets around the globe, as well as smaller, fast-growing companies that should be tomorrow's leaders. Seeking these companies out from markets around the world will provide greater economic diversification and investment growth. These can be bought through mutual funds or you can manage your own portfolio of growth stocks if you have enough interest and dollars to commit to this segment of the market.

Higher still on the pyramid are speculative investments — real estate, tax shelters and private business ventures. These can be particularly risky but particularly rewarding. Some tax advantages can help mitigate the risk inherent in these investments and provide a better opportunity for solid returns. But you should not invest in these unless your foundation is firmly in place and your tax rate

will allow you to benefit from tax savings if the investments go sour.

At the apex of the pyramid are art, gems, collectibles and commodities, a class of investments that usually requires special expertise and generally costs more for retail buyers than professionals. Of course, something atop our pyramid might be a lower-tier investment for you, say, if you're very knowledgeable and experienced with the item. Perhaps you've collected stamps for many years. Other people profitably invest in rare books, Persian rugs or classic cars, combining expertise in investment with personal enjoyment. Inevitably, your pyramid will be different from mine, but everyone can benefit from taking a structured approach to making decisions about investment priorities.

Financial assessment

Let's consolidate the information you have on your current financial position and identify problems and opportunities. To provide a framework for this review, first list your financial priorities. We'll start at the bottom of the pyramid. Study your control over your expenses with a view to starting to build assets and reduce debts. Take a good look at your insurance and the protection it provides you and your family. Then look at the organization of your financial affairs. Are the details of your assets and debts and other financial matters organized so that your family will be able to understand them? If not, then this should be a priority in getting your estate in order.

Next, ensure that you have established safe and solid savings. Make sure you are using all available means to reduce your taxes, especially tax deferrals and incentives such as RRSPs. Consider extending these tax advantages by sharing income with other family members where possible.

Finally, you will want to examine your investments to make sure your hard-earned money is invested for the highest possible return consistent with the amount of risk you can accept.

With this in mind, we can review the financial information you've assembled. There are a number of questions to be answered but for the rest of this chapter we'll concentrate on controlling the flow of cash through our hands.

Finding more cash

Over your lifetime, you will receive millions of dollars and will spend millions of dollars. The trick is to hang on to some of it as it passes by. This isn't easy. For the first twenty to thirty years of your career it seems like you spend everything you receive — on raising and educating children, insurance, buying a home, and just trying to keep up. You hope that on the way through you build up some value in a company pension plan, in RRSPs, or at least in the Canada or Quebec pension plans.

As you've seen, it takes an enormous amount of savings to finance retirement. It's possible that the savings you have already accumulated along with the savings you put aside every year will give you plenty of money in retirement; if not, cash management becomes your number one priority.

How do you get more cash? There are a number of ways:

- make your savings work harder
- reduce your income taxes
- earn more
- spend less
- tap the cash value in insurance policies
- tap your hidden assets; your home, personal belongings and investments that are lagging
- receive an inheritance

If you truly want to retire in style, you should try to turn as much cash into savings using as many methods as possible. Effective investment planning is so critical to improving

your earning power in the future that I'll discuss it in detail in chapter twelve. Tax strategies can also be very powerful, so we devote chapter eleven to taxes. Meanwhile, you have to put aside cash today, and every month, to create a pool of funds that can be effectively invested for tomorrow.

Earning more

How can you earn more in today's tough economy? It's not easy. In fact, many people are struggling to ensure that they don't earn less, let alone earn more. It's beyond the scope of this book to deal in depth with gaining employment or business income. But as a financial planner I have seen many people who learned the hard way that you must constantly improve your skills, adapting to the new environment.

Talented people are always in demand; and busy people seem to manage their time so well they get more done. There is no room for complacency. You are either improving your expertise or you are falling back. This sounds tough and it is. But if you have health, energy and the support of friends and family, you can find ways to improve your earnings, and add to your savings.

One of the problems with earning more is that you will have to pay more in income taxes. You might even end up giving up 30 to 50 percent of your new earnings to Revenue Canada. And there may be expenses incurred by taking on a new or extra job — the cost of getting to work, clothing, child care, lunches. We are often asked if a second job is worth it. I've always felt that as long as you enjoy what you are doing, then it's worth it. As for income taxes and job-related costs, it's always better to have fifty cents more than nothing at all.

Controlling your spending

One of the most powerful ways to improve your immediate financial position is to control your spending. Sometimes this can seem impossible; we often already feel as though we're scrimping and doing without. In fact, you can reduce expenses often simply by studying spending patterns. Look at the expenses you detailed in chapter nine. Can you identify immediate savings opportunities? Often you can reduce spending by ensuring that each expense is essential in its own right and cannot be achieved more economically in some other way. For example, if you spend $1,000 a month on dining out, consider whether this expense is essential (perhaps because you don't cook and the pleasure of dining out is more important to you than taking a lavish vacation) or whether you could cut down on these costs by organizing barbecues at home. If you spend $500 a year on magazine subscriptions, make sure that you are actually reading the magazines, not leaving them in a pile in the family room.

Examining income and expenses to establish greater control over costs is, of course, called budgeting. I've avoided using this word so far because it carries notions of deprivation and constraint. But a budget should be a good thing, for it can help you spend money more intelligently and enjoyably.

The expense forecasts you prepared in chapter nine can be turned into a monthly cash budget — or you can use the current numbers in those forecasts to do a review of your spending habits. Consider whether each expenditure is a "need" or a "want" and look for ways to cut costs. The very act of preparing an annual budget may be all that's needed to ensure a constant awareness of spending and saving. Although some people prefer to keep regular records of the coming and going of cash and to compare them to their budgets on a monthly basis, there are an infinite number of ways to use a budget. It all depends on your personal style and comfort with your financial affairs. However you do it, preparing a budget

How Canadians spend their money   **TABLE 11**

Item	Families earning $35,000 to $39,000	Families earning over $85,000
Food bought in stores	$4,563	$6,261
Restaurants	1,213	3,421
Shelter	7,601	13,049
Transportation	5,326	10,552
Household goods and furniture	2,945	6,688
Clothing	2,021	5,564
Life insurance premiums	212	616
Recreation	2,025	5,056
Education	350	1,102
Tobacco and alcohol	1,253	1,838
Personal care	866	1,421
Health care	793	1,410
Pet care	185	330
Personal taxes	5,765	31,278
Pensions and RRSPs	770	2,617
Gifts and charity	1,984	3,948
Lottery tickets	154	152

NOTE: This information is compiled from data obtained in January, February and March 1991 on Canadian household spending during 1990. Family expendure surveys have been conducted approximately every two years since 1953.

SOURCE: STATISTICS CANADA, FAMILY EXPENDITURES IN CANADA, 1990

and examining spending at least once a year are valuable exercises for anyone serious about financial planning.

I'm constantly being asked by clients about whether they should "loosen up and live for today" or "smarten up and save for tomorrow." People have been facing this battle for years; I tend to talk as if I'm in the save-for-tomorrow camp, but I don't often act like it. My dad was the serious saver type and today he and my mother are able to live comfortably in their older years. I remember a man who worked for Dad who was on the live-for-today side and he too seems to be living well in retirement. It is hard to say who's right.

What is terribly sad is to see someone die prematurely, having saved all his or her life and having never been able to enjoy it. So we must do those important things in life that allow us to enjoy family and friends. But there are a great many other things we do and ways we spend money that may not be so important. And it is from these that we should choose to do without and save for the future.

Perhaps you could switch from downhill to cross-country skiing. Cross-country is cheaper and healthier and can be just as enjoyable. You can spend your vacations in Canada and spend less on air fares, hotels, expensive meals. You could keep your old car running. Sure it costs more for repairs than a new car (usually) but it's still less than the $5,000 or so annual depreciation in value of a new car. Or you could cut back on expensive gifts for birthdays and holidays. They'll still love you.

This is a good time to make the change. It has become fashionable to save money and ostentatious consumption is frowned upon.

Tapping the cash in insurance policies

During your retirement-planning years, from age forty-five to sixty-five, your need for insurance tends to decline as your children become self-sufficient (more or less), your mortgage debt begins to dwindle and your wealth begins to build. Your thoughts might be turning to the cash value in that whole life policy you bought when the kids were little. If so, don't do it hastily.

First, ask a professional to make sure this is the best option. Whole life insurance is complex and it is not easy to determine whether it's a good idea to take the cash from a policy — and if it is, the best way to do it.

Second, you might find you need your insurance in retirement. Your group insurance will either be cancelled or reduced to a small sum. We often find people need insurance for about ten years into retirement, until age seventy-five. If they've let their policies go, there's a gap. You can't buy insurance at that age for an affordable price. Finally, if the policies are inexpensive you might find they expand your options when choosing your pension or RRSP survivorship options.

On the other hand, keeping insurance policies that are not needed is poor planning. This is particularly true if your family investments and your spouse's own retirement income will protect him or her if you were to die. It's also possible that the survivor's rights in your pensions and annuities provide all the protection that's needed. The premiums that keep the insurance in force should be invested; if they're invested well they could produce more wealth than the insurance policy ever will. Again, a warning. Before you cancel any insurance policy believing you have plenty of income, have your calculations verified by an expert. The projections are complex and an error in judgment could lead to years of discomfort.

Rather than cashing in a whole-life policy, you could look at the various options available for tapping the cash. Those options might include converting to another insurance product, some of which are eligible as RRSP contributions. Or, it can be converted to a paid-up policy. Such a policy will pay a reduced death benefit but you will not have to pay any more premiums. Finally, you could simply borrow against the policy, usually at a very low interest rate. Again, make sure your family is protected before making the change.

Hidden assets

We have many hidden assets. The ability to reduce our spending is one; using our time more profitably, perhaps through a second job, is another. A third is doing things around the house which we pay others to do for us. Improving our skills and studying at night to improve our job prospects is yet a fourth.

Another hidden asset is your home. You own your home because it provides you with shelter and it's part of your lifestyle. However, your home also shelters a good deal of your wealth — wealth you can only tap by selling. As your life changes and your children leave home, your need for your home may have also changed. Among the most difficult decisions to make as we organize our financial affairs for retirement is whether or not to keep the family house, especially if you've spent most of your adult life in it. A great deal of emotion is attached to the place where you've lived and raised your family. The benefits — garden, workshop, comfortable living space, the very familiarity of the home — may be unavailable in other places. If these considerations are important, perhaps you shouldn't look at the decision in financial terms.

The financial decision is closely tied to your need for cash. If you are concerned about having enough cash, now or in the future, and it's emotionally acceptable to move, you should carefully study the potential savings involved in selling your home. The proceeds could represent a significant pile of cash that could be invested to boost your pension income. On the other hand, it could trigger the claw-back of the Old Age Security pension. Your analysis, therefore, must examine housing expenses that might be saved, investment income that might be earned from the proceeds of the sale, and the costs of finding a new home. These numbers will allow you to determine the cash flow improvement you can expect from selling your home.

Take a look at the worksheet "The costs of relocating." We've provided an example and left a blank column for you to do your own analysis. In the first part of the worksheet, list all of your current housing costs — the cost of staying in your home. Then estimate the cost of moving. To do this, start with an estimate of the gross proceeds. Deduct from this the expenses of the sale — you can use 10 percent of the gross proceeds as an estimate of these expenses. This will leave you with the net proceeds you will receive from the sale. Then determine what after-tax cash flow you will derive from investing these funds. The example

assumes a 10-percent investment return and a 40-percent income tax rate.

Finally, estimate the costs of your new location, assuming you will rent a condominium or apartment. These costs will include rent, parking, tenants' insurance and might also include the cost of utilities and heat if these are not included in your rent. With these calculations done, you can now determine whether selling your house will provide you with a cash flow improvement and how significant that will be. You will save the amount you currently spend on housing costs and you will earn investment income. These savings will then be reduced by the rental costs you will need to incur. In our example, selling the house and moving to a rented apartment would result in a saving of $4,500 a year. How much would you save?

If you've decided that it is financially worthwhile to sell, you must turn your thoughts to the investment value of your house and the optimum time to sell. If you think house prices will rise, assuming that you don't need the money right away it will be wise to hold on, remembering that capital gains on the sale of personal residences in Canada are tax-free.

Another hidden asset is a cottage. You've got some great memories there and you love to go up and putter around. But you only went up three weekends last year and the kids have moved away. So let's look at the cottage from a financial viewpoint. If you believe cottage values are going up, it's probably wise to keep it, particularly if maintenance costs aren't too high. If you're less confident of its future value, you could sell it and invest the funds. You can still go to the country for three or four weekends a year, and stay at a bed-and-breakfast or inn. Better still, you might stay at a neighbour's cottage. Let him carry the cost of the property, while you help him enjoy it.

Another asset you might consider selling is a second car, although this decision will clearly

The costs of relocating

	Example	Your Situation
Current residential costs		
Property taxes	$2,200	_____
Insurance*	$600	_____
Repairs and maintenance	$600	_____
Heating	$1,200	_____
Snow clearing and lawn care	$500	_____
Total house ownership costs	$5,100	_____
Investment income from proceeds of house sale		
Proceeds from the sale	$185,000	_____
Expenses of sale	$18,500	_____
Net proceeds	$166,500	_____
Investment return	10%	_____
Annual income from proceeds	$16,650	_____
Your personal tax rate	40%	_____
After-tax income	$10,000	_____
Cost of new accommodation		
Apartment rent	$9,600	_____
Tenant's insurance	$100	_____
Car parking fee	$600	_____
Repairs and miscellaneous	$300	_____
Total rental costs	$10,600	_____
Improvement in your cash flow		
House costs which you not have to pay	$5,100	_____
Add to this your investment income	+$10,000	_____
Deduct the cost of renting	-$10,600	_____
Improvement in your financial position	=$4,500	_____

*Don't include the cost of the insurance on your home's contents. You'll need this no matter where you live.

depend on whether you'll need it more or less in retirement. How about a garage sale? This can raise lots of cash and clean up the garage or basement at the same time. Just make sure you don't give away any $50 comic books or $500 baseball cards: items that have gained collectors' appeal while gathering dust.

The point is not to turn your life upside down. It's simply to look at things you own and see if there's a better use to which their value can be put. From a financial standpoint, the trick is to project the future value of your hidden assets — house, cottage, cars, comic books — compared to other forms of investment. But money is only one consideration. It's not healthy to sell all your possessions just to put cash in the bank. In the end, bank books and stock certificates provide very little enjoyment in and of themselves.

Having your cake, and eating it, too!

Much of your life has probably been spent paying off your mortgage. As your retirement years progress and inflation eats into your cash flow, you might find yourself in the position of many seniors — house-rich and cash-poor. If you find the idea of selling your home unappealing, there is an alternative — the reverse mortgage. You enter into an arrangement with a financial institution to borrow money against the security of your debt-free home, usually a single-family, detached house. A reverse mortgage converts your home equity into cash — it is truly a mortgage in reverse. Instead of making monthly payments to the lender, the lender gives you a monthly cheque.

The mortgage holder will only lend a portion of the equity in the home (usually about 35 percent), expecting that the value of the home will increase more than the debt increases. The monthly income you receive depends on the value of your home, your age, your life expectancy and the age and life expectancy of your spouse.

The money advanced for the mortgage is used to purchase an annuity that provides a monthly income to you. Some plans offer the option of a healthy payment up front as well as monthly cheques. You owe the mortgage funds advanced to you plus the interest that accumulates each month. The mortgage rate is usually locked in for the life of the contract. The interest builds but isn't collected until the house is sold or the contract expires. The best plan is not to have to pay off the loan until the home is sold. You don't want to be forced to sell because the contract has ended.

There are now two reverse mortgage plans available:

1. Canadian Home Income Corporation's Canadian Home Income Plan (CHIP) purchases joint-survivor annuities guaranteed for the life of both partners. Based in Vancouver, it also operates in Toronto. Seaboard Life Insurance Co. provides the funding.

2. Security Life Insurance Co.'s Home Equity Plan (HEP) sets the income for life, but fixes the mortgage interest rate for five years at a time. Both plans allow you to tap into 35 percent or less of the present value of your home. Your legal costs will range from $100 to $500.

Royal Trust has offered a type of reverse mortgage, but their loan must be repaid after five years. In most cases, it would be necessary to sell the home to raise money to pay the loan.

One word of caution. Although you initially borrow only 35 percent of your home's value, the interest compounding for several years could eventually equal the total value of your home. For example, at 10 percent interest, a $35,000 loan would cost $95,000 to repay in ten years. A $70,000 loan on a $200,000 house would cost $190,000 to repay in ten years. If the house does not go up in value, you come close to using up its full value.

Be sure that any contract you sign does not make you liable for any costs that exceed the value of your home when it's sold. There should also be a guarantee against foreclosure, so that no one can cast you out of your own home. This is the time to use an experienced lawyer to protect your most valuable asset. Know the total costs, as well as the benefits of the plan.

Do I think the reverse mortgage is a good idea? In general, no, because you should never borrow for personal living costs. There are times when it will be useful, however, such as for short-term arrangements of one to three years, after which moving to a nursing home is expected. Or it might be critical to one's mental well-being to stay in the family home, near friends and relatives. Let me give you an example: One of our clients is an elderly East European who owns a big home in central Montreal. He and his wife are just over eighty and are short of money. He won't sell the house because he sees it as the only security for his wife and two daughters, both of whom are married and financially insecure. If he sold, he would have more than he needs for the rest of his and her days, but he won't part with it. The answer was a reverse mortgage, but this need for real estate security is costing the family and the estate, at the rate of 10 percent a year. For more information, write:

1. Canadian Home Income Corporation, 2590 Granville Street, Suite 202, Vancouver, British Columbia V6H 3H1. Telephone (604) 737-2447.

2. Consumers for Home Equity Conversion, P.O. Box 623, Streetsville Post Office, Mississauga, Ontario L5M 2C1. Telephone (416) 858-1396. There is a small fee for information.

3. Public Interest Advocacy Centre, 1 Nicholas Street, Suite 410, Ottawa, Ontario K1N 7D7. Telephone (613) 563-0734.

4. Security Life Insurance Home Equity Plan, 1200 Sheppard Avenue East, Suite 404, Willowdale, Ontario M2K 2S5. Telephone (416) 494-2497.

Your financial position and priorities   WORKSHEET 29

Jot down your priorities and opportunities arising from the review of your financial position.

1. _____

_____

2. _____

_____

3. _____

_____

4. _____

_____

5. _____

_____

6. _____

_____

7. _____

_____

8. _____

_____

9. _____

_____

10. _____

_____

Inheritances

It might seem strange to include inheritances as a method of maximizing savings. Most people feel uncomfortable considering the deaths of their loved ones and the wealth it will bring them. But there are things that you can do. You can help your parents to draft their wills. You can help them to get the right investment management so that they don't lose money.

You can help them consider whether there are means of income-splitting that can be considered in their wills, perhaps by having assets pass to your children to provide for their college educations rather than to you. Or you can help them consider an estate freeze. Such a step would allow them to enjoy the income generated by their current assets, but future growth in value will benefit you or your children. (For a discussion on estate freezes, see chapter fifteen.) This planning need not be considered uncomfortable. Instead you should focus on helping your loved ones to manage their affairs and provide future benefits to their descendants.

Building toward your goal

The goal of financial independence is formidable and not many people will reach it easily. It's possible they will have to delay their retirement or lower their expectations unless they seriously commit to achieving financial independence. This chapter sets out a number of financial planning strategies that deal with sound money management and your priorities. It is easy to come up with a number of good financial strategies, but which should you do first? When faced with this problem, think of the priority pyramid, and make sure you have a solid base in place before reaching for the top. If your financial structure is solid, you can afford to take greater risks with your investments, and move ahead at a faster pace.

Chapter 11

Forty ways to reduce your tax bill

In 1993, tax freedom day arrived June 11. Until that day, every dollar you earned went to pay federal, provincial and local taxes plus a wide range of government fees. On average, 44 percent of our income goes to one kind of tax or another. It is your legal right and responsibility to arrange your affairs to reduce this tax burden. What is not acceptable is using illegal means to evade taxes.

Knowing the income tax rules and regulations can provide many opportunities to save on income taxes, leaving more of your earnings for saving and spending. Such tax-saving steps are perfectly legal and available to everyone. Each device on its own might give you only a small saving but, together, the reduction in taxes could be significant. And these savings can be made year after year.

Before you start looking for tax savings, find out just how much tax you really pay. The table in the appendix shows the marginal tax rates at various levels of taxable income for residents in various provinces of Canada. Your marginal tax rate is the rate of tax that applies to each additional dollar of income you earn.

You'll notice that our tax system uses a "progressive" tax rate structure. The rate at which you pay tax increases progressively as your personal income rises. It's a bit like climbing stairs: You move up the stairs until you reach a plateau. Once past the plateau, there are more stairs, only steeper. Then another plateau followed by even steeper stairs. It's important to be aware of the high cost of tax at the top levels of your income. Reducing taxable income at those levels can yield big tax savings. Taxpayers rise toward the 50 percent level quickly — jumping over that with ease with provincial surtaxes. That's the bad news. The good news is that even small

reductions from your income can generate significant tax savings.

In general, there are three principles of tax savings:

- Deduct. Take advantage of every available tax deduction and tax credit.
- Defer. Delay paying taxes until the future by taking advantage of tax deferrals such as RRSPs and pension plans.
- Divide. Move income into the hands of family members with lower marginal tax rates.

There are many ways that you can apply these three principles of tax reduction. We've explained forty tax-saving strategies and more than fifty tips to help you reduce your tax bill. They won't all be useful to each of you but those few that you can use could have a dramatic impact over time.

Tax deductions and credits

Taking advantage of legitimate tax deductions and credits is the first principle of effective tax planning. You can determine if you're getting all the breaks you're due by reviewing your last tax return. To do a more detailed review, you can turn to the annual Revenue Canada Income Tax Guide. During tax season, this guide is available at your local post office or you can phone the number of your local

Revenue Canada office located in the blue pages of your telephone directory to obtain this guide. The guide lists many deductions and credits to which you might be entitled along with a summary of the requirements for each deduction and credit.

The following are the most commonly overlooked deductions and credits.

1. Interest expenses

You can deduct from your income the interest you pay on a loan incurred for the purpose of earning income. This could be a loan you took out to buy stocks, business equipment or rental real estate. It's not necessary that the investment earn income for the interest expense to be deductible — if you borrow money to invest in a portfolio that realizes some capital losses, you can still deduct the interest on the loan — but there must be a reasonable expectation of earning a profit through future income or capital gains.

TIP: Many people will decide to finance the purchase of a new car while maintaining savings or other investments they have. This can be appropriate for self-employed business people or commissioned salespeople who can deduct the cost of their cars against their business income. But for the rest of us this means that we continue to pay tax on the income generated by our investment and do not get a tax deduction for the interest expense on the car loan. Non-deductible debt is very expensive; for example, if you're paying 10-percent interest on a car loan and have a 40-percent marginal tax rate, you would have to earn about 17 percent on your investment to break even — a very difficult rate of return to achieve today without accepting a high degree of risk.

Instead, you should use your investment assets to pay for the car. Then you can borrow the funds to invest and deduct the interest payments against your income. This makes

sense as long as the investment will yield a return greater than the after-tax cost of the loan. For example, if your investment yields 8 percent and the investment loan bears interest at 10 percent, then, assuming a 40-percent tax rate, your overall after-tax investment return, after deducting the cost of the investment loan, will be 2 percent — therefore borrowing would make sense. If you take out the same loan, however, and invest in a security that will only yield 5 percent, then the after-tax cost of the loan will be higher than the investment yield, and it would not be beneficial to do this.

A word of caution: Before implementing this strategy, you should look closely at the costs for selling your investments. Term deposits or GICs can carry penalties for early withdrawal. Selling shares in a mutual fund could result in redemption fees or could trigger a taxable capital gain.

TIP: If you have fully paid-up investment assets and non-deductible interest such as a mortgage or car loan, consult your financial planner or accountant to determine if the structure of your affairs could be more tax efficient. You must be careful not to use investment assets to repay the mortgage, and then take out an investment loan to buy the same assets again. Revenue Canada can see through this arrangement and will disallow the deductibility of the interest.

2. Carrying charges

Deductible carrying charges include charges for the safekeeping and custody of investments, safety deposit box and accounting fees, as well as retirement and investment counsel fees.

TIP: For married or common-law couples, the spouse with the higher marginal tax rate should pay these fees and get the benefit of the tax deduction.

TIP: Administration fees for self-directed RRSPs are tax-deductible if paid outside the plan. Make sure that you pay your RRSP administration fee personally rather than allow the trustee to take the fees out of the plan.

3. Moving expenses

Moving expenses are deductible if you move within Canada to earn wages or self-employment income at a new home that is at least forty kilometres closer to your workplace than your previous home. Deductible expenses include the cost of meals and lodging near the old or new home for up to fifteen days, and your old home's selling costs, including commissions and legal fees, as well as land transfer taxes if you purchase a new home. However, deductions claimed cannot exceed income earned at the new location. Any excess expenses can be carried to the following year.

TIP: Students can also claim moving expenses if they move to take a job, including a summer job, or start a business. This deduction will reduce the student's net income, which could otherwise reduce or block the dependent tax credit available.

Students can also claim moving expenses if they move to attend full-time post-secondary education, but only against income from a scholarship or research grant.

4. Alimony, separation allowance and child maintenance payments

These payments are deductible, but only if they are made on a regular basis under a decree, order, judgment or written agreement. Just as you can deduct such payments if you make them, you must include the payments as taxable income if you receive them.

TIP: To ensure that you take maximum advantage of this provision, consult competent tax and legal advisers upon separation, even if you and your former partner agree amicably on the terms of payment. It is sometimes possible to have the agreement apply retroactively to payments already made.

5. Age sixty-five credit

An additional tax credit of $3,482 is allowed for taxpayers age sixty-five and over. Lie about your age to everyone else if you want, but let the government know when you reach age sixty-five so you can take advantage of this credit.

TIP: If your spouse is sixty-five or older and cannot fully use this exemption, the unused portion can be transferred to your own return.

6. Married tax credit and equivalent-to-married tax credit

This credit was $5,380 in 1993, and is subject to a reduction of 17 percent of net income in excess of $538. You should make sure that your spouse claims every possible deduction and credit and makes the maximum RRSP contribution.

TIP: A special provision allows your spouse's dividends to be taxed in your hands, which can be profitable if it frees up or increases the married tax credit you can claim.

TIP: If you're single, divorced, separated or widowed, you can claim an amount equivalent to the married tax credit for a dependent relative who resides with you, such as a child under age nineteen, a parent, grandparent or infirm relative.

7. Charitable donation credits

You can claim a tax credit of 17 percent on the first $250 of charitable donations you make, and 29 percent on the remainder, up to 20 percent of your net income. You must attach all receipts to your tax return to support your claim. You can carry forward excess credits for up to five years from the year in which the donation was made.

TIP: Either spouse can claim a donation, regardless of whose name is on the receipt. It helps to have the higher income earner claim all the donations. If, for example, you each donate $250 to charity, rather than each of you getting a tax credit of 17 percent times $250, one spouse can claim the full $500 and reduce their taxes by 17 percent on the first $250 and by 29 percent on the second $250.

TIP: Let's say you've already donated $250 late in the year and intend to donate more money early in the new year. It's actually better to make the additional donations in the old year to take advantage of the 29-percent credit on contributions in excess of $250, as well as to realize the tax savings one year earlier.

8. Medical expense credit

You can claim a credit for medical expenses for 17 percent of the amount by which they exceed $1,614 or 3 percent of your net income, whichever is less. You must attach receipts to your income tax return for amounts claimed. The expenses must have been paid in any twelve-month period ending in the taxation year and cannot include amounts already claimed in the previous year or amounts reimbursed by medical insurance plans. You can claim medical expenses incurred by yourself, your spouse or by persons for whom you are entitled to claim the dependent tax credit, such as a dependent child under age nineteen, grandchild or a parent.

TIP: It's usually profitable to claim the tax credit for medical expenses on the return of the spouse with lower income because the 3-percent income threshold will be lower. However, if all of the credits can't be used by the low-income spouse, you and your spouse should share the expenses in a way that provides the maximum tax relief.

TIP: A special provision allows you to deduct the medical expenses which you have paid for a dependent child who doesn't qualify as your dependent because his or her income is too high. This "notch provision" allows you to deduct these expenses less 68 percent of the amount by which your child's income for the

year exceeds $6,456. You should compare the tax payable if your child claims the credit compared to the tax payable if you use the notch provision to determine which is to your advantage.

TIP: You might be surprised at the types of medical expenses Revenue Canada will allow. Don't overlook such expenses as wheelchairs, crutches and even a whirlpool bath, provided they were prescribed by a medical practitioner. In most cases, if a doctor is willing to prescribe it, you will be able to deduct it.

9. Pension income tax credit

Certain types of pension income qualify for the pension income credit up to the maximum of $1,000. If you are over age sixty-five, the following types of pension income entitle you to claim this tax credit:

- annuity income from superannuation, pension plans, RRSPs, DPSPs;
- payments from a RRIF;
- income from a life or term-certain annuity purchased with non-registered funds;
- income from an income-averaging annuity contract. These contracts can no longer be purchased, but many people still receive income under existing contracts;
- payments from other specified plans, including the taxable portion of foreign pension plans such as U.S. social security.

If you are under age sixty-five, the following income qualifies for the pension credit:

- annuity payments from superannuation or pension plans;
- income arising from the death of your spouse, including a common-law spouse. This includes annuity income from an RRSP, DPSP, or annuity; RRIF payments, and income from other specified plans, including the taxable portion of foreign government pension plans such as U.S. social security.

TIP: Both spouses can claim the pension income tax credit. You should therefore arrange your affairs so that both of you have at least $1,000 of pension income when you retire. If your spouse won't be receiving sufficient pension income to claim the credit, you should build at least $10,000 of RRSPs in your spouse's name through spousal RRSP contributions. Alternatively, you could claim the pension income tax credit by buying a "prescribed" annuity that will produce $1,000 of income. These annuities are similar to a GIC, but can only be purchased from a life insurance company.

10. Goods and services tax (GST) credits

This credit must be applied for, and you can now do this directly on your income tax return. Rather than reducing your income tax payable, the government mails cheques to those eligible applicants twice a year. In 1993, the maximum amount paid for adults is $199 annually, plus an additional $105 a year for each child in the family. This amount is reduced by 5 percent of the family income in excess of $25,921. This means that if you have two dependent children, the credit is wiped out if your family income exceeds $38,081; if you're single the credit will be gone if your income is $29,901.

TIP: Children at least eighteen years old become eligible for the $199 in their own right, as long as their incomes are sufficiently low. In fact, it's probable that they will be more eligible to claim the credit than you. They must file an income tax return to apply for this credit even if they do not have taxable income.

11. Foreign tax credits

Income earned outside Canada must be included when calculating your taxes. However, taxes might have already been withheld in the foreign jurisdiction, or you might be required to file a foreign return and pay tax on the income received. Our tax system allows you a tax credit based on the foreign tax paid or for the Canadian tax levied on the foreign income, whichever is less.

TIP: When claiming foreign tax credits, ensure that you have converted the amount paid to Canadian dollars (which you should also do for the foreign income you declare). You are allowed to use the exchange rate in effect at the time of the transaction or the average exchange rate for the year, which can be obtained by calling your local Bank of Canada office or Revenue Canada.

12. Provincial tax credits

Various provinces allow tax credits to seniors and persons with income below certain limits to offset provincial sales and realty taxes or for other social reasons.

TIP: These credits vary from province to province and you should ensure that you carefully review the available deductions listed in the general income tax guide. Usually this guide is mailed to you each year by Revenue Canada; however, it can also be obtained at your local post office or by calling your local Revenue Canada office.

13. Tuition fees and education deduction

You can claim a credit for tuition fees if the institution, such as a university or college, has a certificate issued by a provincial ministry of education. You must have paid tuition fees of at least $100 to each institution in order to claim these fees as a tax credit. The tuition fee credit is equal to 17 percent of qualifying fees for courses taken during the year.

In addition, students in full-time enrollment can claim $60 (times 17 percent) for each month of attendance at a designated educational institute, or of enrollment in a qualifying program (one that runs for at least three consecutive weeks and requires at least ten hours per week on courses or work in the program).

TIP: Tuition fees and education tax credits can be transferred to a spouse, parent or grandparent, if the student is dependent on that person and cannot use the credits personally. A maximum of $680 of credits can be transferred.

14. Transferring deductions and credits to a spouse

The unused portion of certain tax credits can be transferred from one spouse to the other. The credits you can transfer include the following: age credit (persons sixty-five and over); pension income credit; disability credit; and tuition fee and education credits (to a maximum of $680).

TIP: To determine the amount of transferable credits, your spouse must calculate his or her own taxes payable, and then deduct the basic personal, CPP/QPP and UI credits; if any tax remains payable after those basic credits, then your spouse's transferable credits must be used to eliminate that tax before the balance can be transferred to you.

The value of a tax deferral

Tax deferral is an important income tax concept. Any time you can find a legal way to delay payment of tax you owe, you gain in two ways. First, you can take the money and invest it instead of paying it to the government. Your funds could double or triple in value before you have to pay tax. Second, if you're lucky, when you finally have to pay that tax, your income tax rate will be lower. Usually we try to defer taxes until we're retired and we're earning less income. Deferring taxes allows you to keep your money working for longer. Finally, inflation makes a dollar paid tomorrow worth less than a dollar paid today.

Imagine transferring $10,000 of a severance payment from a company into your RRSP. You won't be taxed on it until it's removed from the RRSP years down the road — probably after you've retired and are subject to a lower tax rate. In the meantime, that $10,000 earns investment income year after year, which compounds on a tax-free basis. If you chose not to roll these funds over to your RRSP, the $10,000 would grow to $25,500 over a twenty-year period if you earned 8 percent a year and have a marginal tax rate of 40 percent. Inside an RRSP, however, you would accumulate $50,300 by the end of the same period — doubling your money.

Revenue Canada has tried to curtail these opportunities, but here are a few still possible:

15. Maximize your RRSP contributions

RRSP contributions do provide an immediate deduction, but are really a tax deferral vehicle because the funds are eventually taxed when you withdraw them — as you must do one day. They are one of the most important tax deductions available. Make every effort to maximize your contributions annually.

TIP: It's easier to contribute smaller amounts on a monthly basis to an RRSP than try to come up with a large payment at the end of the year. Besides, to take advantage of the magic of compounding, the earlier in the year you contribute to your RRSP, the more money you'll earn. Most mutual fund companies and financial institutions will allow you to set up automatic monthly payments to an RRSP.

To help free up the cash to accommodate these payments, you can apply to Revenue Canada for a reduction of the tax withheld by your employer. To obtain the necessary application form, call your local Revenue Canada office and ask to speak to the Source Deduction Department. The application involves completing an estimate of your income and deductions for the year. These numbers are estimates and there will not be a penalty if you're wrong, as long as your estimates are made in good faith. If you radically overestimate deductions or underestimate income, Revenue Canada might very well deny any subsequent application for reduced withholdings.

TIP: Don't neglect to make a final RRSP contribution in the year following retirement; remember, your contributions are based on the previous year's earned income. Also, you might be able to make additional contributions if you exercise stock options, work part-time or start a business after retirement.

16. Choosing a business year-end

If you are starting a new business, you have the opportunity to defer taxes through the selection of a year-end that does not have to coincide with the calendar year-end. You can elect any date within the first twelve-month period you operate the business. This date becomes your fiscal year-end. You pay tax on the income earned by the business in the calendar year in which the company fiscal year-end falls. For example, you can begin a business in February 1993 and declare January 31 to be your fiscal year-end. The income earned from February 1993 through January 31, 1994, will not be taxable until 1994. Once a year-end is adopted, it cannot be changed without the approval of the Minister of National Revenue.

TIP: Consider carefully when establishing a year-end. For example, businesses often incur losses in the initial months of operation. In that case, it might help to realize those losses against current year income by choosing a December 31 year-end. On the other hand, if the new business is profitable right away, choosing a January year-end will maximize deferral of taxes. Consult your financial adviser or accountant and don't forget to deduct their fees against your business income!

17. Registered pension plans

Like RRSPs, you get a deduction for contributions to registered pension plans. Again, because the funds received out of the pension fund will eventually be taxable, these plans are a form of tax deferral.

TIP: Some pension plans allow you to make additional voluntary contributions, which will provide you with a larger pension at retirement. There can also be the opportunity to buy back past service for periods when you worked part-time, or years before you joined the plan. Explore these opportunities with your employer .

18. Rollover of retirement allowance

Payments for long-term service with a company or severance payments are taxable income. However, these payments can be considered retiring allowances, and, as such, you can transfer up to $2,000 for each year or partial year of service to your RRSP. You can transfer an additional $1,500 for each year or partial year of service up to the end of 1988 if you have not benefited from a vested interest in a pension or deferred profit-sharing plan for those years.

TIP: You should have your company transfer these funds directly to your RRSP to avoid having income tax withheld. Contact either your employer or your RRSP trustee to obtain Revenue Canada's TD2 transfer form.

TIP: Even if you think you might need to use some of these funds to cover living expenses if you can't get another job, you should roll over the maximum retiring allowance directly to your RRSP. Simply invest the money inside your RRSP in a liquid vehicle such as a money market fund. That way you can withdraw any funds when you need them. Furthermore, tax withheld on RRSP withdrawals under $5,000 is only 10 percent; chances are your employer would have to withhold substantially more tax if they paid you directly.

19. Life insurance policies as tax shelters

In simple terms, these policies combine insurance with accumulation of interest. Your annual premiums are in excess of those required to pay for the desired insurance coverage (in accordance with a government-approved formula). The excess premiums (cash reserve) are invested and earn income. Like RRSPs, the earnings on the accumulated money compound on a tax-deferred basis until the policy is cashed in. This feature can make saving through insurance policies profitable. These policies are most commonly called universal life insurance policies.

If the policy owner dies, the proceeds are paid free of tax and the income-tax deferral becomes a permanent tax saving. Or, the accumulated cash value can be used to fund the insurance, which means that the premiums are paid out of untaxed income. The policy owner can also elect to draw on these cash reserves to help fund retirement, in which case the interest element is taxed upon withdrawal.

TIP: Don't consider one of these policies unless you have a definite need for insurance. When examining these policies, check the yield on the illustration provided by the agent to ensure that it is reasonable in today's investment environment. Ask the agent to provide you with past returns on similar policies. Make sure that the life insurance cost and administrative costs are fixed and cannot be raised in future. Is there a minimum guaranteed rate of return? Is it reasonable? Evaluate the policy to ensure that the costs do not outweigh the benefits and that the rate of return is competitive with other investments. These policies should only be considered as long-range investments because policy charges in the initial years and early cancellation penalties make them unprofitable as short-term investments.

20. Registered retirement income fund

For maximum tax deferral, you could convert your RRSP to a RRIF by December 31 of the year you turn seventy-one. A RRIF works in the same way as an RRSP, except that instead of making a maximum contribution every year you must make a minimum withdrawal. The withdrawals are taxed but the remaining income in the plan continues to compound tax-free.

TIP: The minimum payments are based on your age. However, you can elect to base the payments on the age of your spouse. If your spouse is younger, this election will maximize your tax deferral.

21. Prescribed annuity

In a prescribed annuity, money is given to an insurance company in return for a commitment to pay interest and return the capital in equal installments over a number of months or years. The beauty is that for tax purposes the interest return is considered to be spread evenly over the lifetime of the annuity, even though more interest is paid in the early years than in later ones.

TIP: The Canadian life insurance industry has established CompCorp, a consumer protection plan that provides some guarantees against the insolvency of member companies. Through CompCorp, annuities are insured to a maximum of $2,000 a month. When considering these investments, make sure that you use only member companies, and more than one insurer if necessary to fall within the insured limits.

TIP: Because of this tax treatment, a high after-tax return is generated. However, many people are reluctant to use these vehicles because they want to keep their capital intact for their estates. To meet this need, insured annuities are available for those in good health. These policies involve the purchase of life insurance for the capital amount used to purchase the annuity. Depending on your age and whether you smoke, after-tax returns will still be higher than those offered by GICs. Ensure that the insurance premiums are guaranteed and don't negate the higher income generated.

TIP: If you are sixty-five or older, you can take advantage of the $1,000 pension income tax credit by purchasing a prescribed annuity.

22. Registered education savings plan

Contributions of up to $1,500 a year for a child of any age can be set aside, up to a total contribution of $31,500, to provide funds for post-secondary education. You do not enjoy a tax deduction by opening an RESP, but the funds grow tax-sheltered for as long as they are in the plan. Although the funds will be taxed when they are withdrawn, there's a good chance that little or no tax will be paid, because the law allows the income to be taxed in the student's rather than the donor's hands. Thus, an RESP combines the principals of tax deferral with income-splitting — tax is deferred until the money is withdrawn, when it will be taxed in the hands of a lower-income family member.

If you invest $1,500 a year for eighteen years at 10 percent, an RESP fund will be worth about $75,000 at the end of the period. Only $48,000 of this is accumulated interest and, therefore, tax will be paid only as that amount is withdrawn, bit by bit, over the years the student is in school. Not only is the income taxed in the student's hands, he or she will have tuition deductions and tax credits to offset the RESP income.

The main drawback to this plan is that if your child does not attend a qualified post-secondary institution, the income is forfeited to a post-secondary institution designated by you at set-up time. The capital, however, can be withdrawn by you tax-free at any time. A broad range of post-secondary institutions qualify, including community colleges and technical schools. The other drawback is that these plans last a maximum of twenty-five years. So for a plan begun at birth, the beneficiary must use the funds before turning twenty-five. Contributions can't be made after the end of the twenty-first year following the year of set-up, but the plan can continue to exist for four more years.

TIP: If you have more than one child, you can set up one plan naming all of your children as beneficiaries. In this way, if only one child goes on to post-secondary education, all of the income can be withdrawn. As contributor, you control the payout of the funds, which can include funds to cover living expenses while attending school.

You can also set up a plan for your grandchildren, or anyone else you wish to assist. There isn't any age restrictions on beneficiaries. More than one plan can be set up for a beneficiary, provided that total contributions don't exceed $1,500 per year per beneficiary.

TIP: Some group plans, such as Canadian Scholarship Trust Plan, pool all contributors' earnings to provide assistance to all beneficiaries of the plan. These plans might not fund the first year of post-secondary school, and can prevent a student from taking a year off before attending. As well, there can be restrictions on changing the beneficiary after a certain age (sometimes as low as age thirteen). The amount of assistance each student receives depends not only on the investment performance experienced, but also on the number of students who attend in any given year.

Individual plans offered through financial institutions and mutual fund companies allow you to control the investment of the funds, and the beneficiaries, as well as the payout of the funds.

Income splitting

It makes sense to redirect income to family members in lower tax brackets. In this way, significant tax savings can be achieved for the entire family. Of course, it might not be practical to include children who have left home, but one spouse often earns more income than the other. The tax spread between a low-income earner and a high-income earner can be as much as 25 percent.

The goal then is to create equal taxable incomes for both. This should be the objective both before and after retirement.

The value is evident in the following example. If Mr. Albert has $40,000 of taxable income, he'll pay approximately $9,400 of tax. If Mr. Albert has $20,000 and Mrs. Albert has $20,000, they will each pay approximately $3,700 of tax, a total of $7,400. This represents a family tax saving of $2,000. (In Quebec, the saving would be about $2,700.)

To split income, you can't merely direct a portion of your salary to your spouse. Nor will you achieve the tax savings you're looking for if you simply give the money as a gift. The government has enacted a complex set of rules called the "income attribution rules," which attributes income to the person who earned it. But there are still some legitimate ways to transfer income to one's spouse and children.

23. Spousal RRSP contributions

If your spouse will have income in retirement that will be much lower than yours, you should make contributions to your spouse's RRSP instead of to your own. To make a spousal contribution, you must open an RRSP account in your spouse's name, and indicate that you are the contributor. You still claim the RRSP tax deduction, but it's your spouse who builds the RRSP funds for retirement.

The benefit comes in the future when the tax on your total family retirement income will be reduced because those spousal RRSP funds will be taxed in the hands of your lower-income spouse. If you need the funds before you retire, they can be removed from the spousal plan and will be taxed at your spouse's lower marginal tax rate, if contributions have not been made to the spousal plan in the three calendar years prior to withdrawal. If a contribution has been made within that time period, the withdrawal will be taxed in the hands of the contributor.

The tax savings from spousal RRSPs can be significant. Suppose one spouse works and will be entitled to a company pension plan of $40,000 at retirement. Currently, this would mean a marginal tax rate of about 40 percent. If this person received RRSP income on top of the company pension, each dollar would be taxed at a minimum of 40 percent. On the other hand, if the RRSP contributions had been made to the non-working spouse's plan, and he or she had no other income, up to $11,000 could be received tax-free by that spouse because of the personal tax credit, age credit and pension income credit.

TIP: If your spouse is able to make personal RRSP contributions based on his or her own earned income, these contributions should be made to a separate RRSP. By keeping spousal and personal plans separate, your spouse will be able to withdraw funds from his or her personal RRSP without running afoul of the attribution rules. Otherwise, if contributions are mingled, any withdrawals made within three years of the last spousal contribution will be attributed back to the spousal contributor.

TIP: On death, the representative of the estate can make one final RRSP contribution to the surviving spouse's RRSP. This final contribution must be made within sixty days following the year of death. This provision should not be overlooked as taxation at death can be quite onerous.

24. Pension income transfer to a spousal RRSP

In 1993 and 1994, a special provision allows you to transfer up to $6,000 of registered pension plan payments or periodic deferred profit-sharing plan income to a spousal RRSP. These transfers are tax-deductible and are another opportunity to transfer money to a lower income spouse.

If both spouses have eligible income, they can roll this amount over to each other to obtain a current tax deduction and to optimize tax deferral.

TIP: If you are rolling pension income into your spouse's RRSP, be sure to retain $1,000 of pension income for yourself so that you can claim the pension income credit.

25. Lending money to your spouse

Before 1985, the acceptable method of transferring investment income between spouses involved one spouse lending funds interest-free to the lower-income spouse, who could then deposit the funds in a bank or invest them. The tax on the investment income would then be calculated in the hands of the lower-income spouse at the lower marginal tax rate. Now, however, income earned on all interest-free or low-interest loans to spouses will attribute back to the spouse who supplied the money and will be taxed at the higher rate. We mention this change because many families act as if it never happened and might be unpleasantly surprised someday.

Although you cannot reduce your tax burden by giving your spouse an interest-free or low-interest loan, you can lend money at a fair rate of interest. This rate can be no less than the prescribed rate or the going commercial rate. The prescribed rate is the rate set each quarter by the federal government. Currently, the prescribed rate is about 8 percent, and you can obtain the current quarterly rate at any time by phoning your local Revenue Canada office.

Provided your spouse pays the interest to you at least once a year and within thirty days of the end of the year (by January 30), attribution will not apply to income earned on the loan proceeds. However, you will have to declare the interest paid by your spouse as income. Because your spouse has invested the loan proceeds to earn income, the interest will be tax-deductible to your spouse.

TIP: You can lend money to your spouse to start or expand a business. Income from an active business does not attribute back to the financing spouse. Therefore, these loans can be made without charging interest.

TIP: You will also run afoul of the attribution rules if you sign as a guarantor on a bank loan to your spouse.

TIP: In certain cases it can still be worthwhile to give or lend money interest-free to a lower-income spouse. Because of the income attribution rules, the income earned on the original amount loaned or given will be taxed in the hands of the higher-income spouse. However, the "second generation" income — income on the income earned — will start building in the hands of the lower-income spouse. This makes sense if one spouse has a large amount of investment capital and the other spouse has none, as long as there is a fairly long horizon before the funds are needed so that the second-generation income can be left alone to grow.

26. Who spends and who invests

One of the easiest steps to create wealth in the hands of the lower-income spouse is to allow that spouse to invest as much of his or her earnings as possible, while the higher-income spouse pays the bills. It can take longer to build a pool of investments in the hands of the spouse in the lower tax bracket but it is still worthwhile.

This strategy often meets with some initial resistance because the lower-income spouse might feel that their money provides them with financial independence — they might not be inclined to tie it up in investments. To overcome this problem, the higher-income spouse can give the lower-income spouse a cheque each month for the same amount that is being allocated to savings. This will leave the low-income spouse in the same cash position and still move money into the hands of the spouse with the lower rate of tax.

The Income Tax Act stipulates that investment income be attributed to the spouse who earned the funds that were used to purchase the asset. For this reason, a separate bank account should be set up for all of the low-income spouse's earnings. Only in this way will a clear trail of income to investment be apparent to Revenue Canada. At no time should the funds be intermingled in a joint bank account or Revenue Canada will then be able to challenge the source of the funds.

If we look at an example of one spouse at the top tax bracket, and the other spouse in the lowest tax bracket, we can see just how effective this strategy can be. At the top tax rate, the high-income earner is only able to keep about $5,000 out of $10,000 of t income; the low-income earner would be able to retain $7,300. You might not be generating $10,000 of investment income today, but if you follow this strategy, you will get there much sooner.

27. Swapping assets

We often encounter situations where the high-income earner has accumulated a significant amount of income-producing investments, while the lower-income spouse has non-income-producing assets, such as a share of the family home. To take advantage of the lower-income spouse's tax rate, you might be able to sell the non-income-producing asset to the high-income earner. For example, if you can

reasonably demonstrate that your husband or wife helped pay for half the family residence, then you could buy his or her share, using up your investment capital and building your spouse's.

Get professional advice before doing this because certain procedures and documentation must be followed on the transfer of property to ensure that you get the desired tax treatment.

The common question that arises when explaining this strategy is what would happen to the wife's rights to the family home if her marriage breaks down. In most provinces, the title of the matrimonial home is not relevant upon a marriage breakdown. When exploring this technique, you should also ask your financial adviser to explain the marital property rights in your province. We recommend that you proceed with this strategy only when both spouses are completely comfortable with the transfer of property.

28. Inheritances

If the lower-income spouse receives an inheritance, take care to segregate it so that any investment income earned will be taxable to that person.

TIP: In some cases, it might be desirable to use the inheritance to pay down a mortgage or other debts that are in the name of the higher-income-earning spouse. In that case, the inheritor should formally lend the funds to the other spouse via a promissory note. The attribution rules won't apply because the funds will not be producing income; therefore, there is no need to charge interest. This strategy will allow the higher-income earner to pay back his or her spouse once money is available for investment. These funds can then be invested in the lower-income earner's hands.

29. Hiring your spouse

If one spouse carries on a business, either personally or through a corporation, the other spouse could be hired to provide services to the business. The services must be necessary to the business and the salary must be "reasonable" in view of the services performed. Such services can include bookkeeping, secretarial work, and acting as a director of the corporation. You can also hire your children in the same manner, although children must be over age eighteen to act as a director.

It is generally acceptable to pay a little more than the going rate for these services as it is probable that family members are being groomed for greater responsibility, and have a position of greater trust than that accorded to a regular employee.

30. Compound income

The Income Tax Act provides that attribution will not apply to reinvested income. This makes possible a two-step strategy: First, you lend or give your spouse investment capital. The income is earned by your spouse but is attributed back to you; you pay the tax but the income belongs to your spouse. The next year, the income on the income will be taxed in your spouse's hands. Over the years, your capital is frozen while your spouse's investments grow. The tax burden has shifted to the lower-taxed spouse.

To illustrate, let's assume that Mr. Martin has $50,000 of investment capital which he gives to his wife. Mrs. Martin invests the funds at 10 percent. The funds earn $5,000 in year one, which is taxable to Mr. Martin. Mrs. Martin invests the $55,000 at 10 percent in the second year. In year two, Mr. Martin pays tax on $5,000 (the amount earned on the original $50,000 gift). Mrs. Martin pays tax on the $500 generated on the $5,000 of compounded income. At the end of twenty years, the original $5,000 of reinvested income will be worth over $33,000.

TIP: Sloppy record-keeping could make it difficult to demonstrate to Revenue Canada

how much compound income is taxable to each spouse. We suggest that you segregate the original investment earnings (the $5,000 in the example above). Interest earned on it will be the amount to be taxed in the low-income spouse's hands.

31. Avoiding the OAS claw-back

High-income earners who receive Old Age Security pension might be subject to the claw-back I discussed in chapter six. The claw-back applies to those pensioners whose income exceeds $53,215 in 1993. For each dollar earned over this threshold, fifteen cents of the pension must be repaid. If you have a net income of approximately $84,000, the total benefit will have to be repaid.

TIP: Use the income-splitting techniques I talked about above to minimize the claw-back.

32. Lending money to your children

When lending money to children, you must beware of the income-attribution rules. If you lend money to your children (regardless of their age), and it is used to generate interest, dividends or other types of investment income (excluding capital gains), the income is taxed back to you unless the loan is made at a "fair market" rate. Note that these attribution rules extend to loans made at below-market rates to "non-arm's-length persons" where one of the main reasons for the loan was to split income. Non-arm's-length persons include:

- children or other descendants, such as grandchildren, nieces and nephews;
- brothers or sisters;
- spouses, including common-law spouses;
- the spouses of your brothers, sisters or descendants mentioned above;
- adopted children, including those adopted by your children or other descendants.

An exception to these rules, and a good planning opportunity, involves capital gains that arise from money lent to children. These capital gains are taxed in the child's hands, regardless of the child's age. You are free to lend money to a child or other relative without charging interest where income is not being generated, such as the purchase of a home.

TIP: You can lend money to a child to start or expand a business without attribution following the same logic that applies to lending money to your spouse to start or expand a business.

TIP: The attribution rules do not apply to loans to a corporation. A corporation can be set up whereby all shares are owned by children over age eighteen. The parents could then lend the corporation money interest-free. If the funds are invested in dividend-paying stock of a taxable Canadian corporation, the dividends would be received tax-free. The corporation could then pay the dividends to the shareholders who could use the funds for education or other personal needs. A taxpayer, provided he or she has no other income, can receive approximately $22,000 of dividends tax-free thanks to the dividend tax credit.

33. Gifts to children

There isn't any attribution on gifts made to children who are over eighteen. However, when money is given to a child under the age of eighteen, any investment income generated (other than capital gains) is taxable to you. For example, if you give your ten-year-old daughter $5,000 to invest in GICs, tax on the interest earned will have to be paid by you. If the same $5,000 gift is invested in stocks, and the investment is sold for $10,000 in five years, the capital gains will not be considered to be yours by Revenue Canada, and will instead be taxed to your daughter. Attribution will cease in the year the child turns eighteen.

It is important to note that such attribution will apply if money or income-producing property such as stocks, bonds or GICs are gifted to a minor child by a non-arm's-length person.

Before making gifts to children and other relatives, you must carefully consider your intentions. Once you have made the gift, those funds belong to that person and can be used by them for any purpose. With minor children, you would be able to maintain control over the funds by investing them in trust; however, control would revert to them once they turn eighteen. You cannot attach any strings that exert control over the use or return of the money, or Revenue Canada will deem the transaction a loan.

Of course, if you are contemplating gifts of a significant amount, you might consider setting up a formal trust. The attribution rules will still apply until age eighteen, but you might control the use of the funds by including terms in the trust document. However, you cannot set up the trust so that the funds would revert back to you at any time, or the attribution rules will apply for the duration of the trust.

TIP: Attribution does not apply to non-residents. Therefore, if a grandparent is a non-resident of Canada for income tax purposes, he or she can give money to a minor grandchild without having the attribution apply.

34. Splitting CPP

You can split Canada Pension Plan retirement benefits between spouses. Both spouses' CPP entitlements are pooled and divided according to the period of time the couple were living together. You must apply to have your benefits split. This can only be done after both spouses reach age sixty and only if both have applied for CPP. QPP does not allow splitting retirement benefits.

35. Investing child tax benefit payments

You should make sure that child tax benefit

payments are invested in the names of your children. These funds are not subject to the attribution rules provided they are invested "in trust" for the child.

36. Generating tax-preferred income on your investments

Beyond the three basic principles of tax saving — deduct, defer and divide — you should consider carefully how your investments will be taxed before making an investment. It's the after-tax return that measures an investment's worth. Of course, some forms of income are exempt from tax. These include:

■ your home. You will not pay tax on the increase in price of your principal residence whether it is a house, town house, condominium, ski chalet, cottage or mobile home. Only one principal residence exemption is allowed for a family (you, your spouse and any unmarried children under eighteen).

If you own a second property, perhaps a vacation home, you can use the exemption on only one. If you decide to sell one of these properties, you will have to decide whether to use the personal residence exemption or to save it for another you own and can sell later.

Before deciding, you must examine the potential capital gains you might realize on the other property. If you feel you will have a bigger gain on the property you are keeping, it might be wise to save your principal residence exemption for that property. The date of purchase of the property and the availability of your lifetime capital gains exemption will also affect your decision. See the discussion on real estate below for an explanation.

TIP: If a member of your family unit has owned a second property since before 1982, a partial exemption might still be available.

Before 1982, each family member could own a property and enjoy the principal residence exemption. Gains accrued on these properties up until January 1, 1982, are exempt from tax. If these properties are held in joint ownership, you might be able to rearrange ownership to benefit from the double principal residence exemption. If this applies to you, it is worth consulting a financial planner or accountant to ensure that you can take advantage of this exemption, and to determine the amount of the gain exempt from tax.

■ gifts and inheritances. Gifts that you receive are free of tax, although the person making the gift might have a taxable gain to explain to Revenue Canada. But that's not your concern. Even if you receive an inheritance, the estate of the deceased might face tax consequences but you'll receive the bequest without having to pay any tax.

■ lottery winnings and prizes of chance. Unless you're actually in the business of pursuing such winnings, you will receive prizes free of tax. The problem starts afterward, when you begin to earn taxable income with your newly acquired wealth. A nice problem to have though.

■ insurance proceeds. The benefits from life insurance or disability insurance, on which you paid the premiums, are free of income tax. So are the insurance proceeds from damage claims or the loss of pproperty.

Your key to freedom in retirement is building sufficient investment capital to provide the income you need to live the life you choose. Managing investments thus becomes extremely important, both before and after retirement. To create an effective investment strategy you have to understand how various types of investment income taxed.

Interest income from all sources — foreign dividends, rental income and withdrawals from

RRSPs — is taxed in the ordinary way, just like salaries and wages. The amount you receive for the year is included as income in your tax return. With compounding investments, such as a five-year GIC or compounding Canada Savings Bond, you are required to include each year's interest income in your tax return, even if you haven't received it. Some income might even be reinvested abroad or remain beyond your control but it must still be reported annually for tax purposes. The exception to this is for investments made before 1990. For these investments, there are three ways to report interest which compounds over a number of years:

- the cash method. You report the income as you receive it, or at least every third complete year after you make the investment.

- the receivable method. You report interest in the year you are entitled to receive it. For example, you would report the interest on a matured bond coupon in the year you actually receive it versus the year it matures. You must also report interest at least every three years.

- annual accrual method. You report the interest yearly as you earn it, regardless of when you are entitled to receive it or when it is actually paid.

In choosing your reporting method for investments made before 1990, you should look at your marginal tax rate and consider whether deferring taxation of income will result in being taxed at a higher rate. For example, you might be in the lowest tax bracket now, but in three years, with salary increases, you might be paying considerably more tax. In that case, it might be best to use the annual accrual method.

Although it is complicated, the tax treatment of dividends from Canadian taxable corporations works to the taxpayer's advantage. Briefly, 125 percent of the cash amount of dividends received must be included in taxable income. This extra 25 percent is later allowed as a full tax credit. For example, a $100 dividend would be included in your taxable income as $125. If your personal tax rate was 40 percent, the tax would be $50. A credit of about $25 would then be allowed against the $50 of tax, leaving only $25 of net tax payable on the $100 of dividend. Compare this to $40 of tax on $100 of interest income. Canadian dividends yield a higher after-tax return than an equivalent payment of interest income.

Capital gains represent the difference between the selling price of investments and their original cost. They receive preferential treatment because they represent the rewards paid for risking money in enterprises that usually stimulate the economy. The first benefit is that only 75 percent of the gain is taxable.

Next, there is a lifetime capital gains exemption of $100,000 on certain types of capital gains. In other words, $100,000 of capital gains can be earned tax-free over your lifetime. However, there are a number of items which can preclude you from claiming this exemption. Let's take a good look at them.

First, your cumulative net investment loss account (CNIL) can block you from claiming the exemption. CNIL is the cumulative amount that investment expenses you have incurred since 1988 exceed investment income during the same period. Any balance in this account can temporarily block the capital gains exemption normally available. Capital gains equal to your CNIL will be taxed at your marginal rate. For example, if you have $3,000 of CNIL, perhaps from interest expenses, and make a capital gain of $4,000 of which $3,000 is taxable (75 percent of $4,000), the capital gains exemption will be offset by the CNIL balance and you will have to pay tax on the $3,000 as if it were income. However, once an amount of CNIL has blocked you from using your capital gains exemption, that amount will not block you again. You will be able to use your capital gains exemption on future gains — unless your CNIL balance grows again.

The capital gains exemption makes investments such as stocks, bonds, businesses and real estate more attractive, but you must never forget that your CNIL might force you to pay taxes on your gains. If you have borrowed to invest in the stock market, you should consider reducing your loans to avoid restrictions on your ability to use your capital gains exemption.

One word about real estate: Until the February 1992 budget, capital gains realized on real estate could be offset by the capital gains exemption. The new rules provide that capital gains on real estate purchased after February 1992, other than qualified farm property, could not be sheltered by the capital gains exemptions. Real estate acquired before March 1992 but sold after that date, will be eligible for a partial exemption. The exemption will be prorated by the months held after February 1992 over the months the property was held in total since acquisition.

TIP: Under the prorated formula, the longer the partially qualified property is held, the greater the erosion of the gain eligible for the capital gains exemption. However, if the property continues to escalate in value, or if the profit is large enough, this might not be the case. Each affected property should be examined for future potential growth, expected holding period and the gain realized to date.

If it appears that the ability to use the capital gains exemption will be eroded over time, it might be prudent to sell the property now or to otherwise crystallize the available exemption. This also makes sense in view of the fact that future budgets might further erode, or even eliminate, the ability to use the capital gains exemption. To trigger the exemption, you can sell the property on the market, give it or sell it to your spouse or children, or transfer the property to a holding company. Consult a financial adviser.

Every taxpayer is required to maintain a record of cumulative capital gains and losses and to file it with the tax authorities on a schedule provided with your annual tax return. Individuals are also required to file income tax returns for each taxation year in which there is a capital gain or loss, regardless of other sources of income, even if tax is not owing. CNIL balances must also be updated every year, and Revenue Canada now confirms this amount on your notice of assessment.

Losses sustained in investing capital property can be deducted to the extent of 75 percent, but only against taxable capital gains. Capital losses first reduce any taxable capital gains. If you have no capital gains in a year you sustain a loss, you should still ensure that the loss is recorded on your tax return.

These losses can be carried back three years to apply against previously reported capital gains. Generally, it is best to carry back capital losses only if you were unable to offset capital gains with the capital gains exemption in the past three years. Otherwise, capital losses can be carried forward indefinitely and applied against future taxable gains.

Capital losses suffered by investing in the shares or debt of Canadian-controlled private corporations are called allowable business investment losses (ABILs). You can deduct 75 percent of the ABIL in calculating your taxable income for the year — this means that an ABIL can reduce taxable employment or investment income. Contrast this with the fact that capital losses on public company securities (those traded on stock exchanges), and other capital property are 75-percent deductible only against capital gains.

The ability to claim a capital gains exemption, and past claims of capital gains exemptions, are affected by ABILs. This is a very complex area, and professional tax advice should be obtained.

The lifetime capital gains exemption is $500,000 on gains arising from the sale of small business corporation shares or an active family farm. There are also rollover provisions available on qualified farm property which allow the transfer of property on death to a spouse or child with no tax consequences. These provisions ensure that families are not forced to sell their farms or businesses in order to pay the income tax liability which arises upon death.

If you have a valuable business or farm you should seek professional advice on how to structure ownership and your estate.

TIP: Because income earned inside an RRSP is sheltered from tax, no tax preferential treatment is available. In other words, if you hold dividend-bearing investments inside your RRSP, you do not benefit from the dividend tax credit. Therefore, when structuring your investments, it is better to hold interest-producing investments inside your RRSP, and tax preferred investments outside your RRSP.

37. Tax shelters

Several investment opportunities have been created in the past by tax incentives designed to encourage investors to put money into unpopular or speculative investments. In fact, investors have been encouraged to invest where nobody of sound mind would invest if it were not for the tax advantages.

Until recently, wealthy taxpayers were clamouring for such opportunities, anything for a tax reduction. Why else would they invest in apartments and town houses where there are rent controls; oil and gas exploration or gold mines when there is little hope of finding anything; or, Canadian-made films? The most head-shaking investments are those in research and development where there isn't proven

product, market, or any certainty of profit — just flimsy promises.

Don't get me wrong. There's nothing wrong with a tax-sheltered investment. If it works. I'm always happy to buy something at discount and sell it for profit. And the tax saving generated by a tax shelter is supposed to reduce your cost to a very reasonable price. Then you can earn a high income from your investment or sell it for a profit. Sounds good, but does it work? In my experience, each year there are about three or four deals that work — out of more than 200 that we examine.

Tax-sheltered investments generally don't work for investors because they're grossly overpriced and ineptly managed. I don't fault good honest attempts. After all, most private businesses fail in their first few years. What I dislike is the extraordinarily high costs of these transactions, overpriced by greedy promoters. Like a top-heavy ship, they're destined to sink.

In most real estate limited partnerships, the land is transferred to the partnership at too high a price. The development costs are too high. The price the partnership paid for the property is at a peak. Management fees are too high. The promotional costs associated with issuing the units of the tax shelter are a bribe to all parties involved. Sales commissions are unfair. The printers and professionals charge too much for the offering document that you're given to review. All these factors conspire to overprice a business; it cannot pay it back unless everything goes incredibly well.

Investors and their advisers often have trouble seeing how unrealistic the propositions are because the forecasts are well organized and seem to make sense. Packaging and presentation are top quality, and of course you want to believe the market is going up and you're going with it.

Should you invest in a tax-advantaged investment? Yes, but only if:

- you are in the top tax bracket and would get a good income tax discount on your purchase;

- you have known some of the investment managers personally and for some time;

- you or your adviser understand the venture thoroughly;

- you have indisputable evidence that the deal makers have proven expertise and sufficient incentive to make it work;

- you allow sufficient time and cost to check everything out;

- you make certain you cannot be held liable for anything more than the risk you knowingly undertake; and

- you consider the tax shelter to be a good investment, even if it does not have the tax breaks associated with it.

This sounds like a time-consuming and expensive checklist, and it is. But it can ensure that you don't lose money. It can also help you find reasonable, tax-enhanced business ventures.

Most tax shelters work the same way. You invest by putting up a small portion of the cash needed and borrowing the rest; you obtain sizable tax deductions in the first few years. You hope to receive enough income to offset your after-tax borrowing cost. You sell some years later for a sizable capital gain.

The projected numbers will probably indicate a very good return on investment. They have to because you are counting on this return to cover the cost of your loan. But the margin of error is very small and the leverage you've used to get into the deal can turn against you, multiplying your losses.

With this dire warning in mind, now might be a good time to investigate solid investment proposals. Prices are down, interest rates low, expectations have been shaken, and quality business people are available to make an honest effort. Every investment entails risk but if you're tempted, the time seems to be right.

TIP: Seek professional, unbiased advice before making these kinds of investments. Don't forget that there is a real relationship between risk and reward. Investments which offer high tax deductions and thereby high after-tax returns have a correspondingly high risk factor. These investments are not suitable for all investors.

38. Special tax measures for Quebec residents

Unlike other provinces and territories in Canada, Quebec requires taxpayers to complete a second tax return, separate and distinct from the federal return completed by all Canadians. There are tax advantages though, and other provinces are negotiating with Ottawa to have distinct provincial tax calculations as well. This will allow a province to encourage certain investments or activities designed to stimulate the economy or favour a certain group of taxpayers. The following are special tax measures affecting Quebec residents.

The dependent personal tax credit for children under eighteen years of age continues to exist for all Quebec taxpayers (the federal government integrated this credit with the new child tax credit). The dependent personal tax credit continues to be available to children over eighteen if they are in full-time attendance at a post-secondary educational institution. This credit is in addition to the credit available to the parent for each semester the student is in full-time attendance. These credits are reduced for every dollar the student earns.

TIP: Students can deduct their tuition fees; a supporting parent cannot get a deduction for these fees. Even if the student has low income, it's still worthwhile claiming the deduction because it will help reduce the student's income, which in turn makes for a larger dependent personal tax credit available to you.

A special tax reduction relieves the tax burden for persons living alone, low-income families, persons over age sixty-five and those earning below a certain income level who pay property taxes on their own home or a portion of property taxes in their rental building.

TIP: If you qualify for this tax reduction, make sure you have your property and school tax bill, or if you are a tenant get your "Relevé 4" from your landlord. The Relevé 4 will show the property taxes allocated to your apartment.

Quebec has an overseas tax credit which substantially eliminates most tax from employment income earned on an overseas construction, engineering, or contracting job lasting thirty days or more. (The federal overseas tax credit available to all Canadians kicks in after six months abroad.)

The province still gives favourable tax treatment to people who had registered home ownership plans back in 1982. RHOSP money can be kept intact and its earnings will not be taxed as they build. If withdrawals are used to purchase an owner-occupied home or to furnish it and buy appliances, there's no tax on the withdrawal of these funds.

TIP: If you still have a RHOSP intact, do not be shy to use the money in your RHOSP to buy furniture or appliances. You never know when the rules will change.

Quebec also has a number of special investment programs to encourage investment in Quebec business and resources. The most important is probably the Quebec Stock Savings Plan (QSSP). The Quebec government allows a deduction for the purchase of the shares of Quebec-based companies. The size of the company determines the percentage which you can deduct. The smaller the company, the more risk inherent in your investment, the greater the percentage deductible. It might be 75 percent of the amount invested in a large,

stable company, 125 percent of the amount invested in a small company. If you buy $1,000 worth of eligible Quebec Stock Savings Plan stock and 75 percent of the amount is deductible, you would be able to deduct $750. If the company is eligible for a 125 percent deduction, you could deduct $1,250.

Your tax saving is equal to the deduction amount times your Quebec marginal tax rate. Say you purchase $1,000 of QSSP stock that is 100-percent deductible and you are in the top tax bracket in Quebec, 27 percent, then you will save $270 of Quebec tax. Note that the deduction reduces your taxable income for Quebec tax purposes only. The maximum amount of deductions you can take is 10 percent of your net income less any deduction for taxable capital gains claimed.

In order to be eligible for the QSSP deduction, shares purchased must be newly issued shares, or treasury shares of a public company based in Quebec. You must open a Quebec Stock Savings Plan account with a stock broker or financial institution and buy your stock through this account.

To avoid abuse of the tax deductions obtainable through the Quebec Stock Savings Plan, the stock must be held for two full calendar years after the year of purchase and the deduction claimed. Alternatively, you can sell this stock and purchase other qualifying stock that offers the same original deduction amount. Otherwise, the deduction obtained in the current year will be recaptured (brought back into taxable income) if the plan's investments are reduced.

This is important for investment management. If you no longer want to sell your shares in a company before the two-year waiting period is up but you do not want to lose your tax savings, then you must purchase another qualifying stock to replace the original deduction you claimed. Once the two-year waiting period is over you are free and clear;

you can sell the stock, or the replacement stock, whenever you wish, and the tax savings are yours forever.

The Quebec government has loosened the eligible stocks for replacement purposes only. The list now includes stocks on the stock market of eligible shares in developing corporations, instead of just newly issued shares. Deductions will be allowed for convertible securities of growth corporations in Quebec until 1994. Only companies with assets of less than $250 million are eligible to issue shares for the Quebec Stock Savings Plan.

Other provinces offering similar plans are Alberta, Saskatchewan, Nova Scotia and Newfoundland, but their plans allow only small deductions and are not as popular as Quebec's.

TIP: As we exit the recession, growing companies might realize above-average returns. Interest rates have fallen and many of us will look to the stock market for better-yielding investment returns. Stocks, especially of growing companies, are not without risk. When looking at the growth stock portion of your portfolio, look to QSSP-eligible growth stocks since Revenue Quebec will reduce your overall investment by granting you a tax deduction.

The Quebec government's desire to make the provincial economy grow gave rise to the Quebec Business Investment Corporation (QBIC). Under this program, companies can obtain financing from outsiders without having to go public. Quebec taxpayers can invest in a QBIC and receive a tax deduction.

A QBIC is a private investment corporation established after April 23, 1985, under the Quebec Companies Act and registered with the Société de development industriel. A QBIC must be a private corporation whose sole purpose is to make an investment in a Canadian company. The investment must be in new share capital providing less than a controlling investment in that company. To be eligible, the receiving company must be a Canadian-controlled private company with assets of less than $25 million or shareholder equity of less than $10 million and must carry on prescribed activities such as manufacturing, tourism, technology, agriculture or export.

When a Quebec taxpayer invests in a QBIC, he or she obtains an income deduction of 125 percent of the investment provided the QBIC itself makes an eligible investment in a Quebec-based operating private company by the end of the taxation year. Higher deductions of 150 to 175 percent are allowed for investments by employees of the eligible corporation or for investment into a regional development QBIC. A 150- to 200-percent deduction is granted if the eligible company makes expenditures on research and development.

QBICs are not as popular as the QSSP because of their investment return. The QBIC is a private investment and the QSSP is public. QSSPs are therefore more readily obtainable by the public, less risky and easier to sell.

The purchase of treasury common shares, which are newly issued shares of a Labour-Sponsored Venture Capital Corporation, or Fonds de Solidarité des travailleurs du Québec (FSTQ), entitles individuals to a provincial tax credit of 20 percent of the investment to a maximum of $1,400. A further 20-percent credit is provided in the federal tax system. In this way, up to 40 percent of the investment cost is recovered.

Unlike the federal tax credit, any unused Quebec tax credit can be carried forward and credited in future years. Once you turn sixty-five, or if you retire as early as age sixty, then you can no longer use this credit. If the shares are then transferred to an RRSP, a further tax recovery of up to 53 percent is possible.

However, there is not much liquidity in these shares. The shares are non-transferable and cannot be redeemed prior to retirement, although they can be redeemed upon death.

TIP: FSTQ shares are not without risk. However, owing to the incredible tax savings, they should not be overlooked. A small investment should be considered if you cannot otherwise afford to contribute to your RRSP or, if you have lots of RRSP contribution room and can afford to make the total contribution, do not hesitate to look at the FSTQ for a small portion of your RRSP portfolio.

The total tax savings can equal up to 93 percent of your contribution. Don't be too concerned about illiquidity; the investment is for the long term anyway. Investing $1,000 will save you $930, reducing the cost of your investment to only $70 if you are in the top marginal tax bracket. The tax savings alone greatly reduce the cost of your investment and your risk. We recommend only a small portion of your RRSP to hold FSTQ shares, and we do not want you using up your entire RRSP contribution room on FSTQ shares. Not more than 5 to 10 percent of your RRSP portfolio should be exposed to such high risk.

Finally, there is the Cooperative Investment Plan. This program was introduced in 1985 to allow Quebec corporations to raise capital. Individuals who purchase units in certified cooperatives (such as a housing co-op) will be entitled to a deduction of 125 percent of their investment or 150 percent if they are employees. Usually, you can't deduct more than 20 percent of net income using these investments.

39. Minimizing the impact of AMT

There are two tax issues that often affect retirees; installment payment requirements and the alternative minimum tax. Understanding the mechanics of these will allow you to minimize taxes, interest and penalties which you might otherwise have to pay. The alternative minimum tax was a measure brought in by the

government to ensure that high-income, low-tax individuals would pay their share of the national tax burden. It was felt that there were many wealthy taxpayers who paid little tax because they received much of their income in tax-preferred ways. When calculating AMT, certain tax shelters and tax preferences are disregarded. Liability for AMT arises when tax payable under the AMT calculation exceeds the tax payable under the normal rules. There is a $40,000 exemption under AMT, which means that individuals with gross incomes of $40,000 or less will not be subject to AMT. The AMT does not apply to corporations but it does apply to trusts.

If your gross income exceeds $40,000 you could be caught by AMT rules if you have the following types of income or deductions:

- deductions for contributions to pensions, RRSPs, DPSPs;
- dividend income;
- taxable capital gains or deductible capital losses;
- tax-shelter losses;
- employee stock option deduction;
- housing loan deduction;
- excluded prospector's income.

The AMT is not difficult to figure out and is clearly explained in Revenue Canada's general tax guide. The calculation begins with your taxable income on your normal return and is then adjusted for the items listed above. The resulting adjusted taxable income is multiplied by 17 percent, and certain tax credits are then deducted. Certain other tax credits, such as those transferred from a spouse or other person and the pension income credit, are not credits for AMT purposes.

If you end up paying AMT, a credit for the additional tax paid can be carried forward for up to seven years and used to reduce the normal tax payable in future years. Normal tax liability in a future year can only be reduced by this minimum tax carryover to the extent that it exceeds the AMT in that year. Because taxes in most provinces are calculated as a percentage of federal taxes payable, AMT will also cause additional provincial tax to be payable. The additional provincial taxes payable also form part of the minimum tax carryover and can be recovered as such.

AMT does not apply to the final return filed for a deceased taxpayer. However, where a taxpayer who has a minimum tax carryover dies, the carryover can only be applied within the normal limits on the main year of death return only. Therefore, it is possible that the carryover might not be fully recoverable.

TIP: One item that often triggers AMT is the transfer of a retiring allowance to an RRSP. If you are retiring late in the year, you might be able to avoid AMT by having the retiring allowance paid out on January 1 of the following year.

40. Tax installments

In retirement, it is possible that a large portion of your income will come from investments and pensions. Tax is usually withheld from company pensions, RRSP annuities and RRIF payments, but it will not be withheld from investment income and government plans such as OAS and CPP. Currently, if more than 25 percent of your income is from sources that do not withhold income taxes, and your prior-year and current-year federal tax liability exceeds $1,000, you must remit your own taxes by quarterly installments. However, effective September 15, 1994, the basis for determining who is required to pay quarterly installments will be changed.

The new rules will relate to the amount of tax not withheld at source versus the proportion of income subject to withholding. You will be required to make quarterly installment payments if the amount of tax

owed at filing time is greater than $2,000 in both the prior year and the current year. The $2,000 refers to both federal and provincial taxes. Since Quebec residents pay their provincial taxes separately, the $2,000 amount will be adjusted to $1,200 of federal tax payable after federal tax withholdings.

There are three methods of determining the amount you need to remit quarterly. The first, and easiest, method is to simply pay the amount indicated by Revenue Canada on the installment reminder notices sent to each taxpayer who is required to pay installments. Under this method Revenue Canada will base the March and June installments on the tax paid in two years prior. Once the prior year's return is assessed, the September and December payments will adjust the installment amounts so that the total installments paid will equal the tax paid in the prior year. If you pay these amounts as requested by Revenue Canada, no interest or penalties will be charged if you end up owing more taxes at filing time.

The second method allows you to base your installments on the prior year's tax. However, if your prior year's return has not yet been assessed, you might in fact owe more taxes than you expect, and therefore your March and June installments might be too low, subjecting you to interest and/or penalties.

The final method involves basing your installments on an estimate of taxes payable for the current year. If you underestimate, and owe additional taxes at filing time, you will be subject to interest charges. If you expect that your current year's income will be substantially less than last year's (often the case for the first year of retirement) you should estimate your taxes payable. You've already forecast your retirement income, so why not summarize it on a tax return using last year's return as a worksheet. You can use last year's tax rates too, because these don't change dramatically from year to year.

Your installments are payable on the fifteenth of March, June, September and December. Make sure, however, that your estimate includes a whole year's income, so you won't be surprised. Remember, failure to make the right installments will cost you interest, usually a few percent higher than the prime rate. So it's probably wise to err on the high side until you develop your retirement pattern.

The best method to use, is the one that results in the smallest amount of tax paid in installments. Of course, there's no penalty for paying installments based on last year's taxes, and then finding the current year is a lot higher. You simply have to pay the difference in April. Just be sure to set aside a fair estimate of what you'll need. Don't rush to pay the government too much, too soon. Keep your money working in your bank account, not theirs — you need it more.

Notes

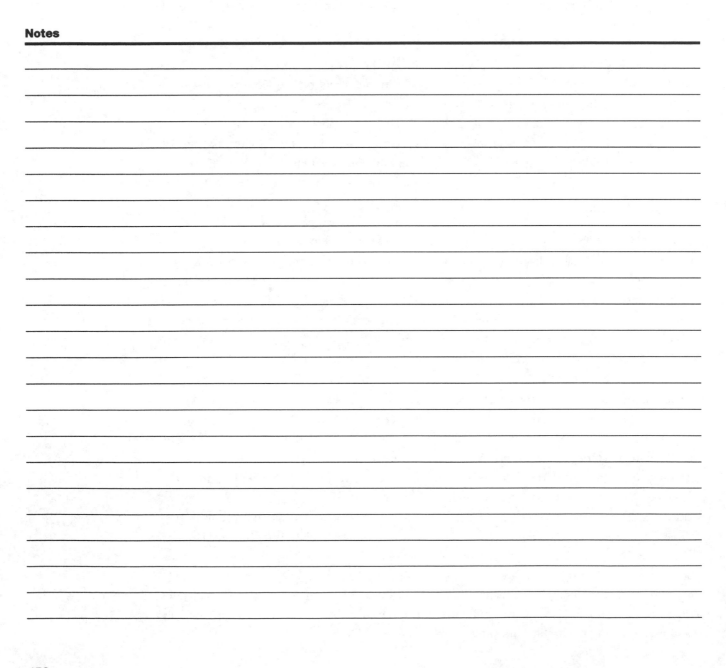

Making the most from your money

We've looked at ways of increasing your savings and controlling spending and we identified forty strategies to save tax dollars. The next step toward financial independence is to make those savings work harder for you, to learn how you can change your financial speed to carry you faster toward a secure and satisfying retirement.

Investing money wisely is a very complicated task. In Canada, we have more than 3,000 different investments to choose from — an exciting prospect to some, confusing to the rest of us. Choosing the right investment is tricky, and many Canadians have little investment experience. Although there is much talk about the stock market, only about 20 percent of Canadians actually venture into it. Far fewer risk investing in gold, German bonds or the future of the American dollar.

You might be happy not to be among these adventurous few. However, in order to make the most of your savings, you must take seriously the task of investing your money. In fact, you must take every possible action to get your money working hard enough for you to stay ahead of taxes and inflation.

You and your partner probably have savings accounts at banks or trust companies, Canada Savings Bonds, term deposits, stocks, bonds or mutual funds. You might also have a good chunk of your family wealth tied up in your family home, cottage, life insurance policies, hobbies and collections; all of which could be made available for investment. There's also a chance you have investments sheltered in your RRSPs. Gradually, over the coming years, you will be adding to this pool of wealth through your savings — if you manage your money well day to day. Your success in achieving

financial independence will depend on how effectively you save and invest.

Although saving money is difficult with mounting bills, mouths to feed, mortgage payments and income taxes, you must make saving a financial priority. Pay yourself first. I know it sounds simple, but it's very practical. One of the reasons owning a home is so rewarding is that it forces you to save a good chunk of your income every month year after year. If you use the same discipline with your savings, even if it is only a few dollars, it will become a painless habit that will allow you to build a hoard of money. You won't even miss the money, but it will be there for you on retirement day!

Unfortunately, being an effective saver is not enough — you must learn to invest. You have to become familiar with the various different kinds of investments, their characteristics and the returns you might expect from each. You need to develop a personal investment strategy and learn how to monitor the security and performance of your retirement nest egg. Don't be tempted to skip this chapter just because you plan to use a professional investment manager; you should become almost as familiar with the investment world as those who handle their own investments so that you can monitor the security and performance of your retirement assets.

The kinds of investments

If you simplify investing, it's really no more than giving or lending your cash today in the hope and expectation that you will get it back at some time in the future, together with a reward for its use. The fear with investing, of course, is that you won't get your money back.

You can view investments on a spectrum, with cash, such as money in a savings account, on the safe end and growth stock, perhaps shares in a gold mining company, at the risky end. If you limit your investing to putting cash in a safety deposit box or under your mattress, you would have no real fear that you won't get your cash back at some time in the future. However, neither will you receive any reward for that investment. Equity investments, on the other hand, will provide you with a greater possibility of growth in value over time — and therefore a greater expectation of reward — but will also carry a risk of investment loss.

The most common investment classification follows this concept and divides investments into three categories, or asset classes: cash, fixed-income investments and equity investments.

Sometimes cash is king

We all think of cash as the paper and coins we carry around in our pockets. In investment lingo, cash is an investment that can be easily turned into money:

- deposits in a savings account. These pay interest monthly, semi-annually or annually;
- term deposits, deposits which are usually locked in for thirty, ninety or 180 days;
- Canada Savings Bonds;
- treasury bills; and
- commercial paper.

These investments make up the "money market." They bear fairly low interest yields today, ranging from 0 percent to about 5 percent, but also carry a relatively low potential for loss. If the investment carries a face value, that price remains steady throughout the investment term. That's because the "term" (the days or weeks over which your funds are invested) is short, usually only a week, a month, ninety or 180 days. When the investment matures you will get your money back. It's also easy to find a buyer if you should decide to sell before maturity — in other words, cash investments are "liquid."

These "cash-equivalent" instruments are offered by banks, trust companies, cooperatives and insurance companies. The rates and terms differ and you should shop around carefully before selecting your investment. Because deposits are so widely used by investors, there is plenty of advice on choosing the right one later in this chapter.

Fixed-income investments

Although the phrase "fixed income" seems foreign to many investors, it's a very sensible term for a whole class of investments. Fixed-income investments are usually loans which you make to governments, financial institutions and companies for a fixed period of time at a fixed interest rate; guaranteed investment certificates (GICs), corporate and government bonds and debentures.

These investments are bought for their guarantee of income; there is some potential for growth and some risk of loss. These investments are slightly riskier because they are issued for longer periods of time than cash investments. They can carry terms to maturity of three, five even thirty years. As a result, their price can move up and down dramatically. The longer the term to maturity, the greater the risk that interest rates will change or borrowers won't have funds to pay you back. To compensate for this higher risk, you can demand a better return or price.

Equity investments

Investing in equities involves buying shares in companies with the expectation that the companies will prosper and the value of their shares will rise over time. As a part-owner, you expect to share in the profits through the distribution of dividends. Of course, the fortunes of a company in which you invest will depend on the state of the economy and of that particular industry as well as the management of the company itself.

Equity investments usually provide a lower current income but offer the most potential for growth — and loss. The risk which you take is lower with "blue chip" stocks, the shares of large, well-established companies of proven worth; it's higher with the stock of younger, smaller companies with fewer individual investors. Stocks are also usually "liquid" but the sometimes seemingly erratic fluctuations in price can make it unappealing to sell at times.

Real estate

There is another category of investment, one which many people do not consider when analyzing their investment portfolio — real estate. Many Canadians have a considerable amount of wealth tied up in their homes, cottages or other vacation or rental properties. For many years, property was considered essential for raising a family and enjoying the Canadian style of living. At retirement, you might choose not to hold on to some of these properties. If your home or cottage is not an integral part of your retirement lifestyle you should look at that property as an investment.

Mutual funds

You can participate in any of these investments by purchasing a stock or bond or certificate. Or, you can invest in them through a mutual fund. Mutual funds are pools of money from many different investors which are invested and managed by professional money managers. The portfolio of a mutual fund is usually spread among a broad diversity of securities, giving every investor, even those with small sums of money, the diversification which you need to achieve the best returns at the least possible risk.

Mutual funds have become one of our nation's most popular investments. There are 120 companies offering more than 750 funds from which you can choose. The funds fall into several broad categories; there are mutual funds which invest primarily in the stock market, those that invest in bonds and mortgages, and those that invest in the money market. There are also a handful which invest in real estate. These broad categories break down into more specific categories: the funds often specialize in a geographic area, such as Canada, the United States, Europe, Japan; others invest in specific sectors of the economy, such as oil and gas, or precious metals. And there are balanced funds which invest in each of the major classes of assets. Almost all of these funds have published track records which you can study before selecting a fund.

Most funds in Canada are "open-ended"; the fund will buy back your shares or units when you wish to sell, or redeem. You are guaranteed a buyer. While you might not be able to withdraw cash from a fund as easily as from savings accounts, it will take only a few days to process the paperwork. (You have to be careful, however. There are still mutual funds which allow redemptions only on one day of the week. A couple restrict sales to a particular day each month.) There are also a few "closed-end" mutual funds, the shares of which are bought and sold on the stock exchange. You won't always find a buyer interested in your shares at your desired price.

Mutual funds might seem to be the perfect investment. However, there is one drawback —

the fees and costs you will have to pay if you invest in a fund, any fund. Even the so-called "no-load" funds, which do not charge you a commission when you buy or sell, will charge the fund a fee every month to cover the management expenses.

Shopping around

A favourite Canadian pastime is the great interest-rate hunt. This hunt becomes most heated during the RRSP season when thousands of Canadians begin searching for the highest rate of return on GICs and term deposits. Your goal should not necessarily be to obtain the highest interest rate possible for the time period chosen. You should also consider flexibility, security and convenience. You can spend a great deal of time, effort and money shopping for that extra quarter of a percentage point.

Shopping is made easier by using the interest rate tables in the newspapers or by phoning the various companies. You could also call a deposit broker to help you. One caution: Sometimes high interest rates can indicate that a financial institution is in trouble. It might be offering the higher rates to compensate for the higher risk they represent. Before you decide to go ahead with the deposit, make sure your deposit is insured by the Canada Deposit Insurance Corporation (CDIC) or Quebec Deposit Insurance Board.

Financial institutions pay different interest rates depending upon how much they can earn with your funds. The risk:reward ratio is at work here, too. When you deposit your money with a bank or trust company, that institution is borrowing your money in order to lend it to other customers who have applied for a loan. If you invest in a five-year GIC, it might turn around and lend the money out on a five-year mortgage.

There are several risks in this transaction.

There is some risk to the financial institution that it won't get the mortgage funds back, more risk than if it were a loan for only a few months. If the institution makes many bad loans and puts itself at risk, you could be at risk of losing your money, if it's not protected by CDIC. There is a second risk: Interest rates might either rise or fall over the five years. Over a long term, the risk of such changes is greater. The bank considers both of these risks when it establishes the interest rates it will pay on deposits. Usually, the longer the term of your deposit, the higher the interest rate your deposit will earn.

So, how do you decide whether to lock your funds up for six months or five years or some period of time in between? There are two questions you have to ask yourself before deciding: When will you need the money and what will interest rates do in the future? Sometimes it is the first question which gives us our answer.

If you need the money in two years to buy a car, then don't lock the money up for five years. On the other hand, if you won't need the money for at least five years, you have to decide whether interest rates are going to increase or decrease over that time. Don't lock in to 6 percent for five years if you believe that rates are probably going to climb to 10 percent within a couple of years. On the other hand, if you think rates are going to fall, you'll want to secure that 6 percent for the full five years.

Here are a few more tips:

1. Make sure your interest compounds daily

When buying short-term deposits of thirty to 360 days, make sure your interest is compounding daily, not monthly or semi-annually. The frequency with which your interest is credited is probably more important than chasing higher rates. Let's look at an example. If you invest $10,000 at 5 percent for three years, your investment will have grown to $11,575 if interest is compounded annually. If interest is compounded semi-annually, your deposit will grow to $11,597; $11,620 with daily compounding.

2. Don't switch without good reason

At 8 percent, your yield will be reduced to 7.5 percent if you miss just two days on deposit each month. This loss of working days for your money is worthwhile if you're switching for a sufficiently higher interest rate and the money will be invested for a reasonably long time. Make sure your increased return will more than cover any fees or charges you might have to pay when switching.

3. Make sure your funds are covered by CDIC

You should always make sure your funds are secure. Historically, investors have had a high level of comfort over the security of their deposits with banks and trust companies. However, in the past couple of years we have seen the decline of several large trust companies.

You can make sure your funds are secure in two ways. First, check the integrity and reliability of the financial institution where you are placing funds. Keep up with financial news and read about the institution you are considering. If you have any concerns, take the time to obtain a copy of the most recent annual report issued by the institution. When reviewing annual reports you should be alert to patterns of persistent losses over the years or high levels of provisions for doubtful loans.

These warning signals could be signals that you should look elsewhere. Also consider the credit rating which the Dominion Bond Rating Service or the Canadian Bond Rating Service have awarded to the institution. Stick with institutions carrying an AA or better rating. Second, only place your funds in deposits with companies that are covered by the guarantee of the Canadian or Quebec governments through the Canada Deposit Insurance Act or its Quebec equivalent, the Quebec Deposit Insurance Board.

The Canada Deposit Insurance Corporation was created in 1967 to protect money on deposit with banks, trust companies and loan companies that are members of the CDIC. Most deposits with a bank or trust company can be guaranteed for up to $60,000 of principal and interest in individual accounts. Insurable deposits must be payable in Canada, in Canadian currency.

The deposits covered include savings and chequing accounts, term deposits locked in for five years or less, money orders, drafts, certified cheques and travellers' cheques. Accounts that are not covered include foreign-currency accounts such as U.S. dollar accounts, term deposits locked in for more than five years, corporate bonds and debentures and investments in equities.

The $60,000 limit applies to all of the eligible deposits held in your personal accounts with that member institution, even if it is in different accounts and different branches. Separate coverage applies to RRSPs, RRIFs, joint accounts and trust deposits. For example, you can be covered for all of the following accounts at one institution: $60,000 in personal accounts, $60,000 in trust for another person, $60,000 in a joint account with your spouse, $60,000 in an RRSP, and $60,000 in a RRIF. Your spouse can have the same coverage. Any money you have contributed to a spousal RRSP will be combined with money in your spouse's name, not yours.

Make sure your funds are protected. If you have significant amounts on deposit you might wish to place them at different financial institutions to ensure all funds are guaranteed. Keep in mind that a $50,000 compound interest deposit will increase in value to over the $60,000 limit fairly quickly. At 5 percent, the $50,000 will be worth over $60,000 in four years, at 10 percent it will exceed the limit after only two years. The excess won't be insured.

Buying Canada Savings Bonds

Canada Savings Bonds aren't really bonds at all, but they've been popular with Canadians for decades. They combine safety, reasonable interest rates and they can be cashed at any time. Canada Savings Bonds are issued on November 1 of each year and usually carry a seven-year term. The interest rate is only guaranteed for one year at a time, then it moves up or down at the whim of the Bank of Canada.

Canada Savings Bonds are an important source of cash for the government and in the past it has attached bonus features to a CSB series to encourage you to hold the bonds to maturity. The importance of these bonus features is twofold. First, a premium interest is paid for retaining the bonds to maturity. Second, you might enjoy preferential tax treatment on the bonus interest. Features of Canada Savings Bonds outstanding are outlined on tables made available annually by the Bank of Canada. They're yours for the asking.

CSBs are a very good short-term deposit. They pay a higher return than bank deposits, they're government guaranteed and cashable any day. But few Canadians use CSBs as short-term deposits — they hold them for years and add more to their investment pile every year. This isn't good. Too much money gets left at low short-term interest rates rather than at the higher rates available in fixed-income investments or in equities.

Treasury bills

Treasury bills are issued by the Canadian government. The bills have maturities of one year or less. They're readily available from banks and brokers, usually in amounts of $5,000 or more. Generally, the larger your purchase, the higher the rate you will be offered. Also, you'll often receive a higher yield from brokers, who compete hard for this money in hopes that you will continue to invest with them.

Because they are guaranteed by the government of Canada, treasury bills provide the least risk of any investment and often provide returns as high as bank and trust company deposits. Technically, treasury bills do not pay interest, although your yield will be taxed as interest. Instead, T-bills are purchased at a discount to their face value and redeemed at full value on maturity. For example, you pay $4,939 now and on maturity ninety days later you get $5,000. This is the equivalent of a 5-percent yield.

The yield is low because the risk is low. However, over the past decade there have been times when short-term rates were higher than long-term rates — referred to as an inverted yield curve. This was abnormal and came about when the Bank of Canada intervened to tighten the availability of short-term funds. Canadians had a delightful time earning very high short-term rates with government guarantees. But the good times came to an end and we are back to more normal times.

Although you can buy T-bills with ease, they are also held through money market mutual funds. These funds pool the dollars of thousands of investors to buy millions of dollars' worth of treasury bills and commercial deposits of the longest possible term. This allows them to command the highest possible interest rates. Mutual funds can provide you with short-term yields superior to what you can achieve on your own.

You should always read the mutual fund prospectus or ask questions carefully before selecting a money market fund. Some funds, although they are called money market funds, invest in longer term deposits of 180 days or so. This is a fairly long term and might not fit your investment objective for the funds you consider to be cash.

Insurance company deposits

Other forms of deposits include endowment policies, deferred annuities and other life insurance products carrying significant savings features. These policies allow you to set aside savings through regular monthly or annual premium payments in a form of forced savings. This isn't a bad thing, but you might be able to achieve higher rates of return by investing your savings in other instruments.

Insurance companies often combine life insurance with investment but it is usually preferable to consider these two important financial needs separately. We've discussed these policies in chapter fifteen. Insurance companies also offer deferred annuities, an investment very similar to guaranteed investment certificates.

In the past, you could earn interest on which tax was not payable until it was received. However, tax legislation has closed this loophole and now you must report accruing interest in such deposits as income every year. There is only one exception: If you purchased a deferred annuity before December 31, 1989, you have to report the interest income at least every three years.

Fixed-income investments

We discussed shopping for guaranteed investment certificates earlier, but bonds, debentures and mortgages make up a significant part of the fixed-income market. Bonds and debentures represent loans made to companies and governments by investors for a specific period of time. The issuer is obliged to pay interest at a fixed rate, usually once a year, and to repay the principal amount on the due date.

The fixed rate of interest is called the

> **Be patient with your CSBs**
>
> You can cash a Canada Savings Bond any day at almost any financial institution. Be patient. You should wait till the beginning of the month; the government only pays interest if the bond is held for the full month. If you cash it in during the last week, you won't get interest for the first three weeks during which they still had your money.

"coupon rate" while the period of time over which the borrower has use of your money is called the "term to maturity." In this way, bonds are deposits. But they also behave like equities because they can be traded on the public markets through stock brokers and bond traders at any time before the redemption date. The price of a bond will move with interest rates — climbing in price when interest rates drop, falling when rates rise.

As with other investments, you want to buy bonds and debentures at a time when prices are low and sell them when prices are high. Because the price of bonds fluctuates in response to interest rates, the decision to buy bonds will depend upon your expectations for future interest rates. The best time to enter the bond market is when interest rates are high and you expect them to start falling. As you will see later in this chapter, you will usually want to maintain a portion of your portfolio in fixed-income securities like bonds at all times. However, in periods when interest rates are low and rising, you will want to hold a smaller portion in bonds, more when interest rates are falling.

In the middle of this century, bonds were a popular investment for individuals seeking high income and security. Then inflation, volatile interest rates and creeping income taxes made bonds less attractive. More recently, plummeting interest rates have resulted in spectacular bond returns.

Bonds are available with a variety of features. Some bonds and debentures can be converted into common shares; others allow investors to apply for earlier redemption, or for an extension of the normal maturity date. Usually, when bonds are issued they comprise two components: the bond itself, which will pay a fixed amount on maturity, and the right to earn interest paid in the years before maturity. This right to earn interest is sometimes represented by coupons

These components can be separated and sold separately — you can buy the stripped bond (the bond without its coupons, also known as a zero-coupon bond) or you can buy the coupons. Because the stripped bond is sold separately from its interest coupons, it will not provide an annual stream of income. Instead, it is sold at a discounted price and held until maturity, at which time you will get the full maturity value. They're convenient because you don't have to worry about reinvesting small amounts of interest each year. Many people choose to hold stripped bonds in their RRSPs.

You can also buy bonds in Canadian dollars or in foreign currencies. I like foreign-currency bonds because they allow you to hedge against losses in Canadian currency when you feel that the dollar is losing value relative to other currencies. They also provide the opportunity to bet on the world's strong currencies while still enjoying the benefits of a stream of fixed income and the lower risk of bonds. You can buy the Export Development Bank bonds or certain Canadian corporate bonds that are denominated in foreign currencies. Or you can buy World Bank bonds denominated in almost any currency. All of these bonds are RRSP-eligible.

You can also buy treasury bonds issued by foreign governments or corporate bonds issued by foreign companies. However, investing in other countries will take you further away from what you know best, and you should consider these investments only on the advice of a

qualified investment adviser or after doing sufficient research on your own to know the political and economic climate of the country in which you are considering investment.

Because it is difficult to buy bonds in small denominations (they are usually offered in multiples of $25,000, $50,000 and $100,000), many Canadians are not active in this market. However, you can participate in this market through the 120 fixed-income mortgage and bond mutual funds available in Canada. Again, similar to the money-market funds, these allow smaller investors to participate in a diversified bond or mortgage portfolio and to enjoy the benefits of professional management of that portfolio.

You can choose a mutual fund that specializes in foreign bonds if you want to invest in these instruments at lower investment levels. Global bond funds can be a convenient way of participating in foreign markets without having to become an expert yourself in changing political and economic climates in foreign countries, or in fluctuating exchange and interest rates.

We are all familiar with mortgages, usually from the borrower's end. Mortgages are also a solid investment opportunity, one which you can tap through mortgage-backed securities and mortgage mutual funds. When you buy a mortgage-backed security, you are buying a share in a fixed pool of mortgage loans made to individuals. These mortgages are guaranteed by the Canada Mortgage and Housing Corporation, thereby reducing your investment risk.

The fixed income you will receive each month will be slightly higher than the interest yield on a bond, because your payments represent the interest payments and principal repayment made by mortgagees. I recommend mortgage-backed securities for individuals who are in the spending cycle of life, want a healthy fixed income that they will spend each month, yet need to know that the capital providing this income is secure. (Avoid these if you do not want to spend the income; you would be faced with constantly having to reinvest little bits of income.)

For other investors who want to invest in mortgages as a fixed-income element in a diversified portfolio, I recommend a mortgage mutual fund. A mortgage mutual fund is similar to a mortgage-backed security but it is continually reinvesting in new mortgages as existing mortgages are paid down. Therefore, the unit value fluctuates as new mortgages are purchased. These investments are best for someone who is looking for a safe, fixed-income security that will provide a slightly higher return than a GIC, with greater flexibility.

Equity investments

Canadians don't like investments without guarantees — and they don't like the stock market. Its movements mirror the health of the Canadian economy, which can be a scary thought in itself, and the potential of the individual companies being traded. If you invest in the shares of a company you are betting that the company will prosper, either because you believe the Canadian economy itself will grow and the company will grow with it or because that company will prosper despite any bumps in the world around it.

Sounds like betting, doesn't it? It's not. The Canadian economy moves through cycles of growth and contraction, pulling the prices on the stock market up and down. At the same time, different industries and the companies within those industries enjoy their own periods of growth and, occasionally, decline. Despite these cycles, Canada's economy has been growing for many decades — a growth that has been fuelled by the companies that provide us with the goods and services we

need. The stock market has proven to provide the most generous rewards to investors — if you are patient. These cycles make it essential that your investing time horizon be long enough to wait out the bad times.

Most of the publicly traded shares are issued by large companies, companies whose names are household words. They have satisfied various government securities commissions that they have fully disclosed their financial position to potential investors. Provided the companies continue to report accurate and timely financial information to the public, the companies' shares can continue to be available on the stock market. Of course, you won't recognize the names of all the companies. The stock market is a major source of funding for Canada's smaller growth companies as well. These are the young companies, companies with new ideas in technology or unproven mines or promising oil finds. They have the potential to strike it rich or go under tomorrow.

It's wise to remember that when you buy shares of a company, another investor is simultaneously selling them. Obviously, you believe the shares will go up in value; the seller either believes he or she can do better with another investment or needs the money for another reason. When there are more buyers than sellers, the stock price will rise. The reverse also holds true: When sellers are anxious to dispose of their shares, the price has to drop to attract buyers. Such is the nature of the stock market.

Company shares constantly change hands based on investors' feelings about the future price movements of a company's shares. The shares of many hundreds of companies in all types of industries are listed on the public stock markets in Montreal, Toronto, Alberta and Vancouver; in the international centres of London, Tokyo, Hong Kong and New York, and in dozens of other stock exchanges worldwide. Investment in the shares of public companies requires a working knowledge of how stock markets work and a good understanding of the prospects for both the economy and the company. Finally, you need reliable investment advice. You can choose to gather this information yourself and invest directly in the stock market, or you can invest in equity mutual funds.

There is a huge variety of equity mutual funds available. You can choose from Canadian, U.S. and international equity funds, or funds which invest in companies within a certain segment of the economy. Canadian equity funds are offered by many different companies and include growth funds that specialize in the younger, smaller and higher risk equities, and blue-chip funds that focus more on larger, established Canadian companies.

International equity funds can participate in a diversified portfolio of stocks from around the world or they can concentrate in a certain geographic area, such as the emerging markets and the Far East. Sector funds can specialize in any segment of the market but resource funds have been most talked about because of their spectacular gains in 1993. The most important consideration in selecting an equity mutual fund is to understand the investments in which the fund is invested. If you invest your money in an international fund without researching the underlying investments, then you might end up with a fund that holds Canadian, U.S. and European stocks when what you really want is participation in the emerging markets in Southeast Asia or South America.

Preferred shares

"Preferreds" do indeed offer you preferential treatment. As a preferred shareholder you have the right to receive dividends each year before common shareholders receive anything. The dividend you'll receive will also be higher than the dividends received by the common shareholders.

While most companies make every effort to pay a dividend (they'll shake the confidence of all investors in the company if they don't), it's not guaranteed. If earnings are low, preferred shareholders might get nothing. Second, if the company runs into trouble, the preferred shareholder has first claim on the company assets. If the company declares bankruptcy, however, creditors might get all the money.

Most preferred shares have a fixed dividend yield; however, some have a floating dividend rate that will fluctuate with interest rates. In addition, preferred shares can be cumulative or non-cumulative. Cumulative preferreds allow any dividends that are not paid in any one year to build on account for the preferred shareholders to be paid eventually, as long as the company has the money. Dividends on non-cumulative preferreds, on the other hand, expire if they are not paid. You should read the features of any preferred shares carefully to understand how dividends are paid and whether there are specifications as to when you can redeem your shares.

There are several other kinds of preferred shares with special features:

- Convertible preferreds: These shares can be converted into common shares during a certain period of time at the investor's discretion at a fixed conversion rate. Convertible preferreds offer the investor the opportunity to enjoy a higher level of income today as well as the right to participate in the future increases in common share prices. The price of convertible preferreds will vary with the price of the common shares.

- Retractable and callable preferreds: can be sold back to the company at some future date for the price originally paid or a specified amount. Because the company is obliged to buy back retractable shares at the shareholder's option, this guarantees that you will at least get your money back. A callable share can be called back by the company for redemption at a specified price after a certain period of time. This allows the issuing company the flexibility to buy back preferred shares if interest rates drop and the yield on the preferreds is relatively high.

Because the dividend is higher and there is greater certainty of receiving it, preferred shares are attractive to investors looking for high-income yields. In addition, dividends from a taxable Canadian corporation receive the benefits of the Canadian dividend tax credit. The after-tax income from preferred shares can be superior to interest received on deposits and bonds because of this beneficial tax treatment of Canadian dividends. On the other hand, preferred shares do not offer any growth in the rate of dividends nor in the value of shares, while common shares do offer these features.

The safety of preferreds can be elusive. Many investors are attracted to preferred shares thinking that the preferential treatment makes them more secure. In fact, this is entirely not the case. The preferential aspect of the shares relates to the fact that dividends will be paid to the preferred shareholder before the common shareholder. Also, on redemption, the preferred shareholder would get a return of his or her investment before the common shareholder. However, preferred shares rank behind all other creditors of a company, including the employees, creditors and bond and debenture holders; they are considerably riskier than bonds or debentures. Yet they do not offer the opportunity for reward offered by common shares.

It's hard to justify the extra risk associated with those preferred shares. Major losses have been sustained by investors seeking high income and safety. You've probably gathered that preferred shares are not my favourite investment.

Derivative investments

Commonly known derivatives are rights, warrants and options. All three represent methods of securing the right to purchase common shares of a company, at a fixed price, until a fixed date in the future. These derivatives can fluctuate in value themselves, mirroring the movements in the price of the common shares. There is an active market for rights, warrants and options. However, derivatives are usually more volatile in their price movements than the underlying shares. To use derivatives most effectively you must understand the stock market implicitly. For investment professionals these instruments can be used to lock in returns and add safety and certainty to a portfolio. However, most investors should leave these investments to sophisticated players or participate only on the advice of an investment counsellor.

Real estate

Although it is not in favour now, real estate has provided Canadian investors with excellent returns over the years. Because the price of land and buildings tends to keep pace with inflation, investing in real estate represents a good hedge against inflation. It has not been only homes and cottages that have proven financially rewarding for Canadians; rental properties, commercial and industrial buildings, public real estate companies, private joint ventures and syndications, real estate trusts and partnerships, and real estate mutual funds have brought rich rewards. When inflation returns to the levels we saw even a few years ago, I predict that real estate prices will begin to rise again.

However, real estate speculating is only for the hardiest investor. It can be a very volatile market. It can be very difficult to time the market well enough to make money selling property over a short period of time. Some investors have undoubtedly been lucky, others who are educated and experienced in certain markets have made wise investments. But real estate demands a long time frame and an informed judgment of social and planning trends and the impact on land values.

If you decide to become a landlord, your investment will require daily management to handle tenant complaints, repairs and maintenance, leasing and rent collection. This may or may not suit you. If not, you should hire an experienced property manager. You will have to pay management fees but a good manager should be able to improve your returns.

Other forms of real estate development or joint venture participations often require expertise, that you might not have. If you want to invest in real estate but have neither the funds nor expertise consider investing in shares of public real estate companies or in real estate investment partnerships, both of which permit the pooling of smaller investor interests into the ownership of a diversified real estate portfolio managed by professionals.

Choosing the right investment

With that explanation of the kinds of investments which you can make, you are left with several critically important questions: Which investment should I buy? What's right for me? Where can I make the best return without risking my money?

I wish I could tell you exactly what you should do today. But I can't. In fact, nobody can tell you with any degree of certainty which investment will be the winner in 1993, 1994 or 1995. Looking back over the past few decades has taught us many important investment lessons. One is that the only thing we can

count on is change. The different investments seem to take turns bringing in the best performance — and it's difficult to know which group will be next to take its place at centre stage.

Few investors are effective market timers, able to enter one market, then another, make a fast buck and get out before they lose their winnings. This is not only a tiring and emotionally consuming process, it's very difficult to do, even for professional managers. Some have made the right investment moves for a few years only to fall from grace (and fortune) later on. Enormous fortunes have been made by putting all the money in one form of investment, only to have it lost when that market collapses.

Look back at the real estate fortunes won and lost by the Reichmann brothers, the Bronfmans, and Robert Campeau. Once you've had tremendous success at one endeavour it becomes impossible to believe that success will fade. You stay too long and then it's too late.

You're much better off developing a personal investment strategy that divides your assets among several types of investments. In this way you can reduce your risk but not your returns. Once your strategy is in place, you have to monitor and rebalance your portfolio to keep it in line with your strategy. You should stick to this strategy over time, it should guide you or your investment advisers in all investment decisions you make. It should be a form of discipline that requires you to return from the vagaries of the investment world to look at your needs and objectives and investment temperament.

Your investment policy will be built on all of the following:

■ your financial goals and objectives,

■ your time horizon,

■ your tolerance of risk,

■ your tax situation,

■ and your management style.

Let's consider each of these in more detail.

Financial goals and objectives

What do you want your investments to do for you? If you're near retirement, you might want as much income as possible from your investments? Are you trying to build your wealth as quickly as possible to allow you to achieve financial independence? Are these funds crucial to your financial well-being in retirement and are you concerned about losing any money at all?

You might answer "yes" to every one of these questions. It is possible you want safety, growth and income. If you plan on spending your funds in the next couple of months you will also want liquidity. Your task is to decide which is your priority and how much of each you need to get the kind of balance of growth, income and safety that best satisfies your needs. If you're close to retirement, concerned about building enough wealth to be secure yet worried about the impact of a poor decision, then safety and growth will both be important investment objectives. If you are most concerned about leaving a healthy estate for your grandchildren, growth might be your most important objective. You should spend some time identifying your overriding objectives, listing them on the worksheet on the next few pages.

Your time horizon

Many people feel that as they approach retirement, they must begin to shorten their time horizon. Perhaps they pull away from those investments that will give them the growth they need to protect them from inflation believing they do not have the ability to wait out a dip in the market. I believe this is short sighted. You could easily live to be ninety

years old; that's twenty-five years after the day you retire. If you stop taking any investment risks beyond that day, you expose yourself to the risk of inflation robbing you of purchasing power. When considering your investing time horizon, you must remember that at least some of your money will remain invested for a quarter of a century.

Risk and return

Although we all seem to be aware of the risks in the stock market, it's important to know that every investment carries some risk. Probably the most insidious risk is the risk of losing purchasing power. The erosion in our wealth caused by income tax and inflation can be so damaging that our wealth can slowly decline over the years if we don't protect ourselves.

Not convinced? Let's say we take the safe route and invest in a $1,000 guaranteed investment certificate earning 5 percent a year. Inflation is running at 3 percent and our marginal tax rate is 40 percent. At the end of the year, we have $1,050, but we have to give 40 percent of our interest ($20) to the government so we only have $1,030 left. Our 5 percent return has been reduced to 3 percent. But inflation has eroded the value of your money by 3 percent, and your original $1,000 only stretches as far as it did last year. Your purchasing power has not increased at all and you've lost one full year of time.

Let's take a little bit of risk. Let's purchase shares of a well-established Canadian company paying a dividend of 4 percent. After tax, this amounts to a return of about 2.4 percent. This return is about the rate of inflation but our stock might go up in price, especially if it has a steady annual growth in earnings and attractive dividend. If the stock rises by 5 percent, our combined return after tax comes to 7.4 percent for the year, a giant step ahead of inflation. Of course, there is some risk that the stock price

**Total rates of returns on treasury bills,
bonds, mortgages and stocks**   **TABLE 12**

December to December
Total return (% change in total return indices)

Year	Cost of mailing a letter	Inflation	91-day T-bills	Long bonds	Residential mortgages	TSE 300 stocks
1958	5 ¢	2.67	2.51	1.92	5.82	31.25
1959	5 ¢	1.30	4.62	-5.07	3.67	4.59
1960	5 ¢	1.28	3.31	12.19	6.81	1.78
1961	5 ¢	0.84	2.89	9.16	5.55	32.75
1962	5 ¢	1.26	4.22	5.03	5.49	-7.09
1963	5 ¢	1.65	3.63	4.58	5.50	15.60
1964	5 ¢	2.03	3.79	6.16	5.43	25.43
1965	5 ¢	2.39	3.92	0.05	3.94	6.68
1966	5 ¢	3.50	5.03	-1.05	4.12	-7.07
1967	5 ¢	3.76	4.59	-0.48	4.51	18.09
1968	6 ¢	3.99	6.44	2.14	5.73	22.45
1969	6 ¢	4.53	7.09	-2.86	3.47	-0.81
1970	6 ¢	3.33	6.70	16.39	11.18	-3.57
1971	8 ¢	2.90	3.81	14.84	12.88	8.01
1972	8 ¢	4.70	3.55	8.11	7.79	27.38
1973	8 ¢	7.78	5.11	1.97	5.55	0.27
1974	8 ¢	10.83	7.85	-4.53	3.44	-25.93
1975	8 ¢	10.78	7.41	8.02	10.86	18.48
1976	10 ¢	7.47	9.27	23.64	13.86	11.02
1977	12 ¢	8.00	7.66	9.04	13.47	10.71
1978	14 ¢	8.97	8.34	4.10	5.23	29.72
1979	17 ¢	9.12	11.41	-2.83	3.79	44.77
1980	17 ¢	10.16	14.97	2.18	6.52	30.13
1981	17 ¢	12.35	18.41	-2.09	12.82	-10.25
1982	30 ¢	10.86	15.42	45.82	28.15	5.54
1983	32 ¢	5.73	9.62	9.61	18.69	35.49
1984	32 ¢	4.41	11.59	16.90	11.79	-2.39
1985	34 ¢	3.90	9.88	26.68	14.42	25.07
1986	34 ¢	4.17	9.33	17.21	10.93	8.95
1987	36 ¢	4.40	8.48	1.78	8.74	5.88
1988	37 ¢	4.02	9.41	11.30	8.31	11.08
1989	38 ¢	4.97	12.36	15.17	12.44	21.37
1990	39 ¢	4.82	13.48	4.32	11.20	-14.80
1991	40 ¢	5.61	9.83	25.30	19.31	12.02
1992	42 ¢	1.50	7.08	11.57	10.08	-1.43
Dec/62-Dec/92 (30-yr.)		5.71	8.45	8.60	9.67	9.81
Dec/67-Dec/92 (25-yr.)		6.33	9.32	10.01	10.69	9.54
Dec/72-Dec/92 (20-yr.)		6.95	10.30	10.65	11.34	9.43
Dec/77-Dec/92 (15-yr.)		6.29	11.27	11.82	12.01	12.71
Dec/82-Dec/92 (10-yr.)		4.35	10.09	13.73	12.53	9.24
Dec/87-Dec/92 (5-yr.)		4.17	10.41	13.33	12.21	4.87

The ScotiaMcLeod long-term bond index measures total performance of issues whose term is greater than ten years and which have an average term of 16.5 years. All total return indices, except the TSE 300, are copyright © ScotiaMcLeod Inc., 1993.

could decline, especially if it was not chosen wisely or the stock market itself declines. Nevertheless, you might take the risk in return for the possibility of staying ahead of inflation.

In determining your risk tolerance, you have to consider your own personality and your reactions to fear and greed. Some people are just more aggressive than others, more ready to accept the risks of the marketplace. This might be obvious in your job, daily activities and attitude toward sports and games. The risk-prone will have taken risks in business, investments, life and been successful with some of those risks. At the other end of the investor personality spectrum are the risk-adverse, passive investors. They have a greater need for security and less tolerance of risk. They might still be very successful people, but have done things more safely.

Your tolerance of risk will also depend on your stage in life. The young have fewer commitments and responsibilities and can afford to take greater risks. And they have time; if things don't work out, they have many years to get back on track. As we move into middle age we have more family responsibilities, children to raise, a mortgage to pay off, a style of life to finance. Our income is growing and there are still many years before retirement. Provided your debt is low, your insurance is adequate and your job secure, you can handle a little more risk.

The next stage in life is the consolidation stage, the ten to fifteen years before retirement during which your earnings are at their peak, your expenses are down and you are focused on saving for retirement. Financially, you might feel better able to handle risk. Although retirement is looming and we begin to feel nervous about losing any capital when we don't have time to replace it, we have to remember that retirement will last for twenty or thirty years.

The spending stage begins in retirement,

although the first few years might surprise you — many continue to save. But for many of our years in retirement, we will draw on our life's savings to provide the income we need. Your investment approach moves toward a concern about loss of capital and a need for income.

It is possible that as time goes on and you are comfortable with your life and finances, your thinking will turn toward giving away some of your wealth and possessions, either before or after you die. Sometimes this means a need for cash, at other times it will mean setting a few investments aside to grow for the benefit of your heirs.

The question is, where do you fit? How comfortable are you with risking some of your funds to build your wealth for the future? If you want to avoid risk, think about the consequences of your decision. Most of us cannot afford to accept the returns that come with investments that do not provide us with growth. Without it, we will never keep ahead of inflation and taxes.

Fortunately, knowledge will help you over your fears. If you look at the history of returns in the investment markets, you might begin to feel more comfortable with risk. You can see in the history of returns compiled by the research staff at ScotiaMcLeod Inc. that the returns from bonds or stocks can climb and drop with unnerving speed. You can also see that if you can keep investments for five, ten or even more years, you will have both good and bad years but time will average your returns and reward you for your patience.

Finding the best after-tax return

When investing, you must never forget that it is the after-tax return that is yours to keep. You must keep the tax treatment of the various types of investments in mind when developing your investment policy and selecting your asset mix. The example in the table illustrates the taxation of various sources of income, assuming a 40-percent tax rate and $1,000 investment.

You can see that even if you have used up your $100,000 lifetime capital gains exemption, your after tax return is greatest from an investment that gives you growth. If you have not used up your exemption, your after tax return on capital gains is close to double your return from an interest-bearing investment. If you have not used your lifetime gains exemption, then you should consider including investments, such as a Canadian equity mutual fund or stocks themselves, in your investment portfolio to take advantage of this tax benefit.

Interest income and foreign dividends are fully taxable, but the tax on Canadian dividends is lower because of the dividend tax credit. You can reduce your tax bill simply by switching from interest-bearing deposits, CSBs and bonds to preferred or common shares that yield dividend income and capital gains when they are sold. In fact, a $1,000 investment in shares yielding a 4-percent dividend and 5-percent annual capital growth will return about $82 after taxes, or 8.2 percent. (There is no certainty, however, that the investment will pay these returns or even retain its original value, but based on historic return information, there is a good likelihood that shares will provide these returns over the long term.)

As a rule of thumb, a Canadian dividend is worth about 1.25 times the after-tax value of the same amount of interest. For this reason, a common share paying 4 percent is more valuable than a deposit paying 4.75 percent. The opportunity to earn tax-free capital gains will also make the share worth even more.

Establishing an asset mix

You can also see in the ScotiaMcLeod history of market returns that while one investment class is faring poorly, another will be bringing in great returns and a third might be simply respectable. This gives rise to an old piece of wisdom that is used in many endeavours in life but is especially apt when it comes to investing: Don't keep all your eggs in one basket.

It's usually wiser to invest in several types of investments, and to own several different investments of a given type. Investing only in the stock of a single pulp and paper company would not be prudent. The company could be badly managed and run into financial difficulty. Or, the industry's paper-making capacity could be excessive at the same time demand for paper begins to drop. The entire industry could go into the doldrums. Or, the Canadian economy could be depressed and the stock market itself drop.

Instead, you should diversify your investments in a balanced mix of investments. Because the different investment classes react in different ways to changes in the economy and in the marketplace, the risk of declines in one category is offset by potential increases in another. This allows you to participate in the solid historical returns for each asset class while reducing your overall risk.

To gain the greatest benefits of diversification, we recommend that you buy twenty or more securities — stocks of different companies and investments in more than one class of investment assets. This diversity allows you to catch the ups (and unfortunately, the downs) of many different sectors of the economy. It will also mean that the investment performance of your portfolio will be close to the average for the market itself.

One way to achieve this balance of asset classes and diverse securities is to invest in a balanced mutual fund. The objective of these funds is to invest in some mixture of securities in the three major investment classes. These funds are a response to modern portfolio theory and the concepts of asset allocation. If you do not want to build a diversified portfolio yourself and choose to buy a balanced fund, make sure that you understand the percentage of underlying securities that will be invested in cash, fixed income and equities.

Fixing your mix

Your first task in creating your personal investment strategy is to establish your "asset mix", the mix of different kinds of investments that best fit your needs and investment personality. Let's take a look at your current portfolio; although you should include both your RRSPs and non-registered assets, list them in separate columns. There's space on the worksheet to divide your investments into the main categories — cash, fixed-income securities, equities and real estate. You probably hold at least a few investments in each group. It would be useful to list your investments separately for you and your spouse. You should then calculate the percentage of investment assets you have as a family in each of the main investment classes.

The next step is to decide whether you want to maintain your current mix of investments or shift the balance, perhaps even making new investments. Your asset mix decision will be based on several factors: your investment objective, your age, and, most importantly, your risk tolerance. To help you establish an appropriate mix, consider the following examples.

Our first investor has an above-average tolerance for risk and is seeking long-term growth. He doesn't need any income from his investments for at least ten years nor does he expect to need to use any of his investments for personal spending in the next couple of years. This investor realizes the value of his investments will rise and fall, he's even prepared for a loss every five years or so, but he wants above-average returns over the long

haul. He wants to keep his taxes as low as possible. I would suggest his portfolio look like this:

- 10 to 20 percent cash,
- 10 to 30 percent fixed-income,.
- 50 to 70 percent common stocks

Our second investor wants a portfolio that will provide moderate growth and income stability, although his income needs from his investments are modest. He is somewhat tolerant of risk. He expects some ups and downs in the value of his assets but will only feel comfortable with small losses, if any. However, he also has a ten-year time horizon as well and he's also hoping to defer and reduce his taxes. His suggested portfolio mix is:

- 10 to 20 percent cash,
- 30 to 50 percent fixed-income securities,
- 30 to 50 percent common stocks.

Finally, we have an investor who cannot sleep if he knows his investments are at risk. Safety comes first in all his investment decisions. This investor has a time horizon of less than ten years before he either spends the wealth he has created or begins to draw an income from it. This investor accepts a lower potential income in favour of safety and avoidance of risk. This portfolio will provide little growth. His suggested portfolio mix is:

- 30 to 50 percent cash,
- 30 to 50 percent fixed income,
- 0 to 30 percent common stocks.

In creating your own mix, look at your investment objectives and the tolerance for risk. Consider the sample cases and your current portfolio. Using this information, try to determine the balance of asset classes that meets your needs. Express this in a range so that your portfolio can fluctuate slightly; if it moves outside the range you've established you will have to reduce your investments in that class which has exceeded its range in

Seeking the best after-tax return TABLE 13

The example in the table illustrates the taxation of various sources of income, assuming a 40-percent tax rate and $1,000 investment.

	Interest	Dividends	Exempt Capital gains	Non-exempt Capital gains
	8%	4%	9%	9%
Income	$80	$40	$90	$90
Taxable amount	$80	$50	$0	$67.50
Income taxes payable	$32	$20	$0	$27
Dividend tax credit		$12		
Taxes payable	$32	$8	$0	$27
After-tax return	$48	$32	$90	$63

order to purchase more of those that will have fallen beneath the limit you've established. This is called rebalancing. Document your choice on the investment strategies worksheet.

Your investment management style

Finally, you should consider the management style with which you will be comfortable. If you're investing mainly for growth, have a high tolerance for risk and have decided that your portfolio can be largely in speculative investments, then you might be able to accept an aggressive management style which calls for many trades and quick investment decisions.

For most people in retirement, a more passive investment style will be acceptable. Such a style involves choosing appropriate investments in keeping with your asset mix and risk tolerance and holding these quality investments over the long term. Some investors will want to play an active role in managing their funds; others will want to be passive. You should consider your knowledge about investments and your desire to be involved in the investment decisions.

If you have identified that you have an aggressive, active investment style and you have the experience, time and interest, you might want to manage your own portfolio of stocks, bonds and deposits. This can be done

quite profitably by making use of the research and information that is available to the public through the financial press and brokerage houses. If you decide to manage your own investments, you must be disciplined about monitoring your results and sticking to the principles in your investment strategy. You might choose to select a broker or you might choose to execute all of your trades on your own through a discount broker.

Many of you, however, will have decided that you do not want to manage your portfolio. Instead, you will want to get the best professional help that you can find, given your level of assets and the fees you are willing to pay.

Selecting a broker

If you have decided that you want to manage your investment portfolio on your own, you might need a broker to buy and sell your stocks or bonds for you. A good broker can be of great assistance in helping you to manage your portfolio, provided that he or she has a full understanding of your financial position, goals and income tax status.

You should also spend some time talking to make sure that you are comfortable with his or her investment style. If you decide to use a broker, you should monitor the transactions in your account monthly when you receive your statement. Although the broker can help you in developing your portfolio, no one will have a greater interest in your investments than you. Review the portfolio to see that it remains in line with your investment policy and the management style you desire.

Mutual funds

If you have $250,000 or less and you want some form of professional management, then you will probably want to invest in mutual funds or through a "wrap account." Mutual

Your portfolio mix   **WORKSHEET 30**

Investment type	My personal assets	My RRSP assets	My spouse's personal assets	My spouse's RRSP assets	Total family assets	% of family portfolio
Cash	$ _____	$ _____	$ _____	$ _____	$ _____	% _____
Fixed income	_____	_____	_____	_____	_____	_____
Equities	_____	_____	_____	_____	_____	_____
Real Estate	_____	_____	_____	_____	_____	_____
Total	_____	_____	_____	_____	_____	_____

funds allow you to participate in a diversified portfolio, chosen and monitored by professional investment managers with a long history of experience managing money. You will pay for this advice through the annual management fees and/or an annual fee. Once you have determined your preferred asset mix, you can achieve this portfolio by buying mutual funds invested in each of the main investment classes.

Although professional management is one of the greatest advantages of mutual funds, investment in these funds does not provide the kind of personal attention that will ensure that the fund's goals match your unique goals and objectives. Choose a fund with great care, paying attention to past performance and the selection of individual securities held by the fund. Don't hesitate to ask for a copy of the fund's portfolio and the range within which the types of securities can vary.

The past performance of the fund might or might not be a crucial factor in your decision to purchase it. It is all too easy to want the fund that was the top performer over the past three months, six months or two years. It might turn out, however, that the investment manager responsible for that performance is no longer

with the fund or that the fund manager chose one or two securities that were winners coming out of the recession but will not do as well as the economy begins to grow again.

Wrap accounts

In the past, mutual funds were the only way for smaller investors to get professional investment expertise. Now, wrap accounts are providing an alternative for those investors with less than $250,000. You open a wrap account through your broker, providing him or her with a minimum amount of capital, usually $50,000 to $150,000. The broker and an investment manager might have established a portfolio managed according to a particular set of objectives in which you can place your funds. Or, they might help you create a custom-tailored portfolio.

The investment manager provides ongoing management of the funds, and your broker will execute and settle trades, maintain custody of the assets and provide you with monthly statements summarizing your portfolio and movements in your portfolio. The professional investment manager participates in the wrap account program because the broker agrees to bring as many individual investors as possible to the program, creating a large pool of investments.

These accounts are interesting in that they allow smaller investors to obtain the same professional management expertise available to the big players. However, the main drawback is cost. The annual fee must cover the investment manager's fee and the brokerage cost. The fee on most wrap accounts is at least 2.5 percent of your assets a year. This is significantly higher than the fees charged by an investment counsellor. Undoubtedly, the increasing competition in the market will lead to a reduction in fees.

Wrap accounts are widespread in the United States and are on the rise in Canada. Because they are still relatively new, you should ask questions about the investment managers involved, especially if the program itself does not have a track record. It is probable, given the U.S. experience, that the number of these account arrangements will grow and become a large factor in the Canadian investment world.

Investment counsellors

If you have investment assets of $250,000 or more, investment counsellors will provide the best independent professional advice you can obtain. Investment counsellors will work with you to develop a personal investment policy, custom-designing a portfolio with your funds to suit your objectives and situation. If you have more than $300,000 to invest, we recommend that you use a professional manager to handle at least some of your assets, even if you have an aggressive investment style and want to actively trade your own account. In this case, you could keep a portion, perhaps 20 percent, with a broker or discount broker.

Investment counsellors are usually paid a percentage of the assets under management. Any bias on their part then will be toward increasing the value of your assets, which is

what you want. Investment counsellors do not have any vested interest in any individual securities or trades on your account.

Selecting an investment counsellor is a lot like finding a financial planner. You must work with someone who you trust and whose style matches your investment management preferences. You should ask about the past performance of assets under management and inquire about the extent of assets under management to get an idea of how successful the investment counsellor has been. Investment counsellors must be licensed by one of the provincial securities commissions. Ask family and friends for recommendations of a good investment counsellor and then meet with the counsellor to determine if he or she is a good fit for you.

Your RRSP and your asset mix

The asset mix you have established in your investment strategy should cover your entire portfolio, including your RRSPs. We have covered the tax advantages of RRSPs in chapter eight but let's look at how you should use those tax elements while balancing your portfolio. If you remember, investment income earned in your RRSP will grow tax-free until you withdraw it.

In addition, if you suffer any losses on investments held in your RRSP, you will not enjoy any tax relief from these losses, as you would if the investments were held outside your RRSP. For these two reasons, it is best to load up your RRSP with the fixed-income investments in your asset mix, and to hold the tax-advantaged equities outside.

For example, let's assume you have $100,000 worth of investments, including $40,000 in your RRSP, you could have 10 percent of those investments in Canada Savings Bonds, 40 percent in bonds and GICs, and 50 percent in equity mutual funds. The $40,000 in

Your investment strategy

Your financial objective

Look at your need for cash, growth and income and establish their importance to you. Indicate that importance by assigning a percentage to each. If you need income from your investments, indicate the annual amount you require. You will know this from your work in chapters five and nine. If your priority is building your wealth, jot down the return you need to achieve. Again, you'll know this from the work you did in chapter nine.

_____

_____

_____

_____

Income tax considerations

For example, have you and your spouse used your lifetime capital gains exemption. If not, how much exemption do you have left? Or, what is your usual RRSP contribution limit? Do you have any carry-forward room that you should use? Have you made your allowed $8,000 overcontribution? Should you be contributing to a spousal RRSP?

_____

_____

_____

_____

_____

Your investment time horizon

_____

_____

Your risk tolerance

_____

Your desired asset mix range for the family

Cash _____

Fixed-income securities _____

Equities _____

Real estate _____

Your management style

Do you want to be actively involved in your investments?

_____

_____

_____

fixed-income securities should be held in your RRSP, and the CSBs and equities outside your RRSP. In this way, you wouldn't have to pay tax on the interest you're earning, since it is sheltered from tax, and you could use your lifetime capital gains exemption on any growth in the equities.

Of course, if the entire $100,000 is in your RRSP, you should maintain this asset mix. You don't have to have a self-directed RRSP to purchase units in Canadian mutual funds, as long as they're RRSP-eligible. The same principles apply to RRIFs as well.

Development of an investment plan that helps you to achieve your goals will help you to proceed at the right financial speed to achieve financial independence. Investing is a complex business and you have to work at it to become familiar with the fundamentals. You have to learn how to use the system to produce the investment returns that will keep you ahead of income taxes and inflation.

There are thousands of investments to pick from, but you will become comfortable with those that fit into your investment plan if you take the time. You can decide to change your portfolio mix, but only do so when conditions merit a change.

Review your investment results every three months to make sure that they are consistent with your strategy and are producing the results you seek. Compare your results to that of the investment averages in the marketplace, the consumer price index for inflation, and the rates of return that you could get on guaranteed investment certificates.

If your performance is lagging, try to figure out why and make changes if necessary. You should know what is happening to your investments, but don't worry constantly about daily changes in the marketplace. Once you have a sound plan in place, your job is to keep feeding the investment pot with more savings, and then to enjoy the results.

Notes

Chapter 13

Crossing the border

Canadians are driven by many factors — adventure, high taxes, cold weather — to retire outside Canada. To some this means an extended trip around the world; to many others it means spending three to six months a year in the warmth of Florida, Arizona or Mexico. To a small but growing number, it means cutting ties with Canada and becoming a resident of another country.

Leaving Canada, even if only for a few months, is not a decision to be taken lightly. There are a great many financial and social considerations. You have to consider the impact on your income taxes, the quality of medical care and its costs, the cost of daily living, the availability of financial services, the opportunity for employment and involvement in community activities, the nearness of family and friends, and the laws concerning immigration.

Leaving Canada's tax system behind

One of the most compelling reasons for leaving Canada is to escape our relatively expensive system of taxation. Other parts of the world have considerably lower taxes, either because they are wealthier in their worldwide trading activities or they provide fewer benefits and services for their citizens. While Canadians are driven daily to escape this considerable tax burden, you should keep in mind that you would also be leaving behind the country that the United Nations placed at the top of the list for general living conditions, a country with one of the world's finest and least expensive medical-care systems.

Avoiding Canada's income tax net is easier said than done. Canada applies taxes based on the residence of an individual and where he or she earns income or carries on a business.

Apart from the fact that we work or carry on a business in Canada, you and I are taxed in Canada because we live here. As residents, we have to report our income from all sources, no matter where that income arises. If you have bank accounts in Australia, a pension from Sweden, rental income on your condo in the United States, you must report all of these incomes on your Canadian tax return.

If you move outside Canada and cease to be a resident in Canada, you will no longer need to complete a tax return for Canada, unless you carry on business activities or earn rental income from property located here. Even if you are not a resident, you will still have Canadian taxes withheld from payments of pensions, RRSP annuities, RRIF payments, and investment income from Canadian sources. So you can see that even when you get away from Canada you don't entirely get away from its taxation.

If you reside outside Canada, however, the Canadian taxes you pay will probably be only 10 to 25 percent of your Canadian income and you will not have to pay any tax on incomes that you receive from other countries. However, your non-Canadian income will be subject to the tax rules of your new country and possibly to the tax rules of the country whose citizenship you adopt. (The United States taxes its citizens no matter where they live; Canada does not.) In most countries, you will either be granted a tax credit for the amount of tax withheld on your income in Canada or your Canadian income will not be taxable at all. If the income isn't taxed in your new country, your tax burden will drop from the 40 to 50 percent you might have paid if you had remained here to only 10 to 25 percent — the withholding tax.

You'll pay a lower withholding tax rate of 10 to 15 percent if you move to a country that has an income tax treaty or agreement with Canada. The high withholding rate of 25 percent is charged when you live in a country with whom we do not have an agreement. This will be particularly true if you move to a tax haven — territories and countries which charge little or no income tax on their citizens and residents. Even this higher withholding will result in a lighter tax burden if you don't have to pay any tax in your new country of residence. Countries with which we do have agreements will probably charge a tax of their own on the income you receive from Canada, but will give you a full or significant credit for taxes withheld in Canada.

In almost every case, you'll pay less tax because most countries have a lower tax rate than Canada. In the United States, your state and federal tax bill could range from 20 to 30 percent of your income. If your income is over $100,000 this could be 30 to 40 percent, still 10 to 20 percent less than your Canadian tax burden. Think about it: If you receive $50,000 income in retirement, you would save $5,000 to $10,000 every year.

But that's not all! U.S. taxes will be even less on certain types of retirement incomes from Canada. Pension income and income from RRSPs are fully taxable for Canadian residents because contributions to these retirement plans enjoyed tax deductions when they were made. In the U.S., however, Canadian pensions and RRSPs are considered to be merely saving and investment accounts that have accumulated over the years. The U.S. system has not given you any deferred tax advantages over the years and seeks to tax only the increase on the RRSP arising from interest, dividends and capital gains from the date on which you became a resident of the U.S. However, this tax can be deferred until you actually receive it.

Income from a pension or RRSP annuity would be taxed in much the same way as a prescribed annuity is taxed in Canada — it is considered to be partially investment income and partially the return of capital. As much as 20 to 50 percent of the income will not be taxable in the U.S., depending on your age or the number of years over which you will receive your retirement income. This reduces your tax burden even more. The combined U.S. income tax and Canadian withholding tax might be around 20 to 30 percent. This is a bargain compared to the 40 to 50 percent you would pay as a Canadian resident.

Cutting your ties

To escape Canadian taxes, you must also give up your status as a resident of Canada. A non-resident of Canada is someone who does not have a permanent home in Canada. If you leave behind a house or a property in Canada, it must be rented out under a lease that cannot be cancelled and is for at least three months. Even the continued ownership of a country property could lead tax authorities to question whether you have really ceased to be a resident of Canada under the suspicion that you might be using your country home as a residence. If you keep your vacation home, you must be able to prove that you reside outside Canada and hold the country home as an investment or for very infrequent vacations.

A non-resident is expected to have a job or business earnings outside of Canada unless he or she is retired. A non-resident would also be expected to have banking and financial services provided at the new residence rather than continued in Canada. Medical care would be provided outside of Canada and social activities would be carried out mainly outside Canada. Your congregation or place of worship would have to be outside of Canada. Any remaining club memberships would be converted to out-of-town, limited-use status. You should be able to demonstrate that if you spend time in Canada at all, it is only for a temporary visit and you are clearly residing in the other country.

Your country of residence is determined by the overall situation and evidence that most of your ties of residency are outside of Canada, even if there are a few still remaining in Canada. The change of status to non-resident is not normally challenged by the Canadian income tax authorities unless there are considerable amounts of annual earnings at stake. In such cases, the Canadian government might make a careful determination of the residency status and someone with high income — and therefore significant tax benefits from not being a Canadian resident — would be wise to be pure in breaking with Canada and establishing complete residential ties in a place outside of Canada. This status should be maintained very clearly for at least two years before any return to Canada.

If you are concerned, income tax bulletin number IT221R2 outlines the Canadian government's understanding of what makes you a resident or a non-resident of Canada. One of the criteria is that you plan to reside outside of Canada for at least two years. You should be careful. If you are in doubt, check it out with a tax adviser who has considerable experience in this area.

Departure tax

You might have to pay a tax to leave the country. What we call a departure tax is really a tax arising from the necessity to include certain special incomes in your final tax return before you might do so if you remained in Canada. When you leave, you are required to file an income tax return covering the period from January 1 to the date of departure. This return would report all of the income you have earned during the period along with some additional items, including:

- Interest income accruing on deposits, GICs, bonds, and other fixed-income instruments, even if you have not yet been paid.

- Taxable capital gains on the "deemed" disposition of capital property on the day you depart. As far as the government is concerned you have sold any capital property which you own on the day you leave the country. In this way the department can capture tax before you leave. You must attach to your tax return a schedule showing all of the investments and capital properties that you own and their fair market value on the date of departure. If you have any capital gains, you can reduce the tax by applying any past capital losses or claiming your capital gains exemption.

- All your earnings to the date of departure. Professionals and other self-employed individuals who often report their taxes on a fiscal year different from the calendar year have to submit a final tax return that reports both the earnings for the normal tax year and for the period up to the date of departure. If your tax year ends January 31 and you leave the country on September 1, you would have to report, and pay taxes on, nineteen months of earnings — the twelve months ended January 31 plus the seven months from February 1 to August 31.

Departure taxes need not be onerous, especially now that Canadians are required to report their interest income every year. Also, the opportunity to use the capital gains exemption and to elect that property be considered as taxable Canadian property allows you to avoid heavy capital gains taxes. Capital property can also be transferred to a Canadian investment holding company. In any event, the departure tax return can require some special consideration and tax planning. It may not be a barrier to your departure from Canada but should be looked at with a professional tax adviser if you have significant amounts of capital property such as a business that you own and operate.

You might also be able to delay the tax on deemed dispositions by declaring them to be taxable Canadian property. Taxable Canadian property includes shares of Canadian-owned corporations, real estate, and such other property as you elect to be considered as taxable Canadian property. In the case of real estate or private company shares, the government knows it will collect its taxes when a sale takes place because the buyer of your property will be responsible for the tax liability unless a significant portion of the proceeds from the sales have been withheld and remitted to the tax department. Or you can make arrangements with the tax department to satisfy it that no tax is payable or provide the department with adequate security to pay the tax that will eventually have to be paid.

Medical costs

The biggest challenge in deciding whether to reside in Canada or the U.S. will be medical care costs. Pick up any newspaper and you will see the raging debates in the United States over escalating health costs. The problem will become worse as the number of seniors grows. Unlike in Canada, the national medical-care system cares only for those citizens over age sixty-five, and only if they have paid into social security over the years. Up to that age, Americans are covered by private insurance.

Almost 33 million U.S. citizens are not covered by medical health insurance at all.

U.S. social security does not cover Canadians who retire to the U.S. And you will lose your medical-care coverage after ceasing to be a resident of Canada or after being out of the country for three to eight months, depending on your province of residence. Even for retired Americans, the cost of a significant operation or a chronic health condition will exceed their protection under their national Medicare plan. Many employers provide their employees with medical insurance in retirement, but it is expected that post-retirement health-care benefits will be curtailed because of the enormous cost. Many retired Americans must buy private health-care insurance to cover those medical costs that won't be paid by Medicare.

For all the complaints about Canada's health-care system, the standard of care is high and the cost is right. One of our clients paid $106,000 for hospitalization in Florida for three weeks, two angioplast angina treatments, physicians, drugs and nursing care arising from a mild heart attack. His insurance paid for $32,000 and the only relief for the remaining $74,000 was an income tax deduction, good for about $30,000. He paid $54,000 for treatments that would have been free in Canada.

As a former Canadian resident and citizen you could return to Canada and establish residency. As a Canadian citizen or landed immigrant and resident of Canada, you have the right to provincial medical care. Although the provinces and territories have the right to impose a waiting period of six months, this does not seem to have been enforced in the past. This could mean that a Canadian who needs an operation or chronic care could return to Canada and come back on to the Medicare system, having given up legal residence elsewhere in the world.

Unfortunately, there is a much greater vigilance in accepting medical-care claims by those who have resided outside Canada. One cannot expect to return automatically to claim Canadian medical care in the future. Your illness might not permit the luxury of returning to Canada and waiting out a period of time before becoming eligible. If you have chosen consciously to give up your provincial medical care by moving outside Canada, you must search diligently for insurance in your new home to replace what you have lost.

In the U.S. this isn't easy. Medicare is available to all working Americans and their family members after age sixty-five and private medical-care insurance policies for people over this age are not available. (If you work for a multinational corporation, you might consider becoming employed by the U.S. operation some months before retiring. Your U.S. service might make you eligible for the company's post-retirement health-care benefits. Be sure to check this out carefully.)

I canvassed several U.S. insurance companies and agents to find some kind of coverage for Canadians who choose to retire in the U.S. This insurance just doesn't appear to exist. The best we could do was build a layer of existing "excess limits policies" which would mean you would not have coverage for basic services, but you would be protected from financial disaster. Several years ago, this would have cost $6,000 a year for $500,000 coverage but you would still have to cover the first $50,000 as a form of self-insurance. Rising insurance costs have probably since pushed the premium for such coverage to at least $20,000 a year.

For some healthy retirees who are saving a great deal on their income taxes and cost of living this might not be a bad proposition. For most others it may be too great a gamble to take with the precious retirement savings.

Estate taxes

You should also give some thought to the implications of estate taxes on your family and dependents. Canada is one of the few countries in the world that does not tax your estate at the time of death. We tax capital gains at the time of death, but this is not comparable in cost unless considerable wealth has been built in a private company or other valuable investment held for a great number of years.

In the U.S., as in many other countries, estate tax is charged at the time of death upon the value of all investments and possessions less debts. These taxes range from 10 to 50 percent. Generally, the imposition of estate tax is delayed if property is left to a spouse, but eventually there will be a considerable cost of transferring your estate from one generation to the next. For a retiree planning to live many years off a retirement income and savings, estate tax might not be relevant. But if you are older or your assets are considerably in excess of your needs, you should not overlook the advantages of being able to pass assets on to your heirs free of tax, which is substantially the case in Canada.

For Canadians choosing to retire in the U.S., the estate tax can be onerous. Americans can leave assets to their husbands or wives and avoid paying any estate tax. You can reduce the impact of estate taxes by making gifts to your family and by passing property during your lifetime into trusts for your children and grandchildren. If you are particularly concerned about estate taxes and the effect they will have on your family, you might consider buying enough life insurance to at least cover your taxes.

Normally, the fact that a country has estate taxes would not stop a Canadian from changing residence in retirement. There are situations where significant estates are being handed down from one generation to another and deserve sophisticated estate planning, perhaps even a move to a country more receptive to your estate plans. In these situations, you will certainly need good professional advice.

Becoming a U.S. resident

If you want to become a permanent resident or citizen of the United States, you will have a tough but not impossible chore. There are seven preferential categories and two acceptable alternatives. The seven categories are:

- Spouses and unmarried minor-aged children of U.S. citizens.

- Unmarried adult children of U.S. citizens.

- Spouses and unmarried children of permanent resident aliens.

- Married sons and daughters of U.S. citizens.

- Professionals and persons with exceptional scientific or artistic abilities, who have job offers.

- Brothers and sisters of U.S. citizens.

- Workers in areas of short supply in the U.S.

The United States also offers entry visas to 12,000 Canadians who are randomly selected from the thousands of Canadians who apply every year. If you don't qualify under the preferences and have not won in the periodic lotteries for U.S. entry, then you might be able to qualify as a business investor who will bring money and jobs to the U.S. by opening a business or as a person of means who can demonstrate that he or she will not need to enter the job market.

While it is possible for you to gain entry to the U.S. in one of these ways it can take years and thousands of dollars in legal fees. As a temporary visitor from Canada you can own property in the U.S., spend most of your time there, and pay U.S. income taxes. You could likely meet the test of residing there even

though you don't have permanent resident status in the U.S. and are not actively seeking it. (We'll discuss "substantial presence" residency later in this chapter.)

With the official signs of residency, you will be considered to be a resident alien and therefore required to file a federal 1040 income tax return reporting your worldwide income expressed in U.S. dollars. You will also have to file a state tax return in most states. A significant exception is Florida.

Incomes to be included in the federal tax return are largely the same as for a Canadian return but there are some differences. Dividends are included at 100 percent of the amount received, they are not grossed up to 125 percent; capital gains are included at 100 percent, rather than 75 percent. The gain is measured from back to the original cost, even if you obtained the property many years ago while you were a resident of Canada. In some cases, social security is tax free; in others only half of the amount received is taxable. Only half of the benefits from Canadian Old Age Security and Canada or Quebec pension plan would be taxable. The capital portion of Canadian pensions and RRSP incomes can be excluded from U.S. income tax.

Deductions from income are similar to those in Canada but you should keep in mind that RRSP contributions do not have any status in the United States. Contributing to a Canadian RRSP will not reduce your taxable income. There are, however, comparable programs in the U.S. if you earn employment income, business income, or professional income.

One of the most interesting deductions allowed in the U.S. is the deduction of interest expense on the purchase of a home or second residence. If you have to borrow to buy a home, this is certainly a welcome improvement; about one-third of your borrowing cost will be recovered from income tax. (If you have the money to buy a home, however, you should think twice about borrowing. You will want to borrow if the after-tax cost of the mortgage is less than the after-tax income you would expect to make on your investment.) Another difference is the deduction of property taxes and your state and municipal taxes from U.S. taxable income.

There are also municipal and state bonds which provide income which is not subject to federal and state income taxes. The returns on these investments are lower because the issuer knows that you are getting a tax break. Another tax advantage can be found in compound interest instruments issued by life insurance companies. The U.S. does not tax the investment income that builds in deferred annuities until the annuities mature or you receive the annuity income.

In most cases, your tax cost under the U.S. tax system will be less than in Canada, often considerably less. We find that Canadians will usually save 15 percent to 20 percent on taxes by moving to the United States. On sufficiently large incomes these savings and the lower cost of living more than offset the loss of free medical coverage. A person retired to the United States will still pay tax on income coming from Canada. The Canadian tax cost, however, will normally be small and fully credited against U.S. taxes. Let's summarize this tax information:

Withholding taxes will not be taken from OAS, CPP or QPP benefits when these are sent to a U.S. resident. And, only half of these payments will be subject to tax in the U.S.

Only the growth in a pension plan, RRSP or RRIF after entering the United States will be subject to U.S. taxation. Receipt of those funds that were in these plans before moving south is considered to be tax free return of capital.

The payment of interest and dividends to a U.S. resident will be subject to withholding tax, usually at the 15 percent rate. There is no need to file a tax return in Canada. The paying agent will simply pay you 85 percent of the dividend or interest and remit the 15 percent tax to the Canadian non-resident tax authorities. At the end of the year you will receive a tax slip showing the gross income and the amount withheld for Canadian tax. In the United States, the gross amount of the dividends or interest from Canada must be reported in your U.S. 1040 return. Tax withheld by Canada will be allowed as a foreign tax credit. Your tax cost will be the same as if you had received your investment income directly as a U.S. taxpayer.

As a U.S. resident, you are not required to file a Canadian tax return if your earned income from Canada is less than $10,000 a year. If, however, you are employed on a regular basis in Canada or carry on a business here, an annual tax return will have to be filed to report the wages or business income. This includes Canadians who receive a bonus or delayed compensation of any kind, including a gain from exercising a stock option granted while employed in Canada. A tax return is completed by the non-resident in the normal way except that personal tax credits are not allowed. At the same time, your income must be included in the U.S. tax return under the requirement that U.S. residents must report their worldwide income. Your tax cost will end up being equal to the amount paid in Canada.

Before you pack your bags: If you have a lot of investment capital and very little income from pensions or RRSPs, the Canadian tax system might be about the same as the U.S. Remember, Canada does not tax your first $100,000 in capital gains and taxes only 75 percent of any gains above that amount. The U.S. taxes all of your gain. Canada also provides a tax credit on dividends from taxable Canadian corporations. The best way to assess the impact of a move on your tax bill is to make several tax estimates using different assumptions, to see what will happen to your tax bill over your retirement years.

Sale of a Canadian house

If you leave Canada without being able to sell your house, but sell it within one year, any gain in value of the home to the date of departure will be tax-free for Canadian purposes. (This house was considered to be your principal residence while a Canadian resident.) You will have to go through a complex procedure, however, to convince the Canadian tax authorities that taxes are not payable on the house and that the purchaser need not withhold a large amount of the purchase price and remit it to the government for taxes.

Canada has a protective mechanism which makes the purchaser liable for any taxes that a non-resident vendor neglects to pay. If you are planning to leave Canada, it would be wise to sell your principal residence before departing. Only in this way can you avoid the cost of professional help to deal with the purchaser's notary and the income tax department to ensure that an income tax liability is not incurred and that the proceeds of sale are not held up for an unduly long period of time. A recent change in the Canada U.S. tax treaty should mean that the capital gain on the sale of your former principal residence in Canada will not be taxable in the United States.

Becoming a U.S. citizen

You are permitted by Canada to continue to be a Canadian citizen even though you become a citizen or permanent resident of the U.S. Being a dual citizen will give you rights of entry and residence in each country. Being a citizen or permanent resident of the U.S. brings with it a number of obligations which can be costly or inconvenient. You are required to file U.S. income tax returns as a U.S. citizen no matter

where you reside in the world, even if you return to Canada.

At death you will also have to file U.S. estate tax returns and pay estate taxes on the value of your worldwide assets. Annual gifts in excess of $10,000 (U.S.) to anyone other than your spouse will give rise to U.S. gift taxes even for a U.S. citizen who no longer resides there.

Ceasing to be a U.S. citizen can be onerous. There is a process to follow that results in a Certificate of Loss of Nationality. But you will continue to be subject to gift and estate taxes for ten years after renouncing your citizenship. This is to ensure that citizens do not shirk their estate tax responsibilities by moving out of the country at an auspicious time. Dual citizenship has some advantages; the disadvantages should be studied carefully.

Flight planning for Canadian snowbirds

You need not become a resident down south to enjoy some of the many benefits of living there. Many Canadians look forward to retiring in the United States and it's not hard to understand the attraction. Not only will your taxes be significantly lower, the cost of living can be 20 percent less south of the border than at home. Housing, food, clothing, entertainment, automobiles, travel, and almost everything else are cheaper. There are only two things you might pay more for, electricity and security if you live in a major city.

It is fairly easy to become a temporary resident visiting the U.S. each year, as long as you do not work. Provided you enter this way each year you are unlikely to have any trouble coming and going, as long as you register with U.S. immigration authorities each year. In fact, snowbirds do not have any immigration problem be it to the U.S., Mexico or the Caribbean. These countries are happy to open their borders to the migrant Canadians who bring their money and stay for only a few months of the year to enjoy the warm weather. Snowbirds can comfortably transfer their funds into the U.S. and out again through the North American banking system. (There can be delays, however, and you should try to establish yourself at a bank that can help you move your money from your Canadian bank to the U.S. in the simplest and fastest way.)

Many snowbirds place money on deposit with the U.S. banks and are happy to do so. Just as your accounts are protected by the CDIC here, your deposits are covered by the U.S. federal deposit insurance up to $100,000, provided the bank is a member of the FDIC. On the other hand, U.S. deposit rates are so appallingly low the Canadian banks and trust companies seem generous. You might choose to keep your money at home, perhaps in a U.S. dollar account.

U.S. deposits do have some attractive features: income tax is not withheld in the U.S. on interest earned by Canadians nor is there any reporting of this interest for tax purposes. This has led many Canadians to the erroneous conclusion that they do not need to report their U.S. interest earnings in their Canadian tax returns. That, however, would be unlawfully evading Canadian tax laws. If caught, you would suffer a penalty of 50 percent of the amount of tax you failed to pay along with an overdue interest charge for the period of time that the tax was overdue. You would also encourage tax authorities to investigate many years of tax returns in the past for similarly evasive activity. It just isn't worth it.

Snowbirds generally continue their investment activities in Canada and have little trouble keeping track of their portfolios and executing transactions through their representatives here or by doing them in the months that they stay here. Government and employee pensions will be received without interruption, either by flowing into your Canadian bank accounts by direct deposit or by having the cheques sent to the U.S. This does not have any bearing on your income tax situation. Nor do the Canadian payers have to withhold taxes of any kind other than the normal tax that is withheld on company pensions paid to Canadian residents.

The only thing the snowbird has to organize is filing a Canadian tax return on time. Of course, you can always arrange to have a professional firm prepare and sign the tax return on your behalf. You must make sure that you take special care to gather all of the various slips and receipts that are needed and pass them to the tax preparer, along with the proper written authorization to sign and file the returns.

As a final legal matter, snowbirds needn't change their wills just because you are spending some time in the U.S., even if there's a chance you will die there. The will from Canada will be valid in the United States, although it might have to go through probate in the state where you have property as well as in Canada. Sometimes this U.S. probating can be avoided by showing the authorities the probate documents from Canada.

Substantial presence

The U.S. has a number of rules that establish residency and will tax anyone it deems to be a resident of the United States. You will be considered a resident if you stay in the U.S. year after year for more than six months and have a home there. One worrisome recent development has been the U.S. "substantial presence" test. The U.S. has developed a test which takes into account the number of days spent in the U.S. over the taxation year and the two previous years — it even includes days visiting for a shopping trip. Under this new test, you must add together all of the days you've spent in the U.S. in the current taxation year plus one-third of the days in the preceding year and one-sixth of the days in the year before that. If this sum exceeds 182 days, then you are deemed to be a resident for U.S. tax purposes.

If you spend just four months of the year in the United States, you would fall into this substantial presence status. If deemed to be a resident, you would have to file a U.S. tax return reporting your worldwide income and pay U.S. income tax. However, the Canada-U.S. tax treaty sets out rules for deciding whether Revenue Canada or the Internal Revenue Service can claim you when you are deemed to be a resident of both countries.

The treaty provides that "factual" residential information should determine to which country you have a closer connection. This criteria for establishing this closer connection is similar to those listed above for proving you are a non-resident of Canada: The authorities will look at the location of your permanent home, your friends and family, your place of worship, and where you undertake certain activities, such as voting, banking and investing.

As a result, Canadians did not worry at all about the substantial presence test in the U.S. — until 1992. In that year, changes to U.S. regulations required that a non-resident demonstrate his or her closer connection to another country when that person is otherwise deemed to be a resident of the United States under the substantial presence test. A special return is to be filed, but to this date this return has not been finalized. Nor has the U.S. put into effect penalties of as much as $1,000 for each income item not reported to the U.S. tax authorities if this statement of closer connection is not filed. As a result, Canadian snowbirds did not know whether or not to file for 1992 by the June 15, 1993, deadline.

It would seem that many Canadians are residents under the substantial presence test and should have filed a statement showing their closer connection to Canada. But not only is there not a prescribed form on which they can do this, the regulations exempt Canadians with incomes of less than U.S. $100,000. It would seem that a great number of people are being asked to file a statement of closer connections to Canada but this information is not really wanted.

Canadian snowbirds might be drawn into filing tax returns in the U.S. for other reasons, particularly if they carry on a business activity or earn an income in the United States. Under the U.S.-Canada tax treaty, a U.S. tax return is not required if the salary, income or fees earned are less than U.S. $10,000. However, if you earn more U.S. income than this you will have to file a U.S. non-resident NR1040 return.

An NR1040 should also be filed to report rental income earned in the United States. If you fail to report this on a tax return, the U.S. authorities might charge tax on the gross rental income rather than the rental income less expenses. It is foolish to take the risk: File your tax return and deduct all valid expenses from rental income. Remember, any tax paid to the U.S. will be a deduction from Canadian taxes on the same rental income reported to Revenue Canada. Many Canadians who rent their homes in the U.S. are playing a doubly dangerous game if they fail to report the income to either the U.S. or Canadian authorities. The U.S. will tax their gross income and the Canadian government will slap them with a penalty and interest charges.

Canadians can also be taxed in the U.S. on capital gains arising from the disposal of U.S. real estate. Rules in both countries require that the attorneys of real estate purchasers withhold significant amounts of the proceeds from the transaction and remit them to tax authorities as payment of income taxes on the gain in value of the property. This tax withholding can be avoided in the United States if a non-resident vendor makes arrangements with the tax authorities in advance of the sale by demonstrating that tax will not be payable or by providing security for the payment of such taxes. In any event, the U.S. non-resident tax return must be filed to report the capital gains or loss arising from the sale of the property.

Any U.S. tax which you, as a Canadian resident, paid on capital gains on the U.S. property could be claimed as a foreign tax credit against Canadian capital gains tax that you might have to pay here. If you still have your lifetime capital gains exemption available, you will have to decide whether to claim the exemption and not incur any tax in Canada or incur the Canadian taxes and claim the foreign tax credit. Usually it's better to use the capital gains exemption for another purpose and recover the U.S. tax paid against the Canadian corresponding taxes.

Snowbirds and estate taxes

If a Canadian dies owning property in the U.S., American tax authorities have the right to require payment of any federal or state estate taxes. (There are U.S. states, such as Florida, that do not collect estate taxes.) A home or condo or other real estate property would constitute U.S. property for estate tax purposes. The value of such a property together with the value of your furnishings, art, jewelry, automobiles, boats and golf club memberships would be added together to calculate your gross taxable estate. Bank accounts and term deposits are excluded in calculating the U.S. estate of non-residents. Stocks and bonds of U.S. corporations are usually included in the taxable estate even if you bought the securities from brokers in Canada and the certificates are sitting in your safety deposit box at home. (These securities can only be transferred from you to another person by a transfer agent in the United States and are therefore considered to be property situated in the United States.)

You can subtract from the value of these items any direct non-recourse debt — loans

secured by the pledged property — that might be attached to U.S. property that you own. The gross taxable estate value can also be reduced by a share of your other worldwide debts. U.S. estate tax rates are applied to this estate value and a credit equal to the estate tax that would arise on the estate value of $60,000 (U.S.) is allowed. You can see that Canadian snowbirds could easily have property that is exposed to U.S. estate taxes.

Canada does not charge an estate tax or succession duty upon death and there aren't any offsetting credits in the Canadian tax system for U.S. estate taxes. In fact, you might be charged a Canadian capital gains tax on an increase in the U.S. property, paying estate taxes on the same property twice.

There are some planning steps that can be taken by Canadians who hold property in the United States. Most important is to hold less than U.S. $60,000 (U.S.) worth of U.S. property at the time you die. This might be done in a few ways. You can dispose of property if you become critically ill. This may or may not be an emotionally acceptable thing to do. It also could result in a loss of value from rushing a sale. It's more easily done if you are selling a portfolio of U.S. securities; the market value is readily available, the attachment to the property is less emotional, and you could always buy back the securities at a later stage.

Second, you can own less in the first place. If you decide to own a home in the United States, it should be purchased by more than one family member. This doesn't mean that you should buy the property and just register it as jointly owned by yourself and your spouse. You should be able to demonstrate that both of you contributed to the purchase of the property. It would be even better if other family members provide their funds to purchase a share of the home. In this way, the value of the property would be divided among several family members and it would be less likely that the estate of any one individual would exceed $60,000 (U.S.).

There are several other ways to lessen exposure to U.S. estate taxes:

- buying the property through a Canadian corporation, Canadian trust, or partnership;
- financing the property using non-recourse debt;
- passing the property to your spouse using a qualified domestic trust which allows an initial estate tax to be deferred until the property is eventually sold or until the death of the surviving spouse.

If your exposure to U.S. estate taxes is relatively large, you would be well advised to seek advice from a Canadian tax specialist who has expertise in this area. U.S. advisers tend to know the U.S. tax situation but do not have an understanding of the workings of the Canada-U.S. tax treaty or the Canadian tax implications of an estate tax avoidance strategy.

Snowbirds and Medicare

Before 1991, most provincial medical-care programs paid the full cost of medical attention received by one of their residents while travelling outside the province. A couple of the provinces paid only the cost of the same treatment in that province. This left many Canadians exposed to the extra charges that might be encountered in the U.S. or other parts of the world. Some snowbirds purchased insurance to protect these uncovered medical costs. It wasn't expensive but there were many Canadians who felt that the risk was small and didn't bother.

Since 1991, however, the provinces and territories have sought to reduce their exposure to the high, and quickly escalating, costs of medical care outside of Canada. They've reduced their out-of-province coverage to what is paid locally, or even less than what is reimbursed in Canada. For example, Ontario has reduced its daily hospital-care subsidy from the full cost to $400 a day. This could be as much as $1,500 less than the amount you might be charged by a U.S. hospital.

The private insurance programs offer significantly different coverage limits and exclusions. They also vary by premiums for different age groups. Don't just buy your insurance from a company because it is the plan a friend has bought; make sure you shop carefully for the best coverage and premiums for you.

You should find out which hospitals, clinics and doctors your insurance company finds acceptable in your winter home location. Ask those medical care givers whether they will accept your private medical insurance program; try to determine the costs not covered by your government and private insurance programs. Consider joining the Canadian Snowbird Association, The Canadian Association of Retired Persons, The American Association of Retired Persons or other such groups which have the resources to study and advise you on changing laws that affect your well-being and enjoyment. These associations also publish newspapers and newsletters that are available to Canadian snowbirds.

Immigration rules and the required visas are well explained by officials at the U.S. Consulate in offices in major cities across Canada or through the U.S. Embassy at Suite 201, 60 Queen Street, Ottawa K1P 5Y7, telephone (613) 238-5335. If you intend to change your citizenship or immigration status, be sure to seek the advice of a qualified immigration lawyer. Be particularly careful if you are a landed immigrant or a holder of temporary status in this country. Your move into the U.S. may jeopardize a return to Canada.

Rites of succession: Estate planning

Estate planning seems intimidating and unpleasant. In reality, it satisfies one of our deepest financial and emotional needs — to organize our financial affairs to ensure the well-being of our family after our death. As reluctant as we are to dwell on our death, being organized when that day comes will make things easier for those we leave behind.

Ideally, you should consider estate planning early in life, since death can strike at any time. In your younger years, your family is usually protected by life insurance. You need insurance because you haven't built enough savings to cover your considerable financial responsibilities, particularly those to your children and their education. As you approach retirement, you must accept that death is that much closer and that all aspects of estate planning merit close attention.

Estate planning includes calculating your estate needs and determining the amount of life insurance, if any, needed to meet those needs; strategies to reduce your income taxes at death; organizing your estate; preparing your will and reviewing the need for powers of attorney. We also consider issues surrounding the settlement of your estate such as appointing an executor and finding ways to minimize probate fees.

Estate needs and insurance

Life insurance provides cash at the time of death to cover two needs: the immediate expenses that will arise upon death and the replacement of income that was being earned by the person who died. Typically, when you are young you have many financial responsibilities, mortgages, car loans, hefty expenses and few savings and investments of your own. As the years go by, your

responsibilities diminish, you rid yourself of debt and you build your personal wealth. Our need for insurance is often greatest in our youth and gradually diminishes until, often, we no longer need any at all. Chances are, you're somewhere in between these two stages.

Let's take a look at your need for insurance. In order to do this, you have to look at two different things. First, how much cash will be needed to settle your expenses at death? Second, if your family still depends upon the income which you bring home every month, how much money will they need to produce enough income to cover their personal and living expenses?

We have provided a worksheet to take you through this analysis. Let's walk through the calculation together. First, let's look at the expenses on death. An average funeral costs about $3,500, but if you plan to have a more elaborate ceremony, you should plan to put aside even more than this. You will need cash to settle outstanding bills. Because your death could occur at any time, use the bills you have outstanding right now. You'll also need cash to cover the mortgage and any other loans.

Then there will be the costs of settling your estate; the professional fees for handling your will and ensuring your belongings pass smoothly to your family. There are different advisers who can help, including financial planners, lawyers or trust companies. A trust company will charge between 3 and 5 percent of your assets. To be conservative you should use 5 percent as an estimate. Probate fees are fees charged by your provincial government to declare your will valid. Quebec does not charge probate fees, Ontario's 1.5 percent fee is the highest in the country. Most of the other provinces charge around 0.5 percent.

Your family should have a cash cushion to make it easier for them to get through the first few months after your death. It can be a confusing time; you don't want them scrambling to buy groceries. The emergency or opportunity fund should be consistent with the one we discussed in chapter ten on identifying your financial priorities. You might want to have enough insurance to create an education fund for your children, if they're not already grown and independent. Your family will need money to pay the income taxes that will be due to the government on your death. We'll discuss income taxes at death later in the chapter so you can come back to this table and complete it once you have read that section.

After calculating your cash needs, you should identify the cash you have already put aside or that will be available on death to satisfy these needs. This includes the value of life insurance policies you already have, death benefits on group life insurance and other retirement programs (this information should be available from your company benefits department) and the CPP/QPP death benefit. We discussed this benefit in chapter six. As you will recall, this death benefit is 10 percent of the yearly maximum pensionable earnings, or six times the contributor's pension. The amount in 1993 is approximately $3,300 — this is a good estimate to use in your calculation. Finally, you should identify liquid and investment assets you have in the bank and your investment portfolio.

The difference between your total cash needs at death and the cash you will have available at that time is the amount you will need from an insurance policy to allow your family to cope with these immediate expenses. If you are lucky and have built up sufficient assets already, then you will have an excess of cash available. If this is so, then the insurance need for this part of the calculation is zero.

Next, you need to estimate the amount of capital that will be required to generate income to supplement your family's income after you're gone. Start with the annual personal and living expenses that your family will need. As an estimate, you can assume they'll need between 60 percent and 75 percent of the annual expenses you incur now. You should be able to determine this from the worksheets you completed in chapter nine.

From this amount, deduct the net income after taxes that your survivors will earn from employment, pensions and from investments that will not have to be cashed in to cover immediate expenses. Include the current salary of your husband or wife and your children, if this makes sense. Don't forget the Canada or Quebec pension amount that your spouse will receive. As discussed in chapter six, the pension depends on your spouse's age and circumstances. If he or she is under age sixty-five, the pension is 37.5 percent of your retirement pension; if over sixty-five, the pension will be 60 percent and will be integrated with his or her own CPP or QPP pension. Review chapter six if you are unsure of the amount of government benefits your spouse and other survivors will be entitled to. You can include the OAS allowance on the same line as the CPP/QPP pension. Use the amount of company pension that you have already earned to estimate the amount your spouse will receive after your death.

To estimate your RRSP annuities look at the RRSP assets you have already accumulated. You will have gathered this information to complete your net worth statement in chapter five. To be precise, you would then look at an annuity table and determine the exact amount of annual income you could expect. As an approximation, take 9 percent of your RRSP assets as the annual annuity.

We suggest that you use an 8-percent investment return to estimate the income your family will earn from the investments you have accumulated but will not be used by your family to meet expenses upon your death.

Now, add up all of the income that your family will have and use the income tax table in the appendix or the average rates provided in chapter nine to estimate the amount of tax your family will pay each year. The after-tax income should then be deducted from your family's personal and living expenses to arrive at the income required, if any.

If there is a need for income, translating this income need into the amount of capital needed is a little tricky. The calculation is similar to the one we considered in chapter nine but we have simplified it here. Take the income required and divide it by 3 percent. We've used 3 percent because historically this is approximately what you would receive after tax and inflation. Let me explain. If your family earns 8 percent on the capital invested, this will be a return of 4.8 percent after tax. If you deduct inflation, the actual return is about 3 percent. In a period of 5 percent inflation, your family might expect a return of 13 percent on their portfolio, 8 percent after tax, 3 percent after inflation.

Your final step is to add the cash required for immediate expenses to the cash needed to produce income. This total is the cash needed by your family — and therefore the amount of insurance you buy to protect them. Many employers offer their employees inexpensive group life insurance coverage when they retire. As a result, most retired Canadians have at least one or two life insurance policies.

Before touching your existing policies, or buying more, take a hard look at the value of your estate upon your death as we have done here and determine whether you should maintain some or all of your insurance policies. If this look into the future indicates a need for more funds at death, you might want to buy more insurance from your employer's group plan, if it's available, or from a professional association, if you belong to one. Private insurance is available but if you're over age fifty-five or so, it could be very expensive.

Once you are retired, your need for life insurance might disappear. Insurance usually provides your family with the income you are no longer able to earn. Such coverage is often unnecessary since your pension, annuities or investments will continue to provide an income when you are gone.

However, you might want to continue your health and medical insurance to supplement the provincial plans. A severe illness could require costly medical attention such as a private nurse in your home, paramedical care or a nursing home. If your supplementary health coverage is paid for by your employer, make arrangements to have the premiums continued after your retirement or to pay the premiums yourself. Like other forms of insurance, if your premiums lapse, coverage will probably cease.

Death and taxes

It's common for governments to apply taxes when people die. If you're not there to argue, how are they to be avoided? Yet we all have the right to reduce the impact of taxes — in death as in life — and it can be done.

First, let's look at the tax rules that we have to abide by at death. (It's true that death and taxes are the only certain things in this world but who would have thought that paying taxes would be the last thing we'd do.) The first rule is that the deceased (actually the executor) must file a tax return for the period from

The only retirement guide you'll ever need

Calculating your insurance needs		WORKSHEET 32
Immediate expenses at death	**You**	**Your spouse**
Funeral		
Bills outstanding		
Mortgage and other loans outstanding		
Estate settlement expenses (such as probate fees and professional expenses)		
Income taxes due on death		
Emergency/opportunity fund		
Education fund		
Total expenses at death (A)		
Cash available on death		
Life insurance policies		
Death benefits from group life insurance and retirement programs		
CPP/QPP lump-sum death benefit		
Liquid assets, such as money in bank account, bonds, money market mutual funds		
Investment assets		
Total cash available (B)		
Difference between (A) and (B) = (C)		
Income replacement needs of survivors		
Income which your survivors earn		
Canada or Quebec pension benefits		
Company pension survivor benefits		
Income from RRSPs		
Income from investments		
Total income available to survivors		
Income taxes on this income		
Income available to cover expenses		
Personal and living expenses of survivors		
Difference between after-tax income and expenses		
Life insurance needed to provide income **(D)**		

This represents the amount of capital required to generate
the income which your family will need. To calculate this amount,
divide the deficiency by the after-tax real rate of return that could
be earned on a life insurance benefit. Typically, we use 3%.

Insurance needs equals the sum of:

Cash required for immediate expenses (C)		
Income replacement fund (D)		
Total need for life insurance		

January 1 to the date of death, a final accounting to the authorities. This return is due within six months of death or April 30, whichever is later. Although the return is completed in the usual way, there are certain important differences:

- As far as Revenue Canada is concerned, you are considered to have sold all of your belongings just before your death — and they'd like to tax the capital gain.

- For all of your capital property — your investment assets, real estate, art, collections — the government deems you to have disposed of the property at its fair market value the day you died. The capital gain is the difference between this fair market value and the amount you paid for the assets.

- If you have any depreciable property — rental property or cars or equipment used for a business — the government deems that you disposed of these assets at the midpoint between their fair market value the day you died and the undepreciated capital cost (the amount you paid for the asset less the capital cost allowance you claimed to reduce your taxes over the years). Because of this calculation, capital cost allowances which you claimed in the years before your death to reduce rental or business income may be recaptured — and therefore increase your income — in your final tax return if the property values have not declined. You might therefore have to pay extra tax, a payback of taxes saved by claiming too much depreciation in those previous years.

Say you had bought a property for $100,000, claimed a $30,000 capital cost allowance and therefore had an undepreciated capital cost of $70,000. If on your death, the fair market value was determined to be $150,000, the tax rules would deem you to have sold the property for $110,000, the midpoint between the undepreciated capital cost of $70,000 and the

assessed fair market value of $150,000. As a result, $30,000 would be added to taxable income as recaptured capital cost allowance, and $7,500, 75 percent of $10,000, as taxable capital gain.

A separate second tax return can be filed for income received after death, such as unpaid bonuses, commissions or dividends declared but not received. Including these items on a second tax return will result in a lower overall income tax bill because you can claim the personal income tax credits again.

The cash value of registered funds, such as RRSPs or RRIFs, will be fully taxable at death unless you transfer the funds to your spouse or to children or grandchildren who are dependent on you. If the funds are transferred to your spouse, then they will be taxed at his or her tax rate unless they are moved to an RRSP or RRIF.

If you are not married when you die and you have children under eighteen who are dependent on you, or adult children who are dependent on you because of mental or physical infirmity, then your RRSP or RRIF funds can pass to them tax-free.

As in a normal return, tax credits for charitable gifts are limited to 20 percent of the net income declared. This can be restricting in the final return for people who plan to make a large donation at death. You could pass the money to your estate and have it distributed in the estate's first tax year. This gives your estate the option of claiming the tax credit in your last tax return or in the income tax return of the estate in any of the first five years.

The Income Tax Act contains a variety of special provisions relating to death. Many relate to income tax deferral programs such as RRSPs and RRIFs, pensions and the depreciation of real estate. The government wants to recover the taxes delayed by these deferral programs or tax shelter schemes. They'd also like to collect, if possible, the taxes on capital gains beyond your $100,000 lifetime capital gains exemption. This last tax grab may seem unfair, especially if gains simply reflect increases owing to inflation. Nevertheless, income taxes at death can be a significant problem if you've held assets that had hefty gains over the years and made maximum use of tax deferrals.

In order to estimate the income tax burden of your estate so that you can include this amount in your estate needs analysis, you should consider these rules. The two main components of taxes payable at death will be any tax due on registered funds such as RRSPs or RRIFs, and taxes payable on capital gains accrued on your assets. Using these two tax amounts should give you a good estimate of your estate's immediate tax burden.

If you pass your RRSP or RRIF to your spouse, the tax burden will be deferred until your spouse dies. If not, you should determine the tax that will be due. You can do this by determining the capital gain that would have to be paid if you sold them today. Deduct any lifetime capital gains deduction and calculate taxes payable on 75 percent of the capital gain not eliminated by the deduction. You can use your marginal tax rate (which you can find in chapter eleven) to calculate the taxes.

Estate planning should protect your estate from taxes by taking advantage of the tax planning strategies available. You should make sure that you've used up your full capital gains tax exemption either by instructing your executor to realize capital gains at death or by disposing of assets during your lifetime. You could pass assets to your family members at their current fair market value — which becomes the new cost base for tax purposes — and any future capital gains will be measured from the current market value. If you have assets that will result in capital gains over and above your exemption, then you should consider transferring these assets to your spouse or to a spousal trust or, if you have a

considerable amount of assets, you might want to look at estate-freezing strategies that will eventually pass the assets on to your children or grandchildren. These strategies will help to reduce your tax problems. If you have significant assets you've owned for many years, it's probably wise to consult a tax adviser when preparing your will or make sure to instruct your executor to consult your adviser when filing your final tax return.

Spousal rollovers

The worst effects of taxation at death can be delayed by transferring assets and benefits to your spouse through your will. This tactic usually delays significant taxation until your husband or wife dies. In the meantime, the full value of your assets and income can be enjoyed. On your spouse's death, the taxes are levied, unless surviving children are young and dependent and the taxes are further delayed.

You can transfer assets that have increased in value over the years but have not been sold — in other words, they have accrued capital gains — and assets that are held within registered programs such as RRSPs, RRIFs and pensions. You are not only transferring the asset, you are also transferring the associated tax problem. Is that fair? It is better for your family to receive the full value of your assets with a deferred tax liability, than for your estate to pay your taxes immediately and leave your family with a diminished amount of money.

A common example of the benefits of delaying taxes is the transfer of an RRSP or RRIF. If your will (or RRSP agreement in provinces other than Quebec) leaves your RRSPs to your husband or wife, every dime will be moved to his or her RRSP or RRIF. If you have not updated your will or RRSP agreement to instruct this, then your final tax return would levy income taxes on the full amount of your RRSP and your loved ones would only get the benefit of the after-tax amount, which could be less than one-half of its value.

This is very important. Always make sure that your registered funds (RRSPs and RRIFs) are transferred to your spouse or to dependent children in case your spouse predeceases you. These assets can be transferred to an existing RRSP in your spouse's name or a new RRSP can be set up. If your RRSP is full of complicated investments that might baffle your spouse, then you can either arrange for an investment counsellor to manage the RRSP after your death, or once the assets are transferred they can be sold and replaced with simpler assets.

If you are already receiving an income from an annuity bought with the funds in an RRSP and your spouse becomes the annuitant on your death, there will not be a tax bill. The payments will continue and the stream of income will be taxable, just as the income is taxable as you receive it. However, if you have not made arrangements for payments to continue to your spouse — and you have not outlived the guarantee period — the annuity might be collapsed and its full value taxed. If you will a RRIF to your spouse, there's a choice between continuing the RRIF payments or transferring the funds to a new RRIF for the spouse. If the RRIF is not passed to a spouse or dependent children, the full value of the RRIF becomes taxable.

Estate freezing

The most effective method to avoid taxes is to give your heirs the belongings you want them to have well before you die. In this way, any increases in value will result in capital gains in their hands, not yours. Usually this means that the capital gains will be taxed at a lower rate or at least that the tax will be deferred until the assets are sold. Taking this step is not as easy as it sounds. You might not want to give control of these assets to your children just yet.

And you don't want to pay income taxes earlier than you have to, which might happen if the transfer of these assets to your heirs is considered to be a taxable sale when it happens.

The trick is to avoid having the transfer of assets viewed as a sale and, if you want, to retain control over the assets. To achieve this, you can use a tax-free transfer of your assets to trusts or investment holding companies. These plans are complicated and you should seek professional advice on them. Putting the assets in a trust or company will involve legal fees to set up the trust (at a minimum of about $2,000), professional fees to help design the most effective strategy and ongoing costs of accounting for and administering the new trust or company, including preparation of income tax returns. The ongoing costs will likely be at least $2,000 or $3,000 per year. If you think you have assets significant enough to warrant such a complex arrangement then you should discuss this with your financial adviser.

There are other ways to pass your estate to your heirs and still have some control over them. You can pass the ownership of assets to your children in your will, while giving the surviving husband or wife use of the assets and any income from them for the rest of his or her life. This spousal trust strategy can solve two problems: Your spouse has income for life, and taxes will not be payable until he or she dies. In a refinement of this approach, trusts can defer capital gains taxes for twenty-one years, a potentially longer delay than under the normal spousal trust which is for the spouse's remaining lifetime.

Estate taxes or succession duties

In Canada, so far, we are not subject to special estate taxes when we die. However, a Canadian who dies owning over $60,000 in U.S. investments or real estate will incur U.S. estate taxes as well as Canadian income taxes.

Rates range from 26 to 55 percent on the amount over $60,000 and are not offset by credits against Canadian income taxes.

U.S. securities are considered to be property located in the U.S. because title to the securities can normally only be transferred by a U.S. stock transfer agent. This includes U.S. stocks that are held with your Canadian broker. In practical terms, however, Canadian brokers have often assisted the estates of deceased holders of U.S. stocks to avoid U.S. estate taxes by keeping the securities in street name and allowing the disposition of such securities. They should, in fact, be denying the sale of these stocks and bonds until they have received proof that the estate has settled its U.S. estate tax liabilities, if any.

Avoiding this tax might seem to you to be an unimportant transgression; after all, we Canadians pay enough taxes as it is without having to pay U.S. taxes as well. To do things properly, however, you should plan on selling such U.S. securities before you die, if possible, or transfer them to a corporation or irrevocable trust so that the "owner" continues to survive after your death, thus denying the imposition of the dreaded U.S. estate tax.

You could also be subject to estate taxes (or your heirs could be subject to inheritance or gift taxes) if you own property in other countries. In fact many countries in the developed world have some form of estate tax, including Australia, Denmark, France, Japan and the United Kingdom, to name a few. If you own or plan to own property outside of Canada, it would be worthwhile for you to investigate ways of avoiding foreign taxes.

Organizing your estate

A less obvious, but equally important, aspect of estate planning is organizing the financial affairs of your estate. This consists of documenting your plans, preparing financial records (and keeping them up to date),

identifying your executor, making your will and acquainting a family member or financial adviser with your affairs. There are few things worse than seeing a family searching for insurance policies, the will, bank accounts or safety deposit boxes as they grieve for the loss of a loved one.

Once the funeral is over, it's necessary to tend to the financial well-being of the survivors and to settle the financial affairs of the deceased. If you've been involved in such a situation, you're aware of the key role played by executors and the importance of good financial records. The executor (a man) or executrix (a woman) is the person (or persons) designated in the will to take charge of the deceased's estate, to administer the financial affairs, and to execute last wishes in accordance with the will. This is often a detailed and time-consuming job, requiring communication with financial institutions and governments, filing returns and reports, and sometimes making decisions about investments and taxes. The process is more complicated today because of the variety of investment products and the complexity of tax regulations.

It's never easy to step into someone else's shoes, pick up their financial affairs and settle their estate in a quick and efficient manner. If the executor is a lawyer, notary, financial adviser or trust company that charges fees for services (or if one of these professionals is engaged by the executor), you will want to save your beneficiaries a good deal of money by turning over a well-organized estate. If you do so, your executors will be better able to manage and distribute the funds during their stewardship.

Preparing your will

With your finances in order and the details shared with your husband or wife, it's time to prepare a will — or update an old one — setting out clearly what's to be done with your

Tips for organizing your estate   **WORKSHEET 33**

Make sure that you provide your family with all of the information they will need to ensure that they can benefit from your assets with the least amount of worry or fuss. This means well-documented financial records, an up-to-date will, and someone who has a full understanding of the family's financial affairs. You can list these critical details here.

Funeral and burial arrangements
_____
_____

The location of your will and marriage contract
_____

Names and addresses of your lawyer, executor and financial advisers
_____
_____
_____

The location of the details of all of your assets, liabilities and obligations
_____

The location of insurance policies, tax returns, and other permanent records
_____
_____
_____

You compiled detailed records of your assets and liabilities in chapter five on your net worth statement. A complete summary should be maintained in the home in a safe, fireproof place, if possible. A duplicate set of records, including a copy of the will, should be held by your executor or a financial adviser or placed in a safety deposit box.

Try to make sure that your records are easy for someone else to follow. Sometimes the way in which we choose to organize something makes sense to us but it might not to others. We once had a situation where one of our clients thought her husband was extremely organized. From the appearance of the neat, well-stocked study in their home this seemed to be true. However, when we began to look for the relevant records to settle his estate, we found ourselves poring over yellowing, sometimes coffee-stained pages in disarray within the neatly closed drawers.

Ask your husband or wife, a family member or friend to become acquainted with your financial affairs. Having someone who is intimately aware of your finances is far more useful than even the best financial records. If your husband or wife knows why you were doing something, then he or she will also be aware of the actions that should be taken to complete your financial intentions. It's also valuable for the executor and advisers to have someone to explain entries in your financial records or to fill in missing information where necessary.

Bypassing probate fees

Probate fees in Ontario just jumped from $5 to $15 for every $1,000 of assets over $50,000, and the topic of how to plan your affairs to reduce probate has become a very hot topic. There are two ways that your assets can pass directly to your beneficiaries without becoming part of your estate and having to be covered in your will:

When a beneficiary is named in a life insurance policy, pension plan, RRSP or RRIF. This is true for all types of annuity issued by any kind of financial institution. Unfortunately, this does not hold true in Quebec except in insurance contracts. Your beneficiary need only prove your death and the institution which issued the insurance policy or holds your funds will immediately turn them over to your beneficiary. If this is your intention, you should review your policies to ensure that your estate is not named as beneficiary; otherwise, the funds will be included as assets of your estate at death and will be subject to the terms of your will.

When property is held in joint tenancy. The person who is named as joint tenant is entitled to all rights to properties held jointly. Joint-tenancy assets are not subject to the terms of the will and automatically become the sole property of the joint tenant. In every province but Quebec, your husband or wife will be able to withdraw money from a joint tenant bank account to which they are named in order to pay bills or cover other expenses they have while the bulk of the estate is awaiting probate. In Quebec, all bank accounts of the deceased and the surviving spouse are frozen at death until some documents allowing release of the funds are completed. Some flexibility is normally provided by bank managers when requested.

---

assets when you die. This sounds daunting, but, simply put, a will is a letter that identifies you, authorizes your choice of an executor to manage and settle your financial affairs, and sets out who gets what from your estate. When you die, your financial affairs go into limbo. No one can spend or invest your money. Your finances pass on to a new legal entity known as a trust, and called the Estate of the Late Deceased Person.

If you don't have a will, your financial affairs continue in limbo after your death and it will take some time before a provincial court will appoint a public executor to take charge of your finances. Without a will, you won't have had the opportunity to put the right person in charge as executor or to designate who will inherit your assets. Family law in the province you live in before your death will decide who will inherit. This can cause some hardships for your spouse because when you have children, your spouse will lose control of more than half the estate (except in Manitoba). Even worse, in Quebec the law provides for distribution of one-third to two-thirds of the estate to surviving parents, siblings and cousins, reducing the share to spouses and children.

Other consequences of dying intestate (without a will) include impersonal treatment of the family by the public executor, loss of the opportunity to name or suggest the name of a guardian for young children, and loss of the opportunity to establish a trust for children or other family members. Such a trust ensures that the children's money is managed carefully over a number of years by the trustee, rather than given outright to family members or a guardian. There have been situations where the family home has had to be sold because it represented most of the estate.

A Trust Companies Association of Canada survey recently found that as many as 50 percent of Canadians do not have a will, and most are ignorant of the consequences. In my mind, leaving your affairs in order, including leaving a clear will that appoints your executor and considers carefully what should happen to your property, is a simple way to make life easier for your survivors during a difficult time. The bills of the estate can be paid, using money transferred from your bank account to the new estate bank account, or funds derived from the receipt of insurance, government death benefits, or the sale of investments. The assets of the estate will be properly safeguarded by the executor, and passed on to the rightful beneficiaries in accordance with your wishes as expressed in the will.

You should also provide a tax-flexibility clause in the will enabling the executor to follow any elections or options provided in the Income Tax Act that will benefit the beneficiaries. This will allow the executor to delay or reduce income taxes which would otherwise arise at death.

A will can be prepared in any one of three ways. It can be holographic, which means handwritten by you. It can be in an English legal form prepared by your lawyer in accordance with English common law. Or, it can be prepared and registered by a notary, as is done in civil law in Quebec. All three forms can be legal wills.

The difference between these wills rests on the ease or difficulty of having them legally accepted as your last will and testament. Holographic and English-form wills must be probated, which means that proof must be brought before a judge that the will was prepared and signed by you, that you were mentally capable at the time, and that it is the most up-to-date will that exists. Legality by probate depends strongly on verification of the handwriting or upon the sworn statement of a witness to your will.

If you prepare a legal or English-form will, make sure that two witnesses watch you sign and that they also sign the will. Obtain the sworn affidavit of one of the witnesses swearing that they saw you and the other witness sign, and attach it to your copie.

The notarized will is already legally registered by a notary as being the legal will of an individual. The only dispute that can arise is whether it's the last will, which can be established by searching the registry of wills in Quebec. If another type of will was prepared and dated after the legal notarized will, then the later dated will would have to be probated before the courts.

The role of the executor

Your will should empower your executor to make decisions on your behalf if there are tax advantages for the beneficiaries, or unforeseen opportunities or problems to be handled. The executor should therefore be a person you trust implicitly for integrity and loyalty to your family and your wishes. He or she should also be respected for financial and managerial talents. Ideally, the executor will have an intimate knowledge of your family's financial affairs. Such people are hard to find, and you may end up choosing someone with most, but not all, of these qualities.

The ideal candidate is your spouse. He or she knows the family, has knowledge of your affairs, and is loyal to your objectives. If you're concerned that the role is upsetting by its nature, or too demanding of time and administration, your spouse can be assisted by an adviser, appointed formally in the will or informally. Additional executors can also be appointed to act with your spouse. Other candidates include sons and daughters, their spouses and long-standing advisers to the family. But executors should be willing to serve. There's lots of paperwork and responsibility. The executor should not be considerably older than you or in ill health — you want to avoid having this person die before you. Your will should name alternative executors, in case your first choice is unable or unwilling to serve.

When wills call for creating trusts that could last years into the future, it might be wise to appoint a trust company or established professional firm to act as trustees, ensuring that the trustee will be around for the necessary period of time. Professional trustees will charge annual fees for this service, and will rigorously enforce the terms of the trust.

You will also need to consider the cost of settling your estate. On top of probate fees, lawyers or trust companies will normally charge 2 percent to 6 percent of the gross value of the estate's assets. Additional costs might include completing tax returns and government forms and reports. Although it might be less expensive to use a family member or friend as an executor, remember that the job involves work and responsibility.

Some provision should be made for the executor to engage professional assistance, where necessary.

Tax planning goes beyond the traditional cradle-to-grave approach. Organizing your estate means compiling good records, involving spouse and family members in your affairs, preparing a straightforward up-to-date will, and appointing an executor who will respect your wishes and settle your affairs efficiently. This knowledge can reduce trauma and uncertainties, and can pay dividends in improved savings and investment income for survivors.

Notes

Your health: Growing old gracefully

George Burns has more to say about growing old than any other human being alive. Here's one: "Every morning I get up and read the obituaries. If I'm not in there I have breakfast." Burns does what we all do and shouldn't: Assume that old age means frailty and death. The truth is, there's plenty of reason to look forward to long life and good health in later years.

Today's seniors are healthier than ever before, thanks partly to improved medical care, but also to greater personal awareness of how to stay healthy and avoid disease. Seniors are taking charge of their own health, understanding how to maintain it and how to talk to doctors when something goes wrong.

Doctors interviewed by Time magazine in 1988 noted that every organ loses reserve capacity with age, making it more difficult to recover from illness and injury. Failure of one organ can cause other organs to fail. The immune system weakens, making disease harder to fight. Metabolism slows and muscle mass shrinks. Together, these developments tend to make people fatter; kidneys, liver and lungs lose capacity and effectiveness; bone mass can reduce dangerously, leading to crippling fractures; senses weaken, causing malnutrition, accidents and discomfort.

But good health and good health practices can reduce the impact of these effects. Be aware of your family's health history: Did your parents have heart disease? Did their parents? Knowing this, and the tendency for certain ailments such as heart disease to run in families, helps you to identify if you're at risk.

But probably more important are lifestyle factors. There is a clear link between smoking and lung cancer. There is a clear link between lack of exercise and heart disease. If you're aware of this, you should make appropriate changes in your life — take control of your own health.

Your current health is influenced 16 percent by genetics, 10 percent by professional health care, 21 percent by your environment and, tellingly, 53 percent by the choices you make in the way you live — whether you smoke, exercise regularly, eat a low-fat diet and so on. That last figure is startling isn't it? You can influence your health. In fact, the changes taking place in the world of medicine oblige you to take a more active role in your own health care. Now and in the future, rising costs will make it improbable that you'll be able to use the health-care system the way you might have in the past. For example, physicians will perform far fewer diagnostic tests as they have in the past. Tests are getting costlier and can only be done when sufficient evidence warrants investigation. Only if you tell your doctor everything that's troubling you can he or she determine whether such expensive tests are warranted. Otherwise, doctors may not order them.

There can be a variety of reasons why you might not tell your doctor everything that's troubling you. Maybe you hate going to doctors and get anxious when you do, forgetting half of what you want to say. Maybe you get the feeling your doctor is rushed and doesn't have time to listen to you, isn't even interested, or makes you feel as if you're a hypochondriac. Another reason for misdiagnosis is when a person gives skimpy information, can't describe the type of pain or didn't notice if a particular action made a difference.

What I'm trying to say is your diagnosis can be affected by the relationship you have with your doctor. It can also affect the treatment. Make sure your doctor completely explains your medical condition and why you have to make changes in the way you live to cope with it. You should know why you are on medications and what their potential side effects are, and you should have some choice in treatment offered you. If you do, you'll feel in control and you'll feel that your physician recognizes you as a responsible adult.

Do you currently feel you have this kind of relationship with doctors? If not, you can learn to be more assertive. They can't do their job effectively without your cooperation. You know when something doesn't seem right with your body, so you're in the best position to describe what's wrong. If your doctor doesn't like you becoming more assertive, you may want to find another doctor.

It's also important to be in close contact with your pharmacist. If you are on any prescription drugs at all, and particularly if you're an over-the-counter medication user of such things as cold or cough preparations and painkillers, you need to develop a relationship with one pharmacist so that you can obtain accurate information on drug use, interaction and toxicity to avoid problems. Other professionals who can help you include dietitians, qualified nutritionists, fitness consultants and practitioners of alternate therapies such as massage and acupuncture.

What about the environmental factors that influence your health? The environment contains many carcinogenic elements, such as asbestos and lead, which have been identified as harmful. Skin cancers have increased dramatically in recent years, apparently because of holes in the atmosphere's ozone layer and the fashion in the last five decades of sun tanning. Such things as work pressures and personal conflicts are increasing stress for many people, causing stress-related disorders such as stomach ulcers and heart disease. Other variables are the mine fields of safety hazards that may be your home, scatter rugs and faulty wiring, as well as those outside your home, reckless drivers, drinking and driving and street crime.

One final variable influencing your health — and the one with the most significant impact — is lifestyle choices: what you choose to do. Those choices involve many health practices you already know such as personal hygiene, proper diet and exercise. Do you make lifestyle choices that are potentially harmful? Do you smoke, drink excessively, use drugs carelessly or fail to deal with stress? If your goal is to improve your overall health, then be sure to be brutally honest with yourself in doing an assessment of your current lifestyle.

Stop illness before it happens

In the past, doctors usually treated illness after it had struck. Today, I'm happy to report, that approach is increasingly questioned. Preventive medicine, which counsels people on how to avoid disease, is gaining momentum. Studies show that treating existing disease can be far less efficient and far more costly than preventing the disease in the first place. Cures, moreover, are never guaranteed, and having one disease often makes you more susceptible to another. The preventive approach, of course, requires cooperation between you and your physician.

Some doctors are more concerned with disease than health, with the cure rather than prevention of the disease. The key question is whether your doctor knows you well enough and cares enough to judge your physical problem. If your doctor tends to dismiss your problems with general statements like, "It's all part of growing old," you may want to find yourself another doctor.

The fact is, doctors and hospitals can be hazardous to your health. We have come to see the doctor as a surrogate God, the expert who can bring us back from the edge of death. We know doctors are not infallible, and that medicine has a long way to go in understanding and curing illness, but we persist in assuming that the doctor is always right, that the hospital stay will cure us, that the medical tests and treatments will be good for us. We adopt this faith based on stunning research advances and outstanding performances by doctors, nurses and hospitals. And of course, we want to believe — have to believe — in order to have hope.

Now many physicians are challenging this blind devotion to the medical system, citing its weaknesses as well as strengths. Dr. Eugene D. Robin, professor of medicine at Stanford Medical School, warned of the risks in his 1984 book, *Matters of Life and Death: Risks versus Benefits of Medical Care.*

Robin cited "serious flaws in the basic processes by which diagnostic and therapeutic measures are introduced and used in medicine." Patients, he said, should "consult doctors only when you believe that you are truly ill. By restricting your medical encounters to those that are absolutely necessary you will be avoiding risks inherent in most diagnostic and therapeutic procedures . . . avoid hospitalization unless you are seriously ill and only (enter) a hospital (that) has the facilities for your treatment. Many hospitalizations are unnecessary. Hospitals," said Robin, "can be dangerous places."

Staying healthy

Now let's take a look at some diseases and conditions associated with growing older. I'll concentrate on what you can do to prevent or reduce the chances of these diseases from getting a foothold. Of course, once you have a condition you must see your doctor and completely describe what you believe you are suffering from. But in the meantime, taking charge of your own health means being armed with information on disease prevention.

Heart disease

Heart disease is the leading cause of death in North America, claiming twice as many victims as cancer. In Canada, 45 percent of all deaths in recent years were from heart disease. And one in two Canadians will suffer from it during their lifetimes.

What are you going to do about it? Most of us do nothing — not until we have chest pains, or a loved one or best friend suffers a heart attack, or the doctor tells us our cholesterol level or smoking has made us high risks. By the time that message strikes home it's often too late; serious damage is already done.

A busy muscle that contracts and relaxes sixty to 100 times a minute, the heart needs its own constant supply of oxygen and nutrients. These come from coronary arteries which cover the surface of the heart. It is these arteries that generally form the crux of the problem. They clog up, become narrowed or blocked, and cannot supply the required blood flow. As a result, the heart can be irreversibly damaged.

Early warning signals include a pressing discomfort in the middle of the chest. The pain is not unlike indigestion, but is a heavier pressure, and will often spread to the back, shoulders or arms. The pain may not last long, only until you stop your activity, or for a few minutes after resting. But if it continues for more than a few minutes, or comes and goes over a period of hours or days, or is accompanied by other symptoms, take action.

Sure, you don't want to alarm your family unnecessarily, to be rushed to the hospital without cause. On the other hand, the consequences of not acting promptly can be enormous. Waiting could cause irreparable damage, future complications or even death.

So despite your uncertainty, you must act fast: Recognize the signals quickly, sit or lie down, overcome expressions of denial, and get to the nearest hospital. Time is critical.

Is there life after heart disease or heart attacks? You bet there is. Many conditions can be treated by medication. Blocked arteries may be opened by an angioplast operation — dilation with balloons threaded into the blocked artery — or bypassed in open heart surgery. Heart patients must pay closer attention to maintaining a proper diet. And they should start a regular regimen of walking, jogging or swimming. There will be few other changes, life will continue much as before, preferably in an atmosphere of less debilitating stress.

The risks of coronary heart disease are known to increase with smoking, high blood pressure, high cholesterol levels (although debate continues to swirl on this subject), lack of exercise, stress, heredity and obesity. The risk of suffering a heart attack becomes pronounced at age forty and grows progressively worse, doubling by age seventy. Regrettably, as more women adapt to the stresses of career and the workplace, the risk for women is catching up with that of men. What can you do?

■ Stop smoking. Not easy to do, but absolutely necessary, because smoking is the number one preventable cause of coronary heart disease. It's never too late to stop smoking. Within a year, the risk of heart attack will decrease. Eventually, it will decline almost to the level of people who never smoked. There are many aids and treatments, but these only testify to how persistent the problem is. The essential need is really your own commitment to stop smoking; the rest is easy.

■ Control high blood pressure. It can be reduced by decreasing salt intake, reducing weight, taking medication, removing stress and quitting smoking.

■ Reduce saturated fats and cholesterol. Sometimes we eat too much cholesterol-laden food. Sometimes our bodies have trouble processing it. Either way, cholesterol may be present in high levels in your bloodstream. Over time, it may clog the blood vessels, causing them to narrow. The result is reduced blood supply and oxygen to the heart and brain, resulting in heart attack and damage or stroke and paralysis. To lower cholesterol and fat levels in the blood, you must alter your diet, exercise regularly, stop smoking, reduce alcohol intake and use prescribed medication.

■ Exercise. Have a medical checkup first, then, with your doctor's approval, adopt a program of rigorous exercise, working out at least three hours a week, and otherwise live a more active life.

■ Be aware of the stress factors in your life, and make changes in your lifestyle to give you greater control over your activities. Balance your life among work, family, friends and personal activities.

■ If you're overweight by 20 percent or more, your blood pressure will probably be high, the level of fat and cholesterol in the bloodstream will be too high, and the heart will have to work harder to circulate blood.

■ If family members have had heart disorders, especially before age sixty, you might be subject to great risk. Get a detailed medical checkup, including blood tests, cholesterol-level tests and stress tests, and make special efforts to control all the other risk factors, so they won't compound the genetic risks you may have inherited.

■ Other factors: Check for diabetes. It frequently appears in middle age, and can sharply increase your risk of heart attack. Once detected, diabetes can be controlled. Birth control pills can raise blood pressure and the risk of heart disease for some women, particularly those who smoke, are overweight, record high blood pressure in pregnancy, suffer kidney infections, or have a family history of high blood pressure. Check with the doctor before using them, and discontinue their use after age thirty-five.

■ It's wise to have an annual physical, preferably with the same doctor, so that he or she will get to know you and your family, and can spot trends and problems that may lead to trouble.

■ Learn to relax. There is evidence that happy, loving people see a reversal in heart disease conditions.

■ Read labels looking for sodium or its chemical symbol Na. Choose foods marked "low sodium." Avoid or minimize your use of monosodium glutamate (MSG), sodium nitrate used as a meat preservative, sodium cyclamate used as a sugar substitute, sodium bicarbonate in baking soda and baked goods, and disodium phosphate found in cereals and cheeses. Use medicines with low sodium on the label. Avoid antacids, pain pills, cough syrups or laxatives with sodium on the label or that effervesce when added to water.

Breast cancer

Some 11,000 new cases are diagnosed each year, making the odds of developing breast cancer one in eleven for Canadian women. More than 85 percent of early-detection cases report five years of disease-free survival; leaving 1,650 women struggling to overcome the disease, sometimes unsuccessfully. The impact of breast cancer, even if it is detected early, is devastating; if it is not detected until the disease has progressed, the outcome could well be death. Your best protection against breast cancer is early detection, through self-examination and annual checkups.

Cervical cancer and pap tests

Again, early detection will permit successful treatment. Detection is provided by regular gynecological examinations and standard pap tests or pap smears. In these tests, cells are removed from the surface of the cervix and examined at the lab. After menopause, it is crucial for women to have this test every year. Yet the *AARP Bulletin* of June 1991 reported that a shocking 72 percent of women over age sixty-five have not had the routine test. Five thousand women die of invasive cervical cancer in the U.S. every year.

Cancer of the prostate

Nearly 50 percent of Canadian men over age forty will have problems with the prostate gland. A number of these will be cancer. In 1987, more than 8,200 men developed cancer of the prostate; 34 percent died. The problem arises when the gland, located just below the bladder and in front of the rectum, grows in size because of multiplying cancer cells. Symptoms of prostate problems include frequent, difficult or painful urination, dribbling urine, blood in the urine, pain in the lower back, pelvic area or upper thighs, or painful ejaculation. If any symptom continues, see your doctor. If you are over forty, make sure that a rectal examination is part of your annual physical, and reduce the fatty foods you eat.

Skin cancer

The sun is the main cause of skin cancer, the most common cancer in Canada. Symptoms can include a spreading skin growth which is tan, brown, black or bluish-black, which itches or bleeds; a mole, birthmark or beauty spot that changes or has an odd shape; or an open sore that doesn't heal. The cure rate is 90 percent, so detect it early. Use sun screens with high ultraviolet sun protection factors of thirty or over. Don't sunbathe.

Osteoporosis

This bone disease threatens 25 percent of Canadian women over the age of forty-five. Bone mass gradually decreases, leading to fragile, brittle bones which fracture easily or bend out of shape. The cause is demineralization, the loss from the bones of calcium needed by the body's nerves, muscles and bones. Short on calcium, the body draws on the calcium in the skeleton and bone structure. Women are particularly susceptible after menopause, owing to the loss of estrogen. Removal of ovaries doubles the odds of contracting osteoporosis.

The condition cannot be cured, but it can be prevented and its effects slowed or suspended by the following measures. Consume more calcium, 800 to 1,200 milligrams a day before menopause, and 1,500 milligrams a day after menopause. Some calcium-rich foods include: milk, yogurt, cheese, dry figs, rhubarb, sardines, canned salmon with bones and unsalted sesame seeds. Take vitamin D (from milk and fish oils), exercise daily to stimulate bone growth, stop smoking and eat a balanced diet. The sooner you start, the better off you'll be.

Claudication/arteriosclerosis

A leg that causes pain when you walk and stops aching when you rest may signal that not enough oxygen is getting to the leg muscles.

This is claudication, a condition that affects thousands of Canadians over age fifty. It requires prompt attention because it is often a precursor to arteriosclerosis, or hardening of the arteries, which can lead to heart attacks and strokes.

Early diagnosis will permit treatment by way of lifestyle changes and walking. Walking may be painful, but you need to walk thirty minutes a day beyond normal activities. Better still, take preventive measures — the same as those for avoiding cardiovascular problems — reduce blood pressure, weight and cholesterol, identify and treat diabetes, and stop smoking. One Mayo Clinic study showed that 11 percent of claudication patients who smoked had to undergo limb amputation within five years. Not a single member of the comparison group which had quit smoking required amputation.

Liver diseases

The liver is a vital organ and, unlike kidneys, you only have one. More than two million Canadians suffer from liver diseases each year. The only cure for the most serious of these diseases is a liver transplant. The doctor should check your liver regularly, but you can help by treating it better. Cut down on alcohol and drugs, avoid breathing fumes from toxic cleaners, insecticides and poisons such as garden and lawn chemicals, watch out for hepatitis viruses passed on in body fluids from intimate contact, and avoid cholesterol and fatty foods.

Arthritis

Arthritis is a common name for a long list of conditions that cause aches and pain in the body's joints and connective tissues. Some forms of the disease can lead to severe pain and disability; others produce discomfort, but can be controlled with care and treatment. If diagnosed early, arthritis can be treated successfully, resulting in less discomfort and prevention or reduction of disability. It will not go away entirely, but it can be lived with. Treatment involves medications, rest, special exercises and supports.

Constipation

The solution here is to eat fibre and drink lots of water. Fibre sources include fruits, whole grains and vegetables. Dr. Frank MacInnis, a syndicated columnist on health matters, calls psyllium seeds one of the most powerful sources of fibre. These are natural and non-addictive. But be sure to use them with lots of water. You can buy psyllium seeds, in bulk or in capsules, in health food stores.

Incontinence

An estimated one million Canadians of all ages experience lack of bladder control. In fact, more than half of them are under age fifty-five. The cause is usually an infection of the bladder, kidney, prostate, nerves, discs or even the spine. The degree of involuntary urination may vary, from minor to extreme. Incontinence can often be medically treated and cured through surgery, drugs or exercise. In other cases, it can be managed through use of absorbent undergarments.

Memory

Many people fear that, with age, their memory will start to fade, and that this may be a precursor of Alzheimer's disease or senility. As usual, people worry too much. True, our memory will fail us more often after age forty-five. Small memory problems are not unusual and shouldn't frighten you. Only 5 percent of people over sixty-five suffer from acute mental disorders. With age, the brain contains fewer neurons, the nerve cells responsible for looping and networking to retain facts and memories. But not to worry: We are blessed with far more neurons than we need.

"If you decide it is important, turn on your attention radar; if not, let it pass right by," says Alan S. Brown, author of How to Improve Your Memory. With all the noise and activity in the world, we must listen hard to really hear the things that are important. By the time we realize what we are hearing, the message may be over. The key to better memory, then, may be to listen and watch more carefully, to hone in on what is important, and let the rest pass by.

Dr. Monique Le Poncin, a French psychologist who wrote Gym Cerveau, insists that you must believe in yourself, because you can remember everything you want to. She recommends exercising the brain by giving it a variety of intellectual stimulants, challenging and using it; keeping healthy through exercise, diet and good sleep. Protect yourself from overmedication, depression, illness, malnutrition. Keep socially active and involved. "Treat your brain well," says Dr. Le Poncin. "It is your wealth because it is your autonomy."

Backache

The back needs to be exercised through stretching and flexing, but it also needs protection and rest whenever possible. Good posture is essential to back care, and it helps you look your best as well. Good posture keeps a balance among the three natural curves in your back — neck, chest and lower back. When standing, don't try to be rigidly straight. Instead, let your knees flex and your shoulders relax. Ensure that your ears are straight in line with your shoulders, hips and ankles. I find that if I suck in my stomach a little, everything else falls into place.

When sitting, align your ears with your shoulders, shoulders with hips. Keep your feet flat on the ground. Your mid-back naturally bends inward, and should be supported for comfort and to avoid strain. Good posture lying down can be practiced in a modified fetal position — on your side, with your knees bent slightly toward the chest, or on your back with a pillow beneath your knees. Use a firm mattress and only one pillow.

Take other measures to look after your back. Select furniture for proper support: upright contoured chairs, high and firm sofas, elevated seats to allow for easier access and egress. Avoid sudden movements, and use your legs and arms to get you up and moving from a bed, a car or a bathtub.

One good thing about backache is that it usually appears in the thirties and forties, so the worst may already be behind you, as it were. But if you suffer, don't let backache immobilize you. Staying sedentary won't help. Keep active and involved.

You don't have to get sick and frail when you grow old. You can decrease the chance of your health taking control of your retirement if you take control of your own health care. It's not possible in this book to cover health management completely. I just want you to understand how increased awareness of the causes of health problems and cooperation with your physician can reduce the havoc they can cause. In the following chapters, I'll talk about stress, nutrition and fitness to round out your understanding of how your lifestyle will affect your health and well-being in retirement.

As the French say, "To your health."

Notes

Stressing the best things in life

Stress is a normal part of life. It's present every day and it's not necessarily bad. In fact, it's sometimes very beneficial because it can help you save your life, such as when you need a burst of energy to flee from a fire. The body responds by accelerating some functions and decreasing others to help you act in the face of danger. Of course, too often in modern life, there is bad stress, the kind that builds up from daily pressures, sudden events or changes and acts insidiously, making life difficult and even compromising your health.

Don't think that just because you're going to retire that stress, both good and bad, is going to go away. Although retirement isn't intrinsically stressful, it can sometimes be one of the most upsetting things that can happen to you. However, there are ways to be aware of the effects of stress and to control them. By doing so you'll not only enjoy your retirement years more, you'll be ensuring better health.

Positive and negative stress is associated with change or a sudden event. These circumstances force us to cope, adapt or change to some degree. Stress can be caused by anything — too much or too little time, too many demands, somebody's annoying habit, adult children, the boss, the neighbour, the list is endless.

I feel stess watching my son compete in golf tournaments, listening to someone crunch an apple while they stand too close to me, driving in the rain at night on unfamiliar roads. I enjoy the stress of speaking in front of crowds or on radio. It's different for everybody and only you know what causes you stress. How do you know? Because your body tells you. Maybe it's the migraine headache, stiffness in the neck muscles, a tight knot in the stomach, nervousness or a pent-up feeling, but you know something is bothering you.

Stress occurs when we feel that we can't adapt or cope to changes and sudden events as much as we'd like to. Of course, some people thrive on stress. They are energized by competition and deadlines. But one man's stress is another man's shrug of the shoulders. Other people function better without stress. Don't compare yourself to others and assume that perhaps you're not as competent as someone else who seems to handle stress a lot better than you. After all, not only are you different, but your circumstances are probably different too. What is important is that you don't exceed the level of stress you can handle comfortably. You'll know that if you pay attention to your body's stress cues — various physical or emotional signals — such as sudden weight change, increased smoking or drinking, anxiety, hyperactivity, headaches, stomach aches, short temper, skin disorders, back pain, negative reactions, an inability to concentrate, fatigue, high blood pressure and heart irregularities.

Retirement, like any other stage in life, means change and adjustment. How you have coped with similar change in the past will largely determine how you cope with retirement. People who expect change, rather than allow themselves to be taken by surprise, adjust better in retirement. By preparing for retirement, you are planning for change. It isn't always easy. It takes effort, constant awareness of what you are actually doing and what you wish to do.

Consider the following questions:

■ What causes you stress?

■ Do you know how much stress you can handle before it becomes too much?

■ What ways do you use to reduce stress effectively?

We'll help you address these questions in the rest of this chapter.

Managing stress

The psychiatrists Thomas M. Holms and Richard Rahe, who developed the social readjustment rating scale, found that some happy events, such as marriage, can be far more stressful than a financial disaster like bankruptcy. The death of close friends is usually considered very stressful, but it ranks well below retirement or job dismissal. All stressful events, positive or negative, force us to cope, adapt or change to some degree.

The original social readjustment rating scale, adapted for older adults and reprinted on the next page, has special significance for people at retirement. The life change units constitute various interactions of people with their environment and make up essentially all of the changes we have to deal with, or reflect the fact that significant changes have occurred. The number in the right-hand column of the chart represents the amount, duration and severity of change required to cope with each item, averaged from the responses of hundreds of people.

Marriage was arbitrarily assigned fifty points. The more changes you undergo in a period of time, the more points you accumulate. The higher the score, the more probable it is that you will have a stress-related health problem.

Serious illnesses, injuries, surgical operations and psychiatric disorders have been found to follow high life change scores. The higher your score, the more serious the health change will likely be. For example, if you have more than 300 units in one year, you are more susceptible to health risks the following year.

Use the accompanying chart to see how your life stresses affect you. First, circle the values of the life change units that applied to you in the last year. Add up your total score. Then circle the values of life change units that you expect in retirement. Add up your total score.

How stressful a period do you foresee? If you scored below 150 points, you are on safe ground — about a 33-percent chance of serious health change in the next two years. If you scored between 150 and 300 points, your chances rise to about fifty-fifty.

If you scored more than 300 points, your chances are almost 90 percent.

Change is not entirely random. You have a great deal of personal control over some events — marriage, having children, going to university. You may have little control over whether to get divorced, change jobs or retire. But you do have a fairly good idea of when these events will take place. Because you can predict your future to a degree, you can order your life by managing the change. You can weigh the benefits of change against its costs, pace the timing of inevitable changes and regulate the occurrence of voluntary changes to keep your life-change score out of the danger zone. Preparing for your retirement may help you plan for change and pinpoint stressful situations.

It's important to recognize, respond to and manage your own stress signals. Here are a few tips for dealing with a stressful situation:

■ Minimize its seriousness — laugh a lot, look for the humour in it.

The social readjustment rating scale	TABLE 14
Life event	**Stress value**
The death of your husband or wife	100
Divorce	73
Marital separation	65
The death of a close family member	63
Personal injury or illness	53
Getting married	50
Getting fired from your job	47
Marital reconciliation	45
Retirement	45
Change in health of a family member	44
Difficulties with sex	39
A change in your financial state	38
The death of a close friend	37
A change in the number of arguments you have with your husband or wife	35
Change in your responsibilities at work	29
A son or daughter leaving home	29
Trouble with your in-laws	29
Outstanding personal achievement	28
A change in living conditions	25
A change in personal habits	24
A change in work hours or conditions	20
A change in residence	20
A change in recreation	19
A change in church activities	19
A change in social activities	18
A change in sleeping habits	16
A change in number of family get-togethers	15
A change in eating habits	15
A vacation	13

This scales was created by Thomas Holmes and Richard Rahe. This list does not include all of the items which they ranked.

- Seek out facts, not negative possibilities.
- Ask others to help you; talk about it. Share your worries with someone you trust.
- Set short-range goals. Do one thing at a time. Know your own needs and control your priorities. Say no to other demands.
- Work off your anger. Relax.
- Think about different possible outcomes. Try to develop choices.

- Find a general pattern of meaning to life. Change your routine. Slow down.
- Balance work and leisure in daily routine. Develop periods of complete relaxation.
- Cooperate rather than compete. Accept what you cannot change. Don't challenge every situation. Take time to enjoy balanced meals with family and friends. Learn to listen carefully to others without interrupting. Control your temper and moderate your opinions. Be less cynical, more open-minded. Be less of a perfectionist.
- Balance difficult tasks with less demanding ones.
- Exercise regularly to feel in control and to feel good.
- Avoid over-the-counter medicines where possible, avoid drugs and tobacco, moderate your drinking.
- At work, reduce conflict and develop more control over your situation.
- Get counselling from your doctor.

Other methods include keeping a tennis ball in your desk and squeezing or pounding it the next time someone irritates you, buying a large bean bag and punching it when frustrated, finding yourself an open space and letting out primal screams or four-letter words, running or jogging in place for at least five minutes while thinking of something pleasant, climbing a flight of stairs two steps at a time, taking a quick walk around the building and doing some deep breathing, holding a telephone book in each hand and lifting them like weights. Remember, the better you take care of yourself, the greater your peace of mind. Get into the habit of stopping, looking and listening to yourself.

Get a good night's sleep

For some people, getting a good night's sleep is impossible. They suffer terribly as a result.

Causes of sleeping difficulties include anxiety (worrying about retirement, work or family problems), physical problems such as chronic back pain or arthritis, unsuitable medications, and poor eating and drinking habits. The syndrome can also be self-perpetuating: Inability to sleep well may erode your ability to sleep.

Whatever the cause, do something about it. Your health and happiness depend on getting the right amount of solid sleep. The right amount may be less than the eight-plus hours you were once used to. Seven hours could be fine. Winston Churchill did all right on four to five hours. Mahatma Gandhi needed only three.

Your doctor can identify and treat medical problems, or may prescribe painkillers or relaxing drugs. If they work, fine; but don't increase the dosage to get better results.

Good sleeping habits can overcome the problem:

■ Go to bed and get up at the same times every day. Don't take naps during the day.

■ If you aren't sleepy, don't go to bed until you are; get up and read or watch TV for a while. You will sleep best if you are sleepy, not just because you are lying there.

■ If you don't fall asleep after twenty minutes of trying, get up. Waiting for sleep to happen can result in worrying that it will not come. Go to another room, read or do something else.

■ Exercise each day or in the early evening, but not close to bedtime.

■ Make your bedroom a better place to sleep. It should be dark, quiet, and have a comfortable bed. Don't use your bedroom for work, meetings or TV. The temperature should be somewhat cooler than the living room.

■ Try to solve your problems before bed. If you can't solve them, forget about them

until the next day. Working on them in bed is not productive.

■ Avoid big evening meals, especially those that are spicy, acidic or fatty. If you have such a meal, stay up for a few extra hours, dance or walk it off, giving your digestion a chance to do its job. Eat larger meals for breakfast and lunch, or in the late afternoon.

■ Go easy on alcohol, caffeine and nicotine, all of which are stimulants which keep you awake.

■ If you're hungry before bed, eat a light snack, consisting of yogurt, milk, fruit, cookies or crackers.

■ Avoid sleeping pills. Use them only as directed by your doctor, and only for a few nights or occasionally, as needed. They are designed for special stress situations, not daily use.

Depression

Depression is one of the most common problems of people over age sixty; it can be difficult to accept the losses that come with older age. Often, on the surface, there seems to be nothing wrong with your life — no money problems, good relationships and comfortable lifestyle — yet you are still depressed. Prompted by underlying feelings of uselessness and hopelessness, depression can be caused by the fact that you are no longer working or that your children no longer depend on you for advice and support. Or you may be disappointed with the shape your retirement is taking. Loss of friends and loved ones, aging itself, as well as society's dismissive attitude of the elderly, can contribute to depression.

One study of women reported in *Foresight Magazine* in its September/ October 1988 issue suggested that depression happens when tumultuous events occur at the worst time — the death of a child or grandchild, a divorce in retirement years, children remaining home or returning to live at home when they should be on their own. These events, serious in themselves, can cause serious psychological trouble if they happen at a propitious time.

Since depression is such a common illness, how do you know when to be concerned? Everyone has periods when they feel "blue," "moody," "down," or even "depressed." In mentally well people, these feelings can last for up to two weeks but then they come out of it by drawing on personal strengths, a positive attitude, as well as family, friends and a recognition of what they're going through.

But for the clinically depressed, the feeling doesn't pass. They begin to feel the situation is hopeless and they're unable to lift themselves out of the negative rut. They don't care how they look and stop paying attention to personal appearance. They come to not like themselves and are convinced others don't like them either. This represents the slide to clinical depression requiring professional treatment.

It's important to be sensitive not only to your own moods but also to mood changes in family members, friends and work associates. If you sense that someone doesn't seem to be him- or herself, don't hesitate to ask if you can help.

Other signs of depression can include loss of appetite, fitful sleep, early morning awakening, weight loss, loss of energy and motivation, perhaps even thoughts of suicide. Having some of these symptoms is normal, but a combination of all of them signals a serious condition. See a doctor and start treating this easily preventable illness. Dr. David D. Burns' book *Feeling Good — The New Mood Therapy* is an excellent resource for people dealing with someone who is depressed. With professional care, and support from family and friends, depression is curable.

Treatment of depression usually begins with antidepressant medications. But they only work to bring patients to a state of equilibrium, so that they can begin to identify and deal with the concerns in their lives. You can feel better with antidepressants, but if nothing is done to include other aspects of treatment, you usually begin to see cyclical episodes occurring. Depressed people can learn helpful techniques to boost self-esteem, assertiveness and effective communication.

Incorrect use of prescription drugs, usually by overdose, is responsible for many mental disorders in seniors. The *AARP Bulletin* reports that nearly one-half of the people in hospitals for drug overdoses in 1989 were age sixty and over; of these, about two-thirds suffer mental impairment as a result. The overdoses are self-administered or given by caring persons at home and in nursing homes.

Excess use of another drug, alcohol, is also a major contributor to depression. Some people choose alcohol to cope with excessive worries, stress or significant changes in life. Unhappy about retirement or unprepared for a changed lifestyle they move up the cocktail hour to compensate for the boredom, stress, unhappiness and even depression associated with too much time available and lack of rewarding interests and activities.

The mind can have a big impact on the body. As you grow older you have to take care of your mind every bit as much as you do your body. You've got to be able to recognize stress and long-term emotional problems. Likewise, even in your later years, you can learn ways to deal with stress and its results that will help you flourish in retirement. The choice to do something is yours.

Chapter 17

Good nutrition
never retires

I approach this subject with great trepidation. I hate the four food groups of Canada's Food Guide: meat and its alternatives, milk products, grains, and fruits and vegetables. I like potato chips, French fries, chocolate chip cookies and chocolate cake. And I hate the word moderation. I always throw myself fully into everything I do, especially eating.

Still, my reading leads me to conclude that there is little hope for an illness-free retirement unless I pay close attention to what I eat now as well as later in life. The human body is a finely tuned machine. How it performs will depend on what you feed it, especially in later years.

The health experts seem to keep changing the rules. When I was a kid, I was encouraged to eat a healthy breakfast of bacon and eggs. Now the Boston School of Medicine has found that cereal and fruit should replace bacon and eggs at breakfast, thereby reducing daily fat content by almost 25 percent and cholesterol intake by 66 percent.

Knowledge of how diet interacts with the body and various diseases has increased tremendously in the last twenty years. And more people are living longer, so the effects of risky dietary habits become more pronounced. To help make some sense out of all the confusion, in 1990 Health and Welfare Canada released Canada's Guidelines for Healthy Eating, which suggest we:

- enjoy a variety of foods;
- emphasize cereals, breads and other grain products, vegetables and fruits;
- choose low fat dairy products, lean meats and foods prepared with little or no fat;
- achieve and maintain a healthy body weight by enjoying regular physical activity and healthy eating; and

- limit salt, alcohol and caffeine.

A variety of foods makes it easier to get all fifty nutrients you need to keep healthy. When you're young you can eat more, which makes this easier to do. But as you get older, your metabolism slows down and you need fewer calories. This means that all fifty essential nutrients must be provided by a smaller amount of food, because our other nutrient needs remain as high as ever. In fact, some nutrients may be needed in higher amounts. Although the nutritional needs of seniors vary widely and will depend on the individual, after age sixty-five you need extra minerals, especially calcium. As for the B-complex and C vitamins, some nutritionists believe you need more while others feel you need less.

It's unrealistic to expect to keep your youthful figure forever. Mary Holder, a nurse and retirement counsellor, keeps reminding me: "If your input exceeds your output then the food stays put!" Even if you do not gain any weight, some of what you have tends to gravitate downward! Regular exercise helps minimize this.

An average man over age fifty requires about 2,300 calories a day, which is about 400 fewer than he needed at age thirty. The average woman over age fifty needs only 100 calories fewer each day, lowering her average daily intake to 1,800 calories. This is the minimum level, by the way, that Health and

Welfare Canada considers desirable for good health. Intakes below this increase the risk of not getting all those essential nutrients.

Saving just 100 calories a day adds up to 36,500 calories or a little over ten pounds of fat in one year. You burn about 100 calories walking one mile or eat that amount in a medium apple. That should give you an idea of how easy it should be to save calories, but before you start any exercise program, check first with your physician. Keeping a healthy weight reduces the risk of developing diabetes, cardiovascular disease (heart attack, stroke and high blood pressure) and certain types of cancer. Cutting back sensibly and keeping active now is one of the best retirement presents you can give yourself. And you don't even have to wait for it!

Getting all the facts about fat and cholesterol isn't easy. Advertising stresses foods that are "cholesterol free," which makes us think that the cholesterol has been removed, when in actual fact it was often never there in the first place! As Sheila Murphy, a Montreal dietitian-nutritionist has said, "Headlines don't teach sound nutrition." Cholesterol is found only in foods that come from animals, so you won't find it in vegetable oil.

More important than the amount of cholesterol in the food we eat is the amount of saturated fat it contains (animal fats are higher in saturated fats). High intakes of this have been associated with low-density lipoprotein cholesterol, the bad kind of cholesterol your body produces. We also produce a good kind of cholesterol, high-density lipoprotein cholesterol, but how much we make is determined not so much by what we eat, as by how well we've chosen our parents! Lean meat and milk products are good sources of protein, vitamins and minerals and they come in a variety of lower fat selections.

You don't have to eat meat to stay healthy but if you do, rather than cutting it out of your diet, you should cut back on high-fat items like double cheese hamburgers and fried foods. Unfortunately, you can't change habits quickly. So do yourself a favour, introduce small diet changes gradually. Switch from homogenized to 2 percent milk over several weeks, and then to 1 percent and so on to allow your taste to change at its own speed. Recently, a U.S. Food Marketing Institute study confirmed that people tend to rank taste before nutrition in their selection of food. Since fat contains much of the flavour you enjoy, eating slim but deliciously is a challenge. There are excellent cookbooks on the market developed with this in mind; *The Lighthearted Cookbook* and *Lighthearted Everyday Cooking* by Anne Lindsay are examples.

Dietary fibre has been getting a great deal of attention. Actually there are different kinds of fibre: soluble fibre found in oatmeal and oat bran and insoluble fibre found in wheat bran. Both types are found in many fruits and vegetables. Eating a wide variety of grain foods, vegetables and fruits will ensure we get a good mix. Dietary fibre helps maintain normal bowel function, reduces elevated blood cholesterol, helps control blood sugar level in diabetics, and may reduce the risk of colon cancer. When you increase your intake of fibre-rich foods it is also important to increase your water intake. Some people find they become more gaseous but this usually adjusts with time. Any diet changes should be introduced slowly over a matter of several weeks or months.

Health and Welfare Canada's Expert Advisory Committee on Dietary Fibre has determined that Canadian diets are lacking sufficiently in fibre. The average diet provides about half (fifteen grams) the required fibre you need, and many people do not even get this limited amount! It's not difficult to increase your fibre:

Food shorts

- Eat fruit and vegetables raw. If you must cook them, use steam or the microwave. Keep them crisp.
- Chew your food thoroughly, it's easier to digest and might result in eating less and enjoying it more.
- If you suffer from stomach acid, drink water to dilute the acid. Eat crackers and avoid milk and antacid remedies.
- Eat breakfast like a king, lunch like a prince, and supper like a pauper.
- Use a smaller plate and fool your brain into thinking you had your usual big meal.
- Eat with someone else and listen to music. You will eat less and feel fuller than if you eat alone and gulp it down.

- Eat bran cereals, the ones that look like buds have three times as much fibre as a bran flake, whole wheat bread instead of white bread, peanut butter instead of cheese.
- Add a banana to your cereal, tomatoes to your salad.
- Include bran in stews, casseroles, ground meat mixtures and in mixtures used for coating meat and chicken.
- Have fibre-rich fruit for snacks as well as carrots and celery sticks. Apples have more fibre than grapes, corn and peas have more fibre than cauliflower.
- Add nuts to salads and sandwich spreads or eat them alone as a snack.

A friend of mine, years ago, decided she preferred to eat rather than drink calories. She told me that four ounces of Sangria punch has more calories than a chocolate chip cookie. While she only worried about the arithmetic, she had the right idea. Eating food instead of drinking it is more satisfying, it takes longer, and often, as in the case of fruit versus fruit juices, gives you more fibre. Her other example was a six-ounce glass of orange juice (84 calories) as opposed to a medium-sized orange (65). If the juice has had sugar added, as it often does, the difference will be even greater.

As you age, your body's ability to assimilate drugs and alcohol is reduced. They can also interfere with nutrient absorption. When taking medication or drinking alcohol, you should consider your body's reduced tolerance and remember to use alcohol in moderation.

Nutrient deficiencies are more common among older adults and the reasons vary. Often simply eating too little food is a contributing factor. A neighbour of mine used to live on tea and toast because it was easy to make and she couldn't be bothered going to the store. Poor appetite can be caused by medications, a physical disability, dental problems, poverty or depression. Community groups have found that people's appetites are better when meals are shared than when they eat alone.

Making an effort to invite a friend for a meal usually brings a good return. It can be an economical way to share costs and preparation time. Dr. Louise Davis, head of the gerontology nutrition unit at the Royal Free Hospital School of Medicine in England, believes "the aim of practical nutrition is to ensure maximum nourishment with minimum effort."

Local programs like Meals On Wheels and a newer version called Wheels To Meals, which transports people to a central dining area, can provide at least one nourishing meal a day for those who live alone, and cannot prepare for themselves adequately for one reason or another, even temporarily.

Data from the Nationwide Food Consumption Survey by the U.S. Department of Agriculture confirm that people eat better with other people around. Men living alone have poorer diets than men living with wives or women living alone. Even when single men spent more money for food than couples, many still had inferior diets. This suggests a need for better nutrition education, particularly for single men.

Supplemental vitamins and minerals can play a role in assuring adequate nutrition for older adults. It's best to use food sources but sometimes that's not always possible. Some nutrients are toxic, however, when taken in large doses or can interfere with drug action, so don't fall into the trap of thinking that if a little is good, more is better.

If you're worried you're not getting enough of a nutrient, consult your physician or a registered dietitian. Always check with your pharmacist before self-medicating, even with over-the-counter items.

Chewing problems are not uncommon as we age, and account for a lot of the digestive complaints of older adults. Often this is found in those with full or partial dentures. Bone loss, which occurs naturally with age, can alter the fit of dentures, which results in poor chewing ability. Regular dental checkups are never out of style and they can prevent discomfort and help maintain a nutritious diet.

We used to have tables of Ideal Weights. In the late seventies, health professionals began to agree that they did not know what ideal was, so the name was changed to Desirable Weights. In 1983, the name was again changed simply to Table of Weights. These tables have several limitations which have been recognized. The most obvious one is that they do not tell you anything about the kind of weight a person is carrying; is it fat or muscle?

Obesity is a cause for concern because of the disease risk it can pose. Being overweight owing to extra muscle, as is the case with some athletes, does not pose a disease risk. In other words, body composition is important; but the scale tells you nothing about it. It is unrealistic

to evaluate your health status simply by weighing yourself.

Instead of the bathroom scale, a newer measurement called BMI (body mass index) is now used to evaluate weight. This correlates more with the amount of body fat and therefore it better shows excess fat. It too has some limitations (it should not be applied for people under nineteen years, or over sixty-five years or to athletes; muscle tone, or lack of it, can skew the BMI).

Where that fat is located on your body is important as well. Fat that accumulates around the abdomen increases disease risk. This is commonly referred to as the male or android pattern of distribution. Fat that accumulates all over the body or around the hips and buttocks does not carry the same risk. This is referred to as female or gynoid pattern of fat distribution. These two distinct body shapes have been nicknamed the apple and the pear. Fat distribution is inherited to some extent.

Another measure of overall fatness is to determine your waist to hip circumference ratio (WHR). Simply measure your waist and divide this by your hip measurement (taken at the widest point). A desirable WHR for men is 1.0 and 0.8 for women. This allows for the natural greater fat distribution in the hips normally found on women. For example, if a twenty-eight-inch waist is divided by thirty-eight-inch hips it gives a woman a WHR of 0.74. A waist of thirty-four inches and hips thirty-six inches is a WHR of 0.94, which is okay for a male. You may be able to get a cardboard calculator to help you figure out your BMI from the Canadian Dietetic Association or the Canadian Egg Marketing agency.

Fat provides over two and one half times the calories that carbohydrates (starch and sugar) provide (one gram of fat equals nine calories versus one gram starch or sugar equals four calories). This is an obvious reason to reduce your fat intake. But another reason is that the body treats fat calories differently from carbohydrate (CHO) calories. Any extra calories not used will be changed into fat, the body's only way of storing excess energy. The changing of food CHO calories into body fat calories takes up more energy than changing food fat into body fat calories, thus fewer calories are left over to store. In other words, if you overeat it's better to choose foods that are high in complex carbohydrates like bread, rolls, cereals, potatoes, rice, pasta and beans. Traditionally, these foods have been mistakenly labelled fattening. What you add to them (butter, cream sauces, gravy or margarine) is usually far more fattening.

Nutritionists' recommendations for Canadians are that no more than 30 percent of calorie intake be fat; thus on a woman's 1,800-calorie diet this is equal to twelve teaspoons of fat.

As your appetite lessens with age, be sure that what you eat is high in nutrients, not in calories. Variety is important to stimulate the appetite as well as to ensure that your body's need for the fifty nutrients is met. A diet high in fibre as well as plenty of fluids will reduce the need for laxatives. Women should be sure to have adequate calcium in their diet and should exercise, at least by walking, to reduce the possibility of osteoporosis. There are calcium substitutes your doctor can recommend if you have a problem digesting dairy products.

Chapter 18

Don't take it easy: Keeping fit

When was the last time you truly felt physically fit? Was it your teenage years, as it was for me? In those days, I could run for more than an hour, play thirty-six holes of golf, eat and drink as much as I wanted, and stay out all night. There's been squash and golf, and some great skiing since then, but these activities have progressively diminished. That peak level of fitness I once knew has fallen dramatically: I'm a haggard-looking, middle-aged Canadian male, overweight and sedentary. In general, I have the fitness of an eighty-five-year-old Swede.

Like most Canadians, I am convinced I can change my habits whenever I want. Because of this overconfidence, I fail to be motivated by warnings about heart failure, arthritis, arterial sclerosis, or other disabling diseases. We usually have to wait until a heart attack strikes, doing great damage unnecessarily.

How did we ever get like this? The human body was made for hunting; it was made for us to walk or run great distances to track and capture food. Even when humans learned agriculture, growing food and livestock, we still led a physically active existence.

Today, working lives are anything but active. Our exercise has become the turning of our necks to see if cars are approaching, or jostling on a crowded subway or running to catch the elevator. Men and women, once great hunters, spend their days sitting on chairs, talking on the telephone, working at computers or discussing everything from politics to the weather.

True, many people join fitness clubs, sports clubs and health centres. We rush around all day avoiding any hint of physical exertion; then, at great expense, we squeeze in an hour of programmed exercise. We would probably derive the same fitness value (and save money) if we were more active the rest of our day. Still, getting in shape this way is better than not getting in shape at all.

What is getting in shape all about? Consider what happens to the inactive body. It loses bone mass density because of osteoporosis, has reduced blood volume and muscle mass, and an impaired ability to absorb and transport oxygen. The heart rate is considerably faster both at rest and at work. And its recovery rate is much slower than in a fit person.

Almost invariably, those disabled by illness or operations show beneficial results after adopting a physical training program. Maximum oxygen uptake increases. The heart rate slows. They feel better. They become less anxious and more confident. A person out of shape requires a much higher heart rate to carry out a specific physical activity. A fit person will require much less effort. It's interesting that an hour of vigorous exercise makes the heart work harder for this period of time but saves it from working so hard for the rest of the day. Both heart and lungs become much more efficient.

The sedentary person must also watch his or her diet because the same caloric intake is no longer needed. Eating less and eating better, combined with exercise, will help you shed weight and keep more fit.

Your goal should be to be physically active at least thirty minutes every day; or, you should participate in some sort of aerobic exercise lasting about forty-five minutes at least three times a week. If you'd rather spend less time at fitness, keep in mind that exercise has to last at least fifteen minutes to be of any value. You must consider whether to see a doctor before starting a fitness program. Most experts advise getting a checkup before you start to work out but, well, it's easy to use this as an excuse for not working out. Use your common sense, consult a physical therapist or instructor and work at your own pace. If it hurts, stop.

Your workout should include a warm-up, exercises to increase physical strength and endurance, and a cooling-off period which should hone flexibility and involve stretching. Aerobic activity, such as low-impact aerobic classes, jogging, walking and bicycling, should raise your heart rate for a ten- to fifteen-minute period, but should never be so strenuous that you cannot carry on a conversation.

Warm-ups and stretching exercises should take five to ten minutes. These are intended to increase flexibility and circulation, warm up the muscles and prepare the body for more vigorous work. The stretching and rotating movements have changed significantly since my old football days. The old jumping jacks, windmills and straight-knee toe touches are now considered dangerous.

Stretching should be slow, continuing until you feel resistance or a pulling sensation in your muscles. The stretch should be held twenty to thirty seconds without bouncing. Whenever you touch your toes you have to avoid damaging your knees; avoid damage by touching your toes while sitting on the floor with your legs out in front of you. You shouldn't feel pain. And you shouldn't do it so vigorously as to hurt yourself. Remember to breathe out on exertion, and breathe in when you are relaxing.

To exercise your neck, sit comfortably but without slouching in a chair. Slowly drop your chin and head to one shoulder, moving it slowly forward in a smooth semi-circle until it reaches your other shoulder. Repeat in the opposite direction. A second exercise for your neck is to bend your head as if you are trying to touch your ear to your shoulder. Don't bring your shoulder up to your ear as you do this. Now your shoulder joints. As you stand or sit on a chair, shrug your shoulders, bring them up toward your ears, then relax. Now slowly rotate your shoulders, first in one direction, then in the other. Another good exercise for your shoulders is to lie on the floor with your feet tucked up to your buttocks, raise your arms straight up over your head to touch the floor far behind your head.

Rotate your wrists and ankles. While standing bend slightly to right and left, sliding your arms down your legs. Another exercise is rotating your spine; keeping your hips stable, turn very slowly from your waist until you can look behind you. Or, you can sit cross-legged on the floor and make the same turning movements with your arms folded in front.

Stretching the calves and hamstrings is also important. For the calf stretch, stand eighteen to twenty-four inches from a wall, place your hands on the wall in front of you and lean toward it as if you were doing push-ups. Move your weight forward until you feel stretching in your calf muscles. If you repeat the movement, bending your knees, you will give your Achilles tendons a workout. To stretch your hamstrings, sit on the floor, bend one foot so that it crosses over the other leg. Place your hands on the floor for support and bend forward from the hips.

If you want to do strength exercises, you'll need weights. Strength training can increase bone and muscle mass and slow aging but you must be shown how to do it safely. These exercises can easily be done improperly, which can result in injury. Before starting any weight training program consult a fitness counsellor.

Finally, it's important that we devote time to aerobic fitness. You should spend fifteen to thirty minutes walking, jogging, swimming, stair-stepping, bicycling, working hard enough to raise your heart rate. You can also go to fitness classes.

Wait! You're not finished yet. You have to let your body cool down. Walk at a slow pace for two or three minutes. While standing, swing your arms forward and overhead so that you can breathe fully and deeply. Stretch from standing or sitting positions, twisting hips and body slowly, and loosening your neck and shoulders through rotation and shrugging.

The key is to get started — and to stick with it. Get yourself into a regular routine, day in and day out. The best time of day is the time that's best for you. Pick an activity that you enjoy. Fitness is one of the few activities we can all enjoy, no matter what our financial situation. Staying fit need not be costly; you can do your stretches in your living room, you can walk in the park for free.

Staying fit is important and you should handle your fitness regime with the same dedication as any other part of your life. Make the same commitment to it that you would to an appointment or a meeting. And whatever you do, make sure you have fun. If it's not fun, it's going to be hard to keep up.

One of the best ways to commit yourself is to exercise with another person. You can both help each other. This can be complicated if you are not working at the same pace; the runner who tries to change his speed or stride to suit a faster or slower partner might not find the workout enjoyable. If you're the slower partner, as I probably would be, watch that you don't try too hard to keep up. Use the talk test to make sure: If you can't hold a conversation while you're exercising you're doing it too hard. Ease up.

Finally, be sure to take small steps toward fitness. Don't rush. If you set a balanced and scheduled pace, you'll be surprised at how quickly you can improve. If you decide to join a fitness or health club, pay for as few months as possible. Don't take out a three-year membership and pay for it all at once. The reason is twofold: By paying each week or month, you're more aware of the cost and more likely to keep going. Second, there are too many clubs that have gone bankrupt without paying back the fees to members. Make sure you ask if the club has discounts for seniors or for exercising during off-peak hours.

Just as young Canadians are more conscious about fitness so are today's seniors. In fact, the Masters Games have become an important fitness phenomenon. Started in Toronto in 1985, the games bring together athletes over the age of fifty in a wide variety of sports, from track and field to billiards and hang-gliding. Several senior athletes, including Otto Wenk of Little Rock, Arkansas, have set world records for their age group. Wenk set a men's seventy- to seventy-four-year-old record in the 5,000-metre speed-walking. Although the games bring together accomplished older athletes from around the world, you don't have to be an Olympic athlete to participate. Nor do you have to go to the world games to get involved in competitive sports: Many community recreation centres and YMCAs and YMHAs across Canada offer "masters" sports, including basketball, swimming and track and field.

My personal goal is to get my body in shape, modelled somewhere between Woody Allen and Arnold Schwarzenegger. At the moment, I resemble John Candy. But not for long.

Walking

Walking is quickly becoming the most popular exercise for persons age fifty and over. Why? Because it's healthy, convenient, can be done almost anywhere or anytime, alone or with friends. Walking is also inexpensive, although you're advised to buy a good pair of walking shoes. And while other exercises might strain or damage muscles, walking is unlikely to cause injury. I once thought walking required two or three times as much time as jogging to get the same results. In fact, at five miles an hour, the effects of a twenty-minute walk equal those of a twenty-minute run, whatever the speed. Walking will increase your endurance and improve your tone but not strength. There's another compelling reason to walk. According to Dr. James Skinner at Arizona State University, walking can extend the number of years that you remain sexually active — a very good reason to get at it and keep at it.

Before your begin your walk, be sure to stretch your calves and hamstrings to make sure you're limber and won't suffer muscle aches later. Walk for fifteen minutes then cool down with more stretches. When walking, keep your head erect, your back straight and your stomach in. Toes should point ahead with arms swinging naturally at your side. You should land on the heel of your foot and roll forward, off the ball. Breathe evenly and deeply. The speed should be such that it's work, but there should be no pain. You should be able to carry on a conversation. A forty-five-minute walk can burn 300 calories — about the energy in a cheeseburger — and remove stress. It's a great way to get fresh air, meet people, and keep up with what's going on in the neighbourhood.

More adventurous walkers take walking holidays to various parts of the world, hike in woods and mountains, explore cities and small towns in the surrounding areas. In cold weather, many people walk in indoor shopping malls.

Jogging

Jogging is an effective way to get your aerobic exercise and to build endurance. It can, however, be dangerous if your heart is not up to it or your muscles and joints cannot take the strain. Some people are better advised to walk before they run. You should definitely get your doctor's okay to commence a jogging program. Warm-up exercises are critical for joggers, as are good jogging shoes.

Bicycling

Gliding along on a bicycle is a fun, effective and scenic way to exercise. The choice and cost of new bicycles is a little unnerving, so you may be reluctant to get started. But many good bikes can be purchased secondhand or through the police auctions; any bike that's in good condition will be fun, you don't have to have one of those twenty-speed mountain bikes or space-age speed bikes.

Also, most towns and cities provide safe bicycling routes and zones. Cycling has strong aerobic benefits, burning upward of 400 calories an hour, depending on how hilly your terrain is. Don't even think of getting on your bike without a helmet. Statistics tell us that 45 percent of all deaths from bicycle accidents could have been avoided if the riders wore helmets. In Ontario, legislation has been passed making bicycle helmets mandatory for riders. Other provinces will probably follow.

Swimming and water exercises

Swimming is not only an aerobic activity, it challenges your muscles and joints. The beauty of water is that it provides enough resistance to make swimming good exercise, and at the same time provides support, so that the workout is gentle on our joints. Water exercises or aqua-fitness classes vary from thirty to sixty minutes. They start with stretching warm-up exercises and end with cool-down and relaxing. Classes usually take place in chest-depth water that's warm enough to be comfortable. Because of the water's resistance, you work all parts of the body equally and get exercise no matter what you do. Said one aqua-fitness devotee of fifty-seven to *Good Times* magazine: "Water is my fix! I wouldn't be able to live without that hour a week in the pool." And she lost twenty-five pounds in a matter of months with water exercises and an improved diet.

Tai Chi

This 600-year-old Chinese discipline is increasingly popular among seniors. Deceptively undemanding, Tai Chi combines a uniquely sophisticated set of more than 100 postures to help improve the cardiovascular, skeletal, muscular and nervous systems. A combination of stretching and strengthening exercise, Tai Chi is taught by experts in community and senior citizens' classes throughout Canada. Contact your local Tai Chi organization — there are about forty across Canada — or write the Taoist Tai Chi Society of Canada, 1376 Bathurst Street, Toronto, Ontario M5R 3J1.

This is hardly an exhaustive list. You can dance, or exercise to music at dance exercise classes. You can cross-country ski; much like walking or jogging, you can cross-country ski at a nice, steady, slow pace or you can whip along. How about canoeing, rowing or kayaking? There are games like tennis, squash, badminton and table tennis. Ballet dancing and yoga don't qualify as aerobic exercises because the heart rate is not always raised high enough but they are good for flexibility and posture. Neither requires much equipment. Both counteract the tendency to tight joints and stiff muscles as we age, making movements less easy. Ballet and yoga exercises tone the body, working muscles and bone structure to relieve

tension and improve overall health. Yoga instructor Lilly Dickson says: "Regular practice of yoga is the most effective and painless way I know to get into shape or keep the body young and supple."

If you can't follow a fitness program, try to develop your own exercise regime, incorporating as many of the following elements as possible:

- Walk, climb, ride a bike, move every day.
- Stretch and breathe deeply throughout the day, particularly when you feel tense.
- Push, pull, bend and twist your body, at least three times a week, carefully.
- Do enough aerobic activity — walking, swimming, dancing, cycling, or skiing — to increase your heart rate for fifteen to twenty minutes at least three times a week.
- Participate in sports, hobbies, or outdoor activities at least once a week for two hours.
- Don't use golf carts. It's a good way to guarantee you won't be playing at all in the future.
- Don't take it easy. Make your body do things the harder, longer way.

A final note of caution

Exercise should make you feel better, not worse. Don't overdo it. Avoid sudden exertions that put undue stress on your heart and lungs. Remember to check with your doctor before embarking on any program, especially if you've been mostly idle for several years.

Notes

Chapter 19

Dealing with loss and grief

Death and bereavement are not easy or pleasant topics to discuss. It's painful to think about not being alive or to imagine your life without a loved one. And it raises fears and anxieties about the unknown — when will it take place, how will it occur, will it be painful?

Why should I talk about death Because it represents another of life's changes, a change that is universal, inevitable but not really predictable. It is also life's ending, the final chapter on a lifetime of purpose, commitment, responsibility, involvement and action. You spend a lifetime concerning yourself with the direction your life takes but you may fall short of carrying that direction to a final destination. If I could convince you that planning and preparing for death would provide you with some beneficial outcomes, would you be more inclined to at least consider some action? Think about the following scenarios.

Bill had been thinking about making some changes to his will for sometime. In the last few years, a number of things had changed in his life. He was now divorced, he felt alienated from one of his sons, the unexpected loss of a daughter had been devastating to him and his marriage. His financial resources had altered, not only because of the divorce settlement but also because of surprise inheritances from family members. Following the divorce, he made some major adjustments in his life. The divorce forced him to give some thought to relationships and involvement. He had found a new meaning in life through volunteering abroad. He met wonderful people, developed close friendships and felt happier than he had in some time. Bill never did get his will revised. He procrastinated and then it was too

late. He died of a massive heart attack. The family found themselves in considerable conflict when the will was read. Bill had lost control of his life's affairs to an outdated will!

Dan provided well for Ruth. She knew how much money she needed to maintain their lifestyle and was able to spend freely. But she had no idea where the money came from, where and how it was deposited, and what plans existed for the future investment of the money. Ruth didn't like to deal with financial matters because they seemed so complex. Certainly she could maintain her chequing account balance but Dan looked after the rest.

In fact, he told her not to worry about it, everything was fine and under control. So Ruth didn't worry because Dan had always taken care of her and would continue to do so. Then in one short moment everything changed. Dan was killed in an automobile accident. Ruth was devastated. Everyone was asking her questions — the family, banker, broker and her lawyer — and she didn't know the answers. Where was the will, what were the family assets, their location? What about forms that needed filing, funeral arrangements and money for current expenses? How was she going to straighten everything out? Why didn't they discuss financial matters, the inevitability of death and the need to be ready to live alone?

We discussed this topic in a practical and objective fashion in the financial chapters but here your heart's needs must be considered. These scenarios point out the problems that arise from lack of preparation and planning for death and bereavement. By planning, you gain personal control over the disposition of your possessions and resources, and provide more support for your survivors. Consider your loved ones. Wouldn't you want to do all you could to make death less painful, to show that you cared enough to prepare.

No matter how much you love someone, it's important to keep your individuality in a relationship. Although we all commit to various relationships, it is not wise to become overly dependent because one day the relationship won't be there. Each person needs a strong self-identity to survive and should have in place their own lifestyle, independent of those to whom they are close. It's good to have shared activities, but you should also have something of your own: activities, friendships and interests. They provide the basis for a new lifestyle when your partner dies. People who are too dependent on close relationships often find it difficult in mid- to late-life to begin again — to find new friends and interests.

Death causes an immense sense of loss and grief for survivors. But you're actually more prepared than you might realize. Remember losing a favourite possession, a treasured item, a pet, leaving the family home, losing friends, neighbours, acquaintances, changing jobs, suffering health problems? All these situations caused a sense of loss, some more painful than others and each creating some degree of grief. They all help us to understand and cope with the loss of spouses and work through grief.

Much has been written about grief. Psychiatrist Elisabeth Kubler-Ross was a pioneer in promoting understanding and acceptance of grief. She identified five stages of grief associated with dying: denial, anger, bargaining, depression and acceptance. There is no normal way to grieve; it will vary from person to person. These stages are not necessarily sequential; there is no specified time frame and they can be repeated. What matters is that you and those around you accept that you might go through these stages.

Grief is like a wound that needs time to heal. It can have physical effects: inability to sleep, poor appetite, sense of fatigue and weakness. Psychological effects can include your attitude. There are also social effects: loneliness and isolation despite the support of family and friends.

The degree of grief varies with a number of factors. It is influenced by:

- the age of the person who has died. Generally people accept the death of an older person who has had the opportunity for life more than they can that of a younger person;

- the circumstances of the death. Was it the expected result of terminal illness? Or was it unexpected — an accident, suicide or murder;

- your ability to respond to major change;

- how much individuality you've maintained; and

- the personal and community support you have around you.

Support is necessary to help you cope with a loved one's death. Consider the following sources:

- your own internal strength — a positive attitude, strong religious convictions and the ability to express feelings and concerns;

- your family, both immediate and extended;

- your community, such as self-help groups or social agencies.

Use of these sources can help you resolve your grief and carry on with your life.

People often ask how much time they need to heal, to get over a loss. No one can answer that because of the many factors involved and individual behaviour. The time needed to grieve can be reduced if you know how to cope with death. Do you handle change reasonably or does change handle you and put you out of control? Do you feel you have an adequate support network or do you need to reach out and establish strong links?

There is a time guideline used by professionals to determine if clinical depression is present following bereavement. If a survivor is not back to the business of living, coping with daily activities and getting out to some activities within two years of bereavement, they should be assessed for possible depression. This is not to suggest that they should be finished their grieving but rather that they should be able to function adequately.

Too often, well-meaning family members or friends may advise that certain actions be done now. For instance, they may say: "You should move out of the house — it's too big and there are too many memories." They must not presume responses to loss and grief. For some people, memories are sustaining and they need to stay where those memories linger. For others, memories are too painful — they need to get away for a time.

Financially, it is particularly important not to make rash decisions. If you've done your planning, only those matters which must be attended to, such as the funeral arrangements and executing the will, will be dealt with. So, rather than pressuring the grieving to respond, be supportive and encouraging instead. Usually, the individual will come to a time when they know their grieving is done and they are ready to carry on.

Review the financial chapters dealing with having a will and estate planning and get a lawyer's or financial adviser's advice if you still don't know what to do. Most important, talk about it with your loved ones. If that's too uncomfortable for you to talk about it, write your wishes down and be sure others know

where to find them.

Making arrangements or leaving specific instructions regarding funeral arrangements ensures that your wishes in this regard are considered and that decisions need not be made by vulnerable family members. Disposal of personal possessions can sometimes cause family conflict, particularly if two people want the same item. You know your family, who might really appreciate something of yours, whom you might like to have a certain item or perhaps you would like a friend to have something. This, of course, will not occur without some direction from you.

Perhaps you feel strongly about organ donation and have signed the donor card attached to your driver's licence. If you have not conveyed your wishes to family members and stressed your hope that they will comply, they may not do so. If there is disagreement among immediate family members, the donation will not be accepted. In the eyes of the law, the body belongs to the living — their wishes take precedent.

If you don't want to be kept on life-support systems should you become gravely ill you may be interested in an enduring power of attorney. This enpowers a person close to you to make medical decisions for you. Such arrangements are currently not legal in Canada, except in Quebec, but are in some U.S. states. For physicians to turn off life-sustaining equipment legally, there must be an agreement by people affected by the decision. That means the person concerned, if he or she is capable of responding, the immediate family and the attending physician. With no mutual agreement, life support must continue. This is a very personal and sensitive issue which could cause considerable emotional pain and suffering if you don't discuss it. Again, it's better to discuss this beforehand.

Dealing with the loss of a loved one is very painful. You can help your family at the time of your death by having your personal and financial affairs organized. As for your own feelings on the death of someone close, open yourself to your friends and family and to God. Let time help you to cherish your memories.

Notes

_____

_____

_____

_____

_____

_____

_____

_____

_____

_____

_____

_____

_____

_____

_____

_____

_____

_____

_____

_____

_____

Creating an action plan

You have covered a great deal in the last nineteen chapters. You started with a look at how you want to spend your time in retirement, analyzed your current home and future housing needs, and considered the impact of this lifestyle change on your most important personal relationships. Then you worked on setting your financial goals and objectives, established your financial targets, priorities and opportunities. Finally, you looked at your health.

Now it is time to pull everything together to develop a comprehensive plan — an action plan — to help you to achieve security and independence in retirement. You have the tools, now let's use them.

Focus on goals

The first step is to focus on your personal goals. You identified these goals in chapters two and five. Go back and review them now. You will harness tremendous power if you can focus on a small number of clear statements about those things you want to achieve between now and retirement and after retirement. Any broadly stated general goals should be more clearly defined with action-oriented statements. For instance, it's useful to say you want financial security in retirement. But this is usually coupled with the fact that you want to live a full and complete life today — a desire that often runs in conflict with your first goal. The vagueness of these two statements allows you to fudge on your own goals so that they become merely words and not commitments.

We spent time reviewing your current financial situation and determining how much money you will have to amass to achieve financial independence, because I believe in merging the American concept of visualizing your goals with the Japanese concept of seeing the reality and reacting to it. Too often we sit back dreaming and don't get on with making things happen. We are lulled by a general complacency which leads us to believe we will achieve our goals without blood, sweat and tears. It's not going to happen so easily, as we know when we look back at some of our dreams of youth that have passed us by. We now know the enormity of the goal of financial independence in retirement, and I believe that doing the calculations will cause you to act so that you can achieve your independence goal.

Let's look at the kind of precise statement you need to make. For example: You will retire at age sixty-two. You will have sufficient resources to provide an income of $50,000 after tax in today's dollars each year for the rest of your life. You will apply a small number of financial strategies designed to achieve the savings and investment returns necessary to accumulate the required pensions, RRSPs and investment capital to provide this security. Once you refine your goal statements and commit them to paper, you will have identified achievable targets that you can focus on and against which you can measure your performance.

The shape of retirement

Retirement planning begins by looking at the way you want to spend your time in retirement. So many of the retirees we meet are leading full, active and satisfying lives travelling, learning new skills or giving back to their communities through volunteer work. With a little planning and thought you can make retirement the time of your life with opportunities to do all of the things you wanted, but didn't have time, to do in your working years.

Make sure your action plan identifies the things you want to accomplish in retirement. Do you want to find a part-time job? Start your own business? Volunteer in the local community? Go on safari in Africa? Commit yourself to whatever it is that you dream of doing, then list all the things you need to do to achieve that dream. What research needs to be done? To whom can you talk for more information? By what date will you meet with them? All of the financial planning for retirement is really only important so that you can do the things you want to do for the rest of your life. So take some time to set your lifestyle goals and objectives before concentrating on your financial strategies.

Your financial goals

Your ultimate financial retirement goal is to achieve financial independence in retirement. By determining your net worth in chapter five you looked at where you are today. Then with the information from chapters six to eight, you calculated your retirement income and expenses and the retirement income gap that you must fill before you retire. The amount of capital that you need to fill your gap is your financial destination — where you want to be on your chosen retirement date.

Your action plan should specify when you want to retire, what your retirement spending needs will be, how much capital you will need

and the amount you have to save every year from now to retirement. You went through these calculations in chapter nine. Use the action plan worksheet to summarize these objectives.

Next, you will want to list the financial planning strategies that you will use to meet your annual savings goals and proceed toward your financial independence target at the right financial speed. You studied priorities and opportunities in chapter ten using a pyramid approach. Starting at the base of the pyramid, identify what you are going to do to control costs and reduce debt. List immediate savings opportunities that you can achieve by reducing current spending on expenses that aren't essential to you. If you are in debt, list the steps that you will take to pay down and manage your debt load. Set the date when you will have paid off each obligation.

Next, establish financial strategies for avoiding financial loss. Take steps to secure sufficient financial protection for your loved ones and for your house and goods against fire and theft. Review precisely the amount of life and disability insurance you need and the amount of insurance you should have for fire, theft and public liability in relation to your home, automobiles and other possessions. If you identify a need for increased insurance then make sure you plan to fill this need as soon as possible.

Chapter eleven provides forty strategies for reducing your income taxes. Cutting your tax burden will help you to free more funds for investment for retirement. Spend the time to review your current tax position and include some of these strategies in your action plan.

After covering these basic financial objectives, you should identify the investment strategies that will allow you to achieve the returns you need to build your annual savings toward your financial independence goal. In chapter eight, you saw that your money will grow up to three times as fast in your RRSP or registered pension as it will in your personal portfolio. One of your commitments should be to contribute the maximum to your pension and RRSP every year. Then you should use the RRSP investment strategies to provide the best possible returns manner.

Develop your investment plan as outlined in chapter twelve. Set your target asset allocation mix in your action plan and specify the length of time you will take to move from your current mix to your target.

Remember that you will likely live for twenty to forty years in retirement and that your financial objectives should extend into this time line. Plan to begin cashing your RRSPs in the most effective manner at the end of the year that you turn seventy-one. You might plan to buy a RRIF to take advantage of the flexibility and continued tax deferral or to buy an annuity if you will need the cash flow. With a RRIF, you will want to identify RRIF investment strategies that will continue to provide the growth and security you want. You will also want to plan your portfolio investment objectives into retirement and to put appropriate investment management strategies in place.

Next, consider your estate plan. You owe it to your loved ones to take this personal responsibility seriously and to leave your estate in order. If you do not have an up-to-date will and power of attorney then an important part of your action plan will be to get them. Chapter fifteen provided some tips for preparing these documents. Use these to make up a new will and power of attorney or to review your existing ones. Take the time to organize your estate and update records of key advisers and financial information. File all of this documentation in a secure place and let your family know where things are. Then life will be easier for them.

Health, energy and harmony

Finally, it is essential that you have health, energy and harmony on your side when pursuing your retirement objectives. Your action plan should incorporate plans to maintain and improve your physical health and fitness. Things don't come easily in today's world of slow economic growth and restructuring. You will have setbacks along the way, things that will knock you off your feet. You will have to get up and get going again. You need to have all the positive forces working for you, and to approach life with zest, good humour and optimism. In this way you will see the good in every situation and in all the people you meet.

Today is a time for keeping your present job, but more so, for improving your productivity and abilities so that you are the best at your job, and you are prepared to take on new challenges. It is not enough today to do just what is required. In your job and in business today it is necessary to strive for improvement, to be finding new and better ways to do things, to be learning and applying new skills. Organizations of all sizes, have been threatened by excessive debt and loss of growth opportunities. This restructuring and reawakening will take some time to unfold but should result in opportunities for real personal growth over the balance of this decade. Whether it is in managing your career or your own business, you will need energy, good health and a personal desire to learn and improve if you are going to achieve your goals for retirement.

Monitor and review your plan

Once you have summarized all of these objectives in your action plan, you are ready to implement the strategies that will lead you to a healthy and happy retirement. Your objectives should be specific, identifying who will take what action and by what date. You should also identify the result expected from successful completion of each action. Doing this gives you an incentive to stick to your plan.

Retirement planning is a continuous process. Once you complete your action plan, you will have set out a comprehensive plan to help you achieve security, independence and enjoyment in retirement. On a regular basis, once a year or so, you should measure your success. Update your net worth to see how far you have moved toward your retirement goals. Check off the actions which you successfully completed and set new objectives for the coming year.

Make sure you involve your loved ones in your retirement plan. Your spouse or life partner and your family will also need to adapt positively to the challenging new economic realities. If you are going to achieve your goals, you need the whole family working together, and the support of friends and business associates. The successful person is the one who can develop teamwork and a common approach to achieving everyone's goals. If you can awaken in others the desire to be at their best, they will be better equipped to serve themselves in the achievement of their own goals and to work along with you to achieve your retirement success.

Above all, have a ball. Life is an adventure, and you can achieve great things if you plan carefully for the best years of your life!

Your action plan

An action plan is a goal-oriented list of what you have to do with specific achievement dates, who will help you, and the measurable result you expect. You should complete this action plan with specific objectives in each of the areas identified for you.

Activities in retirement

For example, you might have decided that you would like to volunteer in your community in retirement. If so, list the specific actions you need to take to make this happen: Contact your local volunteer bureau by a particular date so that you can identify the charities or groups you might want to work with. Set a deadline for meeting with representatives from those charities to find the best fit for you. Set a goal; perhaps it could be to begin a new volunteer job one year from today.

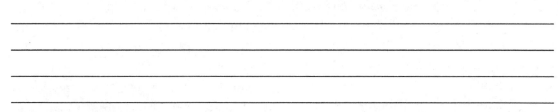

Housing

Where will you live? If you've decided that you want to move to the countryside in retirement, your action plan might include contacting real estate agents in the area you like before the end of the year. If you want to move to the Sunbelt, write to each state and ask for information on retirement villages. You might also list the repairs or improvements needed on your home to make it more appealing to potential buyers, with a deadline for each task.

Relationships

Make a date with your husband, wife or partner to sit down and discuss your plans for retirement. If you know there are going to be problems, such as deciding how to split household chores, you might resolve to arrive at an agreement by a particular date.

_____

_____

_____

_____

_____

Financial independence and security

Your first step is to summarize your financial goals so that they will form an integral part of your action plan and will be close at hand for you to review.

Year of retirement   _____

Spending needs in retirement   _____

Capital required   _____

Annual savings required to retirement _____

Then list the specific actions you will take to reach these goals:

Savings and control

List the immediate savings you can achieve by cutting your expenditures today. If you have debts, you should identify target dates for eliminating your debts.

_____

_____

_____

_____

_____

Income tax strategies

List the strategies you can take to reduce your tax burden. Are there deductions or credits which you have neglected to claim in the past? Are you claiming those in the most effective manner? Are you taking advantage of income-splitting strategies such as spousal RRSPs or letting your spouse earn income on income?

_____

_____

_____

_____

_____

_____

Investment strategies

You prepared your investment policy in chapter twelve. How and when are you going to implement that policy?

Changes required to asset mix: _____

_____

By what date will the change be completed: _____

_____

How are you going to do it: _____

_____

_____

_____

RRSP strategies

Are you making the maximum contribution every year? If not, how can you arrange your finances so that this becomes possible? Will you start to swap equity investments in your RRSP for fixed-income investments? Set a date for choosing your RRSP-maturity options.

_____

_____

_____

Estate planning

If you haven't looked at your will recently, set a deadline for doing this. For a new will and enduring power of attorney, make an appointment to see a lawyer or notary. Plan to get your affairs in order by the end of this year.

_____

_____

_____

Fitness

If you do not have a regular exercise program today, write down your promise to begin some stretching and walking exercises before the end of the month. Set your goals: To do some stretches for ten minutes as you watch the news each evening, take the stairs instead of the elevator three times a week, walk for at least half an hour 3 days a week. Visit a fitness club and decide whether or not you'd like to join. If you jog, you could choose a charity marathon you'd like to run in.

_____

_____

Nutrition

Most of us can improve the way we eat. Perhaps you'll resist the temptation to have chocolate cake and have fruit for dessert instead (except on weekends). You could decide to eat a well-balanced breakfast every morning. You know your weaknesses; set deadlines for getting them under control.

_____

_____

_____

Appendix

1993 Combined federal and provincial marginal tax rates (%)

Your marginal tax rate is the rate at which you would pay tax on the next dollar you earn and depends on whether it is salary, interest income, dividends or capital gains. The numbers in this table are reproduced with the permission of KPMG Peat Marwick Thorne.

Taxable income brackets

	$6,750 to 29,590	$29,591 to 33,400	$33,401 to 38,740	$38,741 to 59,180	$59,181 to 63,315	$63,316 and over
BRITISH COLUMBIA						
Salary	24.98	38.98	39.64	40.43/43.16	48.14	49.59/51.11
Interest	26.44	40.43	40.43	40.43/43.16	48.14	49.59/51.11
Dividends	7.13	24.62	24.62	24.62/26.28	32.51	33.49/34.52
Capital gains	19.83	30.32	30.32	30.32/32.37	36.11	37.10/38.33
ALBERTA						
Salary	24.36	37.72	38.35	39.11/40.06	44.62	46.07
Interest	25.75	39.11	39.11	39.11/40.06	44.62	46.07
Dividends	7.43	24.14	24.14	24.14/24.71	30.42	31.40
Capital gains	19.31	29.33	29.33	29.33/30.04	33.47	34.55
SASKATCHEWAN						
Salary	27.58	41.80	42.47	42.28/45.53	50.50	51.95
Interest	29.06	43.28	43.28	43.28/45.53	50.50	51.95
Dividends	9.99	27.77	27.77	27.77/29.33	35.54	36.51
Capital gains	21.80	32.46	32.46	32.46/34.15	37.87	38.96
MANITOBA						
Salary	26.90	40.85/42.85	43.51	44.30	48.95	50.40
Interest	28.35	42.30/44.30	44.30	44.30	48.95	50.40
Dividends	9.60	27.04/29.54	29.54	29.54	35.35	36.33
Capital gains	21.26	31.73/33.23	33.23	33.23	36.71	37.80
ONTARIO						
Salary	25.86	40.35	41.04	41.86/44.42	49.55	51.00/52.35
Interest	27.37	41.86	41.86	41.86/44.42	49.55	51.00/52.35
Dividends	7.38	25.49	25.49	25.49/27.05	33.46	34.44/35.35
Capital gains	20.53	31.40	31.40	31.40/33.32	37.16	38.25/39.26
NEW BRUNSWICK						
Salary	26.51	41.36	42.06	42.90	47.85	49.30/50.74
Interest	28.05	42.90	42.90	42.90	47.85	49.30/50.74
Dividends	7.56	26.13	26.13	26.13	32.31	33.29/34.26
Capital gains	21.04	32.18	32.18	32.18	35.89	36.98/38.05

Taxable income brackets

	$6,750 to 29,590	$29,591 to 33,400	$33,401 to 38,740	$38,741 to 59,180	$59,181 to 63,315	$63,316 and over
NOVA SCOTIA						
Salary	26.11	40.73	41.42	42.25	47.13	48.58/50.30
Interest	27.63	42.25	42.25	42.25	47.13	48.58/50.30
Dividends	7.45	25.73	25.73	25.73	31.82	32.80/33.97
Capital gains	20.72	31.69	31.69	31.69	35.34	36.43/37.73
PRINCE EDWARD ISLAND						
Salary	26.11	40.73	41.42	42.25	47.13	48.58/50.30
Interest	27.63	42.25	42.25	42.25	47.13	48.58/50.30
Dividends	7.45	25.73	25.73	25.73	31.82	32.80/33.97
Capital gains	20.72	31.69	31.69	31.69	35.34	36.43/37.73
NEWFOUNDLAND						
Salary	27.63	43.11	43.84	44.72	49.88	51.33
Interest	29.24	44.72	44.72	44.72	49.88	51.33
Dividends	7.88	27.23	27.23	27.23	33.68	34.66
Capital gains	21.93	33.54	33.54	33.54	37.41	38.50
YUKON TERRITORY						
Salary	24.58	38.35	39.00	39.78	44.37/45.10	46.55
Interest	26.01	39.78	39.78	39.78	44.37/45.10	46.55
Dividends	7.01	24.23	24.23	24.23	29.96/30.94	31.43
Capital gains	19.51	29.84	29.84	29.84	33.28/33.82	34.91
NORTHWEST TERRITORIES						
Salary	23.78	37.10	37.73	38.48	42.92	44.37
Interest	25.16	38.48	38.48	38.48	42.92	44.37
Dividends	6.78	23.43	23.43	23.43	28.98	29.96
Capital gains	18.87	28.86	28.86	28.86	32.19	33.28

1993 combined federal and Quebec marginal tax rates

Salary	Rate %	Investment income	Interest	Dividends	Capital Gains
6,750 to 7,674	13.9	$6,459 to 7,315	14.7	4.0	11.0
7,675 to 14,000	31.8	7,316 to 14,000	33.7	16.6	25.3
14,001 to 23,000	33.8	14,001 to 23,000	35.7	19.1	26.8
23,001 to 29,590	35.8	23,001 to 29,590	37.7	21.6	28.3
29591 to 32,484	43.6	29,591 to 31,000	45.5	31.4	34.1
32,485 to 38,740	44.7/45.6	31,001 to 50,000	46.6	32.2	35.0
38,741 to 50,000	46.6	50,001 to 52,625	47.7	33.6	35.8
50,001 to 54,220	47.7	52,626 to 59,180	48.9	34.5	36.7
54,221 to 59,180	48.9	59,181 to 62,195	51.5	37.7	38.6
59,181 to 63,320	51.5	62,196 and over	52.9	38.7	39.7

These rates and brackets assume a base salary income. They take into account federal tax, federal surtax (including the 3% low rate and the 5% high-income surtax), provincial tax, provincial surtax, and provincial flat tax. Provincial tax reductions are not taken into account. The personal tax credit available to all taxpayers is taken into account in the above rates, as well as the federal tax credits allowed for CPP/QPP contributions on salary up to $33,400 and for UI premiums on salary up to $38,740. No other credits are calculated as they vary with the circumstances of the taxpayer. It is assumed that no minimun tax is payable.

The secondary marginal tax rates apply when taxable income reaches the thresholds shown below within a particular tax bracket. For example, in the fourth column above, a marginal tax rate of 43.28% applies to Saskatchewan salary or interest income between $38,741 and $40,290 (which is the threshold for the Saskatchewan surtax). The rate increases to 45.53% for income between $40,291 and $59,180

British Columbia	$54,548 (B.C. low-rate surtax), $79,325 (B.C. high-rate surtax)
Alberta	$45,300 (Alberta surtax)
Saskatchewan	$40,290 (Saskatchewan surtax)
Manitoba	$30,000 (Manitoba surtax)
Ontario	$52,193 (Ontario low-rate surtax), $67,776 (Ontario high-rate surtax)
New Brunswick	$95,295 (New Brunswick surtax)
Nova Scotia	$78,170 (Nova Scotia surtax)
Prince Edward Island	$92,655 (P.E.I. surtax)
Yukon	$61,590 (Yukon surtax)

The calculations for interest, dividends and capital gains assume you have a base salary. To find the appropriate tax rate: Determine the taxable amount. Gross up dividends actually received by 125%. For example,if you receive $1,000 in dividends, the taxable amount would be $1,250. For capital gains, the inclusion rate is 75%. Therefore, the taxable amount on a $1,000 capital gain would be $750. Add the taxable investment income to your taxable salary and locate your tax bracket. If you have taxable salary of $63,000 plus $2,000 in actual dividends ($2,500 taxable) and $10,000 in capital gains ($7,500 taxable), locate the bracket for $73,000.

Read down to the lines for your province. If that's Alberta, for example, the marginal rates in this case would be 46.07% for salary and interest income, 31.4% for dividends and 34.55% for capital gains. Watch the secondary marginal tax rate thresholds noted in (b) above when reading these figures.

The appropriate rate for capital gains is applied to the entire gain, not just the taxable portion. In Quebec, the marginal rates for dividends are calculated using the Quebec dividend tax credit rate of 8.87% of the taxable dividend (11.08% of the actual dividend). Marginal tax rates for net rental income would be the same as for interest.

Bibliography

Publications & memberships

You could check out publications at the newsstand or in the library. If you find them useful you could subscribe and have information and ideas arriving in your mailbox regularly.

American Association of Retired Persons
3200 E. Carson Street
Lakewood, CA 90712
(310) 496-2277

ACA News
Alberta Council on Aging
501 - 10506 Jasper Avenue
Edmonton, Alberta T5J 2W9
(403) 423-7781

Canadian Money Saver
P.O. Box 370
Bath, Ontario K0H 1G0
(613) 352-7448

Canadian Association of Retired Persons
1304 - 27 Queen Street East
Toronto, Ontario M5C 2M6
(416) 363-8748

Creative Grandparenting
609 Blackgates Road
Willmington, Delaware 19803

Expression
(National Advisory Council on Aging)
Ottawa, Ontario K1A 0K9
(613) 957-1968

Good Times Magazines
204 - 1340 Bay Street
Toronto, Ontario M5R 2A
(800) 465-8443

Horizon Lifestyle
16815 - 117 Avenue
Edmonton, Alberta T5M 3V6
(403) 242-3101

Intrepid Traveller
RR # 2
Jasper, Ontario K0G 1G0
(613) 283-4190

Maturity
CYN Investments
Box 397
New Westminster, British Columbia V3L 4Y7
(604) 540-7911

One Voice
901 - 350 Sparks Street
Ottawa, Ontario K1R 7S8
(613) 238-7624

Perspectives
Retirement/Life Challenge Ltd.
9 Elliott Place
St. Albert, Alberta T5N 1Y8
(403) 458-4696

Retirement Lifestyle (Club 55)
Box 468
1755 Robson Street
Vancouver, British Columbia V6G 3B7

Seniors Info Exchange
Seniors Secretariat
Health & Welfare Canada
Ottawa, Ontario K1A 0K9
(613) 952-7605

The Pacific Senior's Review
6100 Francis Road
Richmond, British Columbia V7C 1K5
(604) 274-8010

Today's Seniors
1091 Bravik Place
Mississauga, Ontario L4W 3R7
(800) 387-7682

Today's Times
301 - 1201 West Pender
Vancouver, British Columbia V6E 2V2
(604) 683-1344

Selected reading

Work and career changes

Anderson, N., *Work with Passion*; New York, NY: Carroll & Graff, 1986

Baasta, Nicholas, *Top Professions: The 100 Most Popular, Dynamic and Profitable Careers in America Today*; Princeton, NJ: Peterson's Guides, 1989

Bird, Caroline, *Second Careers: New Ways to Work After 50*; Boston, MA: Little, Brown & Co. Inc., 1991

Birsner, Patricia, *Mid-Career Job Hunting*; New York, NY: Simon & Schuster Inc., 1991

Blocher, Donald H., *Career Actualization and Life Planning*; Denver, CO: Love Publishing Company, 1989

Bolles, Richard, *What Colour Is Your Parachute: A Practical Guide For Job Hunters and Career Changers*; Berkeley, CA: Ten Speed Press, 1985

Bolles, Richard, *The New Quick Job Hunting Map*; Berkeley, CA: Ten Speed Press, 1985

Bolles, Richard, *How to Create a Picture of Your Ideal Job or Next Career*; Berkeley, CA: Ten Speed Press, 1985

Cohen, D., Shannon, K., *The Next Canadian Economy*; Montreal: Eden Press, 1984

Cook, Peter, *Start Your Own Business (The Canadian Entrepreneur's Guide)*; Toronto: Stoddart Publishing, 1986

Dayhoff, Signe A., *Create Your Own Career Opportunities*; Andover, MA: Brick House Publishing Co., 1987

Hammond, James L., *Unlocking the Job Market: A Step-by-Step Guide to Successful Job Hunting*; New Bern, NC: Dunmore Publishing Company, 1989

Houze, William C., Career Veer: *How to Position Yourself for a Prosperous Future*; New York, NY: McGraw Hill Books, 1985

Jaffe, D.T. & Scott, C.O., *Take This Job and Love It*; Toronto, ON: Simon & Schuster, 1988

Kaplan, Robbie Miller, *Sure-Hire Resumes*; New York, NY: Amacom Publishing, 1990

Krannich, R. & Krannich, C.R., *Career Success: The Complete Guide to Creating New Opportunities*; Manassas, VA: Impact Publications, 1989

McDaniels, Carl, *The Changing Workplace: Career Counselling Strategies for the 1990s and Beyond*; San Francisco, CA: Jossey-Bass Publications, 1989

Montana, Patrick J., *Stepping Out, Starting Over, How to Get Your Life on the Right Track: Career Life Planning*; New York, NY: National Centre for Career Life Planning, 1989

O'Hara, Bruce, *Put Work in its Place: How to Redesign Your Job To Fit Your Life*; Victoria, BC: Work Well Publications, 1988

Ray, Samuel N., *Job Hunting After 50*, Toronto, ON: John Wiley & Son Inc., 1991

Schmidt, George R., *Personal & Career Exploration* (2nd edition); Dubuque, IA: Kendall/Hunt Publishing Co., 1989

Retirement planning

Beeman, Eleanor, *Travelling on Your Own*; New York, NY: Clarkson N. Patter Inc., 1990

Bolles, Richard, *How To Find Your Mission in Life*; Berkley, CA: Ten Speed Press, 1991

Boyer, Richard & Savageau, David, *Retirement Places Rated*; New York, NY: Prentice Hall, 1987

Bridges, William, *Managing Transitions: Making The Most of Change*; New York, NY: Addison Wasby, 1991

Brown, Kathleen H., *Personal Finance For Canadians* (4th edition); Scarborough, ON: Prentice Hall, 1991

Busch, Vicky, *Educational Travel Planner*; Athabasca, AB: Department of Student Services - Athabasca University, 1990

Callwood, June, *Twelve Weeks in Spring*; Toronto, ON: Lester & Orpen Dennys Ltd., 1986

Chapman, Elwood, *Enhance Your Destiny: Dare to Build a Second Life*; CA: Crisp Publications, 1992

Chilton, David, *The Wealthy Barber*; Toronto, ON: Stoddard Publishing Co., 1989

Cook. R.J. and Daly, M.A., *Money Making Ideas for Seniors*; Toronto, ON: Stoddart, 1989

Cooper, Marion, *The World's Top Retirement Havens*; Baltimore, MD: Agora Inc., 1991

Drabek, Jan, *The Golden Revolution*; Toronto, ON: MacMillan of Canada, 1986

Fries, James F., *Aging Well*; Don Mills, ON: Addison-Wesley Publishing Co. Inc., 1989

Fromme, A., *Life After Work*; Washington, DC: American Association of Retired Persons, 1984

Gordon, Michael, *An Ounce of Prevention*; Scarborough, ON: Prentice-Hall Canada Inc., 1984

Gose, K. & Levi, G., *Dealing with Memory Changes as You Grow Older*; Toronto, ON: McClelland-Bantam, Inc., 1988

Gross, Andrea, *Shifting Gears: Planning a New Strategy For MidLife*; New York, NY: Crown Publishers, 1991

Hartman, George, *Risk is a Four Letter Word*; Toronto, ON: Hartman & Company, 1992

Heibman, J.R., *Unbelievably Good Deals (Great Adventures That You Absolutely Can't Get Into Unless You're Over 50)*; Markham, ON: Beaverbooks Ltd., 1989

Hesse, Jurgen, *Mobile Retirement Handbook*; Vancouver, BC: International Self-Counsel Press Ltd., 1987

Holbrook, Leslie, *Improving With Age*; Toronto, ON: Deneau Publishers, 1984

Hopson, B. & Scally, Mike, *Build Your Own Rainbow*; Leeds, England: Lifeskills Associates, 1984

Hunnisett, Henry, *Retirement Guide For Canadians*; Vancouver, BC: International Self-Counsel Press, 1988

Karlin, Marie, *Make Your Child a Success*; New York, NY: Putnam, 1983

Kaye, Beverly I., *Up is Not the Only Way*; New Jersey: Prentice Hall, Inc. 1982

Kling, Sidney, *How to Retire and Invest Successfully in Florida: A Guidebook for Canadians*; Toronto, ON: General Publishing, 1982

Kling, Sidney & Levy, *Joseph, It's Never Too Early!*; Toronto, ON: Stoddart Publishing, 1985

Lee, Fred & Alice, *A Field Guide to Retirement*; New York, NY: Doubleday Inc., 1991

MacDonald, Helen Bishop, *Eat Well, Live Well;* Toronto, ON: MacMillan of Canada, 1990

MacDonald, Sylvia, T*rust in God But Tie Your Camel;* Ottawa, ON: Novalis, 1983

McCants, Louise & Cavett, Robert, *Retire to Fun and Freedom;* New York, NY: Warner Books, 1988

Miller, Sigmund Stephen, Asher, Julian, & Miller, Don Ethan, *Conquest of Aging;* New York, NY: MacMillan Publishing, 1986

Milletti, Mario A., *Voices of Experience: 1500 Retired People Talk About Retirement;* New York, NY: Teachers Insurance and Annuity Association, 1984

Oliver, Margo, *Margo Oliver's Cookbook for Seniors;* Vancouver, BC: Self-Counsel Press, 1989

Osgood, Nancy, *Life After Work;* New York, NY: Prager Publishing, 1982

Peck, M.S., *The Road Less Travelled;* New York, NY: Simon & Schuster, 1978

Polson, Kirk & Brett, George, *Retire Right;* Markham, ON: Penguin, 1993

Potter, B., *The Way of the Robin;* New York, NY: Amacom, 1984

Ringer, R.J., *How You Can Find Happiness During the Collapse of Western Civilization;* New York, NY: Harper & Rowe, 1983

Salwen, Judy, *Solo Retirement;* New York, NY: Dodd, Mead & Co., 1983

Schmidt, R., *Tough Times Never Last, Tough People Do;* New York, NY: Random House, 1983

Scissons, Edward, *Happily Ever After;* New York, NY: Dembner Books, 1987

Sheehy, Gail, *Pathfinders;* New York, NY: Bantam Books, 1982

Sher, B. & Gottlieb, A., *Teamworks;* New York, NY: Warner Books, 1989

Sher, B. & Gottlieb, A., Wishcraft: *How to Get What You Really Want;* New York, NY: Ballantine Books, 1983

Smith, Jane, & Flynn, Marlene, *More Power To You;* Calgary, AB: Career Dynamics, 1989

Spencer, Sabina & Adams, John, *Life Changes: Growing Through Personal Transitions;* California: Impact Publishers, 1990

Toffler, A., *Previews and Premises;* New York, NY: Bantam Books, 1983

Warschaw, Tess Albert, *Rich is Better;* New York, NY: Doubleday, 1985

Warschaw, T. & Secunda, V., *Winning with Kids;* New York, NY: Bantam, 1988

Watt, J. & Calder, A., *Taking Care;* North Vancouver, BC: Self Counsel Press, 1986

West, Robin, *Memory Fitness Over 40;* Gainsville, FL: Triad Publishing Co., 1985

Widgor, Blossom, *Planning Your Retirement;* Toronto, ON: Grosvenor House Press Inc., 1985

Wyatt, Elaine, *The Money Companion: How to Manage Your Money and Achieve Financial Freedom* (5th edition); Toronto, ON: Penguin Books, 1993

Zelinski, Ernie, *The Joy of Not Working;* Edmonton, AB: Visions International Publishing, 1991

Relationships

Cainem Lynn, *Widow;* Toronto, ON: Bantam Books, 1987

Chapman, Elwood, *The Unfinished Business of Living: Helping Aging Parents Help Themselves;* California: Crisp Publications, 1989

Isbister, Ruth, *Grandparents Don't Just Babysit;* Toronto, ON: Deneau Pub., 1989

Jarvik, Lissy & Smith, Garry, *Parentcare;* Toronto, ON: Bantam Books, 1984

Thompson, Wendy, *Aging is a Family Affair;* Toronto, ON: Family Books, 1988

Index